SUGAR, SLAVERY, & FREEDOM IN

NINETEENTH-CENTURY

PUERTO RICO

The University *of* North Carolina Press
Chapel Hill

SUGAR, SLAVERY, & FREEDOM IN

NINETEENTH-CENTURY

PUERTO RICO

[Luis A. Figueroa]

Designed by Kimberly Bryant
Set in Minion by Keystone Typesetting, Inc.
Sugarcane ornament from North Wind Picture Archives.

The paper in this book meets the guidelines for
permanence and durability of the Committee on
Production Guidelines for Book Longevity of the
Council on Library Resources.

Library of Congress Cataloging-in-Publication Data
Figueroa, Luis A. (Luis Antonio)
Sugar, slavery, and freedom in nineteenth-century
Puerto Rico / Luis A. Figueroa.
p. cm.
Includes bibliographical references and index.
ISBN 0-8078-2949-8 (cloth: alk. paper)
ISBN 0-8078-5610-X (pbk.: alk. paper)
1. Slavery—Puerto Rico—Guayama Region—History—19th
century. 2. Slaves—Emancipation—Puerto Rico—Guayama
Region—History—19th century. 3. Freedmen—Puerto Rico—
Guayama Region—History—19th century. 4. Labor supply—
Puerto Rico—Guayama Region—History—19th century.
5. Plantation workers—Puerto Rico—Guayama Region—
History—19th century. 6. Sugarcane industry—Puerto Rico—
Guayama Region—History—19th century. 7. Puerto Rico—
Race relations—History—19th century. I. Title.
HT1089.G83F54   2005
306.3′62′0972958—dc22   2005017471

cloth   09 08 07 06 05   5 4 3 2 1
paper   09 08 07 06 05   5 4 3 2 1

THIS BOOK WAS DIGITALLY PRINTED

CONTENTS

TABLES

SUGAR, SLAVERY, & FREEDOM IN

NINETEENTH-CENTURY

PUERTO RICO

INTRODUCTION

This book examines the trials and tribulations, the partial victories, and the defeats of a group of people who happened to share a common history, even if at times they did not realize this fact—or even want to. The setting is the southeastern coast and hinterland of Puerto Rico, centered on the sugar plantation *municipio* of Guayama, from about the middle of the nineteenth century to 1898. This study seeks to bring to the fore how Guayama's subaltern groups, mostly slaves and ex-slaves but also free peasants, journeymen, and artisans, sought to create a space of their own, a terrain of their own, in the face of the local sugar plantations' oppressive demands for labor and in an assortment of other economic activities. This work also seeks to understand the complexities of the planter and merchant class that dominated the region starting around 1800 and of the planters' and merchants' relationship not only with their subalterns but also with the colonial state that sequentially helped to build up the plantation economy, failed to prop it up when the going got tough, and ultimately gave way unwillingly to a new colonial power at the turn of the twentieth century.

Guayama's peoples came from almost everywhere—from as far away as Africa, Catalonia, Bordeaux, New Orleans, Guadeloupe, and Curaçao, for example. These immigrants joined a local population of creole large landholders, peasants, and laborers, among whom qualifying as "native" required only a claim to ancestral residence as far back as the sixteenth century. As such, Guayama had the character of a frontier society with a strongly provincial but also cosmopolitan look. Many languages were spoken there: Puerto Rican Spanish, peninsular Spanish, Catalan, French, English, Danish, and a slew of African and neo-African Caribbean languages. Other types of languages were also spoken: the languages of racism, of slavery, of class oppression, and of course, of colonialism—racial, class, and gendered domination and resistance. Likewise, many individual mentalities informed the collective mentality of people in the Guayama region: the mentality of those seeking mainly to gain quick fortunes on the backs of African and creole slaves, peasants, and free laborers; that of those oppressed peoples struggling for survival; and, eventually, perhaps unintentionally, that of those involved in the formation of a new outlook on nature, life, and society that would eventually be dubbed Puerto Rican national identity.

The common thread in the story is the evolution of sugar plantations and various labor systems over the course of a century and the actions and inactions that resulted in the building of the surrounding society. The story contains all sorts of characters and behaviors, places, and outcomes. One of my aims is to provide the people of Guayama and Puerto Ricans on the island and in the diaspora another piece of the puzzle that has been our often mythologized Puerto Rican past.[1] This does not mean that I, like some of my predecessors, seek the role of myth shatterer or mythmaker. My goal is simpler. I offer this study, first and foremost, to readers interested in local, insular matters. Yet as a historian with more than a passing interest in the "larger" questions of historical interpretation and the zigzagging debates of fellow historians, humanists, and social scientists, I have also gently addressed some of those larger questions concerning the events and processes that took place not too long ago in a dusty corner of the Caribbean. I hope both levels of the narrative will remain visible and intelligible throughout this volume. If the first one goes unnoticed, perhaps my characters and their actions were not as exciting as I imagined while poring over boring notarial records and the confusing script of low-ranking colonial officials. If the second level is unintelligible, perhaps I still have some way to go before mastering my trade.

Checkered Patterns of History and Identity

The title of this book, *Sugar, Slavery, and Freedom in Nineteenth-Century Puerto Rico*, suggests my interest in the relationships among slavery, postemancipation class formation, rural proletarian culture and consciousness, and Afro-Caribbean heritage in Puerto Rico. This interest stems from various sources. One of them is a political and a personal fascination with the subject of Afro-Caribbean heritage in Puerto Rico's past and present. At the root of this fascination is a questioning of some widely held "truths" about Puerto Rican society and culture, about what supposedly constitutes the "true Puerto Rican" or perhaps the "most Puerto Rican of all Puerto Ricans." Within this notion, the mythical figure of a white male *jíbaro* living in the interior mountains emerges as the essence of Puerto Ricanhood. From this essence, in turn, come a number of other "truths" about what constitutes the "most Puerto Rican" cultural manifestations (ranging from race to culture to politics).

But what about those Puerto Ricans who, even before the advent of post–World War II industrialization, urban sprawl, and massive migration to the United States, did not fit this characterization? These other Puerto Ricans seem to be much more skewed toward a certain "blackness" and to cultural manifestations more easily linked to the island's Caribbean surroundings. What of the Martínezes, the Santiagos, and the other families of the rural barrio of my maternal family, barrio San Diego in the *municipio* of Coamo, just northwest of Guayama? They were peasants as well but of an evidently different breed: they were black and mulatto peasants. What about the many similar families of the island's coastal plains, hills, and towns? Were they not also "true Puerto Ricans"? If so, why has their place in defining Puerto Ricanhood been ignored? The history of these black and mulatto Puerto Ricans needs to be rescued from its prolonged neglect.

A second stimulus for writing this book comes from a new Puerto Rican historiography that since the 1970s and 1980s has dramatically recast our understanding of our past. During the 1990s, historiography in the Caribbean and elsewhere in the Americas turned to other matters, especially emphasizing race and cultural discourses around race and slavery.[2] Chapter 1 of this book is especially informed by these issues and by dialogues with central issues associated with race elsewhere in the Caribbean and the Americas.[3]

Since the 1970s, the subjects of slavery and Afro–Puerto Rican heritage have assumed increasing importance in Puerto Rican historiography as a result of a number of factors. Of relevance here was the emergence of new views on Puerto Rican historiography from the mid-1970s to the mid-1980s.[4] The sudden availability of new documentary sources for the study of the island's economic and social history during the last century of Spanish domination was one of the keys to this upsurge. Even more important, however, were the new theoretical and political perspectives of a younger generation of historians, social scientists, and other analysts influenced by anticolonial struggles in the Caribbean and elsewhere as well as by the civil rights struggles of the 1960s in the United States. More recently, the late 1980s and 1990s saw to the emergence of new debates and proposed reassessments of the role of the Afro-Caribbean component of Puerto Rican cultural identity. This phenomenon resulted in large part from works of literature and literary criticism that have appeared since the mid-1970s.[5]

Nonetheless, literary writer and critic José Luis González's 1980 publication of a highly controversial collection of essays, *El país de cuatro pisos y otros ensayos*, piqued the intellectual curiosity of many emerging and aspiring writers, scholars, and artists regarding race and Afro-Caribbean culture in Puerto Rico.[6] González claimed that the principal essay, "El país de cuatro pisos," constituted not a historical article but, as he put it, some "notes on the definition of Puerto Rican culture" that sought only to "enunciate the nucleus for an interpretative essay of Puerto Rican cultural reality."[7] "El país de cuatro pisos" owed its title to a metaphor used by González to illustrate what he saw as the four fundamental layers in the development of the Puerto Rican social formation. The first layer, or floor of the house, represented the earliest stages in the history of the colony, from the early sixteenth to the late eighteenth centuries. During this period, Puerto Rico's economy and society stagnated after the initial destruction of the native population and a subsequent failed attempt at building a slavery-based sugar plantation society. This early process resulted in the development of an Afro-Hispanic peasantry devoted largely to subsistence production.

The building of the second floor, according to González, was carried out by the immigration of those who eventually formed the backbone of the sugar and coffee *hacendado* and merchant elites. These were mainly Spanish and creole royalists who had fled South America during the independence wars along with French planters who had escaped Saint Domingue after the Haitian revolution and other foreigners attracted by the reformist economic policies unleashed by the Spanish government during the first decades of the nineteenth century. A new colonial metropolis, the United States, added the third floor to this structure by invading the island in 1898 and subsequently developing an industrialized capitalist sugar plantation society there in the early decades of the twentieth century. The fourth floor followed under the aegis of U.S. corporate capital with Puerto Rico's industrialization after World War II.

Originally written to address the question of how decades of U.S. colonial intervention have affected Puerto Rican culture, "El país de cuatro pisos" also represents a synthesis of the hypotheses raised by the new Puerto Rican historiography emerging at the time González wrote as well as a very forceful elaboration of some of the political implications of this new historiography. This account of Puerto Rican history was very much at odds not only with the interpretations consistently put forth by colonial elites but also with a number of formulations of the Left. González's synthesizing effort, his argumentative forcefulness, and his new hypotheses on the history of Puerto Rican society and culture raised eyebrows in many quarters. For example, González attempted to reshape commonly accepted notions of Puerto Rican identity and popular culture. In González's view, the Puerto Rican culture that emerged during the first three centuries of Spanish colonial rule (1500s–1700s) was fundamentally Afro-Caribbean: in his provocative formulation, "the first Puerto Ricans were black Puerto Ricans."[8] Most members of Puerto Rican intellectual circles found this statement unacceptable, having glossed over if not outright repressed the study of African heritage; to this day, González's idea remains almost unbelievable to the majority of Puerto Ricans, who, despite our varying degrees of African ancestry, have yet to come to grips with our African heritage.

Notwithstanding the number of criticisms that could be—and, indeed, have been—raised against "El país de cuatro pisos," some specific issues in González's formulations have influenced the writing of this book.[9] For example, while González incisively distinguishes "national culture" and "popular culture," I believe that something is fundamentally wrong with the ways in which González represents the Puerto Rican nineteenth century as the "whitening" of a colored society as it existed until the end of the eighteenth century. How could this characterization adequately represent the full complexity of what took place in a century when more Africans and Afro-Caribbeans were brought in as slaves then ever before, a time just prior to the early decades of the nineteenth century, when more free people of color from the Caribbean region than whites immigrated to Puerto Rico from non-Spanish territories? How could a Puerto Rican society so heavily dependent on slavery for the production of its most important export crop (sugar) and on sugar for its place in the webs of Atlantic capitalism have somehow simultaneously produced as an effect and an affect the erasure of blackness as a fundamental element in the construction of what we would insist on calling *puertorriqueñidad*? Furthermore, González seems to dump into one "popular class" enslaved Africans and Afro-Americans (broadly speaking, Afro–Puerto Ricans and Afro-Caribbean slaves) and free colored and white peasants and artisans, thereby disregarding any concrete historical analysis of the diverse productive arrangements of nineteenth-century Puerto Rico and their concomitant sociocultural formations. This type of dumping is also evident in Gonzalez's depiction of the emancipation of slaves in 1873 as a simple change in their legal status, thus assuming once again that as freedmen and -women the ex-slaves simply continued to form part of the amorphous "popular class."[10]

Likewise, when describing his metaphorical second floor—that is, the nineteenth-century migration of planters and merchants and its impact on Puerto Rican society—González gives no place to the forced immigration of thousands of African and creole Caribbean slaves brought to work on the immigrant and *criollo* planters' lucrative sugar estates as well as in other fields of work. These Africans and non-Hispanic Caribbean slaves, along with the hundreds of Caribbean free colored skilled workers who also came, swelled the ranks of the island's black and mulatto population and had an impact on Puerto Rican society that was at least as important as other nineteenth-century immigrations. Yet if the contributions of Afro-Caribbean heritage to Puerto Rican popular culture are correspondingly even more extensive than González has claimed, specific studies are still lacking of the historical processes by which this social and cultural phenomenon emerged. Likewise, only historical research, broadly defined, could explain in adequate detail how the Puerto Rican variant of Afro-Caribbean class formation and popular culture differs from those of Jamaica, Martinique, and Cuba, for example.

The subject of the subaltern class formation that structured the lives of thousands of Puerto Rican ex-slaves after emancipation must also be addressed as part of this explanation, yet when it comes to discussing the lives of the *libertos* (Puerto Rico's freedmen and -women), the new studies on Puerto Rican slavery typically stopped short of providing much information about the people. Pioneering studies by historians José Curet, Andrés Ramos Mattei, and Teresita Martínez-Vergne, for example, have concentrated more on the economic history of the sugar industry than on the social and cultural aspects of the history of plantation slaves and ex-slaves after 1870.[11]

Moreover, these historians met with some methodological obstacles when they tried to research the history of the ex-slave component of the postemancipation sugar industry's labor force. "It is hard to trace the whereabouts of the bondsmen who obtained their freedom in 1873," Curet points out, adding, "the censuses, prior to 1873 classified the inhabitants according to whether they were white, *pardos libres* [mulatto], *libertos*, or slaves; but those classifications were discontinued thereafter." Ramos Mattei also wonders about the *libertos* postemancipation lives: "It is not known for sure the fate of these *libertos*. Studies of individual municipalities and sugar areas will eventually throw some light on this particular problem."[12]

Tracking Historiographical Coordinates

This book also seeks to connect the aforementioned personal and Puerto Rican historiographical concerns to broader historiographical and theoretical issues and debates regarding the transition from slavery to capitalism and the proletarianization of rural labor, particularly in plantation economies. I originally planned to explore the rich collection of a sugar district's municipal, notarial, and judicial records for insights into the process of transition from slavery to capitalism and the formation of the sugar plantation proletariat and thereby to contribute to the existing literature on plantation societies and on labor history in Latin America and the Caribbean.

Compared to the developments in other fields of Latin American social history from the late 1970s to the late 1980s, both these fields appeared to be slower to develop theoretical and methodological perspectives that went beyond a focus on the logic of capitalist development, relations at the point of production, and political activities and strikes.[13] Conversely, as I suggested, during the 1990s, the works concentrating on race and culture and their relationship tended to deemphasize the social history of slavery and its aftermath that had been emphasized in the 1970s and 1980s.[14] This book attempts to integrate both of these approaches and subjects.

Several studies have already examined the economic and social impact of emancipation, the transition to free labor, and the modernization of sugar industries in the region.[15] Authors have attempted to construct theoretical and/or econometric models of plantation economies[16] and to address many of these economic history issues simultaneously by focusing on the history of a single plantation throughout a rather long time span.[17] Despite some important innovations during the 1980s, these perspectives have continued to hold an attraction. Works on the transition to monopoly capitalism in sugar plantation societies, for example, have remained focused largely on the dynamics of the international market, the initiatives and perils of local planter classes, and foreign capital's role in shaping this transition.[18] Moreover, works on labor control and crime as a form of resistance in postemancipation plantation societies[19] have remained plagued by shallow empirical bases and failures to engage the theoretical and methodological issues raised in the study of labor control, everyday forms of resistance, the formation of working-class culture, and that culture's role in structuring social hierarchies.[20]

At the time I started my research, Latin American labor history had begun to question the problems associated with assuming a dependency/world system approach and to look at the "usefulness of applying to the field concepts and methods drawn by social history."[21] Various scholars were calling for the incorporation of the perspectives of the new social history, for the creative use of new sources, and for histories that would go beyond "institutional" or organized labor by considering workers' daily experiences, unorganized workers' struggles, popular culture, "marginal groups," and ethnicity and race within the Latin American working classes.[22] In addition, scholars predicted the appearance of new "more interdisciplinary micro-studies of towns, class fractions, regions, industries" in the field of Latin American labor history as well as the growing importance of "[l]ess studied areas, especially the Caribbean."[23]

Yet despite all this groundbreaking work on continental Latin America, the field of labor history in the Caribbean region was slow to incorporate these perspectives,[24] more perhaps because the Caribbean was an area where even conventional, institutional-oriented, labor history remained largely absent for the pre–Great Depression period.[25] Thus, the road to incorporating these revisionist perspectives into Caribbean plantation studies looked quite long from the standpoint of the late 1980s. As a mid-1980s conference on "new approaches to Latin American labor history" concluded, the question of "the advantages of broadening the traditional institutional and political concerns of labor history to include cultural and social themes" remained "as yet unresolved."[26]

At that time, it seemed that plantation labor history needed to incorporate the study not only of the labor unions and related political parties and of organized strikes and resistance movements but also of the "inarticulate majority" of plantation workers.[27] So as I embarked on my research on Guayama, I was gratified to sense that the field was moving in this direction and beginning to incorporate into its historical studies anthropological perspectives that would bring community relations and kinship networks and values to bear on the study of the working class and everyday forms of resistance[28] while examining the intersections among gender, race, and class in proletarianization and the formation of practices of resistance.[29]

To address these issues, historical studies of plantation laborers (whether slave or proletarian) had to locate historical sources that would permit the study of how the "inarticulate" and the "unorganized" participated in shaping their material and cultural relations within the constraints of slavery and capitalism. This was certainly an ambitious agenda, one beyond any one individual's capacity, but I envisioned this book as the first installment of a larger study that would include a second volume addressing the crucial early period of U.S. rule in Puerto Rico between the height of the original socialist workers' project around 1917–24, on the one hand, and the collapse of the sugar industry, the populist colonial project, and the emergence of heavy industry and radical politics in the late 1960s and early 1970s on the other. I have now left this project for others to do.

This book begins with the last years of slavery in Puerto Rico— the 1850s and 1860s—and extends to the period immediately following the Spanish-American War of 1898. At the start of this broad span, Puerto Rico's slaveholders were trying to hold onto an institution under attack by external and internal forces—by the British-imposed end to the slave trade, the terrible cholera epidemic of 1855–56, the U.S. Civil War and the defeat of the proslavery South, and the Spanish internal and colonial political vicissitudes of the 1860s. Consequently, the second half of the nineteenth century represented the time of Puerto Rico's transition from slavery and forced labor to free wage labor as well as of the worst nineteenth-century crisis in the Puerto Rican sugar industry,[30] while the early twentieth century witnessed the arrival of American business interests and colonial projects that radically transformed types of domination and subordination of both reconstituted creole elites and subaltern groups. Spurred by post-1898 U.S. colonial policies that privileged sugar over other economic activities, sugar became more dominant than at any other time in Puerto Rican history, and the southern coastal lowlands, under the aegis of American sugar corporations, became synonymous with plantation life and labor.

Guayama, Pueblo Brujo

For several reasons, this study focuses on Guayama.[31] Guayama, along with the municipalities of Ponce and Mayagüez, constituted one of the leading centers of slavery-based sugarcane agriculture in Puerto Rico from the early decades of the nineteenth century (see maps 1 and 2). As a result, throughout the nineteenth century, Guayama had one of the island's largest slave as well as free Afro–Puerto Rican populations.[32] Therefore, Guayama seemed to offer the possibility of examining four related processes connected with the legacy of sugar and slavery: the decline of the island's sugar industry after 1870, the process of post-emancipation ex-slave class formation, the early impact of U.S. colonialism and its sugar revolution, and the social and cultural outlook of one of the island's most strongly Afro-Caribbean municipalities.

As mentioned previously, the issue of postemancipation ex-slave class formation has to date received little empirical attention in Puerto Rican history, and Guayama serves as an excellent case study for throwing light on that grossly neglected subject. Guayama also offers an opportunity to go beyond the current state of the wider Caribbean and Latin American literature on postemancipation class formation.[33] Much of the literature on the transition from slave to free labor in the Caribbean, for example, emphasizes the "reconstitution" of a peasantry after emancipation, when the "protopeasant" adaptation of slave subsistence producers joined other factors such as availability of land to enable the slaves to metamorphose into a new class of autonomous peasants. Guayama, however, like Barbados, does not fit the mold. Access to land and subsistence production by slaves and *libertos*, both before and after emancipation, was weak, and the possibilities for ex-slave peasant class formation were slim. Yet precisely for this reason, Guayama offers the opportunity to examine a possible process of earlier and more rapid postemancipation ex-slave proletarianization.[34]

Moreover, Guayama is the seat of one of Puerto Rico's eight politico-administrative districts, each of which encompasses several coastal and highland *municipios*. As such, Guayama's municipal seat or town (*pueblo*) has historically been the largest urban center (even if of small scale by national standards) in southeastern Puerto Rico; consequently, the "town versus country" dynamic has had greater importance in Guayama than in other sugar districts with the exceptions of Ponce and Mayagüez.[35] The inclusion of this additional town setting—and especially the inclusion of town-based artisans and sugarcane workers—enhances significantly the range of social, economic, and cultural experiences studied.

In addition, Guayama was a center of sugar workers' struggles during the early decades of the twentieth century.[36] Area laborers took a remarkably active part in the rural proletarian militancy that climaxed in the wave of massive strikes of 1915–18 and the Socialist Party's 1917 and 1920 municipal electoral victories.[37] This characteristic provides an excellent opportunity to examine the processes of rural (and urban) proletarian class and culture formation that, shaped by nineteenth-century experiences, contained the potential and the constraints registered in the burst of sugar worker and socialist struggles from the 1900s to the 1930s.

In the evolution of Puerto Rican society, Guayama has constituted one of the strongholds of Afro-Caribbean heritage since early in the 1800s. Throughout the century, the municipality remained one of the country's top three in both absolute number and percentage of slaves and people of color. Even today, fellow Puerto Ricans regard Guayama residents, rightly or not, as more enmeshed than most islanders in Afro–Puerto Rican religious practices. From this derives the label of *brujos* (shamans) commonly given to things Guayaman. Almost all sports teams from Guayama, for example, are nicknamed "los Brujos de Guayama" (the Guayama Shamans), and the city itself is often called la Ciudad Bruja (the Shaman City). Consequently, Guayama is an appropriate place for examining social and cultural interactions among Afro–Puerto Ricans and between them and other racial and class components of society.

To return to González's "El país de los cuatro pisos" and the genesis of my research, I felt that in selecting Guayama I had moved through the justifications that it had quite a rich archive and that no one had written much about it and into a terrain that I could not have imagined being as richly textured in its "Caribbeanness." This discovery was quite ironic, perhaps because as familiar with Guayama and its region as I felt I was, having grown up only a few miles from its core, I was and remain a product of the erasure of blackness that I seemed to ascribe to González's interpretation of the nineteenth-century "second floor" in the formation of Puerto Rican society and identity. The child of a matrifocal kin, or mother-based family network, whose blackness seemed simultaneously there and not there, visible to the eye but refracted through the prism of hinterland *jíbaro* identity; a child, moreover, of the piedmont and not the "black coast"; and inevitably a child formed by master narratives of Puerto Rican history that privileged the "interior" as both a geography and a trope of identity, I was a likely subject to be taken aback by the Caribbeanness of nineteenth-century Guayama.

In this sense, I seek here to draw attention to that hidden transcript of Caribbeanness in Guayama, to the dense webs of social imbrications between this neglected corner of Puerto Rico and its neighbors in St. Thomas, Curaçao, and St. Barthelemy, for example. As a Caribbean site of Caribbeanness in a bastion of white settler Occidentalism arguably constitutes one legitimate way to represent Guayama's place in Puerto Rican history. While the text that follows is not dominated by any overriding concern with proving this representation correct, I do hope that readers will get a sense of the ways in which Guayama was as much a part of the Caribbean as a part of Puerto Rico. I also confess to a desire to offer a counterscript for the ways in which Puerto Rican identity has been insistently fashioned as a sort of an exceptional case in its Caribbean context— exceptional, that is, insofar as slavery, taking the island as an aggregate, was a rather "minority affair" in comparison with its predominance in almost all neighboring countries. And Puerto Rico is also exceptional insofar as its dominant form of collective political consciousness looked first north-northeast to Spain and later northwest to the United States to validate and sustain its existence.

THE CORE OF THIS BOOK consists of seven chapters in which attention to issues of political economy and colonial power is mixed with analysis of culture, hegemony, ideology, and subaltern resistance. Taken as a whole, the text enacts what Greg Dening has labeled a "neomodern" intellectual practice—that is, one that is cognizant of and seeks to engage both modernism and postmodernism.[38] In chapters 1–3 I describe the emergence of a distinctly Caribbean plantation society in Guayama from the late eighteenth century through the first seven decades of the nineteenth century, concentrating on Guayaman society in the final years of slavery (the 1860s). I explore the ways in which both planters and slaves began to adapt to and resist the prospect of emancipation after Puerto Rico's slave trade was curtailed at midcentury.

In the second half of chapter 1, I examine the role of ideologies of race and colonial modernity in the construction of the Puerto Rican plantation complex; I also pay attention to the Spanish colonial state's role through the 1860s, to changing patterns of investments and labor relations (including a nonslave, coerced-labor regime), to demographic changes, to slave manumissions, and to free and manumitted blacks' and mulattoes' strategies for constructing a distinctively Afro–Puerto Rican community before abolition.

In chapter 4, I offer a quick review of the process that led the Spanish Cortes (parliament) to abolish slavery in Puerto Rico through two laws: the 1870 Moret Law, which freed slaves determined to be over sixty years old as well as infants born after 17 September 1868, and the Abolition Law of 1873, which freed Puerto Rican slaves but imposed on them a transition system of forced government-supervised labor contracts until 1876. I return to my focus on Guayama in chapters 5–7, analyzing how planters and former slaves tried to define their new relationships after abolition in 1870–76. Here I follow the trail of literally hundreds of ex-slaves, free laborers, peasants, and planters as they go about negotiating new individual and group identities and relationships given the constraints and opportunities produced by a virtually immediate abolition and the decline of Puerto Rico's sugar industry during the last three decades of the nineteenth century. Quite importantly, this analysis considers the local colonial elite's and the declining Spanish colonial regime's inability to construct a new colonial hegemony adapted to the conditions of the postslavery transition to colonial capitalism. These chapters focus primarily on issues such as peasant and proletarian class formation, forms of resistance, tensions arising from divergent meanings of the idea of free labor, and questions of how class, gender, race, and ethnicity were woven into the fabric of being Afro–Puerto Rican in nineteenth-century Guayama.

Finally, I reflect in the conclusion on how U.S. colonialism and its sugar revolution helped structure the ways in which Guayama's plantation workers and other subalterns responded to the arrival of the United States and to the reconstitution of local creole elites and their newly refashioned political projects. The advent of U.S. domination after the 1898 Spanish-American War meant the pouring of large sums of capital into the development of capitalist sugar plantations, especially on Puerto Rico's southern coast. I also consider the implications of this process for sugar plantation workers in the Guayama region by taking a quick look at key aspects of the history of sugar workers in the region after the U.S. invasion.[39]

CHAPTER 1

RACIAL PROJECTS AND

RACIAL FORMATIONS IN A

FRONTIER CARIBBEAN

SOCIETY

In introducing his 1972 book, *Guayama: Sus hombres y sus instituciones*, local historian Adolfo Porrata-Doria tells readers that the principal stimulus for his endeavor was a 1848 description of Guayama written by Don José Antonio Vázquez. Vázquez was a prominent sugarcane planter (*hacendado*), mayor (*alcalde*) of Guayama at the time, and member of one of the region's elite creole (*criollo*) families. Guayama, said Vázquez, "is not the motherland of anyone distinguished by his hierarchy, education, or feats of arms."[1] Porrata-Doria concedes that by the middle of the nineteenth century, after some three and a half centuries of Spanish rule, Guayama had indeed failed to produce any men prominent in the annals of Puerto Rican history. Porrata-Doria goes on, however, to point out a great period of progress that began, significantly, after 1870—that is, when the dismantling of slavery in Puerto Rico began. Until the mid-1800s, says Porrata-Doria, Guayameses were "living a pastoral life dedicated to the noble goal of organizing a solid economy that could guarantee the future of the community. [Yet w]hat had not happened during the first centuries was shaped into reality and admirable progress during the last century [1870–1970]. Much good has come since the chronicle of Señor Vázquez. New horizons and perspectives have widened the cultural and industrial life of this *municipio*."[2]

Reflecting on Porrata-Doria's work from the vantage point of the early twenty-first century, one cannot help but feel stunned that such views of Guayama's past could be held and that they could pass until quite recently as the authoritative interpretation. My original response to this interpretation was based largely on childhood tales of Guayama's slave and racially oppressive past told by elderly relatives as well as the findings of more recent Puerto Rican historiography and my research into the *municipio*'s past. I began to wonder why such views would come to pass as history. Indeed, since the late 1970s, new works on nineteenth-century Puerto Rico in general and Guayama in particular have presented a view of this *municipio* and its region sharply at odds with Porrata-Doria's. The works of historians Guillermo Baralt, Andrés Ramos Mattei, and Francisco Scarano, among others, have repeatedly mentioned Guayama as one of Puerto Rico's leading slavery-based, sugar-producing centers during the first seven decades of the nineteenth century and as the setting of one of the most remarkable slave conspiracies in the island's history.[3] Moreover, Jalil Sued Badillo's brief general history of the *municipio*, published a decade after Porrata-Doria's book, portrayed a Guayama of sugar haciendas, worked mostly by slaves and owned by wealthy Puerto Rican, Spanish, and French planters, that rivaled those of the rest of the island.[4]

How, then, to explain Vázquez's and Porrata-Doria's visions of Guayama? Why this gesture of silence, this refusal to represent some crucial experiences in nineteenth-century Guayama? Vázquez's remarks can perhaps be understood as the product of a rich creole *hacendado* complaining about what he sees as the disparity between Guayama's leading economic position in mid-nineteenth-century Puerto Rico and the *municipio*'s lack of military, political, and cultural heroes, an argument that might reveal much about the configurations of power at that time in the Spanish colonial space called Puerto Rico. Vázquez was one of the region's leading sugar planters and slave owners, and his essay obliterates the contributions of enslaved Africans and Afro–Puerto Ricans to the development of sugar production in Guayama—that is, their role as the producers of the wealth enjoyed by Vázquez and his peers, which he seems to complain did not translate into the grandeur of military and political power and the exercise of cultural leadership.

Porrata-Doria's glossing over of the crucial period of sugar and slavery in Guayama's history, however, presents what might seem a different set of interpretative hurdles. On the one hand, Porrata-Doria was the descendant of a nineteenth-century Guayama slaveholding family whose moment of economic glory came and passed around the years of Vázquez's leadership position in local affairs. Curiously, Porrata-Doria consistently avoids discussing Guayama's economic and social history for the period between 1810 and 1870.[5] His failure, for example, even to mention the apogee of sugar production in the first half of the nineteenth century is quite stunning, especially since he otherwise made extensive use of Vázquez's 1848 description, which discusses—if only briefly—the emergence of sugar haciendas.

In striking contrast, Vázquez points out, for example, that Guayameses "have, nevertheless, a right to some celebrity for having increased their wealth by very hard work in little more than twenty years, to the rise and apogee in which it is today, with the peculiarity that less than a dozen *hacendados* started their haciendas with sufficient capital. Many of them, possessing almost nothing the day that they planned the establishment of their estates, today could aspire to be counted among the top landlords of the island." He even described, although very briefly, how this prominence came into being: "Until the year of 1815, the residents [of Guayama] were limited to raising large and small cattle in communal *hatos* [ranches], without any other agriculture than the *tala* or the *conuco* [provision grounds] and some tobacco for their consumption. Later, foreigners began to establish themselves here, stimulated by the advantages offered by the Real Cédula de Gracias of that year. In 1825, their products were so insignificant that they were loaded into four brigantines by the only North American merchant who existed at that time, while today more than 100 large ships sail loaded from its port. The number of these ships in 1845 was 125, plus 79 coasting-trade vessels."[6] But how did these haciendas produce sugar? That is, what labor system did these prominent *hacendados* employ? Vázquez conveniently failed to address this question, perhaps an unsurprising move given that, as chapter 2 will demonstrate, the bulk of the African slaves who toiled in Guayama's sugar plantations had been smuggled into the region after Spanish imperial authorities outlawed the slave trade in 1817 (effective 1820), 1835, and 1845.

Porrata-Doria also rarely discusses slavery in his 320-page book, and he never even hints that slavery flourished in Guayama as it did in very few places in Puerto Rico.[7] For example, one of his few comments on the subject describes slavery as an "archaic and rancid system of centuries past, [that has] disappeared for the glory of we who live together in constant struggle to smooth over racial prejudices."[8] In an effort to "smooth over racial prejudices," Porrata-Doria painstakingly glosses over the painful history of slavery and in so doing achieves another purpose: depriving today's Guayameses and other Puerto Ricans of a work of local history that could help them come to grips with their heritage, as painful as it might be.[9] To that extent, Porrata-Doria's book represents another example of that genre of elitist Puerto Rican historiography and literary writing that since the nineteenth century has sought to create a myth of racial and class harmony and to erect a scholarly monument to Guayama's image as an exceptional case in Caribbean history.[10]

One of the goals of this study is precisely to offer some insights into that history. This is a history painfully shaped by broken memories yet filled with testimonials of struggle not to smooth over race, class, and gender oppression but rather to overcome them. In that context, a central aim of this chapter and the next is to examine the historical processes that Porrata-Doria failed to address: the emergence of Guayama as a leading Puerto Rican slave and sugar region during the first half of the nineteenth century, a period that is soft-pedaled and characterized as a "pastoral" way of life. What was Guayama like during the late eighteenth and the early nineteenth centuries, before the flourishing of the "archaic and rancid system" of slavery?

In answering this broad question, I will consider Guayama's and Puerto Rico's history in two separate moments. This chapter explores Porrata-Doria's trope of a "pastoral life," but doing so requires displacing his time frame by focusing first on the final decades of the eighteenth century and the first decade of the nineteenth century—that is, the time before the boom of sugar and slavery swept across the island's southern coast. In this sense, this chapter has four main goals. I first describe Guayama's physical environment, a region I call "greater Guayama," stretching along southeastern Puerto Rico from the arid lowlands and piedmont of Salinas in the west to the more fertile lowlands and piedmont of Patillas in the east. The ecology of this physical environment both helped and constrained the sustained development of sugar plantation agriculture. And, very importantly, the ecology constrained even more severely the ability of free subalterns, either peasants or workers, including free blacks and mulattoes, to establish a viable and flourishing subsistence or cash-crop peasant economy that their peers in other regions of the island used to eke out a living. This specific feature of greater Guayama would also prove crucial in the aftermath of emancipation.

Precisely because much of the scholarly discussion on the fate of slaves revolves around issues of peasantization versus proletarianization, the chapter turns next to a brief examination of land tenure issues before the development of the region's sugar and slavery economy—that is, during the crucial late-eighteenth-century period of imperial reformist policies. This reformist thrust was intimately linked to efforts to impose a "second colonization" of Puerto Rico that was itself part of the advent of a "second empire" period based largely on the insertion of Puerto Rico, via a "second slavery," into the Atlantic world's vast trade networks.[11] I briefly discuss some of the initial moments of this imperial shift as a prelude to more closely examining a discursive instance produced by local elites at the moment when they seemed to sense that the island was ready to take off as a new zone of plantation agriculture. I will focus on petitions by the *cabildos* (town councils) of San Juan and Coamo, which had jurisdiction over greater Guayama at the start of the nineteenth century.

Local elites of the generation that preceded José Antonio Vázquez, including some notables who may have been his forebears, saw the possibility of leaving behind Porrata-Doria's quaint "pastoral way of life" by basing a new economy on the production of export crops using newly imported African slaves. This amounted to no less than the elaboration of a particular class and racial project that would seal the fate of lowland peasant life and would reconfigure Guayama's society along lines closer to its Caribbean neighbors than had previously been the case, intimately linking greater Guayama with Caribbean networks of finance, commerce, and slave trading during the first half of the nineteenth century.[12] A veritable human hurricane would ensue, as chapter 2 will demonstrate: fierce winds cut through the terrain of a "pastoral" frontier society, blazing a path on which the storm's torrential clouds rained down enslaved people from Africa and the surrounding Caribbean islands as well as settlers from as far away as Denmark, Barcelona, and New Orleans.[13]

A Corner of the Caribbean Known as Guayama, Puerto Rico

In his often-moving portrait of Guyanese society in the late nineteenth century, Walter Rodney describes brilliantly how the ecological setting of British Guiana's frequently flooded coastal plain represented a major constraint on the lives of Guyanese people from aspiring peasants to indentured East Indians and of course struggling planters.[14] In Guayama, at a distant, opposite corner of the Caribbean region, local ecological conditions could not have been more different from those of Guyana's coastal plain. While the latter region received water from the ocean or from overflowing rivers and canals, in Guayama the hazards of low rainfall and the deforestation created by demographic expansion and the need for timber fuel exacerbated the problem of rivers and smaller streams that for most of the year were merely dry, stony gutters. These rivers and streams crisscross an otherwise fertile alluvial plain, squeezed between the Caribbean Sea to the south and a belt of hills to the north, that could barely sustain the production of foodstuffs. The terrain then quickly rises to the highlands of the humid and lush Sierra de Cayey Mountains, where, to the chagrin of coastal sugar planters, most of the heavier rainfall flows not toward Guayama's plantation cane fields to the south but to the north. This combination of terrain and contrasting climatological conditions created the ecological predicament faced by planters, peasants, slaves, and laborers living and working on a mosaic of plantations, cattle ranches, subsistence farms, and small freehold lots during and after the era of sugar and slavery.

The *municipio* of Guayama is located on Puerto Rico's southeastern coast, thirty-three miles south of San Juan and thirty-three miles east of Ponce, on the eastern side of the Ponce-Patillas alluvial plain (see maps 1 and 2). This coastal plain is the island's second-largest, smaller only than its north coast counterpart. The Ponce-Patillas plain encompasses 162.5 square miles in a narrow east-west coastal belt with an average width of three to four miles. For almost a century and a half beginning around 1820, the plain's predominant agricultural use was the growing and grinding of sugarcane to produce raw sugar to be refined in North Atlantic countries. As geographer Rafael Picó put it in 1938, "everything from Ponce to Patillas is connected with sugar."[15]

The most important ecological variations in Puerto Rico are related to the island's topography, rainfall, and soil types, since temperature variation is minimal. The Ponce-Patillas plain is characterized by scarcity of rainfall and by good-quality soil. This coastal plain is the second-most arid region in Puerto Rico, after the island's southwestern corner. Indeed, during the 1920s and 1930s, annual mean rainfall increased traveling east from Ponce toward Guayama, rising from about forty inches per year in the vicinity of Ponce to seventy inches per year in Patillas.[16]

High temperatures work in combination with high evaporation rates, relatively low humidity levels, and steady winds to produce semiarid geographical regions such as the Ponce-Patillas coastal plain.[17] Both rainfall and the carrying capacity of local streams are believed to have been somewhat higher at the start of the sugar boom early in the nineteenth century and to have decreased in quantity and regularity as deforestation, stimulated by population and economic growth, increased the acreage dedicated to agriculture and as the fuel needs of the coast's sugar mills took their toll. As average annual rainfall declined and severe droughts became more common, sugar planters began to devise means for irrigating their lands, from private, rudimentary dams and groundwater pumps built by slave and nonslave workers during the 1840s to more ambitious and extensive irrigation projects constructed from the 1860s through the end of the century. In the early twentieth century, the island's new U.S. colonial government created extensive irrigation systems strikingly similar to those proposed as early as the 1860s to supply the Ponce-Patillas coastal plain with increased water for the newly booming capitalist plantation complex.[18]

The plain's soil has elicited much praise.[19] The soil's alluvial origin gives it its quality, and the otherwise detrimental dryness of the climate prevents heavy erosion. Physical and other chemical characteristics made the soil very suitable for agricultural production and allowed relatively high yields per acre of sugarcane. The alluvial plains slope gently toward the sea or toward rivers and creeks, providing generally good natural drainage. The soil that attracted attention and investment from dozens of Puerto Rican and foreign planters beginning in the late eighteenth century was the natural product of material washed down from the uplands by various rivers and creeks. In Guayama in particular, the most important bodies of water that replenished the plain during seasonal floods were the Guamaní River, which served as a natural border between rural barrios Jobos and Machete and was the most important river in the *municipio*; the Río Seco in barrio Jobos; the Piedra Gorda and Corazón *quebradas* (creeks) in barrio Algarrobos; and *quebradas* Guayabo Dulce and Quebrada Honda in barrios Machete and Jobos, respectively.[20]

At the northern edge of the coastal plain, the semiarid southern foothills constitute a narrow piedmont zone that parallels the coastal plain and provides a buffer between the plain and the humid mountains of the Cordillera Central and the Sierra de Cayey. These hills have elevations ranging from 250 to 1,800 feet above sea level, reaching their highest altitudes to the north. Agricultural productivity here was very low, as these lands were mostly suitable for pasture for raising stock (beef, dairy, and oxen production). In Guayama, the semiarid piedmont dominates the lands of old barrio Quebrada Yeguas (now Carmen); most of barrios Palmas, Pozo Hondo, and Caimital; and the northern tier of Algarrobos. The soil here is very shallow and stony, and the steeper the angle of the hill, the less productive the soil. Only on the banks of streams and on terraces does the accumulation of alluviums make it possible to grow some subsistence crops with success, yet over the course of the eighteenth, nineteenth, and early twentieth centuries, thousands of Guayama's peasants, free laborers, and former slaves sought to settle these stony hillsides, which provided refuge or at least some physical and emotional distance from the sugar estates that dominated the region's most fertile lands.

The township or urban zone of Guayama (the *pueblo*) is located on a plateau formed by of one of these foothills and is surrounded to the east and west by two higher foothills. To the north, the coastal foothills begin to rise quite sharply, and several miles up the road to Cayey the foothills turn into the mountains of the Sierra de Cayey, itself an offshoot of the main chain of mountains, the Cordillera Central, that runs west-east across Puerto Rico's interior. A humid upland terrain dominates most of barrio Guamaní and all of barrio Carite, providing good conditions in which to grow subsistence crops, undertake cattle ranching, and cultivate tobacco and some coffee, although both are of inferior quality to crops produced in the island's west-central mountain region. In more than one sense, Guayama's rural folk, including some former slaves, preferred to eke out a living as subsistence peasants here, forming dispersed communities over four centuries of a Spanish colonial regime that focused mainly on the coastal plain until the middle of the nineteenth century.

In all, Guayama's land area totals slightly more than sixty-five square miles, divided into nine rural barrios—Algarrobos, Caimital, Carite, Carmen (Quebrada Yeguas), Guamaní, Jobos, Machete, Palmas, and Pozo Hondo—and the *pueblo*.[21] However, when sugar and slavery began to flourish in the early nineteenth century, the *municipio*'s total area was somewhat larger, with most of the difference accounted for by the small *municipio* of Arroyo (sixteen square miles) to the east-southeast, which separated from Guayama in 1855. Arroyo's importance during the era of sugar was larger than its small size would indicate. It was Guayama's main seaport and mercantile center, where ships docked to unload scores of slaves from Africa and the surrounding Caribbean region, where slave and free dockworkers loaded ships with barrels of brown sugar bound for Liverpool or New York, and where several of the region's most productive estates thrived.

In his 1848 description of Guayama, Vázquez said that the municipal archive possessed no records that could tell his contemporaries about the *municipio*'s foundation and early settlement. Only the existence of parish registers of baptisms and the memories of some elderly Guayamans helped Vázquez to date the establishment of the *municipio* and its parish to around 1740.[22] More recently, however, historians have discovered further details about Guayama's initial settlement. It is now known, for example, that the first Spanish settlers came to the Guayama region as early as the 1520s in pursuit of mineral resources, particularly gold, as well as wild cattle and eventually to develop a contraband trade with the eastern Caribbean. In the second half of the sixteenth century, as sugar production declined in Puerto Rico, Guayama's residents became involved in contraband trading of cattle and of African slaves, turning Guayama into another node in a wide Caribbean smuggling network that included several communities along Puerto Rico's southern coast. This brief period of modest commercial agricultural production and regional trade had largely ended by the turn of the seventeenth century. Like the rest of the island, Guayama entered a phase of economic and demographic decline that produced dramatic outmigration from Puerto Rico in the face of the development of the mainland colonial centers of New Spain and Peru and even Venezuela and Cuba. The remaining population stagnated and apparently did not begin to grow until the eighteenth century.[23]

Local historians date the foundation of the *municipio* of Guayama to 1736, although no documentation for these claims has yet been found. Guayama was the first *municipio* and parish established in southeastern Puerto Rico and the second on the southern coast proper, trailing only Ponce, created in 1692. The original *municipio* encompassed an area stretching from Jobos Bay in the west to the Cape of Mala Pascua on the southeastern corner of the island, where the Sierra de Guardarraya, an offshoot of the larger Sierra de Cayey, terminates the southern coastal plain by reaching the warm waters of the Caribbean Sea. To the east of the original *municipio*, along the banks of the Río Grande de Patillas (at the time known as Río de Guayama), the region's first demographic and economic growth took place between about 1780 and 1810.

A Caribbean Frontier and the Problem of Land

From the last decades of the eighteenth century, Puerto Rico experienced a complex process of demographic and agrarian transformations. As a result, the island passed from being little more than a Spanish military outpost surrounded by a society based on subsistence agriculture and cattle ranching to a society based on an economy geared toward the production of agricultural staples (mostly sugar and coffee) for North Atlantic international markets. The figures for raw sugar production indicate that the process of growth started slowly during the late 1700s and accelerated sharply after 1815. By the mid–nineteenth century, Puerto Rico had become the Caribbean's second major exporter of sugar, trailing only Cuba, which commanded about one-fourth of the world's sugar output.[24]

Puerto Rico had remained a sparsely populated military outpost on the Caribbean fringes of the Spanish empire for the two centuries that followed the decline of the early postconquest settlement in the second half of the sixteenth century. During this period, two main clusters of population sprang up, the first around the capital port and garrison on the Bay of San Juan de Bautista de Puerto Rico on the north-northeastern coast, and the second at the village of San Germán in the southwest. Several smaller settlements, generally hamlets, dotted the coastal valleys, mostly in the west and north. The bulk of the island, the interior range of mountains

and hills, had remained a hinterland since the destruction of the indige-
nous society in the first half of the sixteenth century. As such, this area
provided, among other things, refuge for an undetermined number of
maroons and deserters of all sorts of racial/ethnic backgrounds. The
island developed a society comprised largely of seminomadic free Afro-
Hispanic peasants, a small number of slaves, and a colonial elite of Spanish
military and civil officials and Spanish and creole cattle ranchers and agriculturalists. Trade connections to the outer world were restricted to a very
small volume of commerce with Spain and a larger contraband trade with
foreign countries through their neighboring Caribbean possessions.[25]

Distinctive land tenure and use patterns emerged in Puerto Rico, as in
its sister Spanish Caribbean colony, Cuba: large, open cattle-ranching
hatos, dedicated mainly to the production of beef and hides, "where herds
of cattle roamed freely"; enclosed, smaller ranches, known as *criaderos*
and *corrales*, where an assortment of smaller animals such as pigs, goats,
and sheep were raised; and farms of varying sizes known as *estancias*,
vegas, and *conucos* and dedicated to the production of foodstuffs and such
cash crops as ginger, allspice, and tobacco. The existence and eventual
destruction of *hatos* caused many of the conflicts over land that erupted
in the final decades of the eighteenth century. The *hatos* represented a
low-intensity form of land exploitation. They usually belonged to more
than one individual and passed undivided from one generation to another even when those with usufructuary rights settled on different parts
of a *hato*.[26]

The vast majority, if not all, of these usufruct rights over Crown lands
had been granted during early Spanish colonial times by the municipal
councils (*cabildos*) of San Juan and San Germán, the only two local
bodies recognized by the Spanish colonial regime until the late eighteenth
century.[27] Unsurprisingly, this *cabildo* practice of granting usufruct rights
over Crown lands was believed to lend itself to considerable corruption,
favoring local Spanish and creole elites and permitting the usurpation of
rights from long-term occupants. On different occasions, especially from
the late seventeenth century onward, the Spanish Crown sought to ban
this *cabildo* practice and to transfer land-grant powers to appointed colonial officials allegedly less inclined to engage in local corruption. This
move probably also constituted an effort by the Crown to regain more effective political control over local issues. A protracted conflict began to
develop between what the Spanish government sought and what local au-

thorities did in the matter of land-tenure policies. This conflict brought
to the fore competing vested interests advocating different land-use policies: cattle ranching, subsistence foodstuff production, and commercial,
export agriculture. The San Juan *cabildo*'s aim of guaranteeing a supply of
foodstuffs for the capital city's population and its military garrison, the
Spanish Crown's aim of developing export agriculture, the interests of
groups of *hateros* and *estancieros* in developing export agriculture, and
the interests of landless peasants in acquiring land created cross-cutting
conflicts throughout the eighteenth and early nineteenth centuries.

Rapid demographic expansion during the eighteenth century was a
major factor in generating these conflicts, as thousands of heretofore
seminomadic peasants began to press for the redistribution of Crown
lands. The Puerto Rican population continued to grow throughout this
century, in great contrast to the demographic debacle of the late sixteenth
and seventeenth centuries.[28] Fernando Picó has conservatively estimated
that throughout the seventeenth century, Puerto Rico's population never
surpassed 10,000 and that at the turn of the eighteenth century the total
lay in the neighborhood of 6,000 people. Yet by 1765 a major survey of the
island's population and economic, social, and cultural conditions showed
44,883 inhabitants, a sixfold increase in just over sixty years.[29] In 1776, a
contemporary estimate put the island's population at 80,246, and figures
for the turn of the century put the number at 163,192, suggesting even
faster population growth during the last quarter of the century.[30]

Thus, during the middle decades of the eighteenth century, groups of
hateros and landless peasants (commonly known as *desacomodados*), especially from the northern coast, began to demand the destruction of
hatos and the redistribution of Crown lands, but these groups often had
conflicting goals.[31] On the one hand, landless peasants demanded more
stable access to land, while on the other, many *hateros* sought to secure
individualized control of extensive tracts, presumably the most fertile
sections located in areas with potential for expanded commercial agricultural production. A third party in many of these controversies was
the San Juan *cabildo*, concerned that the disappearance of *hatos* would
undermine the capital's supply of cheap meat by freeing former *hateros*
from subjection to the *sistema de pesa* (beef tax). The picture was further
complicated by repeated charges of corruption among officials in charge
of granting unused Crown lands and among *hatos*, some of whom sold

the plots for their personal benefit instead of distributing the land among the landless, as well as among the recipients of land grants, who subsequently subdivided the lots and sold the pieces at speculative prices.

At the heart of the government corruption lay the system by which the *cabildo* issued land grants. The Crown sought to eliminate this phenomenon several times during the 1700s, but to no avail: the *cabildo* continued to exercise this function even under clearly illegal terms. Island colonial governors also played important roles, in some instances encouraging the redistribution of marginal Crown lands among *desacomodados*. In other instances, governors blocked the implementation of new policies sent from Madrid aimed at granting property rights to those who held lands in usufruct, while other governors sought to destroy *hatos* to stimulate the cultivation of cash crops, particularly sugarcane, around San Juan's periphery. Nonetheless, these colonial authorities always acted with concern for maintaining social and political stability on a frontier island with strategic military importance and surrounded by colonies of rival European powers.[32]

The parties eventually reached a compromise with the apparent intervention of the governor, and out of this agreement emerged some of the foundations on which southeastern Puerto Rico's future land-use and -tenure patterns were built during the next half century. A fence was to be erected for several miles along the northern and eastern perimeter of the district, in generally hilly and mountainous terrain corresponding mostly to the modern municipalities of Patillas and Arroyo (see map 2). The fence was to be financed by both agriculturalists and ranchers and would separate the *hatos* from the *estancias*. The *hatos* within the fence were to be dismantled and used for agriculture; those outside the fence could continue alongside already existing *estancias* whose crops were not guaranteed protection from damage by animals. The agreement entailed the destruction of cattle ranching in the southeastern lowlands around Jacaboa "to satisfy with its land the *vecinos* [local residents] who, lacking lands, had introduced themselves into the *hatos* and *criaderos* of the Puntilla and Aures, Arroyo, Machetes, Carrera, Caimital, Jobos, Palmas, and some other plains, which they will leave free for *hatos* and *criaderos*."[33]

Not surprisingly, then, the district's early sugar estates were located on lands belonging after 1811 to the *municipio* of Patillas, on the southeastern lowlands around the former *hato* of Jacaboa and its future port, and the

coastal lowlands in the western part of the old greater Guayama municipality did not begin sugar plantation agriculture until the 1810s, when the
Spanish government began to dismantle these *hatos* and to grant their
land primarily to more recent immigrants.

Notwithstanding the cases of San Juan's periphery, Guayama's eastern
tier, and a few other areas where *hato* destruction began as early as the
1750s–70s, not until the implementation of a landmark royal decree, the
Real Cédula of January 1778, did the balance began to tip definitely in
favor of the elimination of *cabildo*-centered land-grant policy, the destruction of *hatos*, the establishment of private land property, and the
development of export agriculture.[34] This *cédula* ordered the survey and
distribution of unused Crown lands (*tierras baldías*) according to their
utility (agriculture or cattle raising), ordered the granting of property
titles to land *usufructuarios* with use titles issued either by the *cabildo* or
the governor, created a land tax to pay for the military garrison of San
Juan, and established three new *cabildos* (Aguada, Arecibo, and Coamo)
to promote demographic and economic growth.[35] Yet these land policies
often simply "officially [ratified] what people had already done" by squat-
ting on unused or little-used Crown and ranching lands. This was apparently the case in the Guayama compromise of 1770 and in the foundation
of several municipalities during the late eighteenth century. In this context, the official destruction of *hatos* by the granting of unused Crown
lands for agricultural pursuits and for new townships helped to facilitate
the tremendous population growth of the late eighteenth and early nineteenth centuries.

Flirting with the Demons of the Atlantic World Economy

Changes in Spanish colonial mercantilist policies and structural shifts
in both the North Atlantic and Caribbean economies during the late
1700s and the early 1800s also represented fundamental sources for these
changes in land policies.[36] Spanish reformist policies began as part of the
broad effort, commonly called the Bourbon Reforms, instituted in Spain
and its American colonial possessions during the eighteenth century.
These reforms sought to refurbish Spain as an imperial power by stimulating trade between the metropole and its American colonies based not
only on traditional mining production but also on increased agricultural

output.[37] One of the Crown's first measures relating to Puerto Rico was a 1755 royal decree authorizing commerce between the ports of Barcelona and San Juan and creating the Real Compañía de Barcelona. For more than two centuries, traditional Spanish policy had restricted lawful commerce between the Iberian Peninsula and the Indies to the Spanish ports of Seville and Cádiz in Andalusia. Flouting these restrictions, contraband commerce between Puerto Rico and its non-Hispanic Caribbean neighbors flourished during the eighteenth century. In an effort to increase its share of Puerto Rico's small but growing trade and to eliminate contraband, Spain began to open trade access to non-Andalusian peninsular ports.[38] This major policy shift had long-lasting consequences not only in Spain but in Puerto Rico as well.

One crucial incident that helped to bring about these changes was the British occupation of Havana in 1762–63. Shortly after the end of the war, Spanish Crown authorities dispatched a series of high-ranking military inspectors to survey and propose improvements in both the defense systems and the socioeconomic conditions of the Caribbean colonies. This moment thus produced both the first major portraits of Puerto Rican society since the sixteenth century and the intensification of Bourbon reformist colonial policies. The key text was Marshal Alejandro O'Reilly's "Report . . . to Your Majesty on the Island of Puerto Rico in 1765," although another, more comprehensive, work appeared two decades later, the *Historia geográfica, civil, y natural de la isla de San Juan Bautista de Puerto Rico* (1788), written by Fray Iñigo Abbad y Lassiera, a Benedictine monk who lived on the island during the 1770s.

To some extent, O'Reilly's report and his subsequent work as a virtual Crown adviser at large on Caribbean colonial matters are often reminiscent of the mentality and writings of late-eighteenth-century British colonial officials in India. They too mixed imperial and economic concerns with the need to elaborate a particular form of power emanating from knowledge of local colonial history and conditions to serve those concerns. The comparison, as stretched as it may at first seem, provides a framework for conceptualizing the period from the 1760s to the 1810s, when Spain carried out a second conquest and colonization of Puerto Rico with the assistance of an assortment of state and church "experts," local Hispano–Puerto Rican settlers, and a new, growing auxiliary corps of mostly non-Castilian and non-Spanish settlers and merchants who combined to insert this frontier Caribbean island into the expanding world economy. O'Reilly's report and to some extent Abbad y Lassiera's, as well as a later, still more extensive document produced by Pedro Tomás de Córdova, the chief secretary to the Spanish governor during the 1830s, could thus be described as "attempts at appropriation" to provide ideological, legal, and administrative support for the sorts of new policies that help set up this second colonization of the island.[39]

As a result of O'Reilly's visit, Spanish authorities took a two-pronged approach toward securing their continuing colonial control of Puerto Rico: large investments in reconditioning and expanding the military defenses of San Juan and other island points, and setting up new economic policies. Crucial among the latter were a series of trade-liberalizing decrees released between 1765 and the first decade of the nineteenth century—for example, 1765, 1777, 1778, and 1789 decrees that opened direct trade between Spain's Caribbean possessions and several Spanish peninsular ports. Another 1765 decree reformed the customs system, simplifying bureaucratic procedures and substantially reducing export/import duties on commerce between Spain and its Caribbean colonies. In 1778, the Crown reformed its customs system, eliminating duties on certain peninsular products, particularly textiles, and some colonial agricultural commodities such as coffee and sugar. Finally, in 1804, after years of petitions by Spaniards and creoles from Puerto Rico, the Spanish government announced the end of the port of San Juan's centuries-old commercial monopoly by permitting lawful trade with the Puerto Rican ports of Aguadilla, Mayagüez, and Cabo Rojo on the island's west coast and Ponce and Fajardo on the south and east coasts, respectively.[40]

These trade-liberalization measures also focused more narrowly on the goal of increasing the flow of African slaves to the Spanish Caribbean after the Seven Years' War. The 1762–63 British occupation of Havana marks a well-documented turning point in the history of slavery and the slave trade in Cuba, a time when British mercantile interests impressed Hispano-Cuban elites in Havana by importing slaves and by linking Cuban exports with the era's leading commercial power. In the aftermath, Spanish metropolitan and colonial authorities moved to establish a series of measures that would expand the slave trade not only to Cuba but also to other Spanish Caribbean territories. Thus, officials experimented with the model of a licensed monopoly (the Compañía Aguirre-Aróstegui), that would bring African slaves and sell them from an entrepôt in San

Juan to buyers in Cuba, Puerto Rico, Trinidad, and the island of Margarita off the coast of Venezuela.

Although estimates show that Aguirre-Aróstegui imported some ten thousand slaves between 1766 and 1770, the experiment eventually collapsed. The Crown tried another model during the 1780s, authorizing Spanish Caribbean settlers to deal with existing French slave-trading networks in charge of supplying bonded Africans to French Caribbean possessions until a landmark 1789 royal decree declared the Spanish Caribbean African slave trade fully open. After 1789, colonists would be allowed duty-free importation of slaves and would be permitted to deal with foreign slave-trading networks to establish slave-trading ventures in association with a slew of mercantile interests ranging from the U.S. southern states and Great Britain (until 1808) to France and Spain. African slave imports to Cuba quickly boomed, and significant numbers of slaves seem to have been imported by settlers in Puerto Rico, where the slave population increased from 11,250 in 1780 to 18,053 in 1795.[41]

Although the bulk of these late-eighteenth-century reforms initially had their strongest effects on the periphery of San Juan on the north coast and on the western coast, O'Reilly and Abbad's colonialist efforts permit the drawing of a fuzzy sketch of Guayama's demographic and economic profile in the late eighteenth century. In his 1765 report, O'Reilly put the total number of Guayamans at 2,404, 1,956 free and 447 slave, while eleven years later, Abbad y Lassiera found 5,120 inhabitants—1,064 whites, 3,170 free mulattoes, 124 free blacks, 251 *agregados* (peasants loosely attached to the land), and 511 slaves. These slave population figures are quite intriguing for what was then the rather extensive and thinly populated southeastern corner of the island that was part of the *municipio* of Guayama (present-day Guayama, Arroyo, and Patillas).

The northern *municipio* of Río Piedras, for example, had 325 slaves out of a population of 1,309 in 1776 (24.8 percent) and did not surpass 500 slaves until 1801, when its 671 slaves comprised 32.6 percent of the population, the highest share ever reported. Río Piedras is adjacent to capital city of San Juan, the island's only official seaport, and was one the main participants in the rudimentary sugar industry and the molasses industry in the late eighteenth century. Although Guayama slaves' share of local total population declined from close to a fourth to about 10 percent between 1765 and 1776, this change resulted primarily from the remarkable 136 percent increase in the district's free population. Nonetheless,

Guayama's slave population figures suggest that slavery played an important role in this region even before the expansion of sugar plantations after the turn of the nineteenth century, perhaps in livestock raising or in the production of some cash crops for the intra-Caribbean contraband trade described by contemporary observers such as O'Reilly and Abbad.[42]

Population growth in the period from the 1770s to the early 1810s did not result exclusively from internal dynamics but also occurred partly because of new colonial policies that stimulated foreign immigration and because of events in Europe and the Caribbean that created a pool of available immigrants. The 1778 decree that opened trade between San Juan and non-Andalusian peninsular ports also allowed foreign immigrants to settle in Puerto Rico as long as they were Roman Catholic nationals of "friendly" nations who pledged their loyalty to the Spanish Crown.[43] Perhaps the most important among these were French and French-creole nationals fleeing upheaval caused particularly by the French and Haitian revolutions or the resulting perilous economic situations. These immigrants came from continental France and the French possessions of Corsica in the Mediterranean, Louisiana in North America (especially after its sale to the United States at the turn of the nineteenth century), and Saint Domingue (Haiti), Martinique, Guadeloupe, and Dominica in the Caribbean.

This early Francophone immigration initially settled mostly on the western coast of Puerto Rico, in and around the ports of Mayagüez and Aguadilla and the village of San Germán, and eventually spread along the southeastern coast. The skills, capital, and slaves brought by many of these migrants, mostly white but also free colored, provided fundamental ingredients for the initial development of both sugar and coffee haciendas from the 1790s through the 1810s.[44] These demographic and economic developments arguably ushered in the "second colonization" of Puerto Rico, which entailed the island's definitive insertion into the North Atlantic–centered world economic system, as well as reshaped the complex roots of Puerto Rican ethnicity.[45] Nevertheless, these developments pale in comparison to the transformations that took place beginning in the late 1810s, when, in the context of the previous internal growth, the demise of the two leading Caribbean sugar producers (Saint Domingue and Jamaica), and the expansion of U.S. commercial interests in the Caribbean, the Spanish Crown published the 1815 Real Cédula de Gracias, seeking to stimulate economic growth in Puerto Rico.[46]

Dreaming of Imported Serfs and Slaves

The missing ingredient from this discussion of the changes in Spanish policies during the second colonization period (1760s–1810s) is labor organization. At first glance, on an island experimenting with rapid demographic growth, colonial authorities and settlers would be expected to focus on transforming the growing number of peasants without legal access to land into a pool of nonslave labor for the commercial agricultural sector of the economy. As it turned out, however, converting the island's peasantry into a substantial, steady, and reliable labor force, especially for the growing sugarcane industry, was one of the battles that Spain and colonial settlers lost in Puerto Rico not only in the late eighteenth century but also throughout most of the nineteenth century.

A crucial aspect of the problem has already been suggested. Puerto Rico's largely mixed-race peasantry had a long tradition as a subsistence, seminomadic group on an island that remained largely a frontier society into the early 1800s. Would these "highly idiosyncratic Puerto Rican rural folk," with their "peripatetic origins" and ways, serve well the labor needs of commercial agriculture?[47] In this context, a distinctive form of coercing Puerto Rican peasants into providing some agricultural labor had emerged during earlier colonial times, as island landholders allowed some of the *desacomodado* peasants to settle, however briefly, on farms and ranches in exchange for furnishing cultivation or ranching services— that is, as *agregados*. *Agregado* labor presented problems, however. Not only were these and other *desacomodado* peasants prone to moving on in search of other land where they could squat or become attached as *agregados*, but the island's sparse settlement and expansive land-tenure system and the Crown's inability or unwillingness to foster the foundation of *pueblos* meant that the vast majority of potential agricultural workers were highly dispersed throughout the frontier territory.

This complex reality no doubt formed part of the backdrop for the protracted conflicts that emerged throughout the eighteenth century over colonial land policies, especially the on-and-off redistribution of marginal lands among *desacomodados*. Thus, by the 1780s and 1790s, the interests of landholding settlers and colonial officials began to converge around a new model for the supply and organization of agricultural labor: the concentration of *desacomodado* peasant families in new villages. O'Reilly took up this idea, proposing to the Crown the foundation of new *pueblos* where the *desacomodados* would be herded as potential laborers. Local colonial officials followed suit, encouraging the formation of new parishes and municipalities, a policy that received further encouragement from the 1778 royal decree that sought to regularize private land rights in Puerto Rico. Thus, during the 1770s, north of Guayama, on a fertile valley atop the Sierra de Cayey, arose a new town, Cayey de Muesas, with a majority of its inhabitants supposedly *desacomodado* families; several other new municipalities were also founded before 1800.[48]

Yet by the time a Napoleonic occupation and the wars of independence in the peninsula and its American empire rocked Spain, colonial authorities and settlers had not been able to convert this idea of reconcentrating landless peasants into villages into a successful labor-supply model. Indeed, the reformist thrust of the 1750s–80s had failed to achieve many of its goals, as is evidenced by the highly illustrative *cahiers des doléance*, as Scarano has so aptly labeled them, that the island *cabildos* formulated in 1809 at the behest of Spanish authorities rallying support in Spain and its American colonies for expelling the French forces and reforming the same ancien régime that liberal Spaniards believed responsible for the debacle.[49]

Historians have quite correctly drawn attention to the ideas and demands elaborated by the *cabildos* in 1809.[50] Few documents better illustrate colonial settlers' concerns at such a crucial moment in both Spanish and Spanish American colonial history. Months after the island *cabildos* met to prepare the "instructions" given their delegate to Cádiz, Don Ramón Power y Giralt, revolts that quickly turned into full-fledged independence wars erupted at various points throughout the empire. However, historians have for the most part commented exclusively on the texts produced by the island's two major historic *cabildos*, San Juan and San Germán. San Germán's petitions hold obvious significance because colonial settlers from the southwestern part of the island seem to echo the views of many of their peers elsewhere in the empire in arguing that if Spain could not expel French occupying forces and restore its legitimate government, Puerto Rico "should remain independent and freely allowed to choose the best means of guaranteeing the preservation and sustenance of its habitants."[51] San Juan's petitions, especially the draft prepared by its mayor, Pedro Irizarri, a Creole, have received the bulk of historians' attention, but those prepared by the Coamo *cabildo* have not been studied extensively, although they merit considerable attention here.

Irizarri's views are significant because he voices the opinions of important sectors of the island's creole elite on some of the period's most pressing social, economic, and cultural issues. After starting his comments with what seems a startling cry, "¡Puerto Rico, o amada Patria! [Puerto Rico, oh beloved homeland!]," Irizarri turns to an elaborate discussion of what he considers to be the major problems affecting his "beloved homeland": an underdeveloped agricultural potential, highlighted by an "abundance of uncultivated lands"; the slow population growth; the oppressive property and church fees and taxes for the construction of military barracks and churches; the archaic sales taxes; the excise taxes on the sale and export of cane liquor; the excessive duties and restrictions on the import of wheat flour; an extensive contraband trade; the lack of institutions of primary, secondary, technical, and higher education; and the disruptive and potentially subversive role played by the recent influx of foreigners, especially Protestants. The *cabildo* of the district of Coamo, which at the time included the municipalities from Ponce on the south-central coast to greater Guayama on the southeast, expressed similar views, as did a handful of interior municipalities. Indeed, substantial sections of Coamo's petitions, agreed upon by the councillors on 20 November 1809—that is, two months after Irizarri prepared his draft—repeat Irizarri's text verbatim.[52]

Nevertheless, the sections where these two texts part ways assist in finding an understanding of the conflicting discourses of local elites from the capital region and of those from what remained a largely underpopulated and unexploited frontier region on the opposite, southern side of the central mountain range that virtually splits the island in two. These differences are also important not only because of the opposing views they present on how to solve agricultural labor problems but also because they help in avoiding the common tendency of too many historians and other nineteenth- and twentieth-century intellectuals to draw neat, facile, and essentializing dichotomies between an allegedly liberal, antislavery, Puerto Rican creole elite and a conservative, proslavery Spaniard elite, a trope that until recently has dominated the representation of nineteenth-century Puerto Rican political, cultural, and economic conflicts. Thus, while Irizarri largely neglects the practice that forced cattle ranchers to provide cheap meat to the capital, this issue is the first *doléance* expressed by the southeastern region's creoles. While Irizarri devotes thirty-eight lines to attacking the recent influx of foreigners (especially on the issue of religion), the Coamo *cabildo* dedicates less than half that space to this issue and does so without the sectarian fervor. And while Irizarri spends what amounts now to half a printed page on the contraband issue, the councillors who represented one of the regions most involved in illegal trade failed to even mention this topic.[53]

Yet the San Juan and Coamo *cabildos'* discussions of the intimately linked issues of labor, the peasantry, and slavery illustrate the most radical differences between the views emanating from the capital and from the southeastern frontier. Irizarri fills his text with sweeping attacks on the moral character of the island's peasants, especially its black population, accusing *agregados* of vagrancy, loose sexual practices, and a tendency to spend considerable sums of money (relative to their meager earnings) buying "luxurious" clothing and accessories to "equalize" their social standing. He is particularly furious with black slave men and women who come to the city wearing so many "accessories, clothing, and jewelry that if it was not for the color of their faces, they would be indistinguishable" from the most elite elements of the capital's social hierarchy. Irizarri also vents his spleen against the *agregados*, denouncing the practice of attaching them to farms where they paid no rent and planted only foodstuffs but no cash crops in light of the fact that they rarely stayed on one farm for more than a year before moving on, living "always as vagrants, drifters, and without fixed residence." He sees them as "the repository of idleness and vice," widely regarded as the "ignorant, despicable, unsteady, and undisciplined authors of the destruction of their own homeland."[54]

But if such was the condition of the island's peasantry, could they be reshaped into a reliable labor force? Irizarri offers merely a qualified yes, and he therefore proceeds to consider an alternative: the importation of agricultural laborers. But from where? Under what conditions? This is, he tells us, "a delicate and difficult issue." Yet his preference is clear. Although the importation of African slaves, he argues, had benefited the colonists of the western, French section of neighboring Hispaniola, the practice also eventually resulted in the rich colony's destruction at the hands of rebellious slaves. Should Puerto Rico take a similar risk? Could the island's settlers achieve a better degree of control than the French had? Impossible. Haiti, Irizarri stresses, serves as a "tragic example to remind us constantly that for men born in the wild [*barbarie*] . . . , inhuman by nature, without religion or morality . . . force can only domesticate them externally, but they would continue internally to be bad citizens, disgruntled [*infelices*], and traitors, invisible enemies of their masters, the country and state."

Then, in a highly revealing gesture, Irizarri hints at the existence on the island of what he calls "the Black Party," a group of settlers who favor the massive importation of African slaves. Indeed, Irizarri strongly and explicitly warns his fellow councillors and by extension Spanish colonial authorities that encouraging the importation of slaves will concentrate wealth and power. As he argues, "Ten or twenty planters, with a formidable capital and with their slaves, will become the powerful in every town. But will all the land come under cultivation? Of course not, and therefore I don't believe that the system to follow is that some people cultivate a portion of land but that many cultivate all of it." Vaguely referring again to this group, Irizarri extends his arguments against the expansion of the slave trade in Puerto Rico, alleging that while slaves were few, "there was nothing to fear," but after "importing more everyday, and [after they reproduced] themselves through generations . . . would not they come to form a multitude, which if not now, would become an exterminating thunderbolt for future generations?" Finally, against the Armageddon that then would come, surely assisted by revolutionary Haitians, Irizarri offered the warmed-over alternative pursued by colonial authorities almost a century earlier: the massive importation of free laborers from the Canary Islands as well as New Spain.[55]

Irizarri's text constitutes one of the first and most articulate renditions of a particular vision of Puerto Rican society and its future, a vision that, with time, would become the primary hegemonic project of the island's liberal elites. Key to this project was the view that Puerto Rico was a society with the necessary, if not sufficient, conditions to become an exception to the general, dominant course of Caribbean history—in other words, not a society based on an export agricultural economy mounted on the importation of African slaves and consequently Africanized in radical and substantive terms, but a society dominated by white (or nearly white, light-skinned mulatto) settlers and their descendants, a veritable pearl in a sea of blackness. This vision, furthermore, would have as one of its fundamental tenets a clearly racist view of its surrounding, largely African, Caribbean neighbors, haunted by the specter of slave and free-colored insurrection and the extermination of an Occidentalist settler society.

Moreover, it is quite significant that, like any hegemonic project, Irizarri's identifies its main competing, rival hegemonic project, which he metonymically calls the Black Party: those white (or nearly white) local elites who envision a productive colonial enterprise in Puerto Rico that runs parallel to what has already emerged by 1809 as the dominant form of colonial economic development in neighboring Cuba: the construction of a plantation economy based on the massive importation of African slaves. Irizarri seems to imply that this Black Party of eager slaveholders and planters in the making and their merchant fellow travelers are proposing an alternative hegemonic project that will transform Puerto Rico from a frontier society to one more along the lines of other Caribbean slave societies. Could this be the alternative hegemonic project of those southeastern local elites represented by Coamo's *cabildo*? After all, the southern coastal valley would become Puerto Rico's premiere sugar and slavery zone during the first half of the nineteenth century. Was this what Coamo's *cabildo* envisioned?

As in their discussions of other issues, the authors of Coamo's report spend one-fourth as much space as Irizarri on the disadvantages of *agregado* labor, focusing instead on the solution to the overall labor-supply and -control problem but arguing for exactly the opposite model. As they put it, "It is our experience that every year [farmers] suffer the regrettable loss of large portion of their harvest, lacking hands that would collect it when this need could be supplied by those who have [no lands]. But to improve [our] agriculture, [the lands] are not enough, and it is necessary to acquire blacks from the Coast of Guinea, while monitoring closely that the proportion of slaves in the island does not exceed one-fifth of the population." Later, in the formal listing of petitions to be presented to Power and through him to Spanish authorities in Europe, the representatives of the southern landowning creole elite wrote, "Seventh: That the importation of blacks, so necessary and so lacking in this Island to develop it, be made from the Coast of Guinea, and be free from all [import] duties, and in ships of any neutral or friendly flag; and that the earnings from their production be equally free of taxes; that the government take note only of sales, so that it could not collect more revenues than these . . . ; and that, if it is possible, of this importation one-third be female; and that in [the next] twenty years it does not exceed twenty-five thousand, which would be, more or less, a fifth of the white and free population." Finally, as if to make more obvious what—and who among the local creole elites— was behind this proposal, the authors' fourteenth *súplica* (plea) calls for opening the port of Salinas, just west of Guayama, to legal, free trade as a complement to the recently announced legalization of trade through the port of Ponce. The *súplica* buttresses this petition by pointing out that this area of the southeastern coast has fertile lands for the cultivation of sugarcane, coffee, cotton, indigo, and other commodities.[56]

The views expressed by Coamo's *cabildo*, which included members with creole surnames of long tradition in this region (de Rivera, Vázquez, Colón, de Santiago, and de Torres), crystallized the vision of many area colonial settlers that the southern coast of the island had the potential to become a profitable producer of tropical commodities for North Atlantic markets. This view was consistent with the earlier petition to eliminate *hatos* in eastern Guayama and dovetailed with the views of the group's wealthier Cuban creole counterparts, who had by now very successfully developed their sugar plantations with slave labor imported from the "Coast of Guinea" and elsewhere in West Africa.

These quoted passages draw attention to the peculiar form in which this alternative hegemonic project rendered the strategy of basing the development of plantation agriculture on slave labor. Members of the Coamo *cabildo* clearly focused their sights on Africa and on the expansion of the slave trade free of colonial taxes and shipping restrictions. Knowing that earlier efforts to develop African slave trade based on imperial monopolistic licenses had failed and that Spain lacked established and well-developed networks for slave acquisition in West Africa, southeastern elites demanded that slave shipments use non-Spanish "neutral or friendly" foreign slave mercantile networks, a demand that anticipated the large role that French, Portuguese, and Dutch slave traders would play in the Puerto Rican slave trade from the 1810s to 1840s. However, in an exceedingly revealing move, southeastern elites emphasized twice that such importation of African slaves should be carefully managed: the importation should be limited to the equivalent of one-fifth of the existing free white and colored population, and the population of imported African slaves should contain enough females to make it possible to reproduce locally the slave population over subsequent generations.

In other words, southeastern elites may have been as aware as their San Juan counterparts that the flooding of African slaves into Puerto Rico could radically shift the island's racial and cultural balance and thereby threaten the security of the island's settler society. At the same time, the Coamo elites seemed to believe that the best formula for sustaining a slave labor force at adequate levels would be through a natural reproduction strategy that would generate creolized slaves who might pose less of a threat to the colonial order than Africans did. The importation of twenty-five thousand African slaves could be seen as a necessary condition for the takeoff of plantation agriculture, while the inclusion of eight thousand African women would be viewed as an essential ingredient for the sustainability of the plantation economy. Yet proponents of this strategy hoped that it would preserve the fundamental lineaments of a settler colonial model that diverged from the "exploitative" slave society model that dominated the colonial societies of the British, French, and Dutch Caribbean.

While in some respects these two sets of petitions written for the consumption of Spanish imperial policy makers illustrate two divergent hegemonic projects, one putting its stock in the importation of poor, white Spanish peasant workers, the other in black African slaves with the qualifications introduced by the southeastern elites, the two views shared notions of race and society that ultimately made both sets of demands projects that sought to reshape the racial formation of Puerto Rican society. The concepts of racial formation and racial projects elaborated by Michael Omi and Howard Winant are useful here because they help to provide an understanding of the potentially hegemonic nature of the formulations expressed by each *cabildo*.

Omi and Winant define racial formation as "the sociohistorical process by which racial categories are created, inhabited, transformed, and destroyed." They see racial formation as intimately linked to the elaboration and evolution of hegemony and hegemonic processes and outcomes. As they put it, racial formation "is a kind of synthesis, an outcome, of the interaction of racial projects on a society-wide level." In turn, racial projects are defined as "simultaneously an interpretation, representation, or explanation of racial dynamics, and an effort to reorganize and redistribute resources along particular racial lines." Furthermore, they see racial projects as engaged in linking "what race *means* in particular discursive practice and the ways in which social structures and everyday experiences are racially *organized* based upon that meaning."

For Omi and Winant, racial projects vary widely in both "scope and effect," including "large scale public action, state activities, and interpretations of racial conditions in artistic, journalistic, or academic fora, as well as the seemingly infinite number of racial judgments and practices we carry out at the level of individual experience." Their linking of concepts of racial formation and racial projects with a Gramscian-derived understanding of hegemony is paramount in their theoretical formulations. In their view, racial projects constitute "the building blocks not just of racial formation, but hegemony in general. Hegemony operates by simultaneously structuring and signifying." Finally, taking into consideration that ideological formulations and social practices also are structured and signified along class, gender, and sexual lines, Omi and Winant assert that, along with race, these categories "constitute 'regions' of hegemony, areas in which certain political projects can take shape. They share certain obvious attributes in that they are all 'socially construed,' and they all consist of a field of projects whose common feature is their linkage of social structure and signification."[57]

Conclusion

The remainder of this book will demonstrate that the two divergent racial projects expressed by the San Juan and Coamo *cabildos* came to interact, often in contradictory ways, through the views, policies, and practices of metropolitan and colonial officials and of both planters and other elites and subalterns in Puerto Rico over the course of the nineteenth century. The racial project expressed by Coamo's *cabildo* came to dominate during the first half of the nineteenth century, resulting in a racial formation in which the combined effects of an increase in the slave trade, the rise of hundreds of sugar plantations housing thousands of African and creole captives, the immigration of both white and free colored Europeans and Antilleans, and the increasing need to police and control slaves and free people of color in the context of sporadic rebellions and other forms of overt resistance, along with colonial authorities' and local elites' fears of possible separatist insurrections or a race war, produced a social order that was significantly more repressive in the ways in which it envisioned the exercise of power and the enforcement of social hierarchies. Race now played a more fundamental role.

In this sense, Jorge Chinea has recently raised an important issue that underscores the kind of shift this discussion suggests—from a frontier, sparsely populated island with a small presence of slavery to a society in which slavery came to constitute the principal engine of the island's economy. Chinea points out that runaway slaves escaping to Puerto Rico from neighboring islands were able, under the original racial formation, to "evade detection and capture by joining up with a wide assortment of 'masterless'" subalterns, "*jíbaro* [peasants], seafarers, adventurers, illegal traders, military defectors inhabiting the relatively unguarded and inaccessible regions just outside the colonial reach of the Spanish authorities in San Juan." However, the emergence of slavery as the principal form of labor in the sugar plantation economy, along with the arrival of thousands of African slaves and Spanish authorities' fear of potential separatist or slave and racial revolts, resulted in the emergence of a new, more expansive military regime and local forms of surveillance. This surveillance emanated from within the plantations and extended into townships and other rural areas, seeking to control not only slaves but also free people of color, particularly Caribbean immigrants who had the potential to bring revolutionary ideas to the island's free and enslaved subaltern peoples. As China puts it, the agrarian boom of the 1810s to 1840s "was accomplished by rigorously and harshly controlling the social and working conditions of the nominally free and bonded workers."[58]

The precepts for a different kind of racial project as articulated by the San Juan *cabildo* would remain present during the first half of the nineteenth century and would acquire a more prominent role around mid-century. The subsequent shift has been associated with the rise by the 1860s of creole intellectuals who began to question the nature of the racial formation and social order produced by the growth of slavery, arguing for the need to do away with slavery, to emphasize the racially mixed nature of Puerto Rican society, and to turn to the island's large free rural laboring population as the basis for a plantation economy. This resurgent, counterhegemonic racial project came to be anchored in a creole view that highlighted what it considered to be Puerto Rico's "racial harmony," as illustrated by its high degree of racial mixing, and with it the exceptionalism of Puerto Rico in the Caribbean context. The creole elites saw Puerto Rico as fundamentally a settler society that seemed like an extension of the Spanish homeland (*madre patria*), a position that buttressed efforts to achieve autonomy through the recognition of Puerto Rico as an overseas province of Spain rather than the island's fundamentally Caribbean culture and social organization. From this wellspring emerged Puerto Rican abolitionism in the 1860s, and in the context of the clash between these two alternative racial projects, thirty thousand Puerto Rican slaves sought to define the contours of the freedom from slave labor granted to them by abolition in 1873.[59]

THE HURRICANE OF SUGAR AND SLAVERY AND THE BROKEN MEMORIES IT LEFT BEHIND, 1810S–1860S

It was a bright, sunny day, and, as is usual during the Christmas holiday season, families and friends went on their typical trips, crisscrossing Puerto Rico to visit each other. I was heading toward a rural community just west of Guayama to visit one of my uncles and his family. Traversing the island from north to south, from San Juan to Guayama, the toll highway crosses the Sierra de Cayey, a journey on which the changing ecology is clearly visible. The lush green of the sierra gives way to the virtually barren, dry, southern piedmont hills before reaching the coastal plain. I joined the festivities at my relatives' house, located in a so-called *parcela* community created by Puerto Rican government agrarian reform programs on a former sugar plantation during the 1950s and 1960s.

We exchanged gifts and stories about how grown-up my uncle's grandchildren had become and about the fortunes or misfortunes of relatives who had migrated to the United States. I remember this occasion vividly because of what occurred when the topic switched to my graduate studies and when I would finally finish my degree. As in other moments, I explained what graduate history required and how a research project could be conducted, and I described my research topic. As at other times, however, the discussion of my project, or maybe some of my comments and questions, drew a variety of often befuddled or negative responses. I scrambled not only to explain but also to justify why in the world it would be "important" or "useful" to unearth unpleasant memories and stories so closely associated with racial and class domination.

Someone within a group of cousins and neighbors that included a descendant of Guayama slaves then asked on that unforgettable day in December 1986, "So, why spend time showing that slavery existed around here? After all, that's a thing of the past." To which I uttered a rather naive and clichéd response: "Because learning about the past is important for understanding the present." The rejoinder of one of my interlocutors then stunned me: "But why should *you* bother with this, Luisito? After all, you turned out more light-skinned than many of us around here. Look, you can even pass without many problems. What you will do is bring trouble on yourself! Let it go, or at least remember: try not to offend anyone by pointing out that so-and-so has slave ancestry or that this or that family once held slaves."

I recall similar conversations about these issues during many more recent visits to the southeastern coastal region—especially Guayama, Salinas, and Arroyo—an area I have known through family and friendship networks since the 1960s. On another occasion, I visited the recently opened historical museum at the sumptuous house built by a local merchant-planter family on Guayama's main square. My guide on that occasion was a "mulatto" woman who had been trained by the government's Instituto de Cultura Puertorriqueña (Institute of Puerto Rican Culture), a sort of ministry of cultural affairs. I asked her about when the *instituto* would build a museum to mark the history of slavery and slave life in Guayama and thus highlight Afro-Guayameses' contributions to local and regional history. She replied, "There isn't that much money available now, and maybe not enough people are interested in touching a topic that folks [*la gente*] often find painful and disturbing." Besides, she added, the family that owned the mansion had few slaves, and most local slaveholders treated their slaves well. "After all," she pointed out, "don't you see how well races got along here, where people mixed together [*se mezclaron*] and have left slavery behind them?" "But I know many folks around here who carry surnames inherited from slaveholders," I replied, insisting perhaps too much, "I see one of them on your name tag! What have you heard folks saying about this?" "Not much," she answered tersely, switching the topic in obvious discomfort. It then dawned on me once more why Adolfo Porrata-Doria's portrayal of Guayama's past discussed in chapter 1 would have so much purchase. In a subtle way, of course, I was engaged in questioning, to quote Paul Connerton, "how societies remember."[1]

The beginning of chapter 1 briefly explored Porrata-Doria's problematic misrepresentation of or refusal to represent Guayama's era of slavery in his work. I pointed out that his portrait of mid-nineteenth-century Guayama as having the conditions of a "pastoral life" is highly problematic, given what Porrata-Doria could have learned from looking at some basic, published primary sources available when he was writing during the 1960s. I also mentioned the contrasting views of slavery in nineteenth-century Puerto Rico and Guayama in particular developed by a new generation of historians that came of age in the 1970s and early 1980s. Yet my two personal stories suggest rather powerfully that even after the revisionist historiographical efforts of the 1970s and 1980s—efforts that have subsequently had a substantial impact on literary writing and journalistic discussions—a sort of broken historical memory of this past still permeates Guayama's and Puerto Rico's society. These two stories also serve as powerful antidotes to any romantic pretensions that the work of a small group of intellectuals could, just by itself, alter Puerto Ricans' perceptions of our history.

This chapter will examine in some detail and from a comparative perspective the character and the magnitude of the transformations that turned Guayama from a frontier society into one of Puerto Rico's leading nineteenth-century slave and sugar plantation districts. I do not seek to carry out a full-fledged study of Guayama under slavery, a task that would entail considerably more research.[2]

My goals in this chapter are threefold. First, I offer a brief overview of the emergence of Puerto Rico as a fast-growing and important sugar-producing Caribbean society between the 1810s and the 1840s. Crucial factors in this process included the culmination of imperial policy shifts that had begun in the final decades of the eighteenth century as well as the ascendancy of a creole planter elite that had set its sights on transforming the island's frontier society into a plantation economy since the late eighteenth century. However, a new factor in the equation was the arrival of a new cadre of merchants, planters, and free skilled workers from Europe and the non-Hispanic Caribbean who brought to the island significant amounts of cash, credit lines, machinery, and slaves as well as strategic access to mercantile, financial, and slave-trading networks that spanned the Caribbean archipelago, the North and South Atlantic, and the Mediterranean. Furthermore, even though Puerto Rico had one of the Caribbean's largest free populations, with a remarkable growth rate since the eighteenth century, planters and merchants—Puerto Rican creoles, Spaniards, or newly arriving non-Hispanic Europeans and Antilleans—turned to the African slave trade as the principal source of labor for an expanding sugar economy. This switch is ironic given the fact that such commerce came under increasing attack internationally after 1815, but the change certainly falls within the framework for the development of a plantation economy that the Coamo *cabildo* expressed in its 1809 report: "to improve [our] agriculture, [the lands] are not enough, and it is necessary to acquire blacks from the Coast of Guinea."[3]

A second goal of this chapter is to identify some of the structural constraints faced by the island's sugar plantations after their initial explosive growth of the 1810s–40s. I will focus on the following two decades, when Puerto Rican sugar planters and merchants sought to sustain more modest rates of growth in the face of the end of the slave trade, the potential for abolition in the not-so-distant future, the need to secure alternative sources of labor, a decline in the importation of capital for sugar production, and the need to modernize sugar operations to maintain the Puerto Rican sugar industry's competitiveness.[4] Finally, I will assess the development of Guayama's sugar and slavery hacienda complex relative to developments in other areas of the Caribbean.[5] From the 1810s to the 1830s, Guayama amazingly quickly developed a plantation system that rivaled others in comparable contexts in the greater Caribbean in terms of productivity and that relied more heavily on slave labor than did the most productive slave plantation district in Puerto Rico, the municipality of Ponce on the island's south-central coast. Guayama's planters would attempt to maintain the influx of African slaves even in the face of additional efforts to ban the trade in the 1840s.

The culmination of the long series of new imperial policies, the 1815 Real Cédula de Gracias tried to "systematize" in a single document the trends in Spanish Caribbean policy that had been evolving during the second half of the eighteenth century.[6] The imperial government issued the Cédula de Gracias also partly in response to Puerto Rican residents' and colonial officials' long-standing demands for reforms, as expressed in the petitions to the king after the defeat of the British invasion of 1797 and the 1809 instructions to Puerto Rico's delegate to the Spanish Cortes. The Cédula de Gracias, which was drafted during the liberal interregnum of 1810–14 and issued by King Ferdinand VII a year after he returned Spain to an absolutist monarchical regime, also represented an attempt to dissuade Puerto Ricans from joining the independence movements sweeping across Spain's American continental possessions.[7] However, while those petitions expressed interest in policies favoring local landholders, the *cédula* favored demographic and economic expansion through foreign immigration and investment. Among the most important benefits offered to foreigners interested in settling in Puerto Rico were land grants at the rate of almost seven acres of land per white immigrant head of household and another three-quarters of an acre per slave who entered the island with his or her master. In addition, immigrants would be allowed tax exemptions for fifteen years, including the duty-free importation of capital, slaves, and agricultural and construction equipment and tools, and would be granted naturalization after five years of residence provided that they fulfilled specific requirements set by local colonial authorities. These policies remained in effect until 1830 and helped to foster an unprecedented increase in the movement toward the export economy based largely on plantation agriculture that both colonial policy makers and creole and Spanish colonial elites had begun to envision and had slowly begun to put into practice.

Yet 1815 represents a crucial historical marker in the development of slave-based sugar plantations in nineteenth-century Puerto Rico not only because of the Cédula de Gracias but also because it marked the end of the Napoleonic Wars that had ravaged Europe and had extended to battles for the control of various European colonies in the New World. The end of the wars ushered in a long period of relative peace in the Atlantic world, allowing the resumption of normal conditions for the circulation

TABLE 2.1: Population of Puerto Rico by Race and Legal Status, 1776–1898

| | WHITES | | FREE PEOPLE OF COLOR | | | | | | SLAVES | | TOTAL |
| | | | MULATTOES | | BLACKS | | | | | | |
Year	N	%	N	%	N	%			N	%	N
1776[a]	29,263	36.5	33,808	42.1	2,803	3.5			6,537	8.1	80,246
1802	78,281	48.0	55,164	33.8	16,414	10.1			13,333	8.2	163,192
1815	93,747	42.4	73,540	33.3	13,605	6.2			18,621	8.4	220,886
1820	102,432	44.4	86,269	37.4	20,191	8.8			21,730	9.4	230,622
1827	150,311	49.7	95,430	31.5	25,057	8.3			31,874	10.5	302,672
1830	162,311	50.1	100,430	31.0	26,857	8.3			34,240	10.6	323,838
1834	188,869	52.9	101,275	28.4	25,124	7.0			41,818	11.7	357,086
1846	216,083	48.8	154,300	34.8	21,491	4.8			51,265	11.6	443,139
1860	300,430	51.5	241,015	41.3	—	—			41,736	7.2	583,308
1867	346,984	52.9	265,996	40.5	—	—			43,348	6.6	656,328
1877	411,712	56.3	319,936	43.7	—	—			—	—	731,648
1883	466,981	57.6	343,413	42.4	—	—			—	—	810,394
1887	474,933	59.5	246,647	30.9	76,985	9.6			—	—	798,565
1899	578,009	60.6	304,352	31.9	59,390	6.2			—	—	953,243

Sources: Abbad y Lassiera, Historia, 153; David Turnbull, Cuba, 555; Bergad, Coffee, 14, 69; Acosta, Coleccion, 8; Puerto Rico, Censo; U.S. Department of War, Informe.

Note: Free mulattoes and blacks were not reported separately in figures for 1860, 1867, 1877, and 1883. Data for those years under the "mulattoes" heading includes both free mulattoes and free blacks.

[a] The 1776 total includes 7,835 agregados, or farm residents, not classified by race.

of people, including slaves, as well as capital, agricultural commodities, and manufactured goods across the Atlantic and within the Caribbean region. After 1815, as Dale Tomich wrote more than a decade ago, "Sugar was transformed from a luxury good to an article of mass consumption. Sugar prices soared, and producers rushed to fill the void [left by the destruction of the great producer, French Saint Domingue]. The unparalleled expansion of the world sugar market during the first half of the nineteenth century stimulated the development of new producing areas and hastened the decadence of old ones."[8]

Puerto Rico became one of these new zones of sugar production: although it never matched Cuba's dominant share of the world sugar market, Puerto Rico developed into the second-largest producer of sugar in the Western Hemisphere. The island experienced dramatic demographic changes beginning in the late eighteenth century. From 1765 to 1802, its population grew by 264 percent, a rate of increase that barely abated after the turn of the nineteenth century.[9] Table 2.1 presents data on the island's population in the nineteenth century broken down by race and legal status. From it we can discern that the total population in 1834 represented a 219 percent increase from what had been estimated in 1802. Even more dramatically, sugar production volumes, measured by the export of sugar (not including molasses), grew an incredible 680 percent from 1817 to 1827 and an additional 252 percent by 1862. Judging from sugarcane acreage measured in *cuerdas* (1 *cuerda* equals 0.97 acre), the expansion of cane fields did not definitely take off until the 1820s, when it grew at a remarkable pace. While from 1817 to 1824 total acreage in sugarcane grew at a modest 2.4 percent yearly, from 1824 to 1830 it increased almost 12 percent a year, an average growth rate that continued for more than thirty years. However, the direct impact of sugarcane cultivation extended beyond the total acreage planted. As Francisco Scarano has pointed out, "For every cuerda of cane, of course, several more of pasture, forest, and subsistence crops were needed to graze the draft animals, supply fuel and lumber for the mills, and feed the workers. Thus, the real proportion of economically exploited land invested in sugar-making was enormous, and not necessarily equivalent to the total area occupied [by cane fields]."[10]

The expansion of sugar production in the coastal plains had important consequences for Puerto Rico's historical geography. Scores of coastal peasant rural barrios had hitherto developed a subsistence economy based on the cultivation of various foodstuffs and cattle raising. The growth of coastal sugar plantations displaced literally thousands of peasants from coastal plains and forced them to migrate to the final hinterland frontier, the island's underpopulated interior, between the 1810s and the 1850s. New municipalities were constituted in the interior and thereafter emerged Puerto Rico's counterpoint to the *bajura* (lowlands), where sugar plantations and cattle raising tied to the plantation system predominated over subsistence farming. In this *altura* (uplands), the peasant subsistence economy and society sought refuge, only to face threats as a result of the expansion of coffee cultivation after 1850.[11]

Puerto Rico had been a racially mixed society since the second half of the sixteenth century. In the nineteenth century, the population officially classified as "white" represented about half the total before abolition in 1873. Puerto Ricans classified as "free blacks" and "mulattoes" comprised around 40 percent of the island's total throughout the nineteenth century.[12] The island's slave population, meanwhile, never surpassed 12 percent, approximately one slave per eight inhabitants, even at its peak in the late 1840s and early 1850s, when the already illegal slave trade for all practical purposes was cut off. Therefore, Puerto Rican society sharply contrasted not only with neighboring British and French Caribbean colonies but also with its fellow Spanish colony, Cuba.

In nineteenth-century Cuba, slaves constituted a much higher proportion of the general population, while the free population of color had a much lower share of the total. Slaves represented no less than 20 percent of the Cuban population during the first stages of plantation growth in the last third of the 1700s and reached close to half the total population during the 1840s, when the slave share peaked.[13] Given this contrast, a group of scholars during the 1970s began to raise the question of what role, if any, Puerto Rico's relatively small slave population played in the nineteenth-century development and sustenance of export agriculture. These scholars also wondered about the consequences the peculiarities of the slavery experience in Puerto Rico had had for postemancipation class formation.

Traditional interpretations of slavery's role in the development of Puerto Rico's export economy had until the late 1970s and early 1980s looked on islandwide percentages of slave versus free population and assumed (as well as concluded) that slavery played merely a minor role.[14] This finding is to a certain extent ironic, given the numerous contemporary testimonies regarding the slavery's importance in the sugar industry's development. For example, Lidio Cruz Monclova's monumental, multi-volume history of nineteenth-century Puerto Rico includes a lengthy transcription of a September 1876 letter from Governor Segundo de la Portilla to the Spanish minister of overseas territories that assesses, among other topics, the importance of slave labor in sugar production. Just five months after the end of the period of forced contracting of the ex-slaves, the governor wrote,

> Although slavery was not the only and exclusive instrument of labor used on the sugar plantations, it could be said that it constituted the medullary nerve of production, since the *hacendado*, applying the work of his slaves to the various tasks required to cultivate the planta-tion during the whole year, counted on the [free] peasant only at the precise moment of cutting the cane, with the objective of dedicating the slaves to the task of grinding it. The *jíbaro* laborer who lives on the mountain, where he occupies himself in [the cultivation of] minor crops, taking care at the same time of the tobacco and coffee [crops], comes down to the plains only during [sugar] harvest time, and even then the number who come down is small, because those who live in the interior of the island leave their communities with reluctance.[15]

Other observers confirm de la Portilla's statement. In 1850, when the contraband importation of slaves was being shut down, an eastern coast *hacendado* petitioned the government for a license to buy twenty-five slaves, stressing the importance of slave labor in the sugar industry. Free laborers, he said, "cannot be employed in the cane harvest, because gener-ally they do not want to work, and if they do work it is only for one or two days. Few of the free laborers complete their work, and there are some tasks (as those of the boiling house) . . . that the free laborers do not want to perform."[16]

Revisionist 1970s and early 1980s scholarly work on the nineteenth-century Puerto Rican economy and particularly the sugar industry ques-tioned previous characterizations of slavery as an "accident" in Puerto Rican history or as a mere "archaic vestige complementary to free la-bor."[17] Taking their cue from contemporary observers such as de la Por-tilla and digging out local archival sources, these new studies began to provide important evidence on the central role played by the development of the slave trade and of slave plantations in the growth of the sugar industry.[18]

An important element in this revisionist understanding is the portrait of a complex pattern of regional diversity. Diversity in the sugar and slavery complex was exemplified by the municipalities of Mayagüez (on the west coast) and Ponce and Guayama (on the south coast) along with some adjacent "satellite" districts (for example, Añasco in the case of Mayagüez; Juana Díaz next to Ponce; and Salinas, Arroyo, and Patillas in the vicinity of Guayama). These districts reached their peak dominance in the sugar export economy before the end of the slave trade at midcentury, acquiring a character that resembled the heavy dependence on slave labor found in many districts in western and central Cuba.

Another, earlier pattern evolved in municipalities whose experience with sugar and slavery dated back at least to the latter part of the eighteenth century. Concentrated around the periphery of San Juan on the north-northeastern coast (Bayamón, Río Piedras, and Loíza), around the southwestern township of San Germán (San Germán itself, Cabo Rojo, and Yauco), and on the northwestern corner of the island (especially Aguadilla but also Moca), these districts benefited from their location next to older and larger population centers (San Juan and to a lesser extent San Germán), a heavy influx of migrants from Spanish and French Hispaniola (and particularly from the western end of the island) in the aftermath of the Haitian revolution at the turn of the nineteenth century, or their access to San Juan, the island's only legal port of trade until the 1810s. Some of these early birds, however, were quickly left behind in sugar output and slave population by the Mayagüez, Ponce, and Guayama regions. Later, a third group of *municipios* located mostly on the northern and eastern coasts became integrated into the island's sugar economy. Members of this group increased the pace of their growth as dusk began falling on the era of open—if illicit—slave trade in the late 1830s and early 1840s and reached their consolidation as important sugar-producing centers only after the slave trade had been cut around 1850. Consequently, a lesser dependence on slave labor characterized this group.[19]

The dominant position of Mayagüez, Ponce, and Guayama is clearly demonstrated by the fact that in 1828 these three municipalities combined to produce slightly more than half of the island's total sugar output and close to two-thirds of its molasses; furthermore, within those three locales lived and worked nineteenth-century Puerto Rico's three largest slave populations. The figures for 1828 are all the more impressive since they precede by more than twenty years the peak in the development of these municipalities' slave-plantation complexes. Guayama, for example, had a total 1842 population of 10,391 inhabitants, of whom 4,286 (41.2 percent) were slaves, an amazing and perhaps unparalleled figure in nineteenth-century Puerto Rico.[20] The data in table 2.2 suggest that Mayagüez, Ponce, and Guayama maintained their dependence on slave labor until abolition even as sugar production spread to other parts of the island. From 1828 to 1865, these three *municipios* housed almost one-third of Puerto Rico's slave population.

The most systematic analysis of a leading sugar plantation district available for the first half of the nineteenth century focuses on Ponce, which contains a diverse mix of coastal lowland plain, relatively fertile piedmont (especially by south coast standards), and upland mountains leading toward some of the highest peaks in Puerto Rico. Scarano's landmark study of the region identifies several important features in its midcentury plantation economy, most obviously, from a comparative perspective, the small size of Ponce's sugar plantations vis-à-vis those elsewhere in the Caribbean. Describing Puerto Rican sugar plantations, Scarano argues,

> in one fundamental respect Puerto Rican plantations differed from their counterparts elsewhere, and particularly from those in areas like the British and French West Indies where haciendas had developed after the annihilation of sparse indigenous population—that is, in a virtual vacuum; this fundamental difference was size. By the standards of most premodern sugar systems, even the larger haciendas of Ponce were rather small concerns, both in land area and in required labor. Plantations with thousands of acres and three hundred or four hundred or more slaves never existed in Puerto Rico. Even in nineteenth-century Cuba and eighteenth-century Jamaica estates of that size were exceptional, but the contrast in size remains valid when the average scale of Ponce farms is compared with those of other fully developed plantation systems.[21]

Furthermore, Scarano asserts that compared with either earlier or contemporary prototypes elsewhere, Ponce's sugar plantations were smaller and less capitalized yet had become the most productive in the Caribbean

TABLE 2.2: Changes in Geographical Distribution of Slavery in Puerto Rico:
Top Fifteen Slaveholding *Municipios* in 1828, 1854, and 1865

Rank	1828		1854		1865	
	Municipio	Slaves	*Municipio*	Slaves	*Municipio*	Slaves
1	Mayagüez	3,860	Ponce	4,431	Ponce	4,720
2	Ponce	3,204	Guayama	4,269	Mayagüez	3,823
3	Guayama	2,303	Mayagüez	4,065	Guayama[a]	3,087
4	San Germán	1,673	San Germán	2,761	San Germán	2,885
5	Aguadilla	1,306	Isabela	2,034	Arecibo	1,398
6	Río Piedras	969	Aguadilla	1,950	Añasco	1,298
7	Arecibo	915	San Juan	1,938	Juana Díaz	1,240
8	Bayamón	899	Cabo Rojo	1,660	Cabo Rojo	1,238
9	Cabo Rojo	851	Arecibo	1,603	Aguadilla	1,209
10	Yauco	834	Añasco	1,332	Humacao	958
11	Caguas	808	Vega Alta	1,077	Yabucoa	859
12	Loíza	742	Juana Díaz	1,079	Manatí	769
13	Añasco	627	Guayanilla	895	Isabela	728
14	Moca	625	Yabucoa	777	Cayey	706
15	Cayey	555	Patillas	727	Guayanilla	697
	Island	29,929	Island	46,923	Island	39,057

Sources: Córdova, *Memorias*, vol. 2; AGPR, FGE, box 41.

[a] In 1855 the *municipio* of Arroyo seceded from Guayama, while neither Ponce nor Mayagüez suffered any loss of territory. Thus, to compare more appropriately Guayama's figures with those of other leading slaveholding municipalities, Arroyo's 1,027 slaves were added to Guayama's 2,060 for 1865.

by the mid–nineteenth century, surpassing even the larger and more heavily industrialized Cuban plantations.[22] Three additional characteristics stand out: the evident technological backwardness of the vast majority of sugar estates when compared to those in Cuba; the surprising fact that investments in land constituted the largest portion of all plantation investments (surpassing even the investment in slaves); and the Puerto Rican sugar plantations' dependence on slave labor within the context of a society filled with potential free laborers.[23]

The higher sugar yields per worker and per *cuerda* of land on Ponce's plantations may have resulted not only from the remarkably high productivity of the district's alluvial lowlands but also from rates of slave productivity that have not yet been fully assessed and that would represent an index of the level of intense exploitation of slaves in at least some sugar districts. These high sugar yields, combined with the limited extension of Ponce's coastal valley, created a situation of land scarcity in which many investors sought to establish or control haciendas in Ponce. The fierce struggle for sugarcane land among planters in Ponce, Scarano writes, "was in large part a result of the competition among petty investors rather than among prospective planters with greater resources."[24] An important feature that came out of this process was that the value of land represented between 40 and 50 percent of a plantation's capital investments, while the value of an estate's slave force represented only between 20 and 30 percent of the unit's total capital assets. Given their limited resources in liquid capital and in land, Ponce's haciendas were forced to try to produce more cheaply and more efficiently with smaller farms on (fortunately for the planters) rich alluvial soil. This meant (unfortunately for the slaves) driving harder a much more limited slave labor pool.[25]

This unprecedented and remarkable transformation in the economy of Puerto Rico's leading sugar plantation districts was spurred in large measure by the arrival of Hispanic and non-Hispanic immigrants after the turn of the nineteenth century, a process that intensified with the enactment of the Real Cédula de Gracias in 1815. Assessing the impact of foreign immigration, however, is not as straightforward as it would seem at first sight. Working with a large database of 5,400 immigrant heads of household who came to Puerto Rico between 1800 and 1850, Jorge Chinea finds that foreign immigrants entered with only 1,324 slaves and 1,875 relatives and dependents. However, the impact of *cedulario* immigration on the island's economy, society, politics, and culture went far beyond what these numbers would suggest, numbers that underestimated to some extent actual immigration flows not only because scores of Spanish subjects migrated to the island from the peninsula but also because countless other individuals, usually of modest means, were unable to regularize their migration to the island and remained there as illegal immigrants for considerable periods of time or even permanently.

Perhaps a better measure of the *cédula*'s impact is the fact that 279 prospective planters, merchants, professionals, farmers, and artisans claimed to bring an impressive 1,672,044 pesos on arriving Puerto Rico. This injection allegedly represented three times the total capital circulating as currency on the island in 1815 and slightly surpassed the total value of Puerto Rican exports in 1819.[26] Furthermore, as Joseph Dorsey has recently pointed out, article 23 of the *cédula* "encouraged all residents—Spanish subjects, pre-decree resident foreigners, and foreign newcomers—to import slaves" and "promoted the illicit arrival of much larger numbers" of African and Caribbean bonded workers than of those who entered the island with immigrants covered by the *cédula*. In this sense, the *cédula* went beyond stimulating the entrance of foreign immigrants and their capital, including slaves, opening up a back door for the influx of thousands of African slaves imported through slave-trading networks that Dorsey argues were more Spanish-Caribbean in nature than previous scholars ever imagined, since these networks were allied with existing French and Dutch slave-trading networks.[27]

Notwithstanding these qualifications, foreign immigration contributed significantly to the expansion of the links between Puerto Rico's new plantation economy and the vast Atlantic networks of trade, where capital, slaves, agricultural commodities, manufactured goods and business know-how flowed during the age of second slavery. In Puerto Rico's case, predominant roles went not only to Spanish subjects and their business firms based in Spain, Cuba, and Puerto Rico but also to a substantial number of French immigrants who arrived on the island either directly from France (and its Mediterranean island of Corsica) or from French Caribbean territories (formerly French Saint Domingue [Haiti], Martinique, and Guadeloupe) as well as from islands ruled by other imperial powers that contained significant French populations or simply served as stepping stones for French immigration to Puerto Rico (Dutch St. Barthelemy, Curaçao, Bonaire, and St. Martin; the Danish Virgin Islands; and Louisiana).

Even decades after this immigration wave of the 1810s–20s, Guayama's planter elite still bore the marks of the influx of Catalan, French, Venezuelan (often of Catalan origin), and other assorted Euro-Caribbean planters and merchants who formed veritable clans that often aligned themselves by ethnic origin despite marrying their children to prominent local creole families such as the Vázquezes and de Riveras whose presence in the region harked back at least to the eighteenth century. As late as the 1870s, for example, the surnames of some of the pioneering Guayama planter families of 1820s–40s remained conspicuous, although the plantations were in the hands of the founders' children or grandchildren. Indeed, of the twenty-four haciendas still grinding in 1872, only one had ownership that could be traced back to the original creole families who sought to develop commercial agriculture in the region in the late eighteenth and early nineteenth centuries: Don José Manuel and Don Rafael Vázquez, sons of Don José Antonio Vázquez, the author of the 1848 *Descripción topográfica del pueblo de Guayama*, who were the fictitious and real owners, respectively, of Hacienda Tuna, located in barrio Caimital, on the west end of the township of Guayama.[28] Catalans and their descendants controlled most of the rest of Guayama's sugar plantations: the Gual, Massó, Pica, Sabater, Virella, and Vives families were Catalonians or first-generation Catalans born in Puerto Rico, while the Texidors were in their second creolized generation.

Next in importance were French immigrants and their descendants: the Boyrie, Clausell, Crouzet, Pillot, and Moret families and the Gaudinau and Blondet-Gaudinau families who constituted the Sucesión Gaudinau. All were French or were first-generation French creoles born in Puerto Rico but who retained their French citizenship. All these French *hacendado* families except Don Isidoro Crouzet traced their presence in Guayama to the French and French-Caribbean immigration resulting from the Cédula de Gracias. Among the other *hacendado* families in 1871, the Curets of Hacienda Santa Elena, Don José García of Hacienda Palmira, Don Florencio Capó of Hacienda Olimpo, and the Villodas-Garcías, owners of Hacienda Agueda, were Spanish or Venezuelan immigrants or their descendants who came to Puerto Rico as a result of the defeat of Spain in the Venezuelan wars of independence. Finally, Don Wenceslao Lugo-Viñas y Oliver, owner of Hacienda Carlota, was a Spanish immigrant who traced his roots to the Canary Islands.[29]

The Texidor family, of Catalan origin, was Guayama's largest sugar and

TABLE 2.3: Guayama's Population by Race and Legal Status, 1776–1899

Year	WHITES		FREE MULATTOES		FREE BLACKS		SLAVES		Total[a]
	N	%	N	%	N	%	N	%	
1776	1,064	20.8	3,170	61.9	124	2.4	511	10.0	5,120
1798	1,349	41.2	1,190	36.3	186	5.7	549	16.8	3,274
1812	698	27.7	862	34.2	522	20.7	328	13.0	2,519
1819	634	18.0	1,919	54.6	67	1.9	697	19.8	3,513
1821	761	22.3	1,269	37.2	188	5.5	703	20.6	3,409
1828	1,777	22.6	1,736	22.0	969	12.3	2,373	30.1	7,874
1842	2,119	20.4	3,777	36.3	209	2.0	4,286	41.2	10,391
1854	3,173	26.5	3,968	33.2	542	4.5	4,269	35.7	11,952
1858	2,672	32.0	2,278	27.3	518	6.2	2,874	34.5	8,342
1871	2,376	28.8	3,706	45.0	436	5.3	1,723	20.9	8,241
1878	4,205	39.4	4,203	39.4	2,269	21.3	—	—	10,677
1887	5,893	43.7	5,331	39.6	2,248	16.7	—	—	13,472
1899	6,477	50.8	5,257	41.2	1,015	8.0	—	—	12,749

[a]Totals for 1776, 1812, 1819, 1821, and 1828 include people classified as *agregados*.

slaveholding clan, controlling Hacienda Josefa, the second-most productive estate and the one with the district's largest concentration of bonded people (115 slaves) in 1871.[30] The Texidor brothers, Antonio and Jesús María, had founded a smaller estate, Hacienda Puerto, strategically located on Jobos Bay beside the port's village.[31] Don Jesús María Texidor y Vázquez owned still another plantation, Hacienda Gregoria, a midsize estate that was nevertheless Guayama's fifth-most productive in 1872.[32]

Guayama's most productive estate, Hacienda Santa Elena, was owned by the daughters of Don Pedro Curet and Doña Andrea Lozada, Catalina and Josefa. The Curet family had migrated to Puerto Rico after Venezuela's war of independence. Catalina and Josefa decided to form a joint partnership (Sociedad Agrícola Hermanas Curet) to preserve the estate from subdivision after their father's death.[33] Hacienda Reunión, Guayama's third-most productive plantation in 1872, was owned by a Catalan immigrant, Don José Gual y Frías, whose son would become one of the leading proponents of technological modernization and the reorganization of production in Guayama's sugar industry over the next two decades.[34]

Don Juan Vives de la Rosa, another Catalan, owned Hacienda Esperanza along with his wife, Doña Isabel Rivera y Texidor, who was half creole and half Catalan. This hacienda was the fourth-most productive in 1872; significantly, it became known to Guayameses as Hacienda Vives after its owner at emancipation. Today, visitors to an industrialized Guayama can look at the ruins of the hacienda's sugar mill as well as most of the base of its old windmill, installed early in the nineteenth century by its original owner, Don Jacinto Texidor I. The government has long promised—but never delivered—funds to convert the hacienda's ruins into a historical museum remembering Guayama's sugar and slave heritage.[35]

Guayama's Transformation

Demographic changes reflected Guayama's transformation into a plantation society, as table 2.3 illustrates. The *municipio*'s population stagnated during the 1810s, the stillness that usually precedes a tropical storm, but the tempest followed in the form of tremendous demographic and economic growth sparked by the development of sugarcane agriculture and slavery from the 1820s onward. Table 2.3 shows that in just seven years, from 1821 to 1828, Guayama's total population more than doubled, and that number grew by another 32 percent between 1828 and 1842. The increase in the *municipio*'s slave population was remarkable as well. From 1812 to 1819, Guayama's slave population more than doubled, and by 1828 it had more than tripled again. Indeed, between 1812 and 1842, Guayama's slave population grew a stunning 1,207 percent, a rate of just over 9 percent per year.

From 1817 to 1828, Guayama's acreage in sugarcane grew at an impressive annual rate of 27 percent, and sugar exports jumped from less than a ton per year to almost 1,300 tons in just eleven years. To put this growth in perspective, during this time Puerto Rican acreage in sugarcane grew at a respectable annual rate of 6.4 percent, from 5,600 *cuerdas* in 1817 to 10,436 *cuerdas* in 1827, and sugar exports grew at an impressive annual rate of 23 percent, from 2,340 to 18,277 tons. Yet these figures pale in comparison with those of Guayama, where sugarcane acreage grew thirteen times faster during the period 1817–28 and where sugar production grew almost 250 times faster than in Puerto Rico as a whole.[36]

Another indicator of the transformation of Guayama after 1815 is the number of sugar mills. In 1818, Don Jacinto Texidor I, the Catalan-immigrant mayor of Guayama and one of the top sugar *hacendados* of the boom period, reported to the colonial government in San Juan that the district had twenty-seven sugar mills, twenty-three with grinders made of wood and only four with iron rollers. By 1842, the municipal council reported eighty sugar mills in Guayama, with only one still using the archaic wooden-roller technology. Ten of these mills had introduced modern grinding technology in the form of steam power, showing that by the late 1830s, local *hacendados* were importing some of the best available sugar-processing technology from capital-goods manufacturing countries in Europe and from the United States.[37]

The council also reported additional figures that help to measure the impact of sugarcane plantation agriculture in Guayama. Table 2.4 presents some of these data, along with corresponding data for the *municipio* of Ponce, Puerto Rico's top sugar plantation district. As Scarano found for Ponce, one generation after the start of the export cycle, Guayama had come to be dominated by sugarcane plantation agriculture. Although sugarcane controlled 20 percent less land in Guayama than in Ponce (probably because of Ponce's less fertile piedmont terrain, as described in chapter 1), the crop controlled the value of land and the most productive sector of the local economy just as absolutely as in Ponce: more than

TABLE 2.4: Landholding and Agricultural Production in Ponce (1845) and Guayama (1842)

	PONCE (1845)		GUAYAMA (1842)	
	Sugar	Nonsugar	Sugar	Nonsugar
Landholding (cuerdas)	8.1	1.2	6.7	3.2
	87.1%	12.9%	67.7%	32.3%
Value of land (pesos)	1,629.9	95.3	1,005.0	90.1
	94.5%	5.5%	91.8%	8.2%
Value of production (pesos)	289.1	16.7	378.6	27.2
	94.5%	5.5%	93.3%	6.7%

Sources: Scarano, *Sugar and Slavery*, 61; AGPR, FGE, Censo y Riqueza, box 12.

90 percent of the value of Guayama's agricultural economy lay in its in booming sugar plantations.

Further insights into Guayama's plantation economy can be obtained by examining the 1842 municipal statistical report, which sheds some light on the distribution of the value of the assets of all Guayama's haciendas. The aggregate value of the sugar haciendas' buildings and machinery stood at 1,099,145 pesos, while the land in sugar was valued at 1,005,000 pesos. In 1842, the value of production of sugar, molasses, and rum reached 378,550 pesos, and the value of all Guayama's slaves amounted to 1,956,345 pesos.[38] Since the slave value figure included slaves not owned by sugar haciendas, this figure must be adjusted to represent more accurately the value of sugar plantation slaves. Guayama's municipal council failed to report figures on the urban-rural distribution of slaves, however, so inferences must be made from other documentation. Estimating conservatively, non-sugar-plantation slaves comprised 15 percent of the total slave population and 10 percent of the total slave value, since plantation slaves generally had higher values in a rural *municipios* lacking significant urban economies. Reducing the value of Guayama's slaves by 10 percent indicates that planters seem to have had more capital invested in slaves (42 percent) than in land and crops (33 percent) or in buildings and machinery (24 percent). In other words, the relative value of Guayama's sugar plantation assets differs in important ways from the distribution found by Scarano in Ponce.[39]

What could explain this apparent difference in the relative weight of Ponce's and Guayama's investments in slaves? One possibility is that

Ponce had higher land prices because of more competition for land or because of better accessibility to water for irrigation, since the soil quality is roughly the same in both districts. Two other potential interpretations emerge. It is possible, though perhaps unlikely, that slave prices were higher in Guayama than in Ponce. The proximity of the two locations makes this hypothesis rather weak except in light of the fact that Dorsey has recently pointed out that well into the late 1840s, Guayama, along with Mayagüez, remained prominent among the locales petitioning for the continued importation of African slaves directly from Africa or through neighboring non-Hispanic Caribbean islands.[40]

Guayama also appears as a leading destination for slave-trading ships interdicted in the Atlantic by British naval forces during the final decade of the slave trade to Puerto Rico. Given the fact that British pressure on slave traders increased beginning in the late 1830s, it is quite possible that new slave cargoes in Guayama commanded higher prices that were in turn reflected in higher values for African slaves reported by municipal authorities during the 1840s. In this sense, Scarano's Ponce slave importation figures, which show a decline beginning in the late 1830s, might not be accurate for the island as a whole. As Dorsey has recently argued, "there is proof that in the wake of Ponce's shrinking influx, Mayagüez and Guayama did not follow suit, for they made last-ditch efforts to obtain African captives for their own consumption by way of their own port exclusively."[41]

The second plausible hypothesis for the importance of slave labor in Guayama's sugar plantation economy suggests that Guayama's sugar *hacendados* depended much more heavily on slave labor than did their Ponce peers, a phenomenon that could be explained by the greater availability of free agricultural laborers in more densely populated Ponce than in Guayama. For example, while slaves represented 23 percent of Ponce's total population in 1846, slaves constituted 41 percent of Guayama's total population that year. This apparent disparity may imply that local planters had different perspectives on the intensity of their use of land and slaves and on the viability of nonslave labor in sugar plantation production. Moreover, as table 2.4 suggests, Guayama had higher sugar productivity by *cuerda* than Ponce—56.50 to 35.70 pesos per *cuerda*—when land quality, as influenced especially by access to better piedmont terrain and streams, should have been better in Ponce than in Guayama.

From this alternative view, which does not exclude but perhaps rein-forces the hypothesis of continuing late-1840s efforts to import increas-ingly expensive slaves, the argument for Guayama would then take the shape of what represents a stunning proposition when considered in the context of Puerto Rican history and historiography: given their limited land resources and smaller nonslave population, Guayama's planters' for-tunes literally rested on the hands and shoulders of enslaved women, men, and children to an extent that had few parallels in the island's nineteenth-century experience. This is a sobering thought, not only for its potential implications during the transition from slavery to free labor but, more broadly, for what it could suggest to early-twenty-first century Puerto Ricans, raised amid broken memories and propagandized images that belittle the historic role of slavery and of people of African descent. Perhaps we should rethink our African heritage, going past canonical understandings that bypass or ignore the heavily African experiences of the southern coast while limiting the scope of "*Africanía*" (Afro–Puerto Rican heritage), to the limited though still rich space of Loíza, a munici-pality on the outskirts of San Juan that is frequently identified as the island's only location of Afro–Puerto Rican heritage, often in a highly folklorized and domesticated gaze of things *Afro-Boricua*, more accessible and malleable for the consumption of island and foreign tourists than the hinterland locations on the southern coast.

Retooling for Survival: Confronting the Challenges of Midcentury

While the period from 1815 to 1850 was the time of the development of sugarcane agriculture and slavery in Guayama, the 1850s and 1860s were years of modest growth in the sugar industry and of gradual decline for slavery, as was the case in most of Puerto Rico. The island's sugar exports, which had averaged an impossible-to-sustain annual growth rate of al-most 20 percent from 1828 to 1849, grew at an annual rate of only 2.2 per-cent from 1849 to 1869. The situation in Guayama differed little, and the available export data show the sort of moderate growth rates that can be expected from a mature regional sugar economy. Whereas 6,700 tons of sugar had been exported in 1842, the volume of sugar exports grew to 10,003 tons in 1860 (a 2.6 percent annual growth rate) and to 12,134 tons in 1869 (a 2.1 percent annual growth from 1860 to 1869).[42] In addition, the

TABLE 2.5: Average Sugar Plantations of Guayama (1866), Ponce (1845), Guadeloupe (1830s), and Louisiana (1850)

	Ponce, 1845 (N=86)	Guayama, 1866 (N=29)	Guadeloupe, 1830s (N=124)	Louisiana, 1850 (N=328)
Total land	282	471	365	973
Land in sugarcane	71	201	NA	296
	25.2%	42.7%	—	30.4%
Slaves	40	54	79	46
Sugar production (tons)	94	132	NA	77

Sources: For Guayama, see "Expediente del subsidio, 1865–1866," AGPR, FMG, DM, box 10 (1860–69); for Ponce, see Scarano, Sugar and Slavery, 64; for Guadeloupe, see Schnakenbourg, Histoire, 22; for Louisiana, see Mark Schmitz, "Economic Analysis of Antebellum Sugar Plantations in Louisiana" and "Economies of Scale and Farm Size in the Antebellum Sugar Sector," as cited in Scarano, Sugar and Slavery, 65–66.
Note: All figures are rounded to the nearest integer.

number of sugar haciendas shrank from eighty in 1842 (in the old, larger *municipio*) to only twenty-three in 1864 in Guayama proper and a dozen more in the newly segregated *municipio* of Arroyo.[43]

Negative fluctuations in international sugar market prices do not explain the Puerto Rican sugar industry's more moderate growth rates of the 1850s and 1860s, however, because prices rose until an 1857 recession dropped the prices of various qualities of sugars.[44] Rather, the lower growth rates seem to have reflected problems of adaptation for an industry organized within the framework of a particular mode of production (slavery) that after midcentury became devoid of substantial numbers of fresh African slave imports and failed to marshal effectively a pool of peasant workers that would have solved the labor supply problems.[45]

At the same time, in the lowlands of Ponce, a process of concentration of more sugarcane land on fewer plantations was well under way after midcentury. Whereas 86 haciendas were reported in 1845, only 74 existed in 1861, about 40 in 1876, and only 22 in 1886.[46] Yet while a trend toward latifundia might seem to be present here, at another level the tendency appears to be toward minifundia—the number of medium- and smallholders increased and the size of their landholdings decreased in various lowland rural barrios of Ponce after 1850.[47] Guayama, however, had 80 sugar haciendas in 1842 but only 23 in 1866. Even adding the 10 or so haciendas that remained in operation in Arroyo, this represents only about a third as many haciendas as just a quarter of a century earlier.[48] In fact, the reduction in sugar estates was a trend registered islandwide. In 1820 1,547 haciendas existed, and ten years later, that number remained virtually unchanged at 1,552; by 1860, however, only 550 sugar estates remained, and by 1886 the figure had dropped to 444.[49]

Table 2.5 reexamines the comparative data presented by Scarano in his study of Ponce, offering some general comparisons of the average sugar plantation in Guayama in 1866, exactly a decade before the end of phased-in abolition (1870–76), with similar data for Louisiana in 1850 (a decade before the start of the U.S. Civil War), Guadeloupe in 1848 (about a decade and a half before the end of slavery there), and Ponce in 1845.

It is quite possible that by 1845 Ponce had not reached the peak of its sugar-slavery boom, and other data examined earlier certainly suggest that Ponce, like Guayama, experienced a process of land concentration (and perhaps slave labor concentration), while the Guayama pictured in table 2.5 was in the midst of a process of mild recovery if not stagnation following the demographic and economic crisis associated with the end of the slave trade (circa 1850) and the cholera epidemic of the mid-1850s. I use the 1845 Ponce averages for two reasons: first, Scarano uses these data to compare Ponce's plantations to others elsewhere (especially those of Louisiana); and, second, because no equivalent published data currently exist for Ponce or Mayagüez for the 1860s.

The figures in table 2.5 make four important points: Guayama's 1866 sugar haciendas, on average, were larger, were more intensively cultivated, had more slaves, and were more productive than Ponce's 1845 haciendas. All these differences can be explained in part by the fact that Guayama had fewer sugar haciendas located in its less fertile piedmont (only two, haciendas Tuna and Olimpo in Barrio Caimital); by the more extensive use of steam mill technology in Puerto Rico in the 1860s than in the 1840s; and by the very plausible expansion of some sugar haciendas as others failed and became integrated into the more productive and modern establishments.[50]

The comparison with the Guadeloupean and Louisianan plantations is more plausible, despite limitations in the data. In Guadeloupe (and in Martinique), the slave trade had already ended by the 1830s, and the abolition of slavery was only a decade away. In this respect, Guayama in 1866 and Guadeloupe in the 1830s were quite similar. When compared with Guadeloupean plantations, Guayama's haciendas were, on average, larger in terms of land but used less slave labor.[51] This is a surprising fact, given that Puerto Rican plantations were generally smaller on average than sugar plantations in the rest of the Caribbean.[52] Guayama's haciendas were smaller than the plantations in Louisiana a decade before the Civil War but were more intensively cultivated and productive and had more slaves. If confirmed by future research on Guayama's sugar plantations during slavery, this finding would be remarkable, since it would indicate that Guayama's haciendas fell within the general spectrum of slavery in the circum-Caribbean area except for their more intensive cultivation of the land and higher yield, which could be attributed to the youth of the district's sugar industry.

Indeed, Guayama's sugar mills seem to have achieved a level of modernization above the island average before the end of slavery. By 1866, for example, Guayama had at least fifteen haciendas had steam-powered mills, and two others should have had steam mills, although that information does not exist. Conversely, between seven and ten of the region's haciendas continued to use the centuries-old technology of a *trapiche de bueyes* (oxen-driven mill), as table 2.6 shows. This more than two-to-one ratio of steam- to oxen-powered sugar mills provides a good indicator of Guayama planters' efforts to modernize even before emancipation, especially given that Ponce at the time had fifty-nine sugar haciendas, only twenty-one of them with steam-powered mills.[53]

Guayama also had ample suitable land to supply the demands of more productive sugar mills. As chapter 1 discusses, the *municipio* of Guayama sits on prime sugarcane land in the Ponce-Patillas alluvial plain. Moreover, several Guayamese *hacendados* apparently were intent on further expanding their plantations, as a process of consolidation of haciendas seems to have occurred during the 1860s. In 1864, for example, twenty-nine of Guayama's haciendas exported sugar, but several plantations consolidated later in the decade. The owner of Hacienda Clemencia, Don José Gual y Frías, obtained Hacienda Carmen in 1865 from Don Juan Elías Montaño. Don Félix Gaudinau's Hacienda Melanía absorbed Hacienda Rosa during the late 1860s. Don Wenceslao Lugo-Viñas purchased Hacienda Buena Esperanza in 1870 and integrated it into his Hacienda Carlota. And Don Juan Vives de la Rosa purchased additional land from Haciendas Guayabo Dulce and Emilia as part of his attempts to modernize the irrigation facilities of his estate, Esperanza. As a result of this process, by the mid- to late 1860s Guayama had at least nine sugar haciendas with more than five hundred acres of land and four with more than seven hundred acres. Indeed, the top two haciendas in terms of land, Agueda and Melanía, covered 1,744 and 1,156 *cuerdas*, respectively.[54]

Yet the simple control of large extensions of land did not guarantee survival, let alone modernization. Of those nine plantations, four had ceased operations or had disappeared altogether by the early 1880s, including Agueda and Melanía. Two other haciendas, Olimpo and Esperanza, halted production temporarily during the mid-1870s. One of the key explanations for the failure of haciendas such as Agueda, Adela, and Melanía was the perennial problem of unstable rainfall in the southern coastal plain. The great majority of the plantations that perished in the transition of the 1870s and 1880s were located on the western edge of the *municipio*, where, as discussed in chapter 1, rainfall levels were perhaps as much as ten inches lower than was the case further east.

Moreover, these plantations were located far from the banks of Guayama's principal river, the Guamaní, and its associated creeks that washed

TABLE 2.6: Profile of Guayama's Sugar Haciendas in 1866

	LAND			Number of Slaves	Number of Oxen	Mill Type[a]	PRODUCTION		ESTATE'S VALUE (Pesos)
Hacienda	Cultivated	Total	%				Sugar (Tons)	Molasses (100 Gals.)	
Adela	130	631	21	68	66	s	109	113	60,000
Agueda	1,037	1,744	59	30	2	NA	1	8	NA
Algarrobo	148	248	60	41	46	s	96	68	50,000
Ana	90	560	16	16	0	o	8	15	6,000
Aurora	130	350	37	21	60	o	160	198	50,000
Bardeguez	250	620	40	100	70	s	346	416	100,000
Barrancas	170	237	72	76	100	o	184	225	60,000
Buena Esperanza	80	90	89	16	24	s	88	83	30,000
Cayures	100	140	71	40	80	o	123	178	NA
Esperanza	222	550	40	80	76	s	196	237	150,000
Felicia	120	300	40	47	84	o	65	39	NA
Gregoria	184	270	68	47	76	s	230	211	80,000
Josefa	360	455	79	114	96	s	362	328	160,000

Juana	80	238	34	25	36	O	11	28	25,000
Melanía	250	1,156	22	108	72	S	111	149	62,000
Merced	200	225	89	20	70	S	148	184	45,000
Olimpo	70	680	10	32	60	S	50	0	60,000
Palmira	250	435	57	101	72	S	235	309	80,000
Pica	110	135	81	71	56	S	80	71	50,000
Puerto	NA	NA	NA	43	74	S	94	109	60,000
Reunión	200	368	54	79	80	S	193	305	60,000
Rosario	90	210	43	27	40	O	65	67	40,000
Tuna	150	730	21	40	70	S	88	61	40,000
Total	4,421	10,372		1,242	1,410		3,041	3,399	$1,268,000
Average	201	471	43	54	61		132	148	$63,400
Median	149	359	42	45	70		110	13	$60,000

Sources: AGPR, FMG, DM, box 10 (1860–69); AGPR, PN, Jiménez Sicardó, 197, #249, ff. 91v.–105v., 7 November 1870.

Note: No information is available for the Amparo, Carlota, Estefanía, Rosa, and Santa Elena haciendas. Carlota and Santa Elena were among Guayama's leading slaveholding sugar haciendas.

[a]O = Oxen; S = Steam.

the plain in barrio Machete and the eastern edge of barrio Jobos. Guayama and the neighboring *municipios* of Salinas and Arroyo had battled
recurrent droughts since at least the middle of the nineteenth century. In
the late 1840s and early 1850s, the owners of Haciendas Tuna, Olimpo,
Caimital, Santa Elena, and Esperanza obtained rights to the waters of the
Guamaní River, while planters from barrio Algarrobos wrestled over
rights to the waters of Piedra Gorda Creek, all part of efforts to provide better access to the precious liquid during times of abnormally low
rainfall.[55]

The limited waters of the Guamaní River were, however, insufficient to
guarantee the further expansion of sugar production in the *municipio*.
Therefore, sugar planters from Guayama organized a collective effort in
the 1860s to provide the region with permanent access to an adequate
water supply. They formed an association to propose the construction of
an elaborate irrigation system in the eastern section of the Ponce-Patillas
plain. The plan, designed by a British engineer, called for the building of a
dam in the Sierra de Cayey that would collect and supply water to Salinas, Guayama, and Arroyo by a series of under- and above-ground tun-
nels and canals. To build and administer these regional irrigation works,
planters proposed that the government create a public utility, the Pantano
Real de Carite. Financing for the utility would be obtained through a
foreign loan from London-based investors. But herein lay the central
problem faced by all modernization efforts in the Guayama region both
before and after emancipation: the lack of sufficient capital resources.
Notwithstanding an initially positive recommendation by the local colonial government in San Juan, the project never went beyond its planning
stages, as the Spanish government in Madrid delayed action and the
prospective British bankers apparently lost interest.[56]

The issues of sugar prices and declining market share are also crucial to
understanding Guayama's planters' predicament at the moment of emancipation and for the rest of the century. The volume of Puerto Rican sugar
exports had generally stagnated through the 1850s and most of the 1860s
before a brief but intense period of growth followed by stable or perhaps
rising sugar prices in the late 1860s and early 1870s.[57] Indeed, the 1870s
opened with great prospects for the island's sugar business. As Emma
Dávila Cox argues in her study of Puerto Rico's trade relations with Great
Britain, the island's second-largest sugar market until the 1860s, "Puerto
Rico's sugar industry was riding the crest of a tide," as the island trailed

only Cuba among the Western Hemisphere's sugar-producing nations, accounting for approximately 7 percent of the worldwide sugar output.[58]

Yet sugar prices for the type of low-quality *muscovado* (brown) sugar produced by Puerto Rico collapsed during the 1870s and 1880s, mainly in response to the subsidized competition posed by higher-quality beet sugar in European markets and the extension of sugarcane production to new zones, especially in the Indian Ocean basin.[59] This threat became particularly acute with regard to the British market. Dávila Cox indicates, for example, that the price of sugar exported to the United Kingdom fluctuated between approximately fifteen and twenty-two shillings per pound from 1846 to 1871, with a brief spike around the end of the U.S. Civil War, when prices in the island's largest sugar market jumped from about 3.7 cents to 18–25 cents, apparently in response to the realization that the war had decimated Louisiana's sugar industry in combination with national postwar economic conditions that spurred a rise in the demand for foreign sugar. In the context of these higher prices, planters mortgaged their properties as never before to finance the expansion of their sugar fields as well as technological innovations in both the agricultural and processing phases of sugar production. Unfortunately, however, British prices for Puerto Rican sugar slid from fourteen to seventeen shillings per pound during the early 1870s to as low as around eleven shillings per pound by the 1890s.[60]

As a result, Puerto Rican sugar became increasingly unwanted in Europe and more dependent on the U.S. market. Eventually, however, similar pressures began to arise there, as the Louisiana sugar industry not only recovered but by the mid-1870s surpassed Puerto Rico's sugar production and as refiners purchased raw beet sugar in Europe and the United States began to develop a domestic beet-sugar industry. General prices for Puerto Rican brown sugar had topped out at 7 pesos a hundredweight (*quintal*) before slave emancipation, but by 1886 the price had dropped to 2.8 pesos. Except for early in 1889, when prices rebounded to 5.5–6.25 pesos per *quintal* for the lighter grades of *muscovado*, prices remained around 3.00–3.50 pesos per *quintal* thereafter.[61]

The combined effect of increasing competition from beet sugar and the downward trend in prices dramatically altered the structural underpinnings of the Puerto Rican sugar industry's business model as developed and sustained during the peak years of the slave trade. In this context, planters faced another large challenge: the continuation of slave-based sugar production at a time when Spain was being forced to curtail the vast contraband in African slaves that brought as many as half a million slaves to Cuba and close to fifty thousand slaves to Puerto Rico during the first half of the nineteenth century.[62] The Spanish government, under pressure from Great Britain, entered into various treaties ending the slave trade between 1817 and 1845 and incorporated a slave-trading provision into its penal code in 1845.

Puerto Rican planters experienced a reduction in the tide of slave imports in the wake of the 1835 treaty but continued in their efforts by developing new schemes and resurrecting old ones to secure the importation of more African captives. Two main procedures seem to have emerged: the development of direct African shipments during the 1830s, often benefiting from links to Cuban, Portuguese, French, and Dutch slavers, including the prosecution of Spanish–Puerto Rican expeditions well into the 1840s, and the reactivation of reexport schemes that used non-Hispanic Caribbean islands such as Curaçao, St. Thomas, St. Eustatius, and St. Barthelemy as transshipment points for African imports.

Guayama featured prominently in all these types of operations, coming perhaps to surpass, along with Mayagüez, the preeminent position occupied by Ponce during the 1820s and 1830s. Dorsey documents, for example, the influx of about one thousand African slaves through the inter-Caribbean nexus in 1847 alone.[63] Behind this willingness to risk interdiction by British naval authorities and the eventual confiscation of slaving vessels seemingly lay the planters' continuing belief that only slave labor ensured the productivity of their sugar haciendas. As Guayama planter Simón Moret expressed in his petition to import slaves through St. Thomas and St. Croix in 1847, Puerto Rican free laborers remained unreliable for sugar production, and he lacked the means to pay wages for work. In the end, stricter enforcement of international treaties banning the slave trade did not necessarily in and of itself end the importation of African captives to Puerto Rico; instead, a shortage of capital resources to pay higher slave prices led wealthier Cuban planters and slave merchants to, in Dorsey's words, "squeeze out" Puerto Rican slave traders and planters.[64]

Therefore, as the supply of African slaves dwindled dramatically at the end of the 1840s, planters had increasing difficulty in relying on slave labor. As Andrés Ramos Mattei has argued,

Of all the changes in a unit or plantation under a process of growth [after midcentury], changing the composition and increasing the [total] labor force was the most difficult. The organic growth of a unit first required a quantitative increase in its labor force. This was very difficult to achieve since sugar was a seasonal industry that demanded a great number of workers only during some months. Second, technological improvements, for example, created the need for skilled workers, not only in the industrial phase of the sugar plantation [grinding] but also in other phases. To achieve an adequate supply of laborers, especially during harvest, the growing units had to develop mechanisms of coercion that tied the workforce to the unit.[65]

Reacting to the close of the massive importation of slaves in the late 1840s, the colonial government attempted to solve the labor supply problem with the 1849 promulgation of the Reglamento de Jornaleros (Day Laborer Code), which sought to force smallholders and landless peasants to become plantation day laborers. With the Reglamento de Jornaleros, together with the effective end of the slave trade, colonial authorities expected to open a new phase in the history of Puerto Rican sugar plantations.[66] However, the *reglamento* seems largely to have failed.[67] Even after the close of massive slave imports, Puerto Rico's leading sugar plantation districts continued to rely heavily on slave labor as the "medullary nerve" of their system of production, as the element that could maintain a certain year-round stability of labor input not provided by extensive use of peasant laborers.

Yet the idea of substituting a local forced-laboring class for the importation of thousands African slaves during the 1850s faced an additional structural problem in a sugar plantation district with Guayama's particular combination of ecology and relatively sparse peasant settlement. Indeed, demographically, Guayama's total population hardly reproduced itself from 1842 to 1854 (see table 2.3), growing at an annual rate of only 1.2 percent, and the picture varied sharply among racial and legal groups. Guayama's slave population held steady in absolute numbers but declined as a percentage of the *municipio*'s total population. Moreover, among the free population, from which colonial authorities sought to mold a "free" laboring class, the number of those classified as free mulattoes, the second-largest demographic group of this period, grew only 5.1 percent over this twelve-year period, a meager annual rate of 0.4 percent. In contrast, the population classified as white increased at an annual rate of 3.4 percent from 1842 to 1854, and the small free black population grew from 209 in 1842 to 542 in 1854, an annual growth rate of 8.3 percent, although the overall numbers remained of minimal significance.[68]

To make matters worse, Guayama suffered a sharp demographic decline during the late 1850s as a result of a summer 1856 cholera epidemic. During 1855 and 1856, Puerto Rico as a whole suffered from this terrible epidemic, which can be regarded as the largest demographic disaster in Puerto Rican history since the sixteenth century. Cholera probably caused the deaths of about 30,000 Puerto Ricans, although official government figures put the death toll at 25,820. Afro–Puerto Ricans, both slave and nonslave, were most affected by the cholera, accounting for almost 78 percent of the dead (56 percent free mulattoes and free blacks and 21 percent slaves). Slaves constituted the hardest-hit group based on the island's 1854 slave population: the epidemic killed close to 12 percent of Puerto Rico's slaves, two-thirds of them male.[69]

In Guayama, the cholera epidemic killed more than one hundred more slaves than free Afro–Puerto Ricans. As a result, Guayama lost more than 11 percent of its slave population. Together, free Afro–Puerto Ricans and African and creole slaves accounted for 94 percent of Guayama's dead. The dead had to be buried along the shores of Jobos Bay, far from the township, where a special "cementerio de coléricos" was created. Many years later, the government and the Catholic Church allowed those who wished to move the remains of their relatives to the Catholic cemetery on the west side of the township. As Adolfo Porrata-Doria reports, "The epidemic was so memorable that more than fifty years later people would date events using the year of the cholera epidemic as a point of reference, saying: 'This many years after the cholera.'"[70] In sum, the cholera epidemic represented a major setback for Guayama's population and for planters' ability to maintain an adequate labor supply, in the form of either slaves or free laborers, and substantially contributed to a period of demographic stagnation that lasted at least two decades.[71]

Even after the demographic disaster represented by the 1855–56 cholera epidemic, sugar plantations in the major producing districts continued to depend on slave labor, albeit to varying degrees of intensity, as the major feature in their labor organization. In 1859, slaves still constituted the core of the labor supply on the sugar haciendas of the Ponce–

Juana Díaz region and particularly on the larger, more productive estates, where slaves represented as much as 80 percent of the labor force during the off-season and no less than two-thirds during harvest.[72] In 1865, just five years before the Spanish Parliament enacted the first abolitionist law, the pool of slaves in Ponce, Mayagüez, and Guayama was at least as large as the theoretically available pool of *jornaleros*. As table 2.7 shows, the ratio of slaves to *jornaleros* in Ponce was 1.4 and in Guayama was 2.5.[73]

These figures serve only as crude indicators of the extent to which the dependency on slave labor continued well into the 1860s. The total number of slaves includes an undetermined number of children under age ten (when their incorporation to plantation labor tasks increased) in addition to elderly and disabled slaves. Moreover, given the costs involved in purchasing or rearing slaves and maintaining them year-round, as well as the existence of other agricultural activities in these districts, a considerably higher proportion of *jornaleros* may well have been employed in nonsugar sectors of the economy than in sugar-producing activities. Other evidence reinforces these perceptions regarding slavery's importance in Guayama, including the fact that as the decade unfolded a number of planters resorted increasingly to leasing slaves to continue running their estates with slavery as the dominant form of labor organization.[74]

In this sense, the crux of the planters' labor supply problems beginning well before the 1873 abolition of slavery was that the existing large pool of potential peasant laborers did not translate into a steady, disciplined, reliable wage labor force for the sugar plantations. The great majority of peasants would not regularly accept being driven like slaves in cutting and transporting cane and were even less inclined to work in crowded, noisy sugar mills. This phenomenon resulted in planters' and colonial government officials' previously mentioned negative evaluations of day laborers' work. As Scarano makes the point, "the existence of a large peasant population—a potential supply of non-slave labor—need not be tantamount to an effective labor supply. For such a connection to hold . . . the peasantry would have had to be in an advanced stage of deterioration, particularly in regard to the means of economic independence—the land. [This] was not the situation in Puerto Rico during the first half of the nineteenth century, when land to own or to squat on was still available in the interior sections of the country. . . . As long as these lands remained an alternative to the peasantry, the supply of wage labor to the sugar haciendas was bound to remain scarce and, consequently, expensive."[75] As

TABLE 2.7: Coerced and Enslaved Labor in Puerto Rico's Top Three Slaveholding *Municipios*: *Jornaleros* and Slaves in 185

Municipio	JORNALEROS			SLAVES			Total	Ratio[a]
	Artisan	Laborer	Total	Male	Female	Total		
Ponce	654	2,644	3,298	2,384	2,336	4,720	8,018	1:1.4
Mayagüez	425	3,707	4,132	1,853	1,970	3,823	7,955	1:0.9
Guayama	164	668	832	1,060	1,000	2,060	2,892	1:2.5
Guayama and Arroyo[b]	228	1,027	1,255	1,529	1,558	3,087	4,342	1:2.5
Island	3,953	53,201	57,154	20,871	19,196	40,067	97,221	1:0.7

Source: AGPR, FGE, box 41.

[a]Expresses how many slaves there were for each *jornalero*.

[b]Arroyo was part of the *municipio* of Guayama until 1855, when it became a separate *municipio*. There were no such segregations in Ponce or Mayagüez during these years.

the century progressed, the interior hinterland began to be closed, and by 1870, "in almost all highland municipalities there [was] little land to be distributed [by the government], and it [was] obtained mainly through connections or investments that [were] beyond the reach of the landless majority."[76]

However, not all factors intervening in the configuration of Puerto Rico's sugar industry during the middle decades of the nineteenth century were of an internal order, as illustrated by the termination of the slave trade imposed on island planters sometime around the late 1850s. The development of new and more expensive technologies for sugarcane production, along with the emergence of competing sources of higher-quality beet sugar in Europe, represented the other major threats to the business model implemented during the first half of the century. The expansion of beet-sugar production and the development of new technologies that rendered lighter-colored and higher-quality crystals ushered in a new era in international sugar markets. As a result, prices for the low-grade *muscovado* sugar produced by almost all Puerto Rican plantations declined sharply after the 1840s, forcing cane-sugar producers worldwide to invest substantial capital resources in processing technologies from more efficient steam-powered grinding machines to elaborate mechanisms to boil and evaporate cane juice and separate molasses from sugar crystals.

Many sugar planters sought to modernize their Puerto Rican haciendas during the 1860s and into the 1870s, but these efforts generally failed. Therefore, the moderate growth rate of the 1850s and 1860s that preceded the end of slavery turned into outright decline in production and economic and social crisis in the last quarter of the nineteenth century. Facing the challenges of modernization and the need to effectively organize labor in hacienda sugar production and struggling to achieve these goals in the context of an unresponsive and autocratic colonial regime, Puerto Rico's sugar planter class turned out to be ill prepared for the domestic and international transformations that came during the 1870s.[77]

Conclusion

The social and economic picture painted by the data presented in this chapter is hardly a setting in which Guayama's population was "living a pastoral life dedicated to the noble goal of organizing a solid economy that could guarantee the future of the community," as Porrata-Doria would have us believe. A better description of Guayama's economy as it stood at the middle of the nineteenth century, therefore, is that offered by Don José Antonio Vázquez, a planter and slave owner who at that time controlled not one but two sugar haciendas, La Tuna and Olimpo, both excellently located upstream on the margins of the Guamaní River in barrio Caimital and holding almost 1,900 *cuerdas*, a stunning figure by Puerto Rican standards.[78] Unfortunately, however, Vázquez's brief description of Guayama from the 1820s to the 1840s falls short when discussing the social aspects of the sugar boom period. He neglects to mention the system of slavery on which his wealth and that of several other planter and merchant families depended, perhaps a convenient maneuver for a slaveholding local official who was, like all his peers, involved in procuring slaves at a time when the trade was illicit.

Did this omission result from the clandestine nature of the slave trade on which Guayama's sugar wealth depended? Regardless of Vázquez's silence or Porrata-Doria's twentieth-century misgivings about Guayama's slave past, the fact remains that in two generations the southeastern coast of Puerto Rico was drastically transformed from an area of cattle ranchers and subsistence peasants where plantation slavery had played a minor role and where centuries of miscegenation had produced a society quite different from the plantation societies of neighboring Caribbean islands. Instead, Guayama became one of Puerto Rico's leading plantation districts, with thousands of slaves imported from Africa and the surrounding Caribbean. The coast was deforested to make way for sugarcane to be cultivated, cut, and ground by more than four thousand slaves; for haciendas where planters kept tabs on the fluctuating North Atlantic prices of sugar; and for slave quarters where African, Afro-Caribbean, and Afro–Puerto Rican slaves began to forge the culture and image of Guayama that persists today, if only as a dissipated collection of broken memories.

CHAPTER 3

SEEKING FREEDOM BEFORE

ABOLITION STRATEGIES OF

ADAPTIVE RESISTANCE AMONG

AFRO-GUAYAMESES

In April 1876, just a few days before the end of Puerto Rico's version of "apprenticeship" and the coming of full emancipation for the island's thirty thousand slaves, the Spanish governor, Don Segundo de la Portilla, issued a circular to town and city mayors in which he expressed his feelings about the *libertos* (the newly freed): "The *liberto*, for reasons that need not be addressed here, will start within a few days to become part of a society that he does not know, a society whose characteristics, customs, and governing laws—and the duties that they encompass—he ignores. In short, he does not comprehend even the most essential norms that direct the progressive and well understood moral and material advance by which the civilized world has to obtain its better and natural objectives."[1]

The governor's circular expressed the fear that, once liberated, the ex-slaves would constitute a danger to personal life and property, especially that of the planters. Scores of slaveholders and government officials throughout the Americas had voiced similar fears as slavery was abolished, and Puerto Rico's elite was no exception.

Yet looking closely at Governor de la Portilla's remarks on the eve of full emancipation, one might ask not only why these fears were harbored but also how accurately they reflected the specific realities of Puerto Rican slavery at the time of emancipation. Put differently, what do they shade from view concerning the integration of slaves into the island society before abolition? Were Puerto Rican slaves as alienated from the island's society as the colonial governor portrayed them? Were island slaves and the coastal plantations on which most of them lived virtual enclaves with few organic linkages to the surrounding nonsugar, nonslave society that often seemed to be perched up on neighboring hills and mountains, looking down?

These questions are not merely rhetorical. As I argued previously, until quite recently, the standard interpretation of Puerto Rican society in the nineteenth century was that slavery played but a minor role. In addition, these questions are crucial because some leading interpretations of slavery posit that the chattel property character of the slave (usually considered in singular rather than plural terms) rendered her or him "a socially dead person"—indeed, "truly a genealogical isolate," in the words of Orlando Patterson. As Patterson argues forcefully,

> Alienated from all "rights" or claims of birth, [the slave] ceased to belong in his own right to any legitimate social order. All slaves experienced, at the very least, a secular excommunication.
>
> Not only was the slave denied all claims on, and obligations to, parents and living blood relations but, by extension, all such claims and obligations on his more remote ancestors and on descendants. . . . Slaves differed from other human beings in that they were not allowed freely to integrate the experience of their ancestors into their lives, to inform their understanding of social reality with the inherited meanings of their natural forebearers, or to anchor the living present in any conscious community of memory. That they reached back for the past, as they reached out for the related living, there can be no doubt. Unlike other persons, doing so meant struggling with and penetrating the iron curtain of the master, his community, his laws, his policemen or patrollers, and his heritage.[2]

Slaves suffered from a status of "natal alienation," Patterson adds, that separated and distinguished them from those living under other forms of labor or social domination. Patterson chooses that term "because it goes directly to the heart of what is critical in the slave's forced alienation, the loss of ties of birth in both ascending and descending generations. It also has the important nuance of a loss of native status, of deracination. It was this alienation of the slave from all formal, legally enforceable ties of 'blood,' and from any attachment to groups or localities other than those chosen for him by the master, that gave the relation of slavery its peculiar value to the master."[3]

Patterson tries to preempt a critique that would call attention to a growing body of scholarship that shows how slaves developed intricate social relations among themselves and with many nonslaves in areas where that population was large. Yet he dismisses this potential line of criticism by offering a particular interpretation of relationships he dubs "informal." "The important point," he argues, "is that these relationships were never recognized as legitimate or binding."[4]

It is quite ironic that many of Patterson's scholarly enunciations echo Governor de la Portilla's 1876 discourse of colonial power, and I will scrutinize and question Patterson's perspectives. Were de la Portilla's anxieties about whether the *libertos* would dedicate themselves to forming and supporting nuclear families and to contributing to society with "the product of their labor" really warranted? Do Patterson's notions on the nature of slavery help to characterize the conditions under which Guayama's slaves lived during the nineteenth century? How can we approach these questions in a study focused on the abolition of slavery rather than on the specific nature of slavery in Puerto Rico? Addressing these questions requires us to take stock of a variety of historical experiences that formed the core of the lives and struggles of Guayama's slaves. Particular attention should be devoted to efforts to develop adaptive forms of resistance to the sort of power relations arrayed by Spanish colonial rule and white settler ideologies and practices within the specific experience of colonial slavery in Puerto Rico.

Plantation slaves in the Caribbean and elsewhere during the region's almost four centuries of slavery developed a wide variety of forms of resistance and accommodation to colonial enslavement and racism: collective and individual violent confrontations with planters, overseers, colonial police, and military forces within and beyond their plantations or localities; individual and group escapes from the status of slave, as in forms of *grande* or *petite marronage*; and sabotage of cane fields, livestock, buildings, and machinery.[5]

These slaves also deployed adaptations that did not necessarily seek the short-term destruction of slavery's social relations but provided time and space for autonomous existence and helped reaffirm their humanity in the face of the normative rules of chattel property imposed by slavery: slowdowns while carrying out plantation labor tasks such as harvesting sugarcane, autonomous peasant cultivation and marketing activities, and the complex cultural symbiosis of institutions, beliefs, discourses, and practices that flourished in a variety of forms throughout slave societies in the Americas. In this context, this chapter examines two issues intimately linked to the development of specific forms of adaptive resistance among Guayama's slaves: slave manumissions, especially those achieved by self-purchase or purchase by kin; and the extent of protopeasant slave activities in nineteenth-century Puerto Rico.[6] The chapter will thus illustrate the extent to which Patterson's argument merits reconsideration.

Freedom through Manumission versus Coartación

On 23 May 1873, one month after the Spanish Cortes proclaimed the abolition of slavery in Puerto Rico, Don José Gual y Frías, one of the Guayama's leading Catalan-born sugar *hacendados*, walked into the office of Don Pedro Jiménez Sicardó, one of the *municipio*'s public notaries. By itself, this scene was not unusual. Guayamans, especially planters and merchants, visited notaries' offices almost daily to record all sorts of land, commercial, and financial transactions as well as other deeds.

Yet this time something about the scene was noteworthy. Don José was accompanied not by another *hacendado* or merchant but by a black man in his forties, a native of Africa who until very recently had been Don José's chattel slave. Miguel was his first name, Chivo (Goat) was his nickname. Miguel was trying to obtain a notarized document certifying that he was a free man. Miguel, however, had not been freed by the 1873 Abolition Law or by the 1870 Moret Law, which emancipated slaves over age sixty. Miguel had achieved freedom by virtue of his own actions, purchasing his freedom from his master. In other words, Miguel was a *liberto coartado*. Coming after the abolition decree, the event seems odd, even irrational, an idiosyncrasy to be dismissed.[7]

But Miguel's *coartación* is quite relevant for understanding slavery and emancipation in Guayama. Miguel had privately paid his master 225 pesos in cash on 15 February 1873—that is, just five weeks before the enactment of Puerto Rico's Abolition Law. Did Miguel know that emancipation was so close? Did he realize that he could have spent his hard-earned money elsewhere? Would saving money for other investments have outweighed the importance of the act of self-emancipation?

It is, of course, impossible to know if Miguel was aware of the events leading to abolition in Puerto Rico. It is known, however, that Don José Gual declared to the notary that Miguel had refused a notarized *carta de libertad* (certification of freedom) the preceding February "under the assumption that he did not need one because of his trust in his owner" and because he "continued enjoying the rights of a free man and earning a monthly wage of eight pesos." Nonetheless, Miguel now needed notarized proof that he had been free before abolition to avoid being bound by the terms of the Abolition Law. The *carta de libertad* meant that he could not be forced to engage in a labor contract with his former master or anyone else. As chapter 4 will discuss, the Abolition Law required all slaves freed by the law to enter into labor contracts for no less than three years.

Moreover, the law and the subsequent regulations decreed by the island's Spanish colonial governor dictated that these labor contracts be registered with special local authorities and specified penalties for the violation of the regulations. Therefore, Miguel seems to have confronted problems regarding his status as a freedman, particularly the obligation of *libertos*-by-the-law to engage in written and supervised labor contracts. Without such problems, he would not needed a notarized *carta de libertad*. Miguel wanted written and official proof that he was a *liberto* by *coartación*, by self-initiative, not a *liberto* freed by Spanish decree and therefore obligated to comply with coercive regulations of the transition from slavery to free labor.

Yet the questions do not end here. What could Miguel have done with his 225 pesos if he had waited just little more than a month? What can be said of his master, Don José Gual? Was he not aware of how close abolition was, of the other ways his slave could have used this respectable amount of money if he had been manumitted gratis? Furthermore, how common was it for Guayama's slaves to gain their freedom through self-purchase or masters' manumission in the final years of slavery? Were slaves who used their savings to purchase their freedom before abolition in better or worse condition for eventual class mobility than those who saved money during slavery but did not spend it until after abolition? Or were *libertos coartados* in a worse position for defining their status as freedpeople than slaves manumitted gratis before 1873 and who therefore could spend their money before abolition—that is, before the ranks of land and home buyers were swelled by the mass emancipation of 1873? These are important questions. As this chapter will show, it is necessary to distinguish between *libertos* who gained their freedom before and after 22 March 1873 as well as those whose hard work provided them with enough cash to enter the market for land and homes after freedom was obtained.

Manumission and *coartación* should be seen as two different paths toward freedom. By "manumission," I mean the granting of freedom by the master to the slave under conditions whereby the latter did not have to put up any amount of money—even a fraction of his or her total value—as a subsidy to the master. "*Coartación*" represents a completely different process wherein the slave takes the initiative, paying a sum equal to his/her value as agreed with the master or as assessed by a third party under the supervision of local authorities in cases where the master refused the *coartación* or when no agreement could be reached between master and slave. Freedom was not gained until after the last payment was made, but formalized, legal freedom was followed by an official *carta de libertad* registered with a public notary.[8]

The case of Miguel Gual also helps to raise other questions about the transition from slave to free labor and from slave to *liberto* status in Guayama. Don José Gual declared that Miguel had "continued enjoying the rights of a free man and earning a monthly wage of eight pesos." How does this wage compare to the wages paid to *libertos*-by-the-law after March 1873? Was Miguel in a more privileged position for wage bargaining than that enjoyed by government-freed *libertos*? How important was the enjoyment of the "rights of a free man" in the context of continuing plantation labor rather than peasantization after emancipation? Yet none of these questions should distract from the human drama involving Miguel Gual's May 1873 visit to Don Pedro Jiménez Sicardó's office: Miguel went there to reassert his status as a self-freed African slave as opposed to the recipient of government or planter charity.

Case Studies on the Paths to Freedom

Between 1870 and 1872, sixty of Guayama's slaves obtained their freedom by means of manumission or *coartación*, eleven in 1870, twenty-eight in 1871, and twenty-one in 1872, the final full year of slavery. To put these annual figures in proper context, table 3.1 presents the annual total number of registered manumissions and *coartaciones* for 1860–72.[9] Three aspects of the prevalence of manumission and self-purchase as paths toward freedom in Guayama emerge immediately from the table. First, during this period in general, very few slaves obtained their freedom through either means—from 1860 to 1867, an average of 7.25 slaves per year. This very low level of manumissions/*coartaciones* increased substantially, however, during the final five full years of slavery. From 1868 to 1872, the average number of slaves freed soared to 19.8 per year.

The increase is not only obvious but also abrupt. From five slaves freed in 1867, the total soars to twenty-three in 1868; after decreasing in 1869 and 1870, it leaps again to twenty-eight in 1871 and twenty-one in 1872. What could explain the obvious change from 1860–67 to 1868–72? Who were the masters and the slaves involved in these emancipations? What can be learned by studying these patterns of the functioning of Guayama's slave society at the dusk of the system on which it developed? What implications do these answers have for the mass emancipations set off by the 1870 and 1873 abolition laws?

First, the figures in table 3.1 call into question certain myths in the historiography: that in the 1860s Puerto Rican slave masters, foreseeing the end of slavery, began to manumit large numbers of slaves and did so either as a gesture of humanitarianism or for reasons of pure economic or political opportunism. These popular beliefs have percolated into the minds of authors who otherwise participated in efforts to redraw the prevailing images and understandings of Puerto Rican history. Ricardo Campos, for example, suggests that Puerto Rican planters converted en masse to abolitionism as a result of the realization that their future lay not in slave-based sugar agriculture but rather in the modernization of the sugar industry in terms of both technology and the organization of production, including a free wage labor system. Campos sees an

TABLE 3.1: Free Manumissions and Paid *Coartaciones* in Guayama,
1860–1872

Year	Male	Female	Total	By Planters
1860	4	3	7	2
1861	7	—	7	—
1862	1	5	6	—
1863	5	8	13	5
1864	2	4	6	2
1865	3	6	9[a]	1
1866	—	5	5	1
1867	2	3	5	2
1868	9	14	23	12
1869	2	14	16	13
1870	3	8	11	6
1871	9	19	28	15
1872	9	12	21	13
Total	56	101	157	72

Source: AGPR, PN, Guayama, "Indice general de protocolos notariales de Guayama, 1808–1910."

[a]Six of these nine were freed by Gregoria de Santiago, a mulatto peasant woman from barrio Algarrobos.

"abolitionist conscience on the part of the slave owners, who felt its historical necessity."[10]

Campos mechanically transplants European models of an emergent, class-conscious, modernizing bourgeoisie to the analysis of Puerto Rican slave-owning sugar planters' attitudes regarding abolition; consequently, he fails to close in on the historical process of the transition to free labor. He paints a picture at odds with what happened—or at least with what happened in Guayama. Of Guayama's total slave population of 2,874 in 1858 (see table 2.3), only 2.0 percent (58 slaves) achieved freedom by manumission or self-purchase in 1860–67. Even the 99 slaves liberated in 1868–72 represented only 5.7 percent of the 1,723 slaves living in Guayama when the Moret Law began to be implemented in 1871. Even assuming that masters manumitted all of these slaves, it is evident that Guayama's slave owners held onto their slaves until the last minute.[11]

The growth in individual emancipations beginning in 1868 reflects an increase in the number of freed slaves who had been the property of sugar planters and their immediate families as opposed to those owned by farmers, peasants, merchants, or artisans. As table 3.1 shows, before 1868, one or two sugar planters' slaves per year obtained their freedom through either manumission or self-purchase (with the exception of 1863). In contrast, in 1868, 1869, 1871, and 1872, *hacendados* individually emancipated about a dozen slaves.

When subjected to close scrutiny, these numbers reveal tokenism and opportunism rather than humanitarianism or turncoat abolitionism. With only a few exceptions, the "surge" in the number of slaves being manumitted or allowed self-purchase was almost evenly spread among plantation owners and their immediate families. The pattern was for one, two, or three emancipations per family during the five-year period from 1868 to 1872. Only one slave owned by the following *hacendados* gained freedom in these five years: Don Simón Moret (1868), owner of Hacienda Adela; Don Arístides Pillot (1869) and his son, Mauricio (1871), of Hacienda Barrancas; the Curet sisters (1869), owners of Hacienda Santa Elena, which, as mentioned in chapter 2, had one of Guayama's largest slave contingents; Don Pedro Virella Cassagnes (1869), owner of Hacienda Cayures; Doña Leonor Vázquez (1871), widow of Don Joaquín García Orozco, of Hacienda Estefanía; Don Juan Eugenio Boyrie (1872), of Hacienda Algarrobos; and Don Isidoro Crouzet (1872), of Hacienda Juana. Don José Gual (Hacienda Reunión), Don José Sabater (Hacienda Merced), and Don José García, Count of La Palmira (Hacienda Palmira), registered three manumissions or *coartaciones* each, and Don Jesús María Texidor (owner of Hacienda Gregoria and co-owner of Haciendas Josefa and Puerto) and Don Florencio Capó and his son, Juan Ignacio (administrator of Hacienda Olimpo), each had five slaves who achieved individual emancipation in the period 1868–72.

Only three planter families were particularly conspicuous on the list of *cartas de libertad* issued during this period. The Villodas and the Gaudinau families were involved in eight manumissions/self-purchases each, and those two families owned plantations that became extinct in the early 1870s—Hacienda Agueda and Hacienda Melanía, respectively. Finally, the spouses Don Félix Massó y Soler and Doña Obdulia Verdeguer de Massó, respectively the owners of the contiguous haciendas Aurora and Bardeguez, were involved in ten *cartas de libertad*. First-generation descendants of Catalonians who had migrated to Guayama, members of the

Massó-Verdeguer family left Guayama during these years to reside permanently in Barcelona. Even though we do not know how many of these ten *cartas de libertad* derived from manumissions or self-purchases, it seems likely that the family's departure for Europe played some role.[12]

This procession of *hacendados* signing deeds of freedom for one or perhaps two or three slaves in the final five years of slavery bears little resemblance to the picture of slave owners who, facing the imminent end of slavery, preferred to "graciously" manumit their slaves (or a substantial number of them) in a context in which slavery supposedly came to be seen as little more than a nuisance. Of the fifty-one individual emancipations between 1870 and 1872 for which I found detailed information, only six were true gratis manumissions—that is, 88 percent of these emancipations were *coartaciones*. This is an extremely high proportion compared to the distribution of purchased and gratis manumissions found by other studies of Latin America. In early colonial Lima and Mexico City, late-eighteenth and early-nineteenth-century Buenos Aires and Paraty (Brazil), and nineteenth-century Bahia, the proportion of self-purchased manumissions generally ranged between 30 and 40 percent except in Buenos Aires, where *coartaciones* represented just under 60 percent of the cases.[13]

This high proportion of *coartaciones* vis-à-vis gratis manumissions in Guayama, however, should not be seen as indicating a high prevalence in the use of *coartaciones* as a way for slaves to obtain their freedom in Guayama or in Puerto Rico in general. These forty-five *libertos coartados* represent just around 2.5 percent of Guayama's 1871 slave population.[14] This proportion confirms an earlier study by Benjamín Nistal-Moret, who examined a large sample drawn from the island's 1872 slave registry. Nistal-Moret found that only 3 percent of Puerto Rican slaves were registered as being under the stipulations of a *coartación* agreement—that is, had already given some amount of money toward their eventual self-purchase. Rather, the low ratio of *coartaciones* to gratis manumissions seems to indicate the lack of inclination among Guayama's slaveholders to part with their investment in chattel slaves as the end of slavery neared, perhaps in the hope that the inevitable emancipation would come with a respectable sum of cash by way of indemnification.

Of the six gratis manumissions registered in Guayama from 1870 to 1872, two involved nonsugar masters: María, a fifty-eight-year-old slave of Don Miguel Miranda manumitted on 14 June 1871, and Hermenegilda, a forty-nine-year-old slave of Doña Gregoria Rodríguez, whose heirs manumitted Hermenegilda on 8 February 1872. Both women were freed as a result of their "*buenos servicios*" (good services) to their masters but only when old and probably no longer productive. In fact, the problem of establishing a slave's exact age in the face of African origin or late baptism if creole makes it plausible that the two women—and especially María Miranda—could have been manumitted by the the Moret Law in 1871. The other four gratis manumissions were of Felicidad and her son, Félix, ages nineteen and three, respectively, slaves of Don Mauricio Pillot; Monserrate, age fifty-eight, slave of Don Florencio Capó; and Valentín, age fifty-one, slave of Don José Gual. The Pillot and Gual slaves were freed on the grounds of good service and loyalty. Monserrate was an elderly slave described in her *carta de libertad* as having disfigured fingers on both hands, a likely sign of arthritis.[15]

Other slave owners were not as gracious with elderly slaves who actively sought their freedom through legal means. Don Félix Villodas, one of the heirs of the Villodas estate, received fifty pesos from fifty-eight-year-old Andrea in exchange for her freedom. Fermín also put up fifty pesos to get a *carta de libertad* from Don Luis Texidor, even though the deed clearly stated that his age could be estimated only as "over fifty." This transaction raises questions about the enforcement of the Moret Law, since Fermín obtained his freedom on 7 February 1872, several months after the law began to be implemented in Puerto Rico and four months after he had paid his master.[16]

Other general features of Guayama's fifty-one individual emancipations from 1870 to 1873 are noteworthy. First, the slaves tended to achieve freedom while between fourteen and forty-five years old. In contrast to the situation found elsewhere, very few children under fourteen obtained their freedom by manumission or *coartación*. While Stuart Schwartz's study of colonial Bahia found that nearly half of all manumitted slaves were thirteen or younger, Guayama had only three cases involving children of those ages. Again, the explanation seems to rest in the small number of gratis manumissions, as children were less likely to have accumulated monies for self-purchase and generally depended on third parties to fulfill *coartaciones*.[17]

Second, the average price of a *coartación* was 231 pesos; for slaves aged twenty and older, the average was 247 pesos. These amounts are very close to the average value of slaves sold in Guayama during the same period, 269 pesos. Of the 130 slaves sold in these years, discrete information is available on the value of 112; the rest were sold along with other property (especially farms), and their prices do not appear separately in the documentation

Following Lyman Johnson's approach, I have calculated the number of workdays needed for a slave to accumulate 247 pesos, assuming hypothetically that they could work for wages as laborers on Sundays and holidays. As Johnson argues, this measure gives a more adequate idea of the sacrifices made by individual slaves, members of their families, or free or enslaved friends to accumulate the necessary capital for a *coartación*.[18] In Guayama, a laborer (a free person or a hired-out slave) would have needed 772 workdays to amass 247 pesos at the optimistic but not uncommon wage of four reals (fifty cents) daily. I concur with Johnson's conclusion that without the intervention of free real or fictive kin, an individual slave would have needed most of his or her productive life to accumulate the money needed for a *coartación*.

Finally, almost no differences exist between Guayama in 1870–73 and the other studies of manumission in Latin America with regard to the gender of the freedpeople. Roughly two-thirds of all manumissions (true gratis manumissions and *coartaciones*) involved female slaves. Schwartz attributes this finding to masters' disinclination to free adult male slaves, who had relatively high values and who evoked sexual and physical fears among masters. This explanation, however, does not help in understanding *coartaciones*.

Dealing with a larger number of *coartaciones* in an urban context, Johnson argues that the preponderance of women is related to the occupations available to them in Buenos Aires, where masters sent many female slaves out as peddlers of foodstuffs and as laundresses rather than hiring them out at fixed wages. These occupations allowed women more independence than was available to male slave peons or artisans and offered the ability to gain more income than the earnings owed to masters. In Guayama's mostly rural context, however, both women and men could also accumulate cash by cultivating small gardens on estate plots and by raising small livestock, especially pigs.[19]

Protopeasant Slave Activities

The last two features of Guayama's slave manumissions in the final years of slavery enable me to address, albeit with great difficulty given the paucity of the available evidence, the extent to which Puerto Rican slaves engaged in autonomous economic activities that would have allowed at least a few of them to accumulate the substantial amounts of money needed to manumit themselves or their kin. This topic has gone largely unexamined in the historiography on Puerto Rican slavery, although certain evidence does allow me to draw a rough picture of economic activities associated with a protopeasant culture and formation.

I will begin by examining the legal prescriptions that could have recognized the existence of such activities among slaves in Puerto Rico. Any examination Puerto Rican slaves' autonomous activities, protopeasant or otherwise, must note the island's official regulations on slave life. The primary source of regulations was the slave code decreed by Spanish governor Don Miguel de la Torre on 12 August 1826, which continued in force, slightly amended, until abolition.[20] The 1826 slave code contained various dispositions regarding the treatment of the slaves in an attempt to regulate planters' policies toward the feeding, clothing, religious instruction, work, and punishment of their chattel slaves. Hardly surprisingly, the new code was enacted when slavery on the island was undergoing a quantitative and qualitative transformation as part of the establishment of a sugar plantation economy.

Perhaps one of the most important reasons behind de la Torre's promulgation of this slave code was the number of unsettling slave flights and rebel conspiracies during the early 1820s. Historians Luis Díaz Soler and Guillermo Baralt have pointed to this connection, and according to Baralt, "The principal aim of the 1826 code was to prevent [slave] conspiracies and to threaten the slave with possible punishment as well as other measures that would be taken against him in case of rebellion."[21] Both Díaz Soler and Baralt identify several provisions that seem to support this interpretation, including those concerning the use and custody of instruments of work, leisure activities, movement outside plantations, citizen arrests of wandering slaves, and automatic freedom for any slave who exposed a conspiracy.[22] But Governor de la Torre offers what may be the most illuminating testimony about the 1826 code's aims of repressing slave resistance and rebellion. In its preamble, de la Torre states his duty to maintain public order on the island, a responsibility he says he cannot fulfill unless he applies "a prompt and efficient remedy—that is, the severe cauterization of the disorders, catastrophes, and the grave ills . . . to public tranquillity and security that are being frequently practiced by hacienda slaves."[23]

The code covered three specific aspects of slaves' lives that are of interest here: feeding; daily work during the off-season, during the harvest, and on Sundays and holidays; and control of slaves' autonomous activities. All three were crucial aspects of slave life directly or indirectly influencing the possibility of protopeasant adaptation. In the first area, the 1826 code specified that "masters should give their slaves two or three meals daily, as they see fit. But these should be sufficient, not only for the preservation of the individual, but also to recover from fatigue. It is regulated as absolutely necessary for each [slave] as daily food six or eight plantains (or their equivalent in sweet potatoes, yams, or other roots), eight ounces of meat, codfish, or *macarelas* [fish], and four ounces of rice or other ordinary potage."[24]

These regulations refer only to foods provided by slaveholders to slaves, saying nothing about any policy of encouraging or permitting slaves to produce foodstuffs to supplement those provided by the masters. In Jamaica, for example, slaves were allowed to produce foodstuffs to supplement plantation provisions, and the slaves' subsistence production activities generally took place on weekends. Did similar developments occur in Puerto Rico? Articles 1 and 2 of title IV of the slave code ("On the Work and Occupation of the Slaves") offer some clues to the answer. According to article 1, slaves were supposed to work no more than nine hours daily during the off-season and thirteen hours during harvest. Article 2 then regulated slaves' use of leisure time to engage in autonomous productive activities: "Every [work]day, during the resting hours and on holidays for two hours, it will be permissible to let the slaves dedicate themselves within the hacienda, without detriment to their master, in manufacturing and other occupations that yield for their personal benefit and utility, so that they can acquire small capital and obtain freedom. Masters should respect these legitimate acquisitions and should even help their servants to that end in whatever possible way, especially those [who are] industrious and of good behavior."[25]

Still, these two articles say nothing about Sunday activities, a matter covered in article 3 of title II ("On Religious and Civil Instruction"). This article prohibited planters from working their slaves on hacienda chores for more than two hours each Sunday except during harvest, when planters had more leeway and could use their slaves for longer periods of time.[26] Combined with other regulations limiting the slaves' recreational activities to only a few hours on holidays (and within their estates),[27] these dispositions meant that Puerto Rican slaves would have had only small periods in which to engage in autonomous productive activities. At least in theory and legally, however, slaves were to be encouraged to engage in activities that would render them some small benefit (*peculio*). To a certain extent, a legal statement recognized the slaves' right to obtain, keep, and use the "legitimate acquisitions" that their autonomous activities could produce. However, what type of activities did the code contemplate? The indication of "manufacturing and other occupations" suggests small craft production rather than subsistence farming. Did planters also encourage their slaves to produce foodstuffs?

Other questions arise: how were the slaves to obtain small capital (*peculio*) for production? Were they allowed to market their produce? Title IV did not address the question of marketing, and the provisions that deal with slave transit beyond hacienda perimeters were stringent, with the goal of prohibiting the mingling of slaves from different haciendas, demonstrating an obvious concern with slave conspiracies. Title VI ("Prohibiting Slaves from Dealing with Those from Other Haciendas") banned slaves from visiting other haciendas and specified that slaves could leave their estates only if masters or overseers provided written travel passes. Moreover, title VI authorized citizen arrests of wandering slaves found without properly issued passes.[28]

Two other relevant regulations on slave life help to draw a preliminary picture of bondswomen's and -men's time and resources for engaging in autonomous production activities. Title V restricted use and custody of instruments of labor, again as a result of security concerns: slaves' use of work tools was restricted to supervised activities of daily hacienda work; at all other times, these tools were to be kept under lock and key. Finally, title VIII, which covered slave quarters, ordered that all slaves be locked up at eight or nine o'clock in the evening, depending on the time of year.[29]

Several features begin to emerge. First, it seems obvious that some of the components of the stipulated slave diet—plantains, sweet potatoes, yams, and other roots such as *yuca* (cassava), and *yautias* (*Xanthosoma*)—could be locally produced on estate land.[30] The code implies that Puerto Rican slaves worked six days a week for a minimum of nine to thirteen hours per day. On Sundays and holidays, Puerto Rican slaves were to perform hacienda chores for at least two hours; during harvest, however, they probably worked much longer. If no extra harvest work was imposed on Sundays and holidays, slaves would have been allowed to engage in recreational activities on the hacienda perimeter. Productive activities could occur only during whatever time the slaves could squeeze out of their regular workweeks and Sunday and holiday leisure hours. But how would they market their autonomously produced crafts (or foodstuffs)? Again, the code implies that the slaves would have needed their masters' or overseers' permission to leave the estate to sell in nearby towns or rural settlements.

Yet one question in particular looms large: did the slave code reflect the realities of day-to-day Puerto Rican slavery? Here the testimony of two contemporaries may offer some initial answers. Having visited various Caribbean islands, including Puerto Rico, in 1841–42, renowned French abolitionist Victor Schoelcher expressed a favorable view of Spanish slave codes' provisions regarding the treatment of slaves. However, Schoelcher also noted a dissonance between the legal and real worlds. The Spanish code's provisions were excellent, Schoelcher said, but, "unfortunately one does not see that [officials and planters] have ever wished to enforce them. [They] are an illusion and in fact null."[31] And reflecting less than a decade after abolition, Puerto Rican journalist Salvador Brau recalled the extent of planter noncompliance with slave code regulations ranging from religious instructions to the encouragement of marriages to respect for the slave family.[32]

Even accepting a discrepancy between legal order and planter behavior, what were the realities of day-to-day slavery in Puerto Rico? Unfortunately, systematic studies of Puerto Rican slave plantation life still have not been conducted.[33] Nevertheless, some elements can be combined to bring us a step closer to historical experience than is possible by simply reviewing slave laws. Did the slaves have access to plantation plots to cultivate foodstuffs? Were they restricted in their movement beyond the haciendas, as the slave code specified? Did they manage to accumulate small capital, as could be reflected in slave self-purchases of freedom?

The only published planter account of policies toward slave subsistence production of foodstuffs and surplus marketing is that by Don José Martínez Diez, "Relación del trato que doy a mi peonage en mi Hacienda Pueblo Viejo."[34] Martínez Diez described his policy toward plantation slaves as part of an investigation prompted by a complaint brought by one of his slave drivers, also a slave. Although the circumstances surrounding this description raise questions about Martínez Diez's truthfulness, the document offers some startling information. After describing his slaves' daily work schedule and diet and his clothing policies (which closely followed official regulations), Martínez Diez claimed, "on Sundays and holidays falling within the week, I never occupy them with anything, only on their tasks until eight o'clock on long mornings and until nine on short ones, as is proven by their famous maize, yam, cantaloupes, watermelons, and even plantain plots: [And] at harvest time they ask my permission and go to the city to market [these goods]; I give them oxen and carts to carry them to the beach. Furthermore, this hacienda is plentiful in fruits, and in the forest you find in abundance roots, like the white yam, the guava, and others, which they are permitted to gather and sell to buy their own tobacco."[35]

Martínez Diez's estate was located in the municipality of Guaynabo, just across the bay from San Juan, and "the city" probably refers to the capital. Martínez Diez offered no information regarding the extent of his slaves' "famous" provision plots, although information on the distribution of land within haciendas was rarely reported. Pedro San Miguel provides some scant information on the existence of limited provision cultivation on sugar haciendas in this northern coastal *municipio* at the start of the growth of its sugar industry. According to San Miguel, of the 5,670 *cuerdas* owned by eight leading sugar *hacendados* or their family estates (*sucesiones*), only 86 (1.5 percent) were registered as dedicated to other agricultural uses, usually minor crops, while 435 *cuerdas* (7.7 percent) were planted with sugarcane, 2,512 (44.3 percent) were pasture, and 2,637 (46.5 percent) were forested. Some *hacendados* had less than a single *cuerda* in minor crops, although others dedicated as much as 10.2 percent of their land to that purpose.[36]

In Ponce, on the south coast, in 1823 Hacienda Pámpanos reportedly dedicated about 5.5 percent of its two hundred acres to plantain groves; in nearby Guayanilla, Hacienda María Antonia apparently had about twelve *cuerdas* of plantain groves among its roughly five hundred *cuerdas* of land. Francisco Scarano reports that Hacienda El Quemado, also in Ponce, with 114 slaves and two large animal-powered mills, had "an impressive array of sugar houses, slave quarters, a hospital, and a spacious house for the administrator, in addition to an undetermined expanse of cane fields and plantation groves."[37]

Scarano has criticized the credibility of the author of two of the few surviving accounts of slave life in nineteenth-century Puerto Rico, George Flinter, describing his works as "awkward" and as examples "of the propaganda genre."[38] Flinter, an Irishman who served for twenty-one years as a British military officer in the Caribbean, visited Puerto Rico in 1829–32. Published when slavery in the Caribbean was coming under attack by abolitionist forces elsewhere, Flinter's *A View of the Present Condition of the Slave Population of Puerto Rico* (1832) and *An Account of the Present State of the Island of Puerto Rico* (1834) sought to portray the well-being and "happiness" of slaves in Spanish colonies vis-à-vis other Caribbean experiences and even European peasants.[39]

As Scarano has cogently pointed out, Flinter's central problem was that he needed to explain to British readers how Puerto Rico's slave population could have almost doubled in twenty years despite the fact that the slave trade had been illegal since 1820.[40] Overlooking the formidable increase in slave imports since the 1810s, Flinter had only one other way to explain this demographic increase: Spanish slave laws and the benign treatment of slaves in Spanish colonies accounted for a tremendous "natural" growth of the slave population. Slaves in Puerto Rico, Flinter argued, not only were protected by humane slave laws but also were allowed to own property, cultivate subsistence foodstuffs, and form stable family units within the plantations.[41] As he said, "If tomorrow an offer is made to Puerto Rican slaves to set them free on the condition that they abandon their plots, huts, and stock, and migrate to Africa, I am sure that they would reject such an offer."[42]

Flinter made several remarks about Puerto Rican slaves' autonomous subsistence agriculture. He alleged that slave "cabins are surrounded by plantain groves loaded with fruit, and trees of different sizes, which afford a delightful shade from the heat of the noon-day sun." Furthermore, "almost all of the slaves in this island have fowls and pigs, and many of them possess cows and horses. In their hours of leisure they raise vegetables and roots, to supply the market; and if industrious and frugal, in a short time they are enabled to save money to purchase their freedom, without encroaching on the property of their masters."[43] Puerto Rican slaves had another advantage, according to Flinter: "more holidays and festivals than in the British and Dutch islands; consequently, they have more days of rest or leisure, which the industrious avail themselves of in order to cultivate their provision grounds."[44]

Flinter's view was shared to some extent by a contemporary visitor, Charles Walker, a U.S. citizen who traveled to Puerto Rico during the mid-1830s and stayed with various planter families in the south coast's leading sugar districts, Guayama and Ponce. Writing to relatives in the United States, Walker, a Protestant northerner, expressed his amusement at the nature of Puerto Rico's Catholicism, race relations, and slavery. For example, describing what he interpreted as the advantages of being a slave in a Spanish colony, Walker said that "if the negro [slave] is a little smart, he can by raising a pig and fowls soon obtain the cost [of his freedom] to the master and he is then obliged to set him free. There are Sundays and feast days when a slave can gain a quarter of a dollar a day for on those occasions if he works, it must be voluntarily."[45] Yet a month later, Walker noticed, "One objection to the Catholic religion is the innumerable holy days—they will sometimes be four a month and these days no public business is done, and the working of the slaves is contrary to law, yet they generally work them till ten in the morning and sometimes after dinner."[46]

Neither Flinter nor Walker described how plantation slaves marketed their produce or whether they did so individually or in groups. These observers also failed to mention when, where, and to whom slave-produced foodstuffs were sold, if at all. Answers to these questions may eventually arise in studies of the relationships among plantation slaves and free peasants and town dwellers.

As stated earlier, one of the principal reasons for Governor de la Torre's new slave code was curtailing the growing number of slave flights and rebellion conspiracies. Title VI of the 1826 slave code dealt with one of the phenomena government officials and planters identified as key to controlling the growing slave population: the movement of slaves beyond the perimeters of their haciendas. Slaves were not supposed to leave their plantations without planter or overseer permission and were supposed to be locked up after certain hours every day. But did slaves abide by these regulations at all times?

Available information suggests that they did not necessarily do so. For example, some of the documentation on runaway slaves published by Nistal-Moret draws us closer to Puerto Rican slaves' daily life experiences of social control and resistance. In an 1838 report, for example, the commander of the northwestern military department of Aguadilla, Colonel Ramón Méndez, explained to the governor the problems concerning the region's runaway slaves. According to Méndez, slaves were planning escapes in small numbers because slaves from different estates and even from estates in different municipalities were able to meet beforehand. The root of the problem, Méndez pointed out, was that, "In these towns the slaves are badly controlled, because they are allowed more liberty than necessary and have dances with the permission of authorities until late at night, and among the free colored until after midnight as anyone else, where the slaves come to watch and even to intermingle."[47]

A month later, the *cabildo* of Aguadilla, the department's capital, met to deal with the problem of runaway slaves in the districts. The *cabildo* agreed with Colonel Méndez's analysis and pointed to the "excessive liberty" given to some slaves. The *cabildo* noticed that even when decrees and regulations prohibited certain slave behavior, many slaves continued to engage in it; consequently, the councillors demanded strict planter enforcement of security measures. The *cabildo* instituted several measures to curtail interestate slave gatherings, the intermingling of slave and free people (especially of color), and slaves' access to seaboard transportation that could facilitate escape to Haiti, the slaves' dreamland of freedom. However, the *cabildo* also insisted on interdicting another form of relations between slaves and free persons:

> The slaves are used to making deals with free persons, selling them produce and goods, and this results in losses to the masters, while they obtain enough means for their flight. And since [the prohibition of this practice] has to be enforced strictly, except when the slave carries a license from his master . . . it is necessary to punish the slave with twenty-five lashes if he does not have the necessary [license]. The buyer has to return to the slave's master the produce, which [the master] should credit to the servant [to his *peculio*?], or as he conscientiously sees fit. The buyer will lose the cost of what he bought and should be fined twenty-five pesos, double this fine in case of relapse. These penalties extend to whomever serves or helps, directly or indirectly, the slaves in those sales or contracts.[48]

Later, during the 1840s, colonial governors saw the need to reaffirm the prohibition against allowing slaves to leave their haciendas. In 1842, Governor Santiago Méndez Vigo complained that this provision of the slave code "has been forgotten," thus affecting public tranquillity, and ordered mayors to enforce this regulation.[49] Six years later, when a slave-rebellion conspiracy was discovered in Ponce, Governor Juan Prim y Prats reaffirmed the importance of forbidding slaves from traveling without written licenses; even with licenses, travel should be permitted only when genuinely needed by planters.[50]

The problem of unauthorized slave travel apparently recurred. In the countryside, the establishment of small stores (*ventorrillos*) close to plantations could present problems for planters and government officials. For example, in 1870 the mayor of San Germán argued that the *ventorrillos* constituted his district's second-leading cause of crime. The mayor argued that the *ventorrillos* were "oftentimes established with forty or fifty borrowed pesos by members of the day laborer class. They open usually close to wealthy estates where there are a number of slaves, with the purpose of buying at a low price all the goods stolen from there. These stores, it could be said without being wrong, are generally dens of laborers and many slaves who come to sell the product of their larcenies, to buy on credit or barter for some provisions or liquor, or lured by the card playing or raffles of provisions that go on there. Hence come the many cases of drunkenness that are the origin of contempt, lack of respect [*faltas de respeto*], and resistance to the authorities."[51]

Moreover, the slave code dictated that wandering slaves be arrested and jailed and that their masters be fined and charged with the expenses incurred in incarcerating the slaves. In addition, planters faced economic losses caused by lost slave labor. A *hacendado* from the western coastal municipality of Añasco complained to the governor in 1861 about the injustice of being fined eight pesos every time one of his slaves was found traveling around the town. Don Miguel López had no problems with fines imposed when slaves ran away but found it unjust that slaves were fined simply for visiting the town area. Such a policy would result in bankruptcy for their owners, especially those from plantations close to towns. But why did these slaves go to the town? As he explained, "In effect, Your Excellency, at night the slaves retire themselves from the daily cultivation tasks, and that brief liberty enables them to go to the nearby town to bring their herbs [*haces de yervas*] or to get in exchange for some coins their children's bread or any other needed article [*artículo de primera necesidad*] for themselves."[52]

López urged the governor to amend the regulations so that the slaves could travel into town until a specified hour each evening, thus saving their owners the great expense of repeated fines. However, Añasco's mayor rejected López's proposition, arguing that having slaves wandering around town in the evenings had caused public disorder, including drunkenness, and a large number of thefts before the slave laws were strictly enforced. Slaves from neighboring haciendas, the mayor said, had come to town, "some without a clear purpose, others selling produce that they probably stole from their own masters, [and] with the product [of the sales] most of them got drunk and others committed disorders against public tranquillity and comfort." Only slaves with written transit passes issued by their masters or overseers, said the mayor's decree, would be permitted to come to town in the evenings. In the end, López lost his plea, as the governor reaffirmed these provisions of the slave code.[53]

In a country where slaves had, at least theoretically, a legal option to purchase their freedom, any possible opportunities for bondsmen and -women to accumulate some capital would be expected to be reflected in their use of the *coartación* mechanism. Indeed, a common question in studying *coartaciones* is where the slaves got the money to purchase freedom. Díaz Soler raised this question decades ago and assumed that the slaves obtained money from their autonomous productive activities, though he did not describe the process.[54] María Consuelo Vázquez Arce also raised the question after finding, in a study of the internal slave trade in the eastern-coast municipality of Naguabo, that the majority of the certificates of liberty extended to slaves had been paid for either in currency or in produce and livestock.[55] However, the evidence shows that only a very small fraction of the slave population obtained individual emancipation through self-purchase. In Naguabo, only 8.4 percent of the 1,193 transactions studied by Vázquez Arce involved *coartado* slaves (that is, involved clauses specifying that the slaves had paid installments toward self-purchase). In San Juan, only 3.5 percent of a sample of 2,350 slave transactions studied by Rubén Carbonell Fernández granted slaves certificates of their freedom through completed self-purchase.[56]

Both Vázquez Arce and Carbonell Fernández find that the majority of freed slaves were female, with a particular emphasis on domestics. Carbonell Fernández argues that "the farther a slave was from economically productive labor, the more possibilities existed" that he/she would end up purchasing freedom.[57] Did this mean that female domestic slaves had more access to the means of buying freedom than did male domestics or all field slaves? Vázquez Arce implies that the key was domestic slaves' greater freedom of movement,[58] but did they also have more ways to accumulate capital? Answers to these questions remain distant, but given the problems caused by the end of slave trade and by the failure to incorporate free peasant labor into sugar plantations, Puerto Rican *hacendados* can be expected to have moved slowly in allowing sizable numbers of slaves (particularly field and mill slaves) to acquire their freedom.

Most of Flinter's descriptions of Puerto Rican slaves' daily life in *An Account of the Present State of the Island of Puerto Rico* simply rehashed his earlier remarks in *A View of the President Condition of the Slave Population of Puerto Rico*. *A View of the Present Condition* dwelled on the advantages of free labor over slave labor and on the political and philosophical advantages of gradual, long-term abolition of slavery in the Caribbean, and only a fraction of the book discussed Puerto Rican slaves in particular. However, *An Account* dealt exclusively with Puerto Rico and with more than slave life. At times, Flinter seems to have sought to lure British investors into establishing sugar plantations on the island, and some statements seem to contradict others elsewhere in *An Account* and in *A View*.

Scarano has already drawn attention to Flinter's contradictory observations on the importance of slave labor and the extent of free labor use in sugar production.[59] More pertinent to the discussion here, however, is Flinter's comparison of the microeconomics of a sugar plantation in Puerto Rico and in neighboring Jamaica. Flinter notes, for example, that smaller estates in Puerto Rico could produce as much sugar as larger Jamaican plantations, a finding Scarano has recently confirmed. But Flinter specifies that his calculations are based on the assumption that "the provision of the negroes were purchased—an expense which can be avoided in this island by the least attention to industry."[60] Flinter later adds, "The high price of sugar and coffee in [the 1820s] made the planters look with contempt on the less profitable cultivation of provisions. So much was this branch neglected that the island, though teeming with fertility, depended for provisions, for the slaves and for the generality of the inhabitants, on foreign countries,—when by proper management the inhabitants might have raised abundance of provisions for home consumption and for a foreign market."[61]

If Flinter's criticism of Puerto Rican planters' neglect of provision cultivation was accurate, what had happened to the slaves' subsistence plots? Presumably, they were wiped out by the expansion of cane fields, a process that would have subsumed any "benevolent" recognition of slaves' "rights" to autonomous subsistence production. After high-flying sugar prices had leveled off, Flinter happily notes, the planters began to reinstate a policy of local provision production:

> The planters of [the south] coast, also, formerly depended on foreign countries for the food of their negroes, but since the depression in the price of sugar, they have mostly opened a communication by good roads with the mountains, and cleared land for sowing provisions; and such has been their activity, that [in 1833] they will have an abundant supply [of provisions], and, I trust, henceforward will not need to depend on foreign aid. It is this system of economy and of active industry in the raising of provisions that can alone save this island from the misery into which the low price of sugar has plunged, I fear irretrievably, the French and English colonies.[62]

Indeed, Scarano has found that Ponce's planters began to expand their landed properties onto the mountainside in response to the scarcity of agricultural land in the coastal valley in the face of the need for grazing space and to substitute local production for imported provisions.[63] Thus, the policy of provision cultivation seems to have responded more to local conditions of land tenure and ecology and to the conditions of the international market than to the legal orders from the governor's office in San Juan.

Elsewhere in the Caribbean, however, a combination of such factors as slave access to land and markets for subsistence agricultural production, the concomitant opportunity to accumulate some capital to invest in land for settlement, and the availability of such land provided either stimuli or constraints on the prospect of postemancipation peasant class formation. The historical geography and the history of planters' policies and slaves' responses shaped the context within which various outcomes emerged after emancipation both between colonies and within a single colony.

Conclusion

Much remains to be discovered of Puerto Rican slave plantations' regional and historical patterns of land tenure and use and provision-cultivation policies and slaves' access to time and resources for producing and marketing autonomously foodstuffs, livestock, and crafts. Perhaps this is one of the very few times that the issue of protopeasant slave adaptations has been raised as a legitimate subject in Puerto Rican historiography.[64] The limited published documentation on nineteenth-century slavery, conversely, suggests that the slaves' access to autonomous productive activities in Puerto Rico was much more restricted than is indicated by the rosy pictures offered by some observers, such as Flinter.[65] Yet the opposing depiction of slaves who spent their lives getting up at three o'clock in the morning and going to bed at nine o'clock in the evening, who never attempted to grow plantains or roots (or to raise cows or pigs), who never tried to scurry away from the estates to sell some of their products (or those stolen from the estates) is perhaps as unidimensional as Flinter's.[66]

In sum, the emergence of a *brecha campesina* (peasant breach) in the slavery mode of production in the nineteenth century seems to have been very fragile and heterogeneous. Districts like those of the south and west coasts, where land was scarce and expensive and where droughts remained constant throughout the century, could be expected to have developed different patterns of land use for provision cultivation than districts on the northern and eastern coasts, where rainfall was not a problem, where peasant settlement was more dense, and where slavery did not develop as fully.

Along with factors such as local land-tenure patterns and ecology and international economic fluctuations, another important condition must be considered when studying protopeasant adaptations in Puerto Rico: the underdevelopment of a monetized economy and of an internal market. Nineteenth-century Puerto Rico suffered from constant currency droughts. The Spanish government never solved this problem, which was compounded by the use of various sorts of currencies, denominations, and equivalents—currency from Spain, Mexico, Venezuela, and Cuba circulated (sometimes all at the same time) throughout the century. Along with the lack of currency, the absence of banking institutions and regulated credit procedures resulted in the growth of usury and in the concomitant concentration of economic power in the hands of a merchant elite that controlled most of the circulating liquid capital. This underdevelopment of a monetized economy was reflected at the elite level in conflicting relationships between merchants and planters, a subject that has recently drawn much attention.[67]

At another level, the absence of a more integrated internal market could also have been reflected in planters' options and policies regarding the feeding of plantation slaves. Some 1853 remarks by an anonymous Guayama planter help to raise this issue. While addressing the unreliability of peasant *jornaleros* as a solution to the sugar industry's labor-supply problems, this planter complained about the lack of an internal market in foodstuffs that would have eliminated the sugar estates' need to import provisions. Had peasants dedicated themselves to producing food surpluses, active commerce would have developed between the interior and the coast. However, this planter lamented, this phenomenon did not emerge, and only those plantations that had provision plots had access to locally produced staples, while others were forced to import staples at high prices. The peasants' laziness and indolence, the planter concluded, not only made them an unreliable source of labor power but also was responsible for the absence of an internal market.[68]

Thus, the available evidence calls into question some of Patterson's views as elucidated at the beginning of this chapter. Much more work needs to be done in Puerto Rico and Guayama on the everyday life of slaves at different historical moments before abolition. However, at least some critical practices—manumission and *coartación*—and certain economic activities associated with a protopeasant culture and life connected to the plantation world created spaces of slave life that mitigate against the wholesale acceptance of all aspects of Patterson's "social death" argument. Furthermore, the evidence offered casts doubt on Spanish governor Don Segundo de la Portilla's 1876 characterization of *libertos*.

CHAPTER 4

THE GALE-FORCE WINDS
OF 1868–1873 TEARING DOWN
SLAVERY

The abolition of slavery in Puerto Rico, viewed from a wide angle, was in good measure intimately linked to the initial stages of a haphazardly reached and implemented Spanish policy for the gradual abolition of slavery in its major colonial possession at the time, Cuba. In both colonial siblings, abolition resulted from a complex process influenced by broad tendencies toward the elimination of slave labor in the Americas as well as transformations occurring within Spanish political culture and the contested evolution of the Spanish state during the 1860s–70s.[1] However, the eye also has to focus on the events that began to unfold in the middle and late 1860s and that in the case of Spanish politics resulted in a new, intensive yet unstable revolutionary period between September 1868 and December 1874 known as the Sexenio or the Revolución Gloriosa.[2] For Puerto Rican slaveholders, abolitionists, and slaves perhaps more than for their Cuban counterparts, the pivot point in the process that led to the termination of slavery on the island was September–October 1868. In a revealing coincidence of political tensions boiling since earlier in the decade, three very different revolts shook Spain and its remaining New World colonies: on 17 September, a military coup overthrew the Bourbon monarchy; on 23–24 September, a prematurely executed and failed revolt for independence occurred in Puerto Rico; and on 10 October, the first Cuban war of independence, the Ten Years' War, started.[3]

This chapter does not, however, seek to recount in detail the complex, multilayered history of this process. Rather, I examine, with a close, local-level emphasis, the twists and turns of the highly contested process of achieving first partial and almost immediately thereafter full abolition of slavery in Puerto Rico between 1870 and 1876. I choose this approach for various reasons. The most important one is that Puerto Rican and Spanish Caribbean historiography continue to demand local-level examinations of the transition from slavery to free labor that go beyond the traditional interpretations, which, surprisingly, continue to find supporters who view this process as a rather trouble-free, successful realization of inevitable economic laws and, especially, the "*gran obra*" (great deeds) of enlightened liberal Spanish and Puerto Rican abolitionists. From a different standpoint, even some revisionist Puerto Rican historiography from the 1970s onward should be reexamined critically to question the extent to which teleological, economic interpretations of the transition to free labor misread some of the available evidence, preclude us from mining other evidence, and ultimately result in explanations that are far from as nuanced as some of its initial practitioners surely had hoped to achieve. Following some of the events leading to emancipation should help to provide some sense of the context within which former slaveholders and former slaves tried to adjust to the sudden legal shift to free labor in March 1873 as well as of the ways in which these people subsequently determined the content and limits of freedom. Chapter 5, in turn, will focus on the initial implementation of the forced-labor contract regime mandated by the 1873 Abolition Law, examining the workings of this policy in Guayama and the shift to a more restrictive labor-contracting policy after the end of the radical liberal policies brought forth during the Spanish revolutionary period.

Atlantic Winds of Change:
From Gettysburg to Madrid, Lares, and Yara

In 1870, the Spanish Cortes (parliament) enacted a partial abolition law for Cuba and Puerto Rico; less than three years later, the Republican National Assembly in Madrid haphazardly approved a full abolition law. Both events represented in part the culmination of a series of political processes and events dating at least to the mid-1860s. For narrative if not heuristic purposes, what should first be identified are the winds from North America, shifting and gusting as they did after 1863–65 with the Confederacy's defeat in the U.S. Civil War, and the political and potentially military effects of the North's victory and the exercise of Republican hegemony during the Reconstruction era. Many Spanish and Hispanic-Caribbean authorities and settlers grasped implications of these U.S. events not only for the survival of slavery in the Spanish Antilles but also for the preservation of Spanish colonial rule over Cuba and Puerto Rico.

As early as 1862, for example, General Francisco Serrano, Duke of Torre, warned of the larger North American implications of some of the Union Army's early victories. In a letter to his superiors in Madrid, the captain-general of Cuba wrote, "since the events in the United States have taken the favorable shape they now present for the North, the idea of the increasing proximity of solving the most grave of all issues that can emerge in Cuba—that is, the issue of slavery—has awakened here."[4] Three years later, Antonio María Fabié, a member of the Cortes, expressed the mood of many members of the Spanish and Hispanic-Caribbean elites when he reflected on the potential political and military impact of the Union's defeat of the Confederacy: "The war in the United States is finished and, being finished, slavery on the whole American continent can be taken as finished. Is it possible to keep Spanish provinces . . . while keeping this institution in the dominions? I don't think so, and therefore I say that the question is urgent, that the government must comply with great obligations. . . . I hope that the enlightenment necessary to solve this problem will be sought for cooperation with the Cortes."[5]

In sum, as Arthur Corwin aptly puts it, the outcome of the American Civil War "tore the lid off a suppressed question": the future in Spain's Caribbean possessions. Indeed, the embers in the U.S. South had not been put out yet when a group of Spanish and Hispanic-Caribbean liberals, headed by Puerto Rican Creole Julio Vizcarrondo y Coronado, met in Madrid in 1865 to form the Sociedad Abolicionista Española (Spanish Abolitionist Society). Moreover, as an immediate reaction to intensified pressures from inside and outside, the Cortes began discussing in April 1866 a bill for the "Suppression and Punishment of the Slave Trade" that stiffened penalties and sought strict enforcement of Spain's commitment to ending the importation of slaves to Cuba (principally) and Puerto Rico.[6]

At another level, as Fabié's speech to the Cortes eloquently shows, the North's victory moved many liberals and some conservatives to question whether continued slavery in Cuba and Puerto Rico could provide the perfect pretense for American intervention in Spain's last colonial possessions in the Western Hemisphere. In this context, the Spanish government announced late in 1865 the formation of an ad hoc commission to study the feasibility of adopting legislation to grant special political status to Cuba and Puerto Rico and to reform their colonial relationship with Spain. This Junta de Información de Ultramar (also known as the Junta Informativa de Reformas) would gather the necessary information on Cuba and Puerto Rico's political, economic, and social situation by questioning delegates from both islands. The delegates were elected early the following year, and the reform commission convened in Madrid from 30 October 1866 to 27 April 1867. The work of the Junta Informativa and particularly of the three prominent Puerto Rican abolitionist delegates, José Julián Acosta, Francisco M. Quiñones, and Segundo Ruiz Belvis, is generally considered to be the starting point of the political process that forced the end of slavery in Puerto Rico.[7]

In the hearings, the abolitionist majority of the Puerto Rican delegation, dominated by three prominent liberals, submitted a radical proposal for the end of slavery on the island. The plan called for immediate emancipation, opposed any labor restrictions on former slaves, and called for the payment of indemnities to slaveholders in the amount of 12 million pesos, paid in equal shares by the Spanish and Puerto Rican governments. Significantly, Acosta, Quiñones, and Ruiz Belvis based their arguments for immediate abolition in part on the puzzling notion that the generation of wealth in the Puerto Rican economy was not linked to slave labor, a view that Acosta had held since the early 1850s. In what seems like a contradictory turn, however, they also supported indemnification in the belief that it would help minimize the amount of economic disruption suffered by slaveholders. Nonetheless, the radical perspective of these three men should not be overlooked: Acosta, Quiñones, and Ruiz Belvis ultimately concluded that immediate abolition should be granted with or without indemnification.[8]

This abolitionist proposal stunned everyone both inside and outside the hearings and has subsequently buttressed the impression that Puerto Rican elites championed abolitionism because of the small proportion of the island's population that slaves had represented throughout the century, especially when contrasted with Cuba and the rest of the Caribbean. Yet as chapter 2 demonstrated, contrary to the abolitionist partisan rhetoric, slavery remained the backbone of Puerto Rico's sugar industry. Thus, questions arise: How representative were the views of the three liberal island delegates? What is the explanation for their election and their claim to represent the interests of the island's settler elite?

First, authorities restricted the election of the Puerto Rican delegates to two delegates from San Juan and one each from the four municipalities with the next-largest populations (Ponce, San Germán, Mayagüez, and Arecibo); the electors were limited to the members of the municipal councils plus an equal number of voters from among each district's top taxpayers, with each municipal group meeting in a special session to choose its delegates; and the colonial governor at the time, José María Marchesi, assumed a rather contradictory stance, forbidding public discussion of the issues to be considered by the junta but keeping a hands-off policy with regard to the elections themselves. As events unfolded, the six elected delegates split along important political lines: San Juan chose a noted liberal intellectual, José Julián Acosta y Calvo, and a moderate conservative, Manuel Valdés Linares, a lawyer; Ponce elected a moderate conservative, Luis Antonio Becerra y Delgado; San Germán a liberal, Francisco Mariano Quiñones; and Arecibo a conservative planter then residing in Barcelona, Manuel de Jesús Zeno Correa. In Mayagüez, a district with a tradition of opposition to the authoritarian model of colonial rule revalidated in the 1830s, some members of the special municipal assembly considered the potentially shocking election of Puerto Rico's principal nineteenth-century independence advocate, Ramón Emeterio Betances, a physician widely known for his clandestine abolitionist activities since the late 1850s. However, at the insistence of Betances, who feared that colonial authorities would reject him as a delegate, Mayagüez elected instead a young abolitionist lawyer and close associate of Betances's, Segundo Ruiz Belvis. The participation of Betances, Ruiz Belvis, and other eventual independence activists in these proceedings is significant (despite the fact that historians often gloss over it) because it implied a (temporary) change in the radical liberals' strategy from seeking a revolutionary confrontation to testing the possibility of achieving some reforms, particularly abolition, within the process opened by the Spanish government in Madrid.[9]

In the end, however, events altered the balance of forces within the Puerto Rican delegation. Valdés Linares and Becerra Delgado did not participate in the proceedings. Both delayed for too long their departure for Spain, and in a still-unexplained move, Governor Marchesi, a conservative military officer, deposed them. No replacements were selected. Thus, conservative, proslavery elites from Puerto Rico retained just one or two spokesmen in a reduced total delegation of four, Zeno Correa and another delegate whom Marchesi trusted would defend the continuation of slavery, Quiñones.[10] The Puerto Rican delegates and some of their Cuban counterparts prepared two major reform packages dealing with economic and political issues, but the Puerto Ricans went their own way on the "social question" (slavery) and submitted the proposal for immediate abolition.

Briefly examining the other two reform packages serves two important purposes. First, it highlights the fact that despite Ruiz Belvis's presence, the Puerto Rican reform proposals remained within the boundaries of a white, European settler mind-set that sought to equalize the political and economic status of the Spanish Antilles with that of the peninsular provinces. Second, it helps in avoiding the temptation to homogenize dichotomous approaches to colonial politics that revolve around the creole-peninsular axis. The economic reform package argued for the establishment of reciprocal, free trade between Spain and Puerto Rico (that is, the elimination of import and export duties), the elimination of restrictions and duties on the use of non-Spanish-flag shipping, and the substitution of a flat 6 percent tax on agricultural, commercial, and professional income for trade tariffs and duties. The motive behind these proposals was not simply economic but included part and parcel the political aim of liberating settlers from the domination of Spanish merchants and shipping companies and the tributary colonial system in place at least since the 1830s. The more explicitly political reforms called for granting Cuba and Puerto Rico the status of Spanish provinces, extending civil and political rights allowed under the Spanish constitution to the colonies, expanding the number of local administrative bodies and their jurisdiction over local affairs, separating military and civilian authority and placing both "provinces" under civilian rule, opening employment in government agencies to all qualified applicants, and granting both islands representation in the Spanish parliament. Significantly, the Puerto Rican delegates' liberalism stopped short of endorsing the notion of universal male suffrage that was one the leading principles of their Spanish counterparts, arguing instead for an electoral franchise limited to those paying more than five hundred reals in income taxes—that is, excluding the vast majority of the Puerto Rican male population from the right to participate in the liberal, home-rule system they were trumpeting and would continue to advocate for the rest of the century.[11]

Manuel Zeno Correa, the sole conservative Puerto Rican delegate to participate in the hearings, vehemently opposed his colleagues' abolitionist stand. A planter in the north-central coastal *municipio* of Arecibo, a bastion of antiabolitionism, Zeno's arguments against immediate emancipation raised the specters of a Haitian-style race war and of the collapse of Jamaica's sugar industry in the aftermath of emancipation there in the 1830s. Instead, he argued for gradual abolition while supporting the other economic reforms proposed by Acosta, Ruiz Belvis, and Quiñones. Also a conservative on the issue of political reform, Zeno opposed the dismantling of the islands' authoritarian colonial regime. Yet in the end, Puerto Rican slave owners who opposed immediate abolition were left with only a weak defense of their interests, and the debate focused instead on a radical stand that may not have closely represented the views of the vast majority of Puerto Rico's sugar planters.[12]

This issue became moot, however, when the Madrid government changed after the reform hearings had adjourned from moderately liberal to conservative, killing this and other important reformist proposals presented by the Puerto Rican and Cuban delegates. Aside from a terse statement on Spain's intention to abolish slavery, the new 1868 revolutionary junta took no concrete measures toward the abolition of slavery in its Caribbean colonies until the enactment of the Moret Law in 1870, and both the emancipation of Puerto Rican slaves and the possibility of reforms in a colonial system rooted in the old Leyes de Indias would have to wait until 1873, when the radicalization of the revolution brought a republican regime for the first time in Spanish history.[13]

The failure of the Junta Informativa process had important consequences for both Cuba and Puerto Rico. In the latter, the persecution of liberals that followed the conclusion of the reform hearings led to a split in the coalition between radical and moderate liberals. Betances and Ruiz Belvis escaped their deportation to Spain ordered by Governor Marchesi in 1867 and set out to organize an independence revolution, planned for late in 1868. Their vision of armed struggle, coupled with their insistence in the immediate and full emancipation of slaves, the end of forced-labor regulations, and other radical proposals that would be implemented in the event of national independence alienated the vast majority of Puerto Rico's liberal creole elite. Betances's revolutionary uprising had to be moved up when Spanish authorities learned of the conspiracy. The result was a quick defeat when separatists revolted in the west-central highland town of Lares, a major center of coffee production, on 23 September.

For most Puerto Rican liberals, however, the events in Lares had another significance. The first decree issued by the short-lived provisional revolutionary government of the Republic of Puerto Rico established in Lares declared the immediate and full abolition of slavery and mandated the burning of *jornalero* forced-labor workbooks. The defeat of the Lares revolt did not mean that the threat of Betances's revolutionary project had vanished. No matter how weak his organization and unrealized his dream, his actions threatened the counterhegemonic project of the more moderate, assimilationist vision put forth by Acosta and his major collaborators, including journalist Román Baldorioty de Castro. Thus, the liberal-reformist group would defend the abolitionism and assimilationist colonial reforms in the late 1860s and early 1870s with the idioms of loyalty to Spain and rejections of Betances's or Cuban insurrectionary plans and actions.[14]

Cuba's separatists fared much better than Puerto Rico's: a war for independence started in the fall of 1868 in the eastern province of Oriente, continuing until 1878 and casting a large shadow over the debates on colonial political and economic reforms and the abolition of slavery in both Cuba and Puerto Rico.[15] The winds of change also blew from Andalusia: revolutionary uprisings there in the fall of 1868 spread to other parts of the country, led to the monarchical forces' defeat at the Battle of Alcolea at the hands of none other than General Francisco Serrano, and resulted in a new regime led by Serrano and another former colonial military governor, Juan Prim, of dubious fame as a result of his repressive Puerto Rican tenure in the late 1840s.[16]

The new Spanish revolutionary regime immediately faced pressure from conflicting political groups and events in both Spain and the Antilles. The Cuban war that erupted as Prim and Serrano seized power dictated caution on the issue of colonial reforms, including abolition. Conservative elements sought a defeat of the Cuban rebels and opposed any colonial reforms, while abolitionists intensified their campaign for the termination of slavery in the Spanish Caribbean. From the fall of 1869 onward, a slew of diverse abolitionist projects were proposed, submitted to the Spanish parliament, and debated intensely in the Spanish press, political associations, and street cafés. Some of these proposals had their roots in the abolitionist activism of the late Isabellan monarchy, while others had started in the tactical maneuvering of latter-day proponents of gradual abolition as a means of staving off full and immediate emancipation.

Indeed, some of the gradual plans called for transitory terms as long as twenty-five years (lasting virtually until the dawn of the twentieth century), and most relied solely on convoluted procedures to facilitate the gradual extinction of slavery through free-womb laws, the emancipation of elderly slaves, and the gradual emancipation of slaves in prime-productive age groups through *coartación*. These measures were often coupled with the imposition of stringent postemancipation forced-labor regimes as well as the importation of more Africans as indentured servants. Of course, the full indemnification of slaveholders for what conservatives viewed as the expropriation of valuable assets went hand in hand with these and other proposals.[17] Yet nothing would come of these early debates until the revolutionary regime's more conservative elements cemented their hold on power around 1870 and the forces fighting for Cuban independence took the important step of promising freedom to all slaves who joined the revolution, thereby incorporating scores of slaves into the rebel army. Mediated, gradual abolition consequently became a potentially powerful strategy for maintaining Spain's last colonial holdings in the New World.

A Drifting Imperial State Offers a Compromise

The Cortes's 4 July 1870 approval of a "preparatory law" for the abolition of slavery formally set the process in motion in Cuba and Puerto Rico. Known as the Moret Law, after its sponsor, Spain's minister of overseas territories, Don Segismundo Moret y Pendergast, the act sought to abolish slavery "in principle." However, it restricted emancipation to slaves over sixty years of age and to children of slaves born after the law's publication in Cuba and Puerto Rico.[18] Yet these slave children as well as those born between the beginning of the 1868 Spanish Revolution and the publication of the Moret Law were classified not as fully freed but restricted to what the law called a *patronato*, a form of tutelage under their mothers' owners. The dispositions on the *patronato* implied that in practice, these half-slave, half-free children would be held as virtual slaves by those who would otherwise have become their masters anyway.

According to the law, the *patrono* (the mother's owner) acquired "all the rights of a tutor," providing the *patrocinado* with room and board and in exchange benefiting "from the work of [the *patrocinado*] without any remuneration until the age of eighteen." Moreover, from age eighteen to twenty-two, the *patrocinados* would still be restricted to earning just half of the regular wage paid to a free laborer for the same job. Furthermore, the law retained another vestige of slavery by establishing that the *patrocinados* could be the subject of property transactions as virtual chattel slaves.[19]

The Moret Law represented a compromise, a "*solución conciliadora*," as a Madrid newspaper called it, between a proslavery defense of the status quo and proabolitionist proposals for immediate emancipation.[20] To proslavery forces, the law offered a postponement of the freeing of productive slaves while releasing masters from a commitment to the welfare of elderly slaves no longer useful on plantations. To the abolitionist camp, the Moret Law offered the partial victory that some slaves would be freed plus the mild commitment expressed in article 21 that the government would present a bill to the Cortes for the indemnified emancipation of all slaves after Cuban deputies were admitted to the Spanish parliament.[21]

Indeed, this provision embodied the reality that the Moret Law represented as much as anything else a response to the Spanish government's need to tackle the possibility that the Cuban insurrectionists' offer of emancipation would win to their side the island's large slave population. As Rebecca Scott puts it, the law "was in a sense an effort by Spain to capture the apparent moral high ground from the insurgents and win gratitude from freed slaves and free people of color, while stalling abolition itself."[22] And a Madrid newspaper, *La Iberia*, bluntly pointed out that apart from its humane aspects, the Moret Law had a utilitarian side, constituting a necessary step in handcuffing Cuba's separatist movement as well as any annexationist maneuvers coming from the United States.[23]

The combined efforts of Cuba's planters and colonial officials delayed for several months the Moret Law's publication and resulted in implementation regulations that significantly reduced its impact.[24] But what was the situation in Puerto Rico, given the fact that the Puerto Rican delegates had pressed so strenuously for immediate abolition in 1867? Puerto Rican planters behaved just as straightforwardly as their Cuban counterparts in opposing the new law's prompt enforcement. As in Cuba, tactics in Puerto Rico included delaying the publication of the law, altering population censuses and private documents so that many children and elderly slaves were excluded from the law's provisions, and using the island's forced-labor regulations for "free" laborers to make allegedly liberated elderly slaves continue working.

The Moret Law was not published in Puerto Rico until November 1870, four months after its enactment, and even this delay was at least three months short of Puerto Rican planters' wishes.[25] Puerto Rican colonial officials' scheme called for withholding the publication of the law in the official gazette and trying to persuade planters to voluntarily enforce the law's provisions as if doing so were an act of mercifulness and "grace" toward the bondsmen and -women. This strategy sought to secure the slaves' loyalty and continued deference to masters and Spain, as government officials were concerned about potential disruptions to public order. The "Frankenstein of the present Government," wrote the British consul in San Juan, H. Augustus Cowper, "is an outbreak of the slaves, or at least their refusal to work."[26]

It is not entirely clear how many Puerto Rican planters went along with the proposal, although, as demonstrated in chapter 3, the use of the label "manumitted" to refer to these slaves in the 1871 Guayama census manuscript suggests that the strategy was followed at least there. Other evidence indicates, however, that many elderly slaves remained in bondage for months after the passage of the law and that the whip, prohibited by the Moret Law, remained in use. The law had to be considered "a dead letter," Cowper complained, "and in its effects much worse than a dead letter, for it cannot be kept secret, and already bands of Negroes have seized horses, and, riding madly over the country, have proclaimed that all slaves are free; whilst others have peaceably collected, and going in body to the Alcaldes, have demanded the promulgation of the law, which they believe is much more sweeping in its character than it really is. I hear that the Government intends on suppressing these demonstrations with the utmost rigour, but the whole blame rests in the timidity and mystery of its own acts."[27]

The Spanish government thus seemed to provoke what it sought to avoid. For example, the mayor of Ponce had to act beyond his immediate jurisdiction and intervene personally on a sugar plantation in the municipality of Juana Díaz to the east, where Ponce planters apparently owned many plantations. The 165 slaves of Hacienda Amelia refused to work, claiming that they were all already free and that the Spanish colonial government and the planters were withholding the truth from them. Their demand was clear: no further work until they were all set free. The authorities openly violated the Moret Law by whipping the slave leader of the protest; they also informed the slaves that owners would free the elderly and small children as an act of goodwill.[28]

Before the Puerto Rican publication of the Moret Law, planters and colonial government officials "corrected" the ages of many elderly slaves and slave children in the 1869 census to exclude them from the law's provisions.[29] In addition, Governor Don Gabriel Baldrich issued a secret memorandum to the island's mayors spelling out some preliminary rules for the implementation of the law. The rules restated the dispositions of the Moret Law but added an order to revive Governor Juan de la Pezuela's 1849 forced-labor decree, the Reglamento de Jornaleros, and to issue a *libreta de jornalero* (day laborer workbook) to all elderly slaves freed by the law who refused to continue under the *patronato* of their ex-masters. Such actions imposed forced-laborer status on women and men who had supposedly been freed.[30]

Irregularities in application seem to have continued even after the Moret Law was published. The Spanish colonial government's 1872 census figures showed 665 more slaves than appeared in the separate 1872 slave registry, suggesting the possibility of continued illegal underreporting to avoid having slaves classified as *libertos* or *patrocinados*.[31] Moreover, some registered elderly slaves had to fight for the recognition of their rights under the Moret Law, as the case of Manuel Fígaro shows. Manuel, a slave from the municipality of San Germán in southwestern Puerto Rico, challenged local authorities to recognize that he was over sixty years old, not forty-nine as his *cédula* indicated. In an exceptional case, Manuel had to appeal all the way up to the governor, even when members of the community testified and a medical examination confirmed that he was clearly older than sixty. The governor's decision has not been located, but the case illustrates the persistence of slaves who sought the full enforcement of the Moret Law.[32]

Luis Díaz Soler has said that the Moret Law brought "demoralization" to the Spanish Antilles by stopping well short of the full, immediate emancipation that abolitionists had sought.[33] And the law certainly represented a compromise between an absolute status quo and the radical step of total and immediate abolition. But as Scott has argued in her study of Cuba, the Moret Law "provided a lever—a weak, fragile, awkward lever—that enabled some slaves to exert influence on their condition or that of their relatives." The law, Scott adds, led in Cuba to "institutional and attitudinal changes which—to a limited extent—disrupted the social order of slavery in unintended ways."[34] The law clearly had less profound effects in Puerto Rico than in Cuba, since just two years passed from the beginning of Puerto Rican officials' enforcement of the law and full abolition in March 1873, whereas the passage of a Cuban abolition law remained a decade away.

In Puerto Rico, more than 3,600 elderly slaves and about 7,000 slave children should have been freed. However, since these children (all under five years old) presumably continued to live with their still enslaved mothers, the law probably had little direct effect on their daily lives.[35] Yet in hindsight, the Moret Law—to paraphrase Acosta—hit the whale of slavery with a harpoon, and the fiercely resisting whale came to die on the shore soon thereafter.[36]

Republican Winds Finally Tear Slavery Apart

After the approval of the Moret Law, abolitionist forces in Madrid prepared numerous bills to end slavery in Puerto Rico alone because the continued insurrection in eastern Cuba and efforts by Cuban planters and their Spanish allies in favor of continued slavery made it politically expedient to separate the debates regarding abolition in the two colonies. To Puerto Rican planters, the enactment of the Moret Law and half a dozen abolition bills signaled that the end of slavery was near, as pressures on the Spanish government from internal abolitionist forces and foreign governments such as Great Britain and the United States intensified between 1870 and early 1873.[37] Trying to make the best of a bad situation,

Spanish, Cuban, and Puerto Rican proslavery forces sought to ensure that any abolition bill substantially accommodated their interests and did not create a precedent for an immediate assault on slavery in Cuba. This meant the inclusion of indemnification provisions for the expropriation of chattel slaves, a point that most abolitionists vehemently supported in the Cortes, and the requirement that newly freed slaves serve several years of forced labor at minimal wages.[38]

The original bills submitted to the Cortes by abolitionist deputies or by the Spanish cabinet failed to include forced-labor provisions that were as sweeping as the planters wanted. Laws proposed by Puerto Rico's abolitionist parliamentarians in November 1871 and again in November 1872 called for immediate and full emancipation and subjected the former slaves only to the same inefficient island vagrancy decrees that sought to force landless people to work for wages. These two bills made no mention of a transitory period of apprenticeship or forced contracting.[39] And the December 1872 bill submitted by the Spanish minister of overseas territories, Don Tomás Mosquera García, contained no references to these vagrancy laws, although the planters would have expected the *libreta* system to be imposed on the *libertos*.[40]

In reaction to these bills, conservative forces in the Cortes countered with another project that included some extraordinary provisions for the transition from slavery to "free" labor. The Topete bill called for an initial five-year period during which slaves, now called *emancipados*, would be paid a fixed monthly wage of two pesos, echoing the provisions of the 1833 British West Indian abolition law. But the Topete bill's authors went even further, proposing a second five-year transition period during which *colonos* would receive four pesos a month for their work. Finally, after ten years of disguised slavery at fixed nominal wages, the slaves would be "freed" but would still be obligated to contract themselves to work for their "former" masters.[41]

In the end, the Spanish Cortes passed—without a quorum—an amended Mosquera bill on 22 March 1873.[42] The measure was approved only after abolitionist deputies reached a compromise with conservative forces, including Spanish General José Laureano Sanz, a former colonial governor and now deputy from Puerto Rico who was the vice president of a Madrid proslavery and anti-colonial-reform group, the Círculo Hispano-Ultramarino. The amended bill lacked the extraordinarily harsh and protracted "apprenticeship" terms of the Topete bill but nonetheless contained an apprenticeship period of three years during which Puerto Rican slaves had to contract out for work with their former masters, with someone else, or in public works with the colonial state. The measure offered the slaveholders an indemnification for the loss of their property, a sort of compensation that was almost as attractive to sugar planters as the apprenticeship period. The transitory period of forced labor would postpone full emancipation until 1876, and the law also provided that the freedmen and -women would not receive political rights until 1878, an aspect of the legislation that has attracted little attention from historians and that I will address in chapters 5 and 6.[43]

Conclusion

The debates on slavery, emancipation, free labor, and free trade, Christopher Schmidt-Nowara has written, were intimately linked to shifts in the nature of political discourse and the emergence of a bourgeois public sphere in Spain from the 1850s through 1874. Yet in these debates and in these largely metropolitan squabbles, Puerto Rican slaves remained an elusive subject with no voice other than that of the creole and peninsular liberals who spoke on their behalf. However, Schmidt-Nowara recounts the story of two abolitionist rallies in early 1873 where the remarkable presence of some Afro-Hispanic individuals caught demonstrators' and spectators' attention. One took place in Madrid on 12 January 1873, drawing a crowd estimated at between ten and sixteen thousand people. The marchers in the procession through the streets of the Spanish capital included a "black man [who] carried a Masonic lodge's standard that inserted abolitionism into Spain's revolutionary tradition: 'The Comuneros—The Cortes de Cádiz—The Abolitionist Society—The Puerto Rican Commission, 1866—The Cortes of 1873.'" About two weeks later, the Abolitionist Society's newspaper published a report of a similar demonstration in Seville on 26 January that highlighted the presence of another black man. This man also carried an abolitionist banner, and he "was hailed by a black woman from a balcony. She asked for liberty for her race. The black man answered her, waving his banner. Energetic and frantic applause and cries of long live liberty for the slaves interrupted his sentences."[44]

Who were these Afro-Hispanic abolitionists who paraded through the streets of Spain demanding freedom for their brothers and sisters across the Atlantic? This question may never find an answer, but their fleeting appearance in the abolitionist campaign records might help us reconsider the case of Chivo Gual, the Guayama slave who, apparently uninformed of the events in Spain, apparently unaware that emancipation was so close, spent his savings to purchase his freedom just weeks before the Spanish Cortes abolished slavery in Puerto Rico. Beyond Chivo's action, beyond the gestures of those nameless Afro-Hispanic supporters of abolition, and beyond the pronouncements of many other supporters of emancipation lay the contentious process of implementing the Abolition Law.

With Puerto Rican slavery ended, Spanish politics gravitated in other directions. The Spanish National Assembly adjourned, as if exhausted by a debate that consumed a major portion of its energies from 17 February to late on 22 March. Internal Spanish political conflicts would return to center stage, and while increasing numbers of moderate, conservative, and reactionary factions were working openly or clandestinely to bring down the revolutionary regime, few contemporaries could have realized that the abolition of slavery in Puerto Rico would become one of the few positive, enduring legacies of a revolutionary period that would end in less than a year.

As with the earlier struggles over the Moret Law, the contested terrain of Puerto Rican abolitionist politics would shift its main locus to the Caribbean and the enforcement of the Abolition Law of 1873. Planters, slaves, and colonial officials would focus on working out delayed emancipation and restrictions on slave freedom for at least the next three years. Could slaves and abolitionists finally say that the whale of slavery that had washed ashore was dead? Chapters 5, 6, and 7 will examine at the level of Guayama's society the ways in which former slaveholders, local officials, former slaves, free people of color, and others sought to ascertain the meaning of freedom in one of Puerto Rico's core areas of slavery.

CHAPTER 5

THE CONTESTED TERRAIN
OF "FREE" LABOR, 1873–1876

The news of the Spanish parliament's passage of the Puerto Rican Abolition Law on 22 March 1873 spread like wildfire, especially after Governor Juan Martínez Plowes published its entire text in a special gazette on 30 March. Celebrations abounded across the island. In San Juan, the British consul wrote, "There was a *Te Deum* in the cathedral, and the houses in this capital were generally illuminated for two nights; those of the leading Conservatives and the Casino Español forming the marked exceptions. . . . I hear from the Vice-Consulates that the news has been received in their respective districts with satisfaction." In Ponce, Luis Díaz Soler reports, a two-hour rally took place after the Te Deum in the plaza church, and major celebrations by the slaves on the plantations occurred. In one case, liberated slaves reportedly praised their master and vowed to stay with him forever, while abolitionist and Puerto Rican Liberal Party leader Román Baldorioty de Castro delivered a timely reminder to the *libertos* of the "sacred obligation to work" that the law imposed on them.[1]

One striking aspect of the Abolition Law is its extreme brevity: three articles addressed directly to the slaves and five dealing exclusively with the issue of indemnification for slave owners. One article declared the abolition of slavery forever in Puerto Rico. Another ordered the freed slaves to enter immediately into labor contracts "for a period of time which *shall not be less* than three years." A third specified that the *libertos* would receive political rights five years after the publication of the law. Four articles addressed the controversial issue of government compensation for slaveholders, which the law envisioned as part of an elaborate scheme in which the Spanish government would take out a loan for 35 million pesetas that would be repaid, ironically, using the taxes imposed on Puerto Rico. A final article instructed the island's colonial authorities to draw up the necessary regulations to govern the transition to free labor.[2]

How these mandates translated into practice, however, would be left to Puerto Rico's Spanish colonial governor, whom imperial authorities, abolitionists, and slaveholders alike expected to specify the rules for the forced-labor regime that the Abolition Law mandated until 1876. Significantly, the task fell into the hands of a sympathizer of the cause of abolition and free labor, resulting in a scenario in which Puerto Rican freedmen and -women would try to exercise a degree of freedom that perhaps extended beyond what moderate abolitionists and antiabolitionists had envisioned. This chapter explores the process of *liberto* contracting first by reviewing the ways in which colonial authorities initially sought to manage the labor contracting process and then by closely examining the initial contracting process in Guayama. Finally, I will discuss colonial officials' and planters' efforts to roll back the degree of freedom in labor contracting granted by the 1873 regulations in the wake of the conservative monarchical elites' return to power in Spain in 1874. The conservative backlash of 1874–76 attempted to impose new, long-term, forced-labor regulations that threatened to denude of meaning the freedom granted to slaves in 1873.

A Liberal Regime of Free Labor, 1873

Shortly after the approval of the Abolition Law and its publication in Madrid (26 March 1873) and San Juan (30 March), a new Spanish colonial governor, General Rafael Primo de Rivera y Sobremonte, arrived. Primo de Rivera had served as deputy governor under General José María Marchesi in the mid-1860s and returned to the island with a strong reputation as a liberal and republican member of the Spanish Abolitionist Society and the Spanish parliament, where he had supported reformed colonial policies for Puerto Rico and Cuba.[3] In addition to the perennial liberal-conservative disputes over colonial politics, Primo de Rivera quickly confronted the task of drawing up the necessary regulations to implement the Abolition Law.

Problems with the enforcement of the law did not take long to erupt. After the initial revelry ended, reports began to reach San Juan that ex-slaves were demanding that they now be considered free laborers and accordingly paid wages. The timing could not have been worse for sugar planters or better for the bargaining position of the ex-slaves: it was early April and the sugar harvest was still under way on most haciendas. A number of planter complaints also reached the governor, informing him that since some planters had begun to agree to pay wages to their former slaves, *libertos* from other estates had refused to work unless they were treated like free men and women—that is, they demanded an end to the practice of being locked up in slave *cuarteles* (barracks) on the estates as well as payment of wages for their work. Close to Guayama, in Arroyo, the British vice consul wrote that "when the emancipation was decreed . . . the '*libertos*' were allowed to go altogether free, most of them left off work altogether, and only returned on the condition of exorbitant wages paid by the planters to get off their crop."[4] Confronted with the absence of specific regulations to implement the law, Governor Primo de Rivera reacted by ordering the island's mayors to authorize provisional work contracts between planters and *libertos* that would be recognized and validated when the regulations were finally written and published.[5]

A few days later, on 20 April 1873, Primo de Rivera published the Reglamento para . . . la Contratación del Servicio de los Libertos. The *reglamento* was fairly extensive compared to the Abolition Law, with thirty-seven articles in all. One of its most important provisions specified that *liberto* contracts should be negotiated individually between employers and ex-slaves, barring any sort of collective bargaining on the part of the *libertos*. The contracts were to be formalized at the town halls in the presence of town officials and a *protector de libertos*, or his delegate, the *síndico protector de libertos*, on behalf of each former slave. Although the regulations described at length the position of *protector de libertos*, they provided for only three of these functionaries islandwide; in reality their local deputies, the municipal *síndicos*, dealt with the day-to-day *contrataciones próximas*.[6]

The institution of the *síndico* in fact represented a carryover from the days of slavery, when the slaves' interests were supposed to be looked after by a prominent local figure appointed for that purpose by the municipal council. The *síndico* was responsible by law for representing slaves in disputes—in or out of court—with masters over issues dealing with the fair application of the 1826 slave code's provisions on slave treatment and the slaves' "rights" to obtain their freedom through *coartaciones*. Usually linked by familial or business relations with the planters or planters themselves, the *síndicos* were often biased and compromised in the discharge of their duties. In Guayama, for example, the *síndico* during the 1873 *contratación* was Don Juan Ignacio Capó, son of Don Florencio Capó and administrator of his father's two haciendas, Olimpo and Caimital. Both men contracted with *libertos* in 1873.[7] Similarly, in Ponce, Don Juan Cortada was the *síndico protector de libertos* at the time of the 1873 contracting of *libertos*, yet he and his brother, Ramón, were principal partners in the commercial firm Cortada y Compañía, which loaned working capital to eleven of the district's principal sugar haciendas. Like many merchant-lenders, Cortada also owned sugar estates in Ponce—five during the mid-1870s.[8] It is no wonder, then, that historian Luis Díaz Soler long ago concluded that the *síndicos* represented an instance where "the divorce between law and historical reality was clear. [The *síndico*] turned out to be a defender of proslavery interests."[9] Therefore, serious doubts can be raised about how strongly the *síndicos* would defend *liberto* interests during the triennium of forced work contracts.

Primo de Rivera's regulations also dictated that *liberto* contracts should clearly specify the agreed upon wage and the total daily working hours and, most importantly, that these contracts could be terminated unilaterally by either party. This was a very important provision from the beginning not only because it went a long way toward fulfilling the liberal governor's purported intent of guaranteeing the emergence of a "free labor" system after emancipation but also because it became almost immediately the most contested terrain in the initial phases of that transition. As Primo de Rivera explained at the time of the promulgation of the contracting code, "The freedom of contracting is the basis to start with. If the duty of working under contract for three years is imposed on the *liberto*, that does not mean that that duty has to be for exactly three years with only one contractor, nor is his will limited in the least on the wage and work conditions [to which he agrees]. The *liberto* in that instance should be equivalent to a free man: he should contract himself, but for the time that is convenient to him and with the legal agreements that he wishes. Otherwise this would be for him the continuation of a state of servitude until the triennial period of contracting is expired."[10]

Of course, the regulations also provided for fining and incarcerating *libertos* and for sentencing them to public works if they illegally broke work agreements or refused to enter into contracts. The contracting code also ordered that when fines were imposed on *libertos*, the money should be collected from their *peculio*, or personal savings accumulated from autonomous activities as slaves; only when slaves had no personal savings would fines be subtracted from their daily wages. In addition, the code also terminated the *patronato* of slave children born after 17 September 1868, the day of the beginning of the Spanish Revolution. However, the code required children born before that date to enter work contracts if they were twelve years of age or older and stipulated that children who reached that age between 1873 and 1876 should do the same for the remainder of the period. The *liberto* contracts were generally standard printed forms with blank spaces to fill in the specifics: names of employer, *liberto*, and former master (if different from the contractor) as well as wage and other conditions and concessions.

Yet although the standardized forms represented an effort to facilitate local authorities' control of the process, the details were far from homogeneous. The island's *libertos* entered into all kinds of agreements, from regular day laborer work contracts for wages, with or without nonmonetary compensation, to work in exchange for training as artisans to sharecropping arrangements. This sort of diversity renders most homogenizing interpretative schemes useless: *Libertos*, former masters, and other free people (propertied or not) approached the end of slavery with practical matters in mind.[11]

The process of *liberto* formal contracting began in late April. By 13 May, British Consul H. Augustus Cowper felt confident enough to report to the British Foreign Office from San Juan that "the law has been promptly carried into effect in all its details, and every living being on this island is free."[12] Was the 1873 *contratación* as smooth as Cowper and some subsequent historians have depicted? Did all *libertos* readily enter into work contracts? Did plantation slaves continue with their former masters, working on the same haciendas? Or did they change employers or move into urban areas? These and many other questions must be answered to better understand the process of emancipation and its outcomes in Puerto Rico and to avoid the trap of interpreting the abolitionist process in Puerto Rico mainly from what either the abolitionists or legal codes said at the time. Although this is ostensibly a dated approach, it continued to find adherents as late as the 1980s. Writing in 1987, Spanish historian Concepción Navarro Azcue argued that the application of the 1873 abolition law "was very satisfactory" because

> blacks did not become vagrants, nor was the public altered, no economic dislocation was seen, nor did the island endure the anguish of a race war. There was the forced contracting of the libertos for a period of three years, which helped avoid the ruin of the *hacendados* and which had the support of the great majority of those emancipated, who expressed their desire to remain with their former masters. The forced contracting paved the way for real freedom. . . . The slaveholders obtained the promise of and the enforcement of an honorable indemnification, guaranteed by the Spanish government and local banking institutions. . . . Against the collapse of socioeconomic and political structures experienced in other slave societies, Puerto Rico offered an example of maturity.[13]

Puerto Rican historiography eventually began to move away from these rather simplistic views and to explore the intricacies of the implementation of emancipation from new economic and social history perspectives. José Curet argues that "the first phase of contract-signing proceeded at an unusually rapid pace," and Andrés Ramos Mattei concludes that "the majority of *libertos* stayed working for their former owners and worked in agricultural labor."[14] Yet conclusive data are hard to come by. Curet cites September 1873 figures reported by Governor Primo de Rivera to the Ministry of Overseas Territories that put the number of *libertos* who "signed" contracts (an awkward statement since very few *libertos* were literate) at 27,032 of the island's 29,335 total former slaves, a figure that Curet thought excluded those below twelve and over sixty years of age. Ramos Mattei cited December 1873 figures published by the government in San Juan that gave a total of 21,584 *libertos* working under contract while the remaining 8,000 *libertos* were said to be either under twelve or over sixty. However, the figure of almost 8,000 *libertos* under and over contracting age is questionable, since an ambitious study of the 1872 slave registry found that these two age groups combined to represent slightly less than 20 percent of the enslaved population. Assuming that these proportions still held for 1873, about 5,800 *libertos* would have been under or over contracting age in 1873. Thus, these sets of government statistics not only contradict each other but fail to account for 2,000 *libertos*. Part of the answer may lie in the government's admission that 818 *libertos* had run away from the forced-labor contracts, a figure that may well underestimate this phenomenon. If Puerto Rican slaves, like their peers elsewhere, were at least as prone to running away after emancipation as had been the case during slavery, many of them would likely have felt tempted to get away from the new legal wrinkle of apprenticeship and begin to experiment with their freed status before 1876.[15]

Ramos Mattei and others have agreed with the U.S. consul's opinion, expressed at the time, that by 1878 the majority of the rural *libertos* had stayed living and working on the estates. "Logically," Ramos Mattei argues, "it has to have been that way. The *libertos* possessed some skills in the processing of sugar that they could not transfer to other activities. They occupied a preferential position in the sugar labor organization hierarchy. And with the coming of the end of the period of forced contracting, the planters made concessions on working conditions so that [the *libertos*] stayed on the plantations."[16]

Ramos Mattei also speculates that the ex-slaves of abandoned haciendas could have moved to urban centers (an important hypothesis shared by Curet and Fernando Picó),[17] migrated to other islands such as Cuba or Hispaniola, or become small peasants.[18] Francisco Scarano, for his part, writes, "Because of Puerto Rico's high population density and the safety checks incorporated into the emancipation law, the island did not experience a massive flight of freedmen from the plantations which occurred, for example, in Jamaica after 1838. A majority of the freedmen in Puerto Rico was compelled to remain on the estates as resident workers, without a significant change in living standards or in opportunity for social advancement."[19]

This general understanding of the immediate patterns of *liberto* labor and life would imply that *libertos* remained attached to their preemancipation plantations and masters. However, the same published govern-

TABLE 5.1: Results of the First Forced-Labor Contracting of Freed
Slaves in Puerto Rico, December 1873

Libertos Contracted with:	Gender	Rural	Urban	Total
Former masters	Male	5,720	535	6,255
	Female	3,364	2,051	5,415
	Total	9,084	2,586	11,670
Others	Male	4,105	1,104	5,209
	Female	2,081	2,624	4,705
	Total	6,186	3,728	9,914
Total		15,270	6,314	21,584

Source: Ramos Mattei, "Technical Innovations," 170.

ment figures cited by earlier historians suggest that a substantial number of *libertos* chose to contract with employers other than their former masters, although it is not clear how many of them were plantation slaves and, in such cases, how many found employment with different sugar planters. Even though government-reported data on the "success" of the 1873 *contratación* need to be taken with a grain of salt, these figures help bring into focus some important issues for scholars to tackle.

The government's aggregate data, reproduced in table 5.1, classified contracted *libertos* according to the type of employer for whom they agreed or were compelled to work (their former master or someone else), the rural or urban location where the former slaves would work, and whether they were male or female. The figures suggest that many slaves found different employers: as of December 1873, about 46 percent of the 21,584 *libertos* had contracted to work with someone other than their former masters, a process that probably had some impact on Puerto Rico's sugar industry, at least in the short run. The slaves' reasons for making these changes remain open to speculation: Were they lured by better wages and working conditions, or, as Benjamín Nistal-Moret suggests, was the movement of people part of a process of reunification with relatives and friends?[20] Starting to explore these questions requires moving beyond published government statistics and examining how local authorities, planters, and freedpeople negotiated apprenticeship in Guayama.

The 1873 Contratación in Guayama

As in a few other Puerto Rican *municipios*, the *liberto* contracts of Guayama have not survived intact. What is available is a group of sequentially numbered official transcripts that, as required by the contracting code, local authorities sent to the central San Juan office in charge of supervising the *contratación*. Extant are 614 contracts, about 37 percent of the approximately 1,670 contracts registered in Guayama from 26 April to 20 October 1873.[21] Some important gaps exist within this group of contracts, most notably the absence of 829 contracts registered between 5 and 17 May, during the early, intensive stage of the *contratación*. By 11 June, 1,221 *liberto* contracts had already been registered in Guayama, almost three-fourths of the contracts registered before 20 October. In other words, most efforts to contract Guayama's *libertos* took place in the first month and a half after the official contracting process began. The second major gap in the surviving batch of contracts runs from 11 June to 7 August and covers 217 contracts, 13 percent of the total. The low number of average contracts registered per month late in the year can be attributed to the fact that the sugar harvest, in which most slaves were normally employed, ended around June. From July until December reigned the "*tiempo muerto*" (dead season), a time of limited work seeding and weeding the cane fields.

These gaps—in particular, the earlier, larger one—raise questions about the value of the surviving contracts for analyzing the process of *liberto* contracting in Guayama. However, the extant documents offer important information about some of the general features of the 1873 *contratación*, and in the absence of more complete data, they provide the only lens through which to examine this facet of abolition in Guayama.

The 614 surviving contracts provide a general profile of the contracting process as well as of the *libertos* and employers involved. As noted earlier, one of the most controversial aspects of Governor Primo de Rivera's regulations for contracting *libertos* was the stipulation that either party could terminate the contract unilaterally. In theory, this rule allowed *libertos* to enter into more than one contract during 1873, an aspect often overlooked when discussing published government figures on the 1873 *contratación*. The extant contracts include documents for 527 *libertos*, 87 of whom (16.5 percent) entered into multiple agreements: 80 *libertos* were

TABLE 5.2: Age Distribution of *Libertos* Contracted in Guayama, 1873

Age Group	Percentage among Slaves in 1871 Census (N=1,978)	Percentage among *Libertos* in 1873 *Contratación* (N=614)
10–14	10.9	6.6
15–19	11.5	15.5
20–24	16.1	16.7
25–29	13.5	15.2
30–34	12.7	13.7
35–39	6.9	10.2
40–44	12.5	6.9
45–49	6.0	6.6
50–54	7.3	4.1
55–59	2.6	4.5

Source: AGPR, FGE, Esclavos y Negros, "Contratos de libertos de Guayama," box 74.
Note: Percentages were calculated based on the 10–59-year-old slave population in 1871 and on the entire group of ex-slaves involved in the surviving contracts.

contracted twice, 6 were contracted three times, and 1 appears in four contracts. The fact that two-thirds of Guayama's contracts are missing means that the rate of multiple contracting could have been much higher and again calls into question studies that rely exclusively on summary government statistics, which were compiled by the Negociado de Libertos based on weekly summaries sent by local authorities that did not indicate whether previous contracts had been signed. The accuracy of the government summary statistics will unfortunately never be known.[22]

The contracts themselves illustrate two aspects of the general profile of the *libertos*. First, 53 percent of the contracted *libertos* were male (325 cases), and 47 percent were female. This gender distribution differs just slightly from that of Guayama's 1871 slave population, which showed an almost even split (see chapter 3).

Second, this batch of contracts provides information on the age distribution of the *libertos* contracted, as summarized in table 5.2. Compared to the age distribution of Guayama's 1871 slave population, the contracts show a higher representations for the age categories that include a *liberto*'s prime productive years. This suggests that as a consequence of *liberto* initiative or employer demand, *libertos* aged between ten and fourteen and over forty may not have been as heavily involved in the formal labor contracting process as their proportions of the 1871 slave population would have suggested. While in 1871 almost 11 percent of Guayama's slave population was between ten and fourteen years old, only 6.6 percent of the *libertos* represented in the surviving 1873 contracts were within this age group. Moreover, while in 1871 slaves between forty and fifty-nine years old represented 28.4 percent of the slave population, in the 1873 contracts they constitute 22.1 percent of the *libertos*. Conversely, while in 1871 just under 61 percent of the slaves between ten and fifty-nine years old were aged between fifteen and thirty-nine, the 1873 data show about 71 percent of the contracted *libertos* in these age groups.

One of the most important issues concerning the contracting of *libertos* in 1873 is the question of occupational mobility and whether gender played any role in differentiating trends in occupational mobility after emancipation. "Occupational mobility" in this instance should not necessarily be construed as "upward mobility" in the social class structure but rather should be seen as a more lateral movement between the broad occupational categories of rural field labor and domestic labor. There are two ways of approaching this issue when examining the Guayama contracts: by comparing the occupational distribution of the 1873 contracts to that of the 1871 slave population, and by studying changing occupations as recorded in the contracts themselves.

In describing the *liberto* hired, the contracts indicated previous occupation in broad terms (rural or domestic); in specifying the conditions, the contracts indicated the type of work (rural, domestic, or "any") to be performed by the *liberto*. Table 5.3 presents the data on the occupational distribution by gender of slaves in 1871 and of the *libertos*. A perceptible change seems to have occurred: male *libertos* represent a higher percentage of rural field labor in 1873 than what could be expected based on the 1871 census, while *libertas* (female former slaves) represented a higher percentage of domestic labor in 1873 than what could be expected based on the 1871 census.

The data on gender and changes in occupational classification presented in table 5.4 seem to confirm this finding. While three-fourths of the male *libertos* involved in these contracts did not change in their occupational classification as rural laborers, the same proportion of *libertas* changed occupational classification from rural to domestic labor. This suggests that a substantial proportion of the available pool of rural

TABLE 5.3: Occupational Distribution of Guayama's Ex-Slaves in 1873 Compared to That of Slaves in 1871

Occupation	MALE		FEMALE		TOTAL	
	1871	1873	1871	1873	1871	1873
Rural	627	239	530	108	1,157	347
	84%	74%	68%	38%	76%	57%
Domestic	93	35	251	135	344	170
	12%	11%	32%	47%	23%	28%
Total	745	322	781	285	1,526	607
	49%	53%	51%	47%	100%	100%

Source: AGPR, FGE, Esclavos y Negros, "Contratos de libertos de Guayama, 1873," box 74.
Note: There were 25 artisans in 1871 and 8 in 1873; all of them were male. The columns do not add up because 82 *libertos* (40 male and 42 female) were contracted to do "any type of work" assigned.

field laborers available to Guayama's slave owners at the time of the abolition of slavery was no longer available during the 1873 *contratación*, as one-quarter of the *libertos* and three-quarters of the *libertas* previously engaged in agricultural work seem to have moved to the domestic-labor sector of the postabolition workforce.

Prospective agricultural employers of *libertos* faced not only the possibility of a substantial reduction in the pool of rural field hands but also competition from employers who were not involved in plantation agriculture or were not seeking *libertos* exclusively or primarily for agricultural labor. While 118 different employers were involved in the 614 contracts examined, only 17 of these employers could be classified as *hacendados* or as hacienda administrators for absentee planters. Moreover, not all of the employers of *libertos* belonged to Guayama's economic and racial elite, as can be seen in table 5.5, where the use or absence of the title "Don" or "Doña," at the time reserved almost exclusively for whites, indicates the extent to which colored plebeian employers contracted *libertos*.

Studying the profile of the employers and of the conditions of *liberto* employment brings home the problem of the absence of more of Guayama's *liberto* contracts. Table 5.5 suggests that a substantial number of employers contracted just a few *libertos*, and most of these cases of

TABLE 5.4: Occupational Mobility of Guayama's Ex-Slaves in 1873

Change in Occupation	GENDER		Total
	Male	Female	
Same master	244	128	372
Rural to domestic	29	107	136
Rural to artisan	6	—	6
Total	319	277	596

Source: AGPR, FGE, Esclavos y Negros, "Contratos de libertos de Guayama, 1873," box 74.
Note: There were 82 *libertos* (40 male and 42 female) contracted to do "any type of work" assigned.

employers contracting fewer than five *libertos* occurred after the sugar harvest ended in June. Even assuming that all of the 829 missing contracts registered in May were with Guayama's sugar planters, the data in table 5.5 would remain consistent with the finding discussed in chapter 3 that slaveholding in Guayama was not limited to the slightly more than two dozen haciendas still active in the *municipio* in the early 1870s but that the practice trickled into the middle and lower ranks of society. Furthermore, the data in table 5.5 beg the question of the identity of the employers who contracted only one or two *libertos* (a category that includes 80 percent of the employers and 29 percent of the contracted *libertos*) and the terms of these contracts. Nevertheless, what do the available cases indicate about the pattern of *liberto* contracting by sugar planters?

The typical *liberto* contract obligated a former slave to do rural agricultural work for twelve hours each day, usually from 6:00 A.M. to 6:00 P.M. However, working hours were not marked by a clock, as in factory employment, but "*de sol a sol*" (from dawn to dusk), as is evidenced by the fact that while most of the twelve-hour contracts stated those starting and ending times, other employers put "dawn" at 5:00 A.M. and "dusk" at any time from 5:00 P.M. to 7:00 P.M. The average daily wage and other remuneration varied according to the type of work (rural or domestic), the gender of the laborer, and the policies of particular employers. Most rural laborers earned three or four reals per day (a real equaled 12.5 cents), with 25 percent of the contracts paying three reals and 40 percent paying four. The nonmonetary compensation varied widely: 19 percent of rural laboring *libertos* received only food in addition to their daily wage;

TABLE 5.5: Guayama's *Liberto* Contracts by Number of Contracts and Type of Employer, 1873

Number of Contracts	Number of Employers	% of Employers	Colored Plebeian Employers[a]	Cumulative % of Plebeian Employers	Number of Libertos	Cumulative % of Libertos	Cumulative % of Libertos Hired by Plebeians
1	118	63.4	55	78.6	118	19.2	60.4
2	31	16.7	11	94.3	62	29.3	84.6
3	11	5.9	2	97.1	33	34.7	91.2
4	8	4.3	2	100.0	32	39.9	100.0
5	2	1.1	0	0	10	41.5	0
6	3	1.6	0	0	18	44.5	0
7	4	2.2	0	0	28	49.0	0
10–19	4	2.2	0	0	57	58.3	0
20–29	2	1.1	0	0	45	65.6	0
30–39	—	—	—	—	—	—	—
40–49	1	0.5	0	0	42	72.5	0
50–59	1	0.5	0	0	51	80.8	0
60 and Over	1	0.5	0	0	118	100.0	0
Total	186		70		614		

Source: AGPR, FGE, Esclavos y Negros, "Contratos de libertos de Guayama, 1873," box 74.
[a]"Colored plebeian employers" were those whose names were not preceded by the title "Don" or "Doña," as was common practice in Guayama at least until the late 1870s.

13 percent received food, housing, and medical attention in case of illness; 13 percent received food and medical attention; 11 percent received only medical attention, but their contracts contained no provisions for housing, raising the question of whether these *libertos* and *libertas* were moving to their own shelters. About half of the agricultural workers were offered at least one meal, 20 percent were offered housing, 41 percent were offered medical attention if needed, and only 4 percent were offered clothing. These provisions reflected the customary rights that had existed under slavery, when masters had been expected to provide slaves with food, housing, medical attention (even if limited), and clothing. Notably, one out of three contracts contained no explicit nonmonetary compensation, suggesting that the *libertos* expected to provide these items for themselves or to rely on other former slaves or free people.

Almost all domestic labor contracts (95 percent) specified monthly salaries that were far smaller than the equivalent wages paid to agricultural laborers.[23] Although 85 percent of the *libertos* doing domestic work were paid less than two reals daily, their nonmonetary remuneration was more substantial than that accorded field laborers: 94 percent of domestics received at least one meal, two-thirds received housing, nearly half received medical attention, and 20 percent received clothing.

Conditions of labor contracts also varied according to the type of the employer—for example, whether or not it was a *hacendado*. While *hacendados* contracted almost twice as many male *libertos* as females, non-*hacendado* employers hired more *libertas* than *libertos* by a similar ratio. *Hacendados* preferred to pay wages on a weekly basis (as specified by 88 percent of their contracts), while almost the same percentage of non-*hacendados* preferred to pay monthly, policies that perhaps reflected different cash-flow situations. Not surprisingly, slightly more than 90 percent of the *hacendado* contracts were for rural agricultural work, and the same proportion of *libertos* hired by *hacendados* did not change their occupational classification as rural laborers.[24] Conversely, non-*hacendado* employers hired 83 percent of their *libertos* for domestic or "any type" of work. In both *hacendado* and non-*hacendado* employment, however, about 40 percent of *libertos* received some kind of medical attention.

However, *hacendado* and non-*hacendado* employers varied in the sorts of food, housing, and clothing enticements used. Half of the *libertos* contracted by *hacendados* received food, but 90 percent of the contracts involving non-*hacendados* made no mention of food. Similarly, while one in five *libertos* who contracted with *hacendados* received housing, non-*hacendado* employers provided shelter for two out of three *libertos* contracted. Finally, although the provision of clothing to *libertos* remained limited, it was much more common among non-*hacendado* employers (20 percent) than among *hacendados* (4 percent).

The large gap in the surviving Guayama contracts for the early period of the *contratación*, when sugar planters probably registered large numbers of *liberto* contracts, severely limits the ability to compare planters' labor-contracting policies. Almost all of Guayama's haciendas, however, are represented among the surviving contracts, although some appear only in small numbers. Among the haciendas known to have continued growing and grinding sugarcane after abolition, transcripts are completely missing only for Hacienda Tuna. Other haciendas for which no contracts survive include Juana of Don Isidoro Crouzet, Agueda of the heirs of Don Julián H. Villodas, Rosario of Suliveras y Rivera partnership, and Felícia of the Clausell Hermanos partnership. These haciendas, however, stopped producing sugar in or around 1873, so they would probably have had less need to recruit *libertos* in 1873.

The most *libertos* were hired by Don Wenceslao Lugo-Viñas, an immigrant from the Spanish Canary Islands, owner of Hacienda Carlota, and liberal mayor of Guayama in 1873, who was responsible for 118 of the surviving 614 contracts. The Sociedad Agrícola Hermanas Curet, an enterprise operated by sisters Josefa and Catalina Curet Lozada, owners of Hacienda Santa Elena, contracted the second-highest number of contracts, 51 (and 5 others were hired by Don Joaquín Villodas García, husband of Catalina and administrator of the plantation). Another planter, Don Luis Boyrie, owner of Hacienda Algarrobos, is represented in 42 contracts, but he may have taken these *libertos* to another plantation he owned in the *municipio* of Maunabo to the east of Guayama, since Hacienda Algarrobos ceased to produce sugar in 1873 and other sources indicate that Boyrie had embarked on an ambitious project to convert his Maunabo hacienda into a fully mechanized mill.[25]

A detailed examination Lugo-Viñas's activities during the 1873 *contratación* of former slaves should provide important clues for understanding the dynamics of the contested transition to free labor in Puerto Rico in the 1870s. Lugo-Viñas had envisioned turning his Hacienda Carlota into Guayama's first fully mechanized sugar mill, or *central*. Moreover, Lugo-Viñas became a leading member of the Puerto Rican Liberal-

Reformist Party during the 1870s, first achieving the position of mayor of Guayama and then winning election in 1873 as a deputy to the Spanish Cortes under the Republican regime (a feat he repeated in 1879 under Spain's Restoration regime) as part of an ephemeral "conciliation" between Puerto Rican conservatives and liberals.[26]

As the mayor of Guayama, Lugo-Viñas inaugurated the official *contratación* by bringing 44 *libertos* to the town hall on 26, 27, and 28 April, earlier than the town's other former slaveholders. Don Roque Rubio, the overseer of Carlota, was in charge of hiring these ex-slaves, bringing them to the town hall, and signing the contracts for Lugo-Viñas. Rubio returned to the *alcadía* to register additional contracts on 1–3 May. During the first two weeks of the process, Lugo-Viñas contracted a total of 69 *libertos*. After only a few contracts registered in July and August, Lugo-Viñas contracted 37 former slaves on 23 September, and he may well have hired many more *libertos* for whom records have not been located. In 1871, however, Lugo-Viñas owned only 41 slaves aged ten to fifty-seven who should have been subjected to the obligation of entering into labor contracts in 1873. Of those 41, 38 appear in the 118 contracts, and 28 were hired by Lugo-Viñas himself.

The rest of Lugo-Viñas's contracted *libertos* came from twenty-five different slaveholders, sixteen of them *hacendados*. His use of a large number of *libertos* who had not been his property before emancipation suggests that he might have actively recruited labor around Guayama as part of his strategic plan to transform his hacienda into a *central* in the early 1870s. Such an effort would have required attaching to his plantation as virtual *agregados* a much larger number of workers of prime productive age than he reported in the 1871 slave census. Moreover, at a time when he was embarking on the purchase of a small adjacent hacienda and ordering expensive, modern sugar-processing machinery from abroad, Lugo-Viñas would not have wanted to spend thousands of pesos to purchase eighty or so slaves of prime working age or to spend time and money recruiting emancipated slaves who lacked the restrictions imposed on *liberto* labor and mobility.

Indeed, in 1873 several Guayama planters apparently complained to the governor that Lugo-Viñas was actively recruiting *libertos* away from them by promising to pay their wages in cash, an incentive most planters apparently had not planned to offer because of the limited availability of currency on the island. Lugo-Viñas's efforts to recruit large numbers of *libertos* seem to have been part of his strategic plan to establish a modern *central*.[27] In an earlier discussion of Lugo-Viñas's labor recruitment of *action*, Ramon Mattei mistakenly described the planter's contracts as offering fifty cents a day plus food, lodging, clothing, and medical attention.[28] Although three-fourths of Lugo-Viñas's contracts were indeed for four reals a day, fourteen others paid only two reals per day, and eight provided monthly wages of five, six, seven, or eight pesos. Fifteen of the twenty-two contracts paying less than fifty cents a day involved female ex-slaves, and Lugo-Viñas registered thirty-eight contracts involving *libertas*.

Moreover, an accurate profile of the Lugo-Viñas contracts must take timing into account. The first forty-four contracts registered by his overseer, which, as mentioned earlier, were the first contracts registered in Guayama, involved not a single *liberto* who had been a slave of Lugo-Viñas. The slaves had been the property of seventeen different masters. Their contracts stipulated that they would work as rural field hands for wages of two reals (five cases), three reals (six cases), and four reals (thirty cases) per day, and three contracts specified monthly wages of five, six, and seven pesos. None of these contracts offered *libertos* additional non-cash remuneration, implying that Lugo-Viñas expected a sudden shift away from slaves' customary "rights" to food, clothing, shelter, and medical attention at their masters' expense and toward ideal free labor relations in which workers depended exclusively on wages to provide such basic necessities. In early May, Lugo Viñas's overseer, Don Roque Rubio, brought to the *alcaldía* twenty-four *libertos* who had been slaves at Hacienda Carlota. All of these ex-slaves, bearing their newly imposed surname, Viñas, agreed to contracts that stipulated a daily wage of four reals, with no additional compensation. The only exceptions to this pattern were the cases of Teresa, Damiana, and Ramón Viñas. Teresa and Damiana were contracted to do domestic labor for four and five pesos a month, respectively, and Ramón was contracted to work on "any kind of job," domestic or agricultural, for six pesos a month.

Lugo-Viñas's policy of cash payments but no further benefits seems to have worked well for him in the early part of the *contratación*. However, when Lugo-Viñas contracted thirty-seven *libertos* on 23 September, all of them received an additional incentive: free medical attention in the case of minor illnesses. There is no way of knowing for certain whether this new policy was the product of Lugo-Viñas's or his overseer's initiative or whether it resulted from *libertos'* demands. Nonetheless, it seems reasonable to infer that the change derived from *liberto* demands in a context of labor scarcity and thus added worker leverage. While 78 percent of the surviving contracts registered prior to 17 May did not offer medical attention even in cases of minor illness, 57 percent of the contracts registered 7 August to 20 October included such provisions.

Finally, even though Lugo-Viñas's contracts covered an indefinite period of time, 40 percent of them were terminated during 1873. Indeed, two-thirds of the contracts he registered in April and May were terminated between May and October. Again, the exact motives for the terminations remain unknown, but several patterns are apparent. Only contracts registered from April to early July have marginal annotations indicating that they were "*rescindidos*" (terminated). The most common dates of termination were late July and 23 September, a day when twenty-one contracts were terminated and thirty-seven new contracts were registered. Some of these terminations may have resulted from decreased labor demand after the completion of the harvest; however, others could have resulted from *liberto* demands for the provision of medical assistance. The latter possibility gains credence from the fact that several *libertos* whose original contracts were terminated on 23 September were immediately rehired under new contracts that included provisions for medical attention. This suggests that the conditions of *liberto* labor bargaining may have forced Lugo-Viñas to offer to pay his laborers' medical expenses, a customary right during slavery.

Focusing exclusively on a leading liberal sugar planter such as Wenceslao Lugo-Viñas would distort the diversity of practices and discourses contained in the surviving transcripts of Guayama's 1873 *liberto* contracts. Not all slaves belonged to sugar planters, and given the links between slaves and free people of color it is not to be expected that all *libertos* would seek employment in the harsh conditions found on sugar plantations. Consequently, contracts involving non-*hacendado* employers contain almost all of the more idiosyncratic conditions of work and compensation.

Don Gabriel Moya, a Spaniard listed as an architect in the 1871 census, contracted a fourteen-year-old *liberto*, Lorenzo Adariche, who had been the property of Moya's wife's family. Moya hired Lorenzo as a mason apprentice under very specific conditions. According to the transcript, Lorenzo agreed to be under the orders and command of his master contractor with the aim that he will teach the trade of mason, obeying him in all orders as well as if there is no work in the trade, in which case the contracted [liberto] commits himself to work in whatever jobs [Moya] orders. The *liberto* remains obligated to work for two years without asking for any compensation other than feeding, clothing, medical attention, the costs of medicines, and lodging in [Moya's] house. . . .

This contract is under the conditions of apprenticeship in the said trades, with the parties having agreed that they shall be for the three years bound by the law; the first two under the conditions expressed above, and in the third year [Moya] agrees to pay the *liberto* Lorenzo five pesos a month [and to provide] food and lodging in his house, with clothing, cleanliness [*asearse*], and medical expenses the responsibility of the *liberto*.

The *liberto* contracted is hereby obligated vigorously to observe and comply with the customs of the house, to give respect to the teacher as well as his wife and family, obeying everything that they order him to do that is just.[29]

Lorenzo Adariche's contract, with all its details regarding not only the mason apprenticeship but also the issue of unremunerated work and deferential behavior, perhaps represented an extreme case, although clauses demanding disciplined and deferential behavior appear in several surviving contracts. For example, Don Joaquín Saunión, administrator of Hacienda Palmira, imposed very strict references to *liberto* behavior in his few surviving contracts. On 3 May he contracted Basilio, José Beatriz, and Eustaquio Vives, former slaves of Don Juan Vives de la Rosa, owner of Hacienda Esperanza, at three reals per day, and later in the month Saunión contracted José Pillot, Pedro García, and Isidro García at four reals per day. Saunión specified that the men would be provided with food "in the quantity and quality customary in the plantation, and the type of foods should not give reason for any claims by the *liberto*, as long as the food is healthy." Moreover, the *libertos* were "bound to the most strict obedience to the orders of the owner, administrator, and *mayordomos* of the plantation insofar as complying with the obligations imposed by this contract." Such harsh language indicates the possibility that previous problems with slave discipline had arisen at Hacienda Palmira.[30]

Other examples of employers' rules for *liberto* behavior appear in contracts registered by Don Federico Vázquez, a relatively wealthy *estanciero* who belonged to one of Guayama's oldest creole elite families. (He was either a son or a nephew of José Antonio Vázquez, the author of the 1848 *Memoria* discussed in chapter 1.) Don Federico contracted seven *libertos* on 3 May, and all of them were "rigorously obligated to observe and comply with the customs established in the *estancia*, maintain and make others maintain respect to the owner, the *mayordomo*, and others in charge, obeying in everything that is ordered, as long as it is just and in compliance with the codes."[31]

Among the most intriguing contracts are those involving *libertos* and black and mulatto artisans that included specific clauses for training or education. Francisco Bas Cancina, a mulatto carpenter who had migrated to Guayama from the Danish Virgin Islands, contracted three *libertos*. In 1871, Bas had owned five slaves, four of them female, and had another slave emancipated by the Moret Law. He contracted Julieta and Agustín Moret, former slaves of the Moret family who may have been related to each other, on 4 July. Agustín, a twenty-seven-year-old carpenter born in Curaçao, agreed to work with Bas for four reals per day. Julieta, a thirty-two-year-old Puerto Rican–born woman who was classified as a field slave in both the 1871 census and her *liberta* contract, agreed to work as a domestic for three pesos a month. Both contracts were terminated on 1 May 1874, although the reasons behind the termination remain unknown. Bas also contracted another *liberto*, sixteen-year-old Luis Texidor, a Puerto Rican–born mulatto freedman who had formerly been a slave of Don Jesús M. Texidor. Luis Texidor's contract with Bas was unusual in that its first clause stated that Bas "commits himself to pay the *liberto* one monthly peso as well as to teach him the trade of carpenter and to provide him with food."[32]

Two Puerto Rican mulattoes, Manuel Vázquez Sánchez, a cobbler, and Francisco Nazario Reyes, a carpenter, also contracted *libertos* for the specific purpose of training them in artisan trades. Manuel hired Dionicio Gaudinau, age seventeen, without any monetary compensation but with the provision of food, clothing, and medical attention as well as training as a cobbler. Francisco hired Juan García, age fifteen, also for no wages but with compensation in the form of food, clothing, medical attention, and training as a *latero* (roofer). Other contracts between *liber-*

tos and artisans containing provisions for training or education have survived. For example, Don Manuel Munro hired Ruperto Texidor, age nineteen, to work as a domestic servant and general assistant in exchange for food, clothing, medical attention, and training as a baker.[33]

These contracts between artisans and *libertos* suggest that former slaves redefined their newly acquired status as freedmen and -women in ways quite similar to those developed by free landless laborers when they confronted Governor Juan de la Pezuela's 1849 forced-labor decree. As Fernando Picó has demonstrated in his landmark study of Utuado before the coffee boom, Puerto Rican peasants sought myriad ways to avoid Pezuela's dreaded *libreta* system, renting land from kin and neighbors, entering into sharecropping agreements, purchasing small plots of land, or moving to live with relatives who had access to land in Utuado. Pedro San Miguel has shown how *jornaleros* in what was then the rather marginal sugar district of Vega Baja on the northern coast developed similar tactics to remain independent peasants and to only occasionally provide free labor. This similarity in attitudes and the deployment of networks of solidarity among Guayama's subaltern people should not be surprising, given Puerto Rico's three-centuries-long tradition of peasant resistant adaptation to the demands of the Spanish colonial state and local settler elites.[34]

Backtracking on the Policy of Free Labor: 1874

As mentioned earlier, Governor Primo de Rivera's code for the implementation of the 1873 Abolition Law contained the seeds for potential conflicts, and not just because of loopholes in the code. As a Spanish republican liberal, Primo de Rivera ostensibly believed in the tenets of free market economy, which extended to a free labor market. As José Curet has argued, Primo de Rivera's regulations "provided former slaves and owners a wonderful temptation to mock the spirit of the law. Although almost all of the former slaves signed contracts, many of these were rescinded at the *liberto*'s will—in some instances for trivial reasons— before the term expired. Other contracts were fictitious, since it became common, though it went against the law, for one and the same *liberto* to sign two or more contracts with different owners."[35]

The problems faced by planters and government officials were not simple, even in light of the fact that the overwhelming majority of the former slaves had to eke out livings as day laborers working for someone else rather than as relatively autonomous peasants, apprentices, or artisans. Various island mayors complained to the governor that hundreds of *libertos* no longer resided in the old slave quarters. Many transit passes issued to enable *libertos* to work in other municipalities appear in the records with the notation "the pass arrived, but not the *liberto*." Thus, many *libertos* who sought and obtained the termination of their contracts and then went to work for employers in other districts disappeared somewhere along the way.[36] In the interior *municipio* of Aibonito, which had an unusually high number of *libertos* for a highland, non-sugar-producing district, the municipal council drew up a set of ordinances to deal with the problems of the *contratación*, especially runaway *libertos*. These ordinances prohibited residents from giving shelter to and hiding escaped *libertos* and prohibited former slaves from living anywhere other than their workplaces. Aibonito's authorities thus sought to achieve a degree of employer control, but the *libertos* seem to have eluded these efforts by establishing the sort of distance between workplace and living place that thousands of free *jornaleros* had previously maintained in the face of legal and economic pressures from the colonial state and large landholders.[37]

British consul Cowper had predicted quite accurately the emergence of these problems when he argued in May that the ex-slave contracts were made "in so loose a way that they will not prove very binding upon them, although, in all probability, sufficiently vexatious to their employers. My belief is that this part of the law will fall into desuetude, or will have to be repealed like the apprenticeship in the British possessions; it cannot be satisfactory to either party. The hardworking people do not require it for one reason, the idle for another, and the employers for both reasons, namely, that the good man will work without it, and the bad man will not work with it."[38]

And, indeed, the forced contracts seem to have fallen out of use by late 1873, as Cowper reported and as leading conservative planter José Ramón Fernández complained early in 1874.[39] However, Cowper's somewhat liberal free-labor mentality could not forecast accurately what 1874 would bring to Puerto Rico's ex-slaves. The colonial reality of the island produced an unexpected change of course when a military coup in Spain in early January brought down the first Spanish republic and removed General Primo de Rivera from his post as Puerto Rico's governor. His successor, the strongly conservative General José Laureano Sanz, took charge in February 1874, returning to the island where he had served as governor in 1869–70.[40] Given Sanz's record of repression, it is not surprising to find that in 1874 the colonial government prosecuted a group of Coamo's abolitionists and liberals that included some freedmen. The group members had allegedly conspired to prevent by force Sanz's return to the governorship, fearing that he would reinstate slavery overtly or in a disguised form.[41]

Sanz summed up his view of the contracting situation as he found it upon his return:

> Holding to what has been performed so far, these contracts were illusory, since many slaves arranged four or five contracts in the same day; and thus, such a formality fell into disrepute, since it did not offer the propertied owners any guarantee. It can be said that the majority of the *libertos* had no contract, and that they abided solely by their own free will, enjoying greater liberty than those born free, since the *libertos* roamed around in the greatest licentiousness.
>
> There was another peculiarity in that *jornaleros* or persons without any properties hired *libertos*, making a farce out of the contract signing. This fostered libertinage and vagrancy. Contract signings have been used even to shield or to legalize, let us put it in that way, concubinage and prostitution.[42]

Sanz's report described the *liberto* contracts in such terms as "illusory," "a formality," and "disreput[able]" because, as he put it, the freedmen and -women "abided solely by their own free will," enjoying greater liberty than what he believed they should be allowed. Because they tried to define freedom in ways Sanz had not expected and did so not through the cooperation of elite intellectuals but through solidarity with other oppressed peoples on the island, especially those of the worst kind, those without property, who helped to "shield" and "legalize" in practice the *libertos*' attempts to define the contours of freedom in their own terms. But why did Sanz find this development so abhorrent? Solely because the former slaves foiled attempts to secure a steady, disciplined labor supply?

Slavery, of course, constituted not simply a labor system but also a system of power relations, of behavioral codes that provided a powerful justification for domination, for sorting people out in particular ways, even if those codes were not always followed. Emancipation had brought out into the open a struggle over values: those pigeonholes of domination and subordination were now being contested, not only in elite debates over free labor or civil and political rights for settlers and educated blacks and mulattoes but also in the practices of subaltern peoples. Thus, the *libertos'* exercise of "free will" was problematic, and Sanz and others associated it with "roaming," "licentiousness," "libertinage," "vagrancy," and "prostitution." Sanz gesture of "othering" was justified by the *libertos* violations of the norms they were expected to follow.

The elites' dreams were now turning into a nightmare of a transition they were not sure they could control. Rather than fully constituting *libertos* as subjects within the folds of his discourse, Sanz was reacting and reconfiguring their subjectivity as part of an effort to buttress the abrogation of Primo de Rivera's liberal contracting code and the reimposition of the vagrancy regulations Primo de Rivera had also lifted in 1873. To be sure, Sanz's discourse had had a previous existence. It had been uttered a century earlier by Alejandro O'Reilly and other colonial officials and settler elites when they confronted the need to subdue Puerto Rico's dispersed, roaming peasants. But just as O'Reilly and others writing in the late eighteenth century were elaborating a discourse of colonial domination in mutual contestation with *desacomodado* peasants, Sanz's discourse was the product of the highly contested dynamics of emancipation in the mid-1870s. As *jornaleros*, African and creole slaves, and freedmen and -women had done before full emancipation, the *libertos* of the 1870s attempted then and over the next twenty-five years to cut through the intricate terrain of colonial politics to define, as far and as wide as possible, the meaning of freedom.[43]

Sanz moved quickly to reform Primo de Rivera's much-criticized contracting system and to curtail the "licentious" behavior of laborers, free and freed. After hearing various suggestions from the municipal councils, the governor issued a new code of forced-contracting regulations and tried to impose a new vagrancy law to cover both free laborers and *libertos* after the period of forced contracts ended in 1876. In the preamble to the new regulations, Sanz stated his aim of rescuing the island's planters, who were suffering the effects of a "complete disorganization of labor" and the *libertos'* disproportionate demands. Under the new regulations, all *liberto* contracts should extend at least until the end of the forced-contracting period.

In addition, Sanz's regulations eliminated the ex-slaves' right unilaterally to renounce their contracts. Furthermore, the new rules prohibited the *libertos'* demands for high wages according to their skills and value; the former slaves should now be paid only the "normal" wage rates in their districts; the cost of nonwage compensation, such as meals and clothing, was to be deducted from their daily wages. *Libertos* could be hired only by established planters, merchants, or manufacturers as determined by local authorities. Finally, all contracts that did not meet the new standards were automatically invalidated, and the affected *libertos* were ordered to contract with legitimate employers.[44] For all practical purposes, Sanz's new regulations represented an attempt to impose a system that, except for the sale of these human beings as chattel, was almost as restrictive and domineering as slavery itself—in short, what the alleged Coamo conspirators had feared.

Sanz's strict regulations on the *libertos'* bargaining for higher wages responded to the planters' general complaint that wages in the sugar industry were too high for a country that demographically ought not to have had labor supply problems. Because the first round of *liberto* contracting occurred during the 1873 sugar harvest, many *hacendados* felt that they had been pushed into giving in to the former slaves on the issue of wages and to maintaining the food, shelter, medical attention, and clothing expenses that they had hoped abolition would eliminate. These concessions, in the *hacendados'* minds, went well beyond their cash-flow capacity despite the fact that they had been providing these things to their slaves before abolition. Furthermore, the planters complained, high wages led many *libertos* to work just two or three days a week to cover their bare necessities, remaining idle for the remainder of the workweek. This complaint was not as farfetched as at first might seem to be the case: the nonmonetary compensation covered many of the day-to-day needs of the *libertos* and their families (food, shelter, medical care, and clothing, which masters had provided to their slaves), so cash represented an add-on, something over and above what the former slaves had received prior to emancipation.[45]

As a solution to the labor supply problems created by abolition and the loose enforcement of the forced-labor regulations, many planters not only proposed new schemes of forced labor—like Sanz's *liberto* contracting code and new vagrancy law—but also sought the immigration of agricultural laborers.[46] By the mid-1870s many Puerto Rican planters, especially those on northeastern, eastern, and southern coastal haciendas, began to utilize immigrant laborers brought on one-year contracts from neighboring British West Indian islands, especially Antigua and St. Kitts. Yet the planters confronted a serious lack of government support for these efforts, as Spanish officials feared that the immigration of British West Indian blacks would stir up the recently freed Puerto Rican slaves or create more incidents over broken work contracts and the treatment of British subjects like those that had already occurred in the island municipality of Vieques, just to the east between Puerto Rico and the Virgin and Leeward Islands. The planters were "desirous of obtaining more foreign labor," the British consul reported in 1875, "so that competition may reduce the high rate of wages." In other words, faced with the inability to use Puerto Rico's relatively high population density to create a "reserve army of labor," planters turned to the colonial state for new labor regulation and importation schemes, just as British Caribbean planters had done after emancipation there in the 1830s.[47]

Abolitionists in Puerto Rico and Spain voiced criticism of Sanz's 1874 contracting code, and diplomatic records show that British officials shared their displeasure with the new regulations with their Spanish counterparts.[48] And while praising the new rules, conservative planters warned the government that only the stringent enforcement of the new measures could guarantee their success: planters remained suspicious of the *libertos'* willingness to comply. The ex-slaves had "a great repugnance," the conservative newspaper *Boletín Mercantil* said, "to contract themselves [to work]; [they have] a tendency to live in independence and vagrancy."[49]

But how did the ex-slaves react?[50] The only evidence as yet discovered of *liberto* resistance to Sanz's forced-contracting regulations comes from the late-1874 appeal of a San Germán *hacendado*, who urged the governor to overturn a local decision to rescind the contracts of a group of *libertos* under his control. According to the planter, these *libertos* had not been working regularly and on schedule on his sugar estate. He had yielded to their demand to pay them by the task, only to have them work just a few days a week, enough to cover their consumption needs: "Tired of the continuous faults of these *libertos* using the pretext of being ill to be absent from work, day after day . . . seeing the slowness with which they moved when they pleased [to work] to obtain the wage of a day for each two or three days of indolent rest, and knowing that all were dominated by a desire to do task-work jobs as free laborers are accustomed to, I agreed. [Yet] what the *libertos* wanted was . . . in reality something else: they said that with task work they would . . . gain more [money], but it would really take off their backs the supervision of their master."[51]

In a surprising move, the mayor and the *síndico* ruled against the planter, Don Vicente Sambolín, terminating the *libertos'* contracts when they complained that he had punished them for their behavior. Sambolín appealed to the governor, who promptly ruled in his favor, reinstating the contracts, forcing the *libertos* to return to the estate, and reprimanding the mayor and the *síndico* for their "excesses."[52]

Conclusion

Together with the issuance of special township passes to the *libertos*, the reinforcing of the 1874 vagrancy decree sought to limit their freedom of movement and to help solve a problem that would nevertheless persist in varying degrees in years to come: guaranteeing that the valuable *libertos* would continue to render consistent and continuous labor as they did in slavery. But neither Sanz nor his successor, Segundo de la Portilla, could convince officials in Madrid to authorize a new forced-labor law that would replace the 1849 Reglamento de Jornaleros abolished as part of Governor Primo de Rivera's attempt to establish a system of free labor.[53] Nonetheless, the planters persisted, and, as chapter 6 will discuss, in 1877 they filed a petition to impose a forced-labor scheme that would solve once and for all the sugar industry's labor supply problems. After four years of lobbying in Madrid, however, the planters found that the Spanish government refused to reintroduce forced labor in Puerto Rico, a not particularly surprising stance given that Spain was still fighting an insurrection in Cuba, where the issue of slavery remained crucial.[54]

Undoubtedly with behavior like that of Sambolín's *libertos* in mind, Governor de la Portilla instructed the island's mayors about how to handle full emancipation in 1876 while reaffirming Sanz's vagrancy decree. De la Portilla told the mayors,

> It is, therefore, absolutely necessary that the *liberto* understand that from the moment that he begins to exercise the civil rights granted to mankind, he contracts the inescapable duty of respecting and complying with the laws that govern him; of respecting the authorities, his fellow citizens, property, and everything that is sacred among us; of

forming, legitimately and religiously, a family; of supporting it with the product of his work; and of acquiring by habit the quality of being useful and industrious, to himself and to society as a whole.

These are the dispositions and advice that all the mayors should give to the *libertos* when giving them their citizenship passes.[55]

At the same time, de la Portilla asked the planters to continue giving work to the *libertos* and to permit them to occupy, rent-free, as *agregados* the huts and *cuarteles* where they lived on the estates "until time remedies that special way of being of the *libertos*"[56]—a primary discourse of domination and power that resembled that of his predecessor. No matter how racist or self-serving de la Portilla's words might sound more than a century later, they voiced an attitude of exclusion, a fear that black slaves could pollute and undermine white settler society and values. These words also justified the combination of paternalist attitudes with the unleashing of the coercive instruments of the colonial state through "vagrancy" measures and, as chapters 6 and 7 will illustrate, the expansion of repressive agencies such as urban police forces and the dreaded Spanish Guardia Civil.

How did planters, *libertos*, and officials react to de la Portilla's instructions? And on a larger scale, how did they contest each other's notions of what "free labor" meant? Planters' responses to emancipation would necessarily include adapting to the conditions Caribbean and world sugar producers were experiencing in the last decades of the century and to the peculiarities of the island's colonial politics, which undermined the planters' position at the same time that they were being forced to reorganize their enterprises around free labor relations.

The *libertos*, meanwhile, were legally set free, but the concrete definition of what freedom could and should entail would be resolved not only on the terrain of work relations but also in the many aspects that constitute an individual's and a social group's existences. Subaltern peoples like Guayama's *libertos* sought not only generally to destroy the signs of authority and domination embedded in slavery but more commonly to preserve some of them in reclaiming customary rights, appropriating them as part of a definition of "free labor." In chapters 6 and 7 I address both of these perspectives: a closer look at the experience of Guayama's planter citizens and *liberto* citizens-to-be in the twenty-five years that followed 22 March 1873.[57]

CHAPTER 6

LABOR MOBILITY, PEONIZATION, AND THE PEASANT WAY THAT NEVER WAS

The transition from slavery to free labor, even in societies like Puerto Rico, where slavery coexisted with relations of production based on free or nonslave forms of coerced labor, entailed the disintegration of a social class of slave laborers and their reconstitution into the various social classes of wage laborers, peasants, and artisans. As pigeons theoretically set free to fly in all directions, former slaves could decide or be forced by circumstances beyond their control to build nests elsewhere in the country's social fabric or to stay put even when the cage door at least nominally had been left open.

As chapter 5 demonstrated, in 1873, many *libertos* grabbed onto the promise of freedom and the rhetoric of free labor enshrined in the discourses of abolitionists and the laws and regulations of a liberal republican colonial regime, seeking to put into practice long-held aspirations of freedom in the context of labor relations inside and outside the realm of the sugar plantation economy. This chapter will ask, beyond the formally limited scope of the fleeting, radical context brought to Puerto Rico by the first Spanish Republic, how did Guayama's *libertos* react to the opening of the cage of slavery and the decline of the sugar industry after the mid-1870s? The answer to this question is as multifaceted as the ex-slave population itself.

Some *libertos* sought to acquire land, even in tiny amounts. In Guayama, however, where scarce land resources prevailed, most ex-slaves could be expected to remain dependent on plantation employment for their sustenance and that of their families. But did this mean that they continued to live and work on their former masters' plantations? The evidence in chapter 5 suggests that although a great number of *libertos* continued to perform manual labor, usually in the sugar industry, many former slaves sought to utilize the mechanisms of free labor to define their freedom in terms that many of their former masters were not necessarily willing to accept. This chapter will further explore this theme, examining specific *liberto* strategies for defining their newly acquired freedom. Discussing these strategies requires looking at those who purchased land or independent dwellings as well as those who sought to develop artisan skills or independently to use skills acquired during slavery. I will also address the issue of labor mobility, both within the *municipio* of Guayama and beyond *municipio* boundaries, as part of a discussion of social control and the peasant way that never was.

It has been argued that the transition from slavery to free labor in the Americas constituted one of the most fundamental changes in the nineteenth-century world economy. The historiography of this transition is vast and complicated, especially debates associated with the factors contributing to "peasantization" or "proletarianization" in postemancipation societies in the Americas.[1] Puerto Rico is an appropriate place to engage a range of the central issues discussed in that historiography. The island had a remarkably high population density at the end of the nineteenth century (277 people per square mile in 1899, compared to 36 in Cuba, for example) and thus had land/labor ratios that restricted the peasantization of ex-slaves. At the same time, the island's sugar industry underwent a serious crisis in the last quarter of the century, particularly in regions such as Guayama, creating additional potential for a serious oversupply of rural labor that would dampen *liberto* efforts to reshape labor relations. Conversely, the sugar industry crisis meant that hundreds of acres of coastal lands were now lying fallow or had been transformed into simple pasture lands, a problematic issue since the decline in sugar production might also have meant a decline in the demand for oxen.

Thus, while unfavorable land/labor ratios would have certainly stacked the odds for peasantization against the *libertos*, the decline in the region's sugar industry could have opened various pathways for reshaping their lives away from full dependence on plantation work. Consequently, the question of *liberto* strategies after emancipation remains open, especially because ex-slaves (or free laborers or peasants, for that matter) had to play by the same rules of economic rationality as planters, government officials, and historians. The continuing examination of the *libertos'* efforts to define their freedom should therefore focus on the issue of peasantization or proletarianization in the final decades of the nineteenth century.

The Pursuit of Land, or the Peasant Way That Never Was

A study of Guayama's notarial records from 1870 to the end of Spanish rule in 1898 reveals that very few *libertos* purchased land in Guayama; just as significantly, many of those who did purchase land were not freed by the abolitionist laws of 1870 and 1873 but obtained manumission (purchased or gratis) before abolition.

On 3 September 1872, exactly one month after his manumission, Valentín Gual purchased 5.5 *cuerdas* of land in barrio Algarrobos from Nicomedes Roubert (a preabolition *liberto*) and his wife, Rita Muñoz, paying 350 pesos. Valentín stated in the deed that he had saved the money for his *coartación* but that because he had obtained a gratis manumission, he had been able to purchase the land. However, less than a year later, on 10 August 1874, Valentín sold this plot to a fellow preabolition *liberto* named Ignacio who had also belonged to Don José Gual y Frías. Unlike Valentín, Ignacio Gual had purchased his freedom in December 1871 through a *coartación* valued at 200 pesos. The agreement between Valentín and Ignacio stipulated the price of the land at 400 pesos, of which Valentín had already received half; the balance would be paid in two installments due in January and December 1875. Indeed, in July 1876, Valentín certified that he had received full payment for the purchase. Valentín Gual purchased other land after his manumission. In September 1875 he bought 11.65 *cuerdas* from Doña Barbara Morales de García in a nonplantation barrio of the neighboring coastal *municipio* of Patillas. Valentín retained this property for almost twelve years before selling it on

13 May 1887 to a *jornalero*, Manuel Figueroa Flores, for 125 pesos. This time, the deed described Valentín as a seventy-year-old widowed peasant native of Curaçao, with no reference to his origins as a manumitted *liberto*.[2]

Another case of a pre-1873 *liberto* buying land in Guayama after 1870 is that of Adelaida Texidor. Armed with money inherited from Don Antonio Texidor y Vázquez shortly before the abolition of slavery, it appears that she first purchased her freedom and then bought a relatively large farm consisting of 175 *cuerdas* and a house in the piedmont of barrio Carmen (then known as Quebrada Yeguas), from Don Luis Rodriguez for 875 pesos. In addition, she purchased from Don Bautista Rubio another 25 *cuerdas* that had previously belonged to that farm, paying 125 pesos. Whatever Adelaida's intentions in purchasing these properties, they did not remain in her hands for long. In November 1873, Adelaida sold 40 *cuerdas* of land for 325 pesos to Jaime Cristian. In February 1876, she sold 12 additional *cuerdas* for 108 pesos to a peasant named Santos Morales y Figueroa who owned adjacent land. On 16 March 1876, she sold the remaining portion of the farm to Cristian for 400 pesos, meaning that she lost 42 pesos overall on the transactions.[3]

The limited success of *libertos* freed by the 1870 and 1873 abolition laws in gaining access to land becomes apparent when the few cases of such land purchases between 1873 and 1898 are examined. Indeed, between May 1873 and January 1888, Guayama's *libertos* purchased land in only twenty-four cases, half of them during the first three years after emancipation. During the last ten years of Spanish rule, no people I could identify as *libertos* purchased land. Excluding two relatively large plots of land by Guayaman peasant standards (measuring 110 and 69.5 *cuerdas*, respectively), the average plot bought by *libertos* measured 8.5 *cuerdas*, and the average price paid was about 165 pesos. In all, Guayama's *libertos* bought just 366.35 *cuerdas*, nearly half of that in the two large plots of land mentioned earlier. Twenty-one former slaves, including eight women, bought land after March 1873. Moreover, in four instances, the buyers were two slaves involved in legal or consensual marital relationships, and a pair of brothers also purchased land together. The most common areas in which *libertos* bought land were the highland or piedmont barrios of Guamaní (thirteen cases totaling 76.25 *cuerdas*), Carmen (four cases, forty-four *cuerdas*), and Palmas (one case of 66.5 *cuerdas*). Not a single *liberto* (manumitted or emancipated) purchased land in the remote highland barrio of Carite or in the coastal, plantation-dominated barrio of Machete. Most the plots were small: nine parcels measured less than 5 *cuerdas*, while eight others measured between 5 and 10 *cuerdas*.

Perhaps not by coincidence, the purchase of the largest tract of land by a *liberto* after the abolition of slavery was done by the surviving son of Adelaida Texidor, Pedro Texidor, an endowed ex-slave who appears to have obtained his freedom at an early age. Pedro bought 110 *cuerdas* in the non-sugar-plantation section of Peña Hendida of barrio Pozo Hondo for 1,100 pesos in 1874, right after receiving his inheritance from the estate of Don Antonio Texidor. Unfortunately, like his mother, Pedro failed to hold onto this property for long. In October 1876 he sold 7 *cuerdas* to another peasant, Juan Bautista Lugo, for 31 pesos to compensate for land that Adelaida had "wrongly ceded" to Lugo (part of the land sold to Jaime Cristian in 1873).

One month later, Pedro sold 60 *cuerdas* to Doña Belén García de Sergés for 400 pesos, of which he had previously received 269.05 pesos. That the deed specified such a precise sum as a down payment suggests that Pedro was indebted to Doña Belén or to her husband, Don Luis Sergés. In May 1877, Pedro sold the remainder of his land in Peña Hendida to Doña Belén García, receiving 400 pesos for the 43 *cuerdas*. Like his mother, he lost money on his land transactions—in his case, 269 pesos in three years. The Pozo Hondo property was not, however, the only land Pedro owned: in July 1894, his four sons sold 29 *cuerdas* of land in barrio Palmas. Pedro seems to have obtained this land before 1870, but no notarized transaction has been found.[4]

The final preabolition *liberto* who purchased land after 1873 was Zenón Pillot, who in 1860 either purchased his freedom or received a free *carta de libertad* from his master, a French citizen, Don Arístides Pillot, who owned Hacienda Barrancas. Zenón represents one of the most extraordinary examples of *liberto* peasantization I have discovered. In 1879, he bought a good-sized finca—65.5 *cuerdas*—for the formidable sum of 1,318 pesos: 1,018 at the time of the transaction and 300 promised by March 1880. In July 1887, Zenón Pillot acquired an additional 7 *cuerdas* in barrio Carmen (Quebrada Yeguas) for 300 pesos. Unlike many other ex-slaves, Zenón and his family retained these properties for a considerable time: his widow, Teresa de Jesús, still owned both plots in as late as 1919.[5]

Some of the stories of ex-slaves' efforts to acquire land reveal the dynamics not of peasantization but of proletarianization or, to put it better, of peonization, as historian Fernando Picó has characterized the processes of class transformation experienced by impoverished peasants in the highland coffee district of Utuado during the nineteenth century.[6] One good example is that of the plot of seventeen *cuerdas* of land in Guamaní bought originally by two manumitted brothers, Alfredo and Emilio Boyrié. The men obtained the land from their former master, Don Juan Eugenio Boyrié, in 1869, but the transfer was not formalized until 7 August 1873, when Juan Eugenio conveyed the property to Emilio (the fate of Alfredo's property rights remains unknown). Emilio was interested in obtaining the certified *escritura* (deed) because four days later, he sold ten of the seventeen *cuerdas* to Manuel Rodríguez and José Víctor Rivera for 170 pesos. Manuel and José Víctor, who were obtaining five *cuerdas* each, made a down payment of 75 pesos and obligated themselves to pay the remaining 95 pesos in November 1873. Two years later, on 4 November 1875, Emilio Boyrié sold the remaining seven *cuerdas* to *libertos* Ceferino Vázquez and Ruperta Aguilar for 147 pesos. That money resulted from their savings over a not too short period of time, as shown by the amount and types of currency given to Emilio in the presence of notary Don José Mariano Capó y Alvarez:

=five ounces of Colombian gold coins, at 16.50 pesos
=one-quarter-ounce Californian gold coin, 5.25 pesos
=two one-quarter-ounce Spanish gold coins, 8.50 pesos
=one-eighth-ounce Spanish gold coin, 2.12 pesos
=one one-twentieth-ounce Californian gold coin, 1.00 peso
=three Napoleonic silver coins, 3.00 pesos
=and 24.63 pesos in U.S. silver and copper coins[7]

This assorted collection of coins provides a good indication of the severe currency problems Puerto Rico's nineteenth-century colonial economy. Yet it also testifies to Ceferino and Ruperta's efforts to acquire land even though the small size of the plot precluded any dreams of making it the basis for independence from wage work elsewhere. Their perseverance may have liberated them from the obligation to continue working under the terms of the forced *liberto* labor regulations of 1873–76, if indeed they had not entirely evaded the *contratación*. However, in December 1879 they sold their land to Don Enrique Amy, a landlord who was increasing his holdings in both the highland and lowland barrios of Guayama.[8]

Another *liberto* couple who sought to obtain land in Guayama's non-sugar peasant barrios was Angelina Viñas and Juan de la Cruz Texidor, formerly slaves of Haciendas Carlota and Josefa. On 26 October 1875, Angelina and her "future husband," Juan de la Cruz, came to the notary's office with some of their savings, 76.83 pesos, to register the purchase of 3 *cuerdas* located in Guamaní for 75 pesos. The land had been owned by Doña Damiana de Rivera, a peasant woman from Guamaní. Once again, the *libertos* came with all sorts of coins—gold coins from Spain, Mexico, California, and France. In September 1879 and again in February 1886, Juan de la Cruz returned to the notary's office to purchase adjacent plots of land—4 and 5.58 *cuerdas* at 95 and 55 pesos, respectively. Juan de la Cruz Texidor apparently held onto at least part of his *finquita* (diminutive farm), because the notarial records show the sale of just 7 *cuerdas* to José Delgado Berríos in 1895, and Juan de la Cruz paid property taxes for 6 *cuerdas* in 1885 and for 13 *cuerdas* in 1898.[9]

Other *libertos* apparently obtained access to parcels of land or houses in the township of Guayama, although the local notarial records do not reflect these acquisitions. The 1885 and 1898 property tax lists, for example, show that Micaela García had 20 *cuerdas* in Guamaní in 1885 and 13.5 in 1898, just months before the U.S. invasion of the island. Cornelio Massó appears with 8 *cuerdas* in Guamaní 1885, and his *finquita* was paying taxes for 9 *cuerdas* in 1898. Valentín García, Tomas Gual, and Calixto Massó had small plots of 6, 4, and 1.5 *cuerdas*, respectively, also in Guamaní in 1898, while Francisco (Chiquito) Capó had five *cuerdas* in Jobos the same year.[10] How did these ex-slaves gain access to these pieces of land? In addition to the most obvious explanation—that these properties were purchased informally—some owners could have inherited them from other preabolition *libertos* or from people to whom they were connected by real or fictive kin networks. They also could have received land from generous patrons or even former masters. In all of these instances, the transactions were never notarized in Guayama.

Although I have not identified any cases in which patrons or masters gave land to former slaves, I found two examples in which *libertos* received urban dwellings in this manner. In 1874, Don Carlos Beaulieu transferred gratis a house to Adrián and Constanza, ages twelve and eight,

TABLE 6.1: Land Tenure in Guayama by Barrio and Farm Size, 1885

Farm Size (Cuerdas)	Algarrobos	Caimital	Carite	Carmen (Quebrada Yeguas)	Guamaní	Jobos	Machete	Palmas	Pozo Hondo	GUAYAMA TOTAL	
										N	%
1–10	4	10	4	4	25	3	0	21	0	71	17.2
11–25	0	8	13	22	36	3	4	20	1	107	25.9
26–50	4	11	6	4	17	2	6	10	2	62	15.0
51–100	0	6	8	7	10	2	10	9	7	59	14.3
101–200	5	6	7	4	6	11	18	4	4	65	15.7
201–300	0	0	4	0	0	11	6	2	3	26	6.3
301–400	1	1	2	0	0	—	—	—	2	6	1.5
401–500	2	1	4	1	1	—	—	—	—	9	2.2
501–600	—	—	1	—	—	—	—	—	—	1	0.2
601–700	—	—	—	—	—	2	—	—	1	3	0.7
701–800	—	—	—	—	—	1	—	1	—	2	0.5
Over 800	—	—	—	1	—	—	—	—	1	2	0.5
Total	16	43	49	43	95	35	44	67	21	413	

Source: AGPR, FMG, DM, "Padrón de la riqueza agrícola de Guayama, 1885–1886," box xx (1880–89).

respectively, the children of *liberta* Juliana Boyrié. The deed stated that Don Carlos was very fond of Juliana's children and consequently had decided to cede to them a house worth nine hundred pesos—double the value of the most expensive house bought by any Guayaman *liberto* after abolition. In 1879, one of the owners of the then-abandoned Hacienda Barrancas, Don Mauricio Pillot, purchased another valuable house from Don Francisco Modesto, a well-known mason, for 600 pesos. At the same time, Pillot transferred the ownership of the house to twelve-year-old Félix and ten-year-old Carlota Pillot, the children of Felicidad Pillot and, like their mother, former slaves of Hacienda Barrancas. Don Mauricio included a clause stipulating that although the property was being transferred to the two children, they were required to permit their mother as well as their grandmother, Juana Pillot, another of his family's former slaves, to inhabit it for the rest of their lives. Indeed, Don Mauricio's affection for these *libertos*, the source of which remains open to speculation, had already been expressed in 1871, when he manumitted gratis both Félix and Felicidad.[11]

The small number of Guayama's ex-slaves who gained property rights over land and the small size of almost all of those plots reinforce the notion discussed in chapter 3 that Guayama the lacked of one of the key ingredients for postemancipation peasant class formation identified by Sidney Mintz and others: the preabolition accumulation of capital through protopeasant activities of autonomous production and marketing. But do these phenomena also indicate the unavailability of land for independent peasant class development? The prospects for subsistence peasant class development in Guayama in the final years of the nineteenth century were certainly minimal. To be sure, the total number of farms seems to have increased in the last two decades of the century but appears to have done so as a result of the subdivision of small landholdings into even smaller plots rather than as a result of the breakup of failed large estates.

Tables 6.1 and 6.2 show this pattern by barrio for 1885 and 1898. The information suggests that a remarkable increase occurred in the number of holdings in barrios with sizable peasant populations, such as highland Guamaní and Palmas. Growth also occurred in the number of *finquitas* measuring ten *cuerdas* or less, from 17.2 percent in 1885 to 34.7 percent in 1898. But this increase seems to have taken place at the expense of the number of farms in the next group (between eleven and twenty-five

TABLE 6.2: Land Tenure in Guayama by Barrio and Farm Size, 1898

Farm Size (Cuerdas)	Algarrobos	Caimital	Carite	Carmen (Quebrada Yeguas)	Guamaní	Jobos	Machete	Palmas	Pozo Hondo	GUAYAMA TOTAL #	%
1–10	7	12	8	12	69	23	2	46	4	183	34.7
11–25	1	7	12	21	36	3	2	16	2	100	18.9
26–50	5	9	14	4	20	1	4	18	5	80	15.2
51–100	3	8	5	3	17	5	1	10	2	54	10.2
101–200	6	4	12	5	1	4	2	2	4	40	7.6
201–300	2	3	8	—	1	4	4	2	2	26	4.9
301–400	2	1	3	—	—	3	—	—	3	12	2.3
401–500	—	—	1	—	1	2	3	—	1	7	1.3
501–600	—	—	1	2	—	—	4	—	—	8	1.5
601–700	—	—	—	—	1	1	4	—	—	5	0.9
701–800	—	1	—	—	—	3	4	1	1	10	1.9
Over 800	—	—	—	—	—	1	1	—	1	3	0.6
Total	26	45	64	47	145	50	31	95	25	528	

Source: AGPR, FMG, DM, "Pueblo de Guayama, Padrón general de agrícola . . . , 1898–1899," box xx (1890–99).

cuerdas) as well as in the number of fincas measuring between fifty-one and one hundred *cuerdas*. In other words, more *minifundistas* existed by the end of the century, but they were probably less able to obtain a significant portion of their families' subsistence from these smaller plots. This development represented an ominous reality for Guayama's ex-slaves, many of whom may have dreamed of owning parcels of land, no matter how diminutive: the Puerto Rican peasantry that the *libertos* wished to join was weakening as the century neared its end.

Peonization, Proletarianization, and Liberto *Residential Patterns*

The reduced dimensions of most of the parcels of land bought by *libertos* suggest that in many instances the land was not acquired so that the new owners could immediately become full-time peasants or dependent on even itinerant wage labor. The plots seem to have been obtained as substitutes for the small provision grounds allocated to slaves on some plantations or simply because they represented a locus of independent life away from the plantation perimeter, generally some miles away from the plantation belt. The notarial records, even with their formal and sometimes boilerplate nature, offer examples that can illuminate this understanding of the behavior of many of the *libertos* who purchased land. The case of the twenty-four *cuerdas* bought by Juan Bautista Vázquez in the proximity of Jobos's sugarcane fields constitutes one of these examples. On 8 November 1878, Juan Bautista bought this land in a section of barrio Jobos known as Pozuelo, an area covered with palm trees and mangrove swamps on the Caribbean shoreline. The land is unsuitable for sugarcane agriculture and even the production of many foodstuffs because of the salinity and dampness of the soil, but it is appropriate for raising pigs and goats as well as the collection of coconuts and as a base for fishing activities. The plot sold for 600 pesos, with Juan Bautista paying 300 pesos in cash and agreeing to pay the balance in installments of 100 pesos in November 1879, 1880, and 1881, which he did. On 4 February 1884, however, he sold five *cuerdas* to Francisca Vives, formerly a slave of Hacienda Esperanza, for 125 pesos, and on 25 June 1888, Francisca Vives sold two of her five *cuerdas* to another *liberta*, Francisca Vázquez, for 60 pesos. On 29 April 1904, these two *cuerdas* returned to Juan Bautista, who bought them from Vázquez.[12]

Even smaller than these and the other parcels of land discussed to this point and with an even more obvious rural labor character were the plots bought by siblings Nicasia Texidor and Ignacio Gual in May 1873 and by Felipe Texidor in 1880. Nicasia and Ignacio purchased "*un cuadro de terreno*" (a square of land, meaning one-fourth of a *cuerda*) in the section of barrio Jobos known as La Puente, including a house located on the plot, for 100 pesos. Felipe Texidor paid 250 pesos in September 1880 for a well-built house and its lot located in the port of Jobos, right in front of Hacienda Puerto, one of the plantations of the Texidor family for whom he had toiled as a slave.[13]

The buying or building of such houses dominated the activities of Guayama's *libertos* as far as the legal acquisition of property was concerned. Yet for the most part, former slaves did not buy houses in the countryside, like these two in barrio Jobos, but rather purchased dwellings in the township of Guayama. During the last three years of slavery, for example, preabolition *libertos* purchased houses in the township much more frequently than land. Between June 1871 and December 1872, eleven *libertos* purchased twelve houses for an average price of 123 pesos. Seven of these *libertos* were women: Anastacia Bardeguez, Monserrate García, María Valentína Moret, Martina Pillot, Castora Sánchez, Nicolasa Texidor, and Enriqueta Villodas.[14]

These purchases, along with the construction of new huts on plots granted by the municipal council, were concentrated on the *pueblo*'s outskirts. Indeed, the urbanization experience of ex-slaves after 1870 gave impetus to the formation of plebeian *barriadas* (slums) that would continue and develop further after the turn of the century. Around the period of the transition from slavery to free labor, these sections of the township took their definite shape and were even christened with richly plebeian names. Some of these *barriadas* have disappeared with time, while others have continued to exist, if sometimes only in name, a hundred years later. Places such as Hoya Inglés (literally "English Creek" but more regularly pronounced "Joyinglé"), San Thomas, Canta Gallo, Borínquen, and Pica Pica, for example, date their formation or their growth into full-blown communities from the last three decades of the nineteenth century.

The migration of ex-slaves to the township started slowly with the movement of manumitted *libertos* to the urban area before abolition. The census of 1871, for example, clearly labeled as *libertos* or as born in Africa fifty-five individuals in the three urban barrios of Guayama. Scores of black or mulatto others carried the surnames of Guayama's leading slaveholders but are difficult to clearly identify as having been born in captivity. Within the group of fifty-five ex-slaves, four out of five were women, prominent among them Petrona Pillot, a fifty-year-old African-born domestic who headed a household that included three other *libertas* who worked as laundresses; Victoriana García, forty years old, who did ironing and headed a household of at least six others, including four additional women who ironed, a domestic, and a male apprentice; and Castora Sánchez, a fifty-year-old peddler born in Africa.

Indeed, the urban female ex-slaves included nine who ironed, eight laundresses, six peddlers or owners of small grocery stores (*ventorrilleras*), three seamstress, three cooks, and five women simply listed as "domestics" or "servants." The twelve men included only three peons (*braceros*) and five artisans (including two coopers and two masons). This profile of preemancipation urban *libertos* suggests one of the most common paths ex-slaves took to redefine their lives: moving to the township represented an opportunity for gainful employment quite distant from the rigors of plantation field work, but the path was more easily trod by women, who often had skills in peddling produce and preparing food, than by men, who had no particular skills other than manual agricultural labor.

Libertos' efforts to seek an independent shelter away from the perimeter of the sugar plantations must also be put into the context of many surviving sugar haciendas' apparent early success in attracting laborers to live inside or very close to the plantation perimeters. In 1878, Manuel Ubeda y Delgado published figures for the number of dwellings and number of households, permitting the calculation of a ratio of households to dwellings for each individual barrio and the *municipio* of Guayama as a whole. The index shows that an inordinate concentration of households in sugar barrios in relation to the number of dwellings reported. For example, barrio Machete, which was overwhelmingly controlled by sugar plantations, had 8.6 households per dwelling, whereas Jobos, which had a mixture of plantations and small peasants, had 2.2 households per dwelling. These figures contrast sharply with the *municipio* as a whole, where the overall ratio of households to dwellings was less than 1.3 to 1. Moreover, Machete's concentration (more than 6.5 times higher than that of the *municipio* as a whole) suggests that a number of haciendas retained laborers living in the old slave quarters or perhaps in new huts built expressly to attract and retain workers.[15]

Indeed, by the mid- to late 1870s, planters around the island were beginning to develop strategies for maintaining a dependent labor force on the hacienda that did not rely on state-imposed coercion. In his study of Hacienda Mercedita in Ponce, for example, Andrés Ramos Mattei identified various mechanisms used to maintain a dependent resident labor force. Following similar patterns uncovered by Mintz in his research in Santa Isabel,[16] Ramos Mattei found that Mercedita had begun to grant garden plots for subsistence production in lots within and outside the hacienda on lands belonging to the *hacendado*. The planters also established on the estate a *tienda de raya* (plantation grocery and general store), where laborers bought goods on credit from the planter. In Guayama, Haciendas Carlota and Merced had similar plantation stores by the 1890s.[17] Planters paid wages in tokens that could only be used to buy goods at the *tienda de raya*, thus hoping to create a cycle of indebtedness that would bind workers to their estates as well as to hold onto their limited specie in an economy that, as mentioned earlier, suffered from chronic shortages of currency. Finally, planters also built individual huts for hacienda laborers. These huts initially occupied hacienda grounds, but as Mercedita turned almost all arable land over to sugarcane cultivation, the construction of houses later moved to a growing working-class slum on the outskirts of the local township.[18]

These policies had in fact been initiated during the last years of slavery, when the haciendas resorted to the increased use of free *jornaleros* and the forced-labor laws became more unenforceable. Ramos Mattei mentions, for example, how many haciendas used debt schemes to snare free laborers to complement the enslaved labor force during the peak of harvest season. The planters sold these landless peasants goods on credit during the off-season and then later secured court orders sentencing the indebted peasants to work to repay the planters.[19] These policies hardly represented a clear path toward the formation of a free labor market but rather created what Rebecca Scott calls "a conflict between the search for new forms of labor, and an allegiance to the old methods of dealing with labor—an allegiance stemming not from mere traditionalism, but from a need and a desire to maintain certain kinds of social and economic control" of the plantation's labor force.[20]

Where did Guayama stand between the opposite poles of ex-slave peasantization and early proletarianization? Some *libertos* clearly sought to acquire land, even in small plots, not just as a means of providing for their sustenance or as a springboard to peasantization but also as the basis for establishing and reaffirming an independent existence in relation to the plantation and its unstable provision grounds. With land/labor ratios stacked against them, other *libertos* simply sought to base their existences on the acquisition of nonplantation rural huts or urban dwellings, perhaps so that even if the former slaves remained dependent on plantation employment, they could establish an independent basis unlike the haciendas' old *cuarteles de esclavos* (communal slave barracks). Other *libertos* seemed bound to the *cuarteles* by economic, kinship, or individual reasons, at least in the years immediately following emancipation. But the ability to purchase plots of land or to buy or build diminutive straw huts in townships did not represent *libertos'* entire universe of possibilities for defining their relations to their old masters and plantations. Other *libertos* unable or unwilling to put up cash or to indebt themselves to obtain land or houses based their attempts to exercise their new freedom on the most simple definition of emancipation: the liberty to move from one plantation, barrio, or *municipio* to another, seeking employment wherever they deemed material or spiritual conditions more attractive.

Social Control and Peonization

From the perspective of sugar planters everywhere in the Caribbean, including those in Puerto Rico, the main objective of the inevitable transition from slave to free labor was to guarantee the existence of a steady supply of disciplined and cheap labor. In essence, Puerto Rican planters had to modernize and restructure their industry or risk a drop in prices for their low-quality sugars, which would eventually result in bankruptcy. But these changes had to take place in the midst of an economy characterized by a lack of banks and by limited access to reliable and cheap sources of credit. Therefore, the planters needed to secure a cheap and reliable supply of workers that would not divert efforts and scarce capital resources to a competition among planters for labor.

Moreover, unlike in most other Caribbean plantation societies, Puerto Rico's sugar sector generally operated throughout most of the nineteenth century within an economy in which slave, free, and coerced labor had coexisted. In this sense, landlords' and government officials' experiences in attempting to coerce the labor of free landless peasants necessarily shaped the leading sugar-producing regions' approaches to the transition from slavery to free labor. As discussed in chapter 2, planters generally had negative attitudes toward the use of free laborers before abolition.

With the end of the slave trade at midcentury and facing a labor shortage for export agriculture, the colonial government devised in 1849 the Reglamento de Jornaleros, a coerced-labor code that sought to force free peasants with access to less than two acres of land to hire themselves out to work as day laborers on the island's sugar and coffee haciendas.[21] The imposition of the *libreta* system (thus known because of the labor-contract booklet that *jornaleros* had to carry at all times) constituted part of a larger process of intrusion by the colonial state in the lives of the island's free rural folk. This "progressive intrusion," Fernando Picó has called it, resulted from colonial state attempts to foster the development of commercial agriculture that dated from the last quarter of the eighteenth century.

Studies of the eighteenth century tend to present a view of the Puerto Rican free rural folk as a seminomadic peasantry dependent on subsistence agriculture in a context where private control of land was minimal—or minimally enforced—as communal *hatos* and slash-and-burn agriculture dominated the settled areas.[22] Not surprisingly, therefore, within this context, the Spanish colonial state made control of the places of residence and movement of people a key ingredient in the strategy to compel free people to work on the new sugar and coffee haciendas. Picó dates these efforts to the regulations imposed by Governor Miguel de Muesas in the 1770s. In 1783, under Governor Juan Dabán y Nogueras, the state restricted the free movement of people throughout the island by requiring them first to obtain from local authorities a license or internal passport. Yet these restrictions appear to have been enforced loosely, at least in the highland frontier, until the 1840s—that is, until after Governor Miguel López de Baños promulgated a vagrancy law in 1838. The legal screws further tightened during the 1850s in the wake of Governor Juan de la Pezuela's even more draconian Reglamento de Jornaleros. However, Picó concludes that the forced-labor system remained mostly unenforced as late as the 1860s except in specific cases when it was needed to repress particular individuals who demonstrated nonconformist behavior or to settle political vendettas.

Indeed, in the mid-1860s, the government carried out an extensive inquiry into the continued usefulness and viability of the Reglamento de Jornaleros and other vagrancy laws, seeking to determine whether the regulation of labor and vagrancy could be revitalized by the imposition of new government laws. Guayama's local authorities prepared a set of regulations for the work of female free laborers and expressed their support for further strengthening the forced-labor code. However, the *libreta* system seems to have gradually unraveled in much of the island by the late 1860s. Finally, on 16 July 1873, liberal Governor Rafael Primo de Rivera y Sobremonte abolished the *libreta* system.[23]

The pre-1873 labor regulations sought more than merely forcing the landless peasantry to work on sugar and coffee haciendas. After 1848, the government also sought to restrict the free movement of people across municipal boundaries without government supervision. Moving to a different *municipio* could provide landless peasants with the opportunity to evade the *libreta* labor system, and the authorities were concerned that local officials have records of the moral and labor conduct of newly arrived *jornaleros*. As in the case of the *libreta* system, the enforcement of restrictions on internal migration apparently fell off by the early 1870s, because in 1874 some newly installed conservative municipal councils petitioned Governor José Laureano Sanz to severely curtail freedom of migration within the island. The municipal council of Coamo asked for a reimposition of López de Baños's 1839 restrictions on *jornaleros'* changing their *municipios* of residence, and the councils from the coastal *municipios* of Dorado and Guayanilla suggested that local officials should have the power to take away *cédulas de vecindad* (residence certificate) from laborers deemed vagrants, thereby restricting their movements.[24]

In addition to dodging the *libreta* system by moving from one *municipio* to another, free laborers could potentially evade the payment in cash or labor of their share of the cost of maintaining rural roads, the "*prestaciones personales*," a tax system that Governor López de Baños had instituted in 1838.[25] In 1879, Guayama's municipal council approved a resolution asking the governor to reimpose the requirement of a passport issued by the *alcaldía* for travel within the island. The aim of this measure, as expressed by Juan Ignacio Capó, the resolution's author and administrator of his father's Hacienda Olimpo, was to guarantee that the road tax was paid by all the *vecinos* of a *municipio* by restricting the movement of people among *municipios*. The method would be to press them to pay (usually with their labor) the road tax. Under Capó's idea, the *vecinos* of a *municipio* could not move to another one unless they had already paid their *prestación de caminos*. Capó alleged that in recent years, "many with their *cédulas de vecindad* move frequently to a very distant town, and when [their road tax liability is claimed,] they abandon the town where they lived and leave for another one." Indeed, Capó added, "we now see in this town an endless number of *jornaleros* from other towns, while at the same time we notice the absence of many from this one, and both could be dodging the payment" of the road tax. Capó's idea apparently was not well received by the central government in San Juan, because such passports apparently were not reestablished in the last two decades of Spanish rule over Puerto Rico.[26]

I question historians' conclusions, based, in Ramos Mattei's view, on insufficient attention to the subject, that the abolition of the *libreta* reflected the growth of a consensus among planters that the modernization of the sugar industry perforce required the creation of a full-fledged free labor market. "Free" refers both to the sense that labor is a commodity rather than an embedded aspect of human life and the social relations irreducible to commodity transactions and to the sense of labor's freedom to move where it was needed and to employers' freedom to dispense with labor when it was not needed. In Ramos Mattei's words, "It was therefore necessary to end the geographic constraints that had immobilized workers. First, slavery had to be eliminated; then the legal obligations to work for a whole year for a single owner had to be eliminated. The landowners knew full well that they needed a large number of workers only during the harvest. . . . Theoretically, a market of free laborers was preferable to laborers who could be used only for a short time but for whom the landowners were responsible for the entire year."[27]

Yet contrary to this view, the end of slavery and the *libreta* system did not cause planters to abandon efforts to impose disguised forms of coerced labor and measures to guarantee the fixity of residence. As mentioned in chapter 5, the fall of the Spanish Republic returned conservative general José Laureano Sanz y Posse to Puerto Rico as governor in early 1874, and he moved quickly to "reform" Primo de Rivera's much-criticized *liberto* contracting system and to curtail the "vagrant" behavior of laborers, free and freed. After hearing various suggestions from the municipal councils, Sanz issued new regulations for the forced contracting of the ex-slaves and imposed a new vagrancy law to cover free laborers and the ex-slaves after the period of forced contracts ended. Although the Spanish Ministry of Overseas Territories eventually disallowed the new vagrancy code, prominent groups of planters remained intent on obtaining strict new labor regulations.

That many planters continued to favor such measures is quite clear in light of the fact that in early 1876 they undertook a major effort to impose a new labor code that restricted the same labor mobility that Ramos Mattei views as one of the goals of the Puerto Rican planter class in the 1870s. As the three-year *liberto* forced-labor period was coming to an end, Governor Segundo de la Portilla convened a commission of leading "men of all political persuasions and social positions" to draft a new labor code for the island. This blue-ribbon commission seems to have been headed by Don José Ramón Fernández, the ultraconservative Marquis of La Esperanza, and to have included among its fifty-two members several prominent sugar planters, including Salvador Calaf of Manatí, C. F. Storer of Arecibo, Eduardo Lind of Arroyo, and Guayama's Jesús María Texidor y Vázquez and Wenceslao Lugo-Viñas y Oliver. On 17 February 1876, the commission presented a Proyecto de Reglamento sobre las Relaciones entre el Capital y el Trabajo Destinados a la Industria Agrícola.[28]

The details of this project shatter the idea that an elite consensus supported the implementation of free labor relations. The proposed regulations included, among other things, the definition of the "moral and social" obligations of *jornaleros*:

1. To work every working day of the year.
2. To be in his workplace at dawn.
3. To work from that hour to sunset, except for the customary time for eating [lunch], which will not be less than an hour.
4. To fulfill religiously all the commitments he makes.

Furthermore, the plan proposed restricting the laborers' ability to move from *municipio* to *municipio* by forcing them to obtain from the *alcalde* transit papers valid only for three-day expeditions to seek work in other *municipios*; such transit papers could be obtained only three times a year. Furthermore, *jornaleros* who were ex-slaves could not leave their *municipios* until all labor contracts had been fulfilled and new contracts had been established in other *municipios*. Moreover, *libertos* could not leave their living quarters on the plantations or farms where they worked without showing that they had obtained new dwellings on their own and even then had to have the conditions of their new homes approved by local labor boards to be established by the code.

The commission clearly wanted some kind of a return to the old *libreta* system, because it also proposed that all agricultural labor contracts be registered at the *alcaldías*, where new "*registros de jornaleros*" would be kept. The idea was that laborers would have to relinquish their *cédulas de vecindad* for new "*cédulas de contratación*" (labor contract certificates) until their labor contracts had expired. This was another clever way to restrict laborers' mobility, because Puerto Ricans could not legally leave their *municipios* of residence without their *cédulas de vecindad*. The project also specified a series of penalties for laborers who violated the provisions of the new labor code, including loss of wages commensurate with the length of a laborer's absence from or abandonment of his or her job and assignment to build and repair public roads for up to two weeks.

Governor de la Portilla submitted the text of the proposed labor code to the Ministry of Overseas Territories on 14 March 1876. He accompanied the commission's proposal with his own version of the code, which excluded women from the definition of *jornaleros* and substituted cash fines for forced labor in public works. Fortunately for Puerto Rican free laborers and ex-slaves, the Spanish government in Madrid rejected the entire project on 16 April 1876, calling on the governor to utilize existing measures to deal with vagrancy "except those that in any form limit free labor."[29] The still unresolved Ten Years' War in Cuba, where slavery and emancipation remained major issues of contention, may have played a role in the Spain's rejection of new coercive labor regulations in Puerto Rico, although this subject has not yet been raised in Puerto Rican historiography.

Puerto Rico's planters continued to express their displeasure with the absence of strict regulations for agricultural laborers. As mentioned in chapter 5, in 1876–77 the Ponce Agricultural Society initiated a long process of lobbying the Spanish government in Madrid to impose a new labor code.[30] Guayama's planters prepared their own study of the "labor question" in 1877, expressing their solidarity with the Ponce group as well as with the rest of the island's planters' associations.[31]

Guayama's planter elite, like others on the island, reduced the "labor question" to the problem of the moral character of Puerto Rico's agricultural laborers; consequently, the government had to impose regulations "to moralize, regulate, and channel the customs of the people." As the report of the Guayama's Agricultural Society put it,

> The Puerto Rican *bracero*, and especially those who work in sugar agriculture, does not have the powerful sting of necessities. He is by nature, and by the climatological conditions in which he lives, indolent; he also does not have well developed sentiments of love for his family and of social improvement in the different spheres in which man evolves his legitimate aspirations; in one word, neither by condition nor by social status does he offer warranties of stability to the agriculture that provides his subsistence in exchange for his manual labor.
>
> [Thus,] we are forced to conclude that one of the principal origins of the decline observed in sugar agriculture is the present abnormal situation of the *jornalero*: his lack of education, his absolute lack of responsibility, the relaxation of family and civil ties in which he lives, and the inability of the landlord to force him to comply with the obligations that he voluntarily enters into and on which the possibility of production depends on a given moment.

The report then denounced labor relations in sugar agriculture whereby *jornaleros*, contracted by day, by week, or by task, did not necessarily finish their work but rather abandoned their tasks on whims or when they felt that they had earned enough wages to cover their bare necessities. This instability in the fulfillment of labor contracts, the report argued, was particularly hard on sugarcane agriculture "because the work in sugarcane has to be carried out on time and with keen regularity." This misconduct had to be "repressed" because it amounted to "what could be called a passive but constant and unmistaken strike of the jornaleros [lo que prodría llamarse la huelga pasiva pero constante e indudable de los jornaleros]." To solve this problem, the Guayama planters' association proposed the establishment of special judicial proceedings directed by the mayors or by the justices of peace and situated outside of the country's normal civil or criminal legal structure. These special proceedings would adjudicate conflicts between "capital and labor" expeditiously and without the regular delays found in the judicial system. The enforcement of sentences favorable to planters would then fall to local authorities (presumably the mayor and the municipal and paramilitary rural police), and the town halls would keep a registry of claims against *jornaleros* that could also be used to monitor their overall behavior.[32]

The government never accepted these and other proposals, but the discussion on "morality" and "vagrancy" (code words for the planters' frustration with their inability to mold laborers into a steady, disciplined, and fully dependent labor force) continued through the 1880s and into the 1890s. Once again, a gap appeared to exist between important segments of the local planter elite's strategies for maintaining forms of pre-capitalist control over the labor force and the Spanish colonial government's actions. Yet these proposals suggest that many planters did not buy the idea of a full-fledged transition to a new society based on a free capitalist labor market. They seem to have considered the issue of the modernization of the sugar industry at one level but hesitated to bring along the concomitant social changes associated with capitalism.

Conclusion

Even if the colonial state did not feed some planter cravings for old and new measures of labor control, at the local level at least, vagrancy and residency regulations remained selectively enforced after emancipation. The surviving records of Guayama's *alcaldía* include extensive correspondence between the mayors of Guayama and of other surrounding municipalities claiming that countless individuals had been arrested for living in *municipios* without proper *cédulas de vecindad*, for engaging in "undesirable" behavior (which could include vagrancy, the failure to hold a steady job, disturbing the peace, drunkenness, and the evasion of family responsibilities), or simply for being "suspected" of being or "seeming to be" vagrants or criminals. In 1874 and 1875, the many individuals who appear in the mayor of Guayama's correspondence include *vecinos* of Guayama found *indocumentados* both in nearby *municipios* (Arroyo, Cayey, Salinas, Patillas, Maunabo, Yabucoa, Coamo, and Ponce) and as far away as Bayamón (on the north-central coast) and Fajardo (on the island's extreme northeastern tip). The mayor also reported that police in Guayama had arrested undocumented individuals from Patillas, Yabucoa, and Caguas as well as San Lorenzo, *municipios* located in the central part of the island north and northeast of Guayama. The local police had even picked up others for whom *municipios* of origin could not be specified.

In all cases where origin could be ascertained, the individuals were arrested and escorted by the rural police back to their home districts.[33] In other instances, the mayors asked their colleagues to order the return of specific individuals sought by the authorities for failure to pay taxes (mostly the road tax) or to fulfill family duties and responsibilities.[34] The mayor of Bayamón expressed some local authorities' attitudes toward the control the immigration of *jornaleros* from other districts in a letter to his counterpart in Guayama: "Francisco Santiago has presented himself to me with a license of residence issued by yourself with the object of fixing his residence in this town, but it draws my attention that an individual from the *jornalero* class with his demeanor and manners could come from that [distant] district without a specific objective. I have been driven to believe that he is a vagrant, and I am taking care to evict him from this town along with many others in the same predicament." The mayor of Bayamón then expressed his suspicions that Francisco had stolen a horse on his way to the northern coast and sent him back to Guayama "because his residence in this town is undesirable, and because it is necessary to find out the origin of the horse that he is riding."[35]

This and other evidence registered the fact that social control over former slaves in this newly "emancipated society" originated in very old struggles over labor and its mobility. The period of forced-labor contracting mainly added a new twist to authorities' efforts to account for the whereabouts of landless peasants for taxing and social control purposes.

CHAPTER 7

CONFLICTS AND
SOLIDARITIES
ON THE PATH TO
PROLETARIANIZATION

The study of postemancipation society needs to include more than just the analysis of continuities and shifts at the level of the sugar plantation economy and the study of the strategies used by planters and ex-slaves to sustain or redefine class relations and alternatives to sugar plantation proletarianization. To grasp more fully the picture of postemancipation Guayama, it is necessary to probe deeper into the fabric of this society. Many questions need to be addressed. How did the colonial state deal with the society that emerged after emancipation? Did it actively favor the planter class? Conversely, how did the slave plantation communities change after 1873? What were the characteristics of the new communities of ex-slaves and free laborers? What patterns of conflict and solidarity emerged within these and other plebeian communities of the coastland as Guayama entered into a decline as a major sugar-producing district?

This chapter will turn to two additional aspects of the transition from slavery to free labor on southeastern Puerto Rico's coastal plains that seem crucial to understanding postabolition society, the problems in the area of discipline and social control that represented a crucial terrain of conflict between laborers and peasants, on the one hand, and planters and local authorities, on the other, and the reconfiguration of practices and mentalities that led to conflicts and solidarities within those communities.

Social Control, Proletarianization, and the Colonial State

The propertied classes and the colonial state were of course not preoccupied solely with offering steady work in export agriculture or controlling the mobility of landless laborers, whether *libertos* or not; a key aspect of attitudes and policies toward both rural and urban folk was control of social behavior. Just as important as a steady plantation labor supply was the "disciplined" behavior of rural- and urban-based laboring classes. "Discipline" meant not only orderly completion of assigned tasks during the workday but also good behavior during leisure time. Indeed, this aspect of the relationship between the propertied classes and rural and urban folk went beyond the issue of labor supply and into the heart of social relations in a society stratified by class, race, gender, and national/ethnic identity.

Cuba and Puerto Rico were Spain's sole remaining colonial possessions in the Americas in the second half of the nineteenth century. The pillars of colonial domination included not only the military and bureaucratic apparatus that ruled both islands but also the allegiance to imperial power of the resident Spanish population, the foreign element in the propertied classes, and the overwhelmingly white creole elite. Together, state military and civil officials, planters, merchants, and professionals—whether Spanish, non-Spanish foreigners, or creole Puerto Ricans—constituted just a small fraction of the island's population, but this group ruled over a mostly Puerto Rican–born mass of peasants, rural and urban laborers, artisans, and petty traders. In lowland areas like Guayama's southeastern region, where the racial stratification was even more pronounced than in the interior, an acute need existed to maintain clear boundaries of "proper" behavior.

By the early 1870s, as the island embarked on the transition from slave and coerced labor to free wage labor, the Spanish colonial state had reorganized the functions of local-level social control with institutions and methods that lasted until the end of Spanish rule. What can be regarded as the executive and judicial aspects of social control consistently overlapped. At the municipal level, the head of the apparatus was the mayor, who was an elected official only during the brief early 1870s interlude covering first the military and then the republican regime in Spain. At all other times, the mayors of the *municipios* were designated by the local municipal council, directly or indirectly under the orders of the Spanish military governors of Puerto Rico.

Under the *alcaldes* were the *comisarios de barrios*, deputies within an urban or rural barrio, group of barrios, or subdivision of a barrio. The *comisarios de barrios* collected information for the preparation of tax lists or for censuses of inhabitants, livestock, or vehicles and reported criminal or other incidents that might require the attention of the mayor, the district judge, or the rural police. The files of Guayama's *alcaldía* and judicial district contain numerous instances in which rural or urban folk resisted the mandates of the *comisarios de barrios* or the municipal police. In some instances, these people simply resisted arrest for minor infractions, but in others they were defending themselves against the *comisarios'* abuses in policing the barrios and enforcing payment of property and road taxes.[1]

However, neither the *alcaldes* nor the *comisarios de barrio* were the major enforcers of law and order, especially when some degree of implicit or explicit violence was required. This was the job of the urban and rural police forces created in 1870–73. Within the urban perimeter of the *municipio*, the Spanish regime organized and supervised from San Juan a police force called the Cuerpo de Seguridad y Orden Público. These *guardias de orden público* were generally assigned to watch over a specific street or group of streets, and a few of them were allowed to carry handguns. Some of these urban policemen were Puerto Rican–born, as was the chief of the Cuerpo de Orden Público in Guayama for most of the period under discussion here. The rural areas were ruled by the dreaded Guardia Civil, a paramilitary force established on the island in 1869, after the force had been developed in Spain.[2] The Guardia Civil was composed exclusively of Spaniards, or *peninsulares*, and was much more tightly supervised by the central government in San Juan than was the Cuerpo de Orden Público. This collection of officials bore responsibility for enforcing administrative regulations and criminal laws, serving as the Spanish colonial regime's local-level eyes and ears as it sought to keep the free and freed popular classes in their "proper" place in colonial society.[3]

The goal of keeping everyone in their social place was also not too far from planters' minds, especially in the context of the 1870s, when the elites tried to manage an orderly transition away from slavery-based social relations. An initial set of examples comes from the 1873 *contratación* period. The French-born administrator and later part-owner of Hacienda Palmira, Don Joaquín Saunión, included very strict rules for *liberto* behavior, as evidenced by the few hacienda's few surviving contracts. As discussed in chapter 5, Saunión's *liberto* contracts included specific provisions for the ex-slave's subordination to the plantation's *mayordomos* (overseers). Similar stipulations appear in the contracts of other landlords, such as Don Federico Vázquez, also with an emphasis on the workers' obligation to "maintain respect" when dealing with *mayordomos* and other supervisory personnel.

One of the best demonstrations of the propertied classes' and the state's views toward rural laborers emerged in the 1884 criminal case against Don José González, the overseer of Hacienda Felicidad, for physically assaulting Angel María Ledeé, a minor who was one of the hacienda's peons.[4] On 28 April 1884, González and a group of other *jornaleros*, including Ledeé, were repairing some carts. Ledeé apparently tried to liven up the work by joking that González was on his "way to becoming a *carpintero de mocho*" (literally a "dull-saw carpenter" but more accurately a "know-nothing carpenter"). González responded angrily, yelling at Ledeé, firing him, and throwing him off the plantation.

Witness accounts of what followed differed to some degree. Ledeé said that González not only expelled him from the hacienda but hit him with a large, heavy piece of iron, part of the cart's wheel assembly, causing serious injury. Two weeks passed before he had recovered enough from the injury to return to work elsewhere. Three *libertos* present when the attack occurred, Miguel Martínez, Juan Domingo Vives, and Valentín Gual, agreed with Ledeé's story, adding that the *mayordomo* had hit him as he was about to leave the hacienda. Don José González arranged to have four other *jornaleros*, none of them a *liberto* and two of them recent arrivals from another *municipio*, testify that although the overseer had hit Ledeé, the *jornalero* had first menaced González with a long sharp stick.

González's efforts to avoid punishment for the incident did not rest solely or primarily on his witnesses' testimony. When Rosalía Ledeé,

Angel María's mother, complained at the *alcaldía* about her son's injury on the day it occurred, Guayama Mayor Don Agustín Calimano Martínez, the brother-in-law of Hacienda Felicidad's co-owner, Don Joaquín Villodas García, did nothing. Three days later, she filed a formal complaint with the municipal judge about the attack and Calimano Martínez's inaction. Because of the seriousness of the injury, the case fell under the jurisdiction of the Guayama district judge, Don Miguel Monreal, who eventually directed the investigation and trial of González on charges of assault.

The significance of this case lies not merely in González's reaction to what he perceived as an insult and a lack of discipline and respect on the part of one of his plantation subordinates or in the fact that González almost escaped punishment as a result of the connections between the hacienda's co-owner and local authorities. It is also noteworthy because the testimony of González's defense counsels, Don Guillermo Alvarez and plantation co-owner Don Joaquín Villodas, also a lawyer, provide a glimpse into the internal dynamics of sugar plantations and the view of some of those dynamics prominent members of the local elite a decade after the abolition of slavery. Alvarez was a medium-sized merchant, former slave owner, and member on various occasions of the Guayama municipal council by appointment of the island's Spanish governors. Villodas not only in practical terms co-owned the plantation where the incident happened but had been part owner (along with his siblings and Calimano Martínez) of the now-defunct Hacienda Agueda. Alvarez and Villodas argued to Judge Monreal that it was imperative that plantation overseers such as González be allowed to severely punish insubordination by their peons. As an overseer in charge of a sugar plantation, González

> needs . . . all the moral prestige and authority that should be part [of the privileges] of the representatives of other interests that as in this case have been conferred upon him; and it is the duty of all authorities to give their help and support to the honest and laborious man that is put in these circumstances, especially in the time that we are experiencing now, in which demoralization and disorder are spreading and undermining the *jornalero* masses, who fail to provide respect other than to the authorities who repress and punish their excesses.

> As your honor will understand, the position of a *mayordomo* such as González is made difficult and painful when he lives isolated on

a farm located near the shoreline, far from the township, and surrounded by *jornaleros*, men formed in the utmost ignorance by lack of
education and resolute and constant enemies of the person directly in
charge of overseeing the completion of the responsibilities of their
assigned tasks.

This unjustified animosity, which unfortunately has progressively
increased in recent times, provoked the incident that occurred between the *jornalero* Angel Ledeé [*sic*] and the *mayordomo* Don José
González. . . .

González is not a genteel man, but he is faithful in carrying out his
mission of not allowing his *jornaleros* familiarities and liberties im-
proper for their condition, and this provokes among them the desire
to tease him, to aggravate [him], and to make him desperate, and in
the end to take him to extremes like the one that motivated these
charges.

Alvarez and Villodas continued to address the need to uphold the authority of plantation *mayordomos* over and above any considerations of criminal justice, stating that Ledeé had been "carried away by the desire, inherent among this sort of peoples, to mortify and mock their superiors."
Alvarez and Villodas interpreted Ledeé's comment as meaning that the
mayordomo was a "useless, laughable, and despicable being," since this
was the "genuine" meaning of the phrase "*carpintero de mocho*" "in the
jargon of the *jornalero* people of this country." This phrase was so inju-
rious that it would have "blind[ed] and enrage[d] the most prudent
man." Such arguments, however, failed to sway the judge, and on 24
November 1884, seven months after the incident took place, the Juzgado
de Primera Instancia found Don José González guilty and sentenced him
to one month in jail plus indemnification of medical expenses and lost
wages to Ledeé.[5]

Planter concerns that the *libertos* maintain "proper" conduct were not
restricted to openly deferential behavior in the workplace or toward colo-
nial/local authorities. There was also an underlying sensitivity to the issue
of people's "proper place" in society, a sense of place derived from slavery.
Only from this perspective is it possible to understand why municipal
council of Guayama, with one of the island's largest concentration of
people of African descent, would prohibit the celebration *bailes de bomba*
inside the township. The *bomba* was the foremost Afro–Puerto Rican

musical genre in the nineteenth and very early twentieth centuries and had evolved in a process of syncretism of African, Spanish, and non-Spanish Caribbean cultures. These dances, possibly named for one of the Bantu words for "drum," consisted primarily of an ensemble of musicians who played drums varying in size, form, and pitch; singers who performed songs that included words of seemingly African origin; and dancers who danced in time to the beat of the leading drum.[6]

The *bailes de bomba* had been commonplace on the sugar plantations since slavery times, and on some occasions slaves used the celebrations to conspire to rebel against their oppression.[7] Indeed, the 1826 slave *reglamento* decreed that slave owners should allow their slaves to engage in their "*bailes de bombas de pellejo*" but restricted the gatherings to the slaves of each specific plantation and ordered that they could be held only on Sunday afternoons (in broad daylight) within the hacienda compound and within clear view of the slave owners or the overseers.[8]

These restrictions apparently were not uniformly enforced: for example, slaves seem to have enjoyed *bailes de bomba* on Saturday evenings, with the participation of slaves from different haciendas, and with little direct supervision by their masters or overseers, as is evidenced by the details of the 1871 criminal case against Sebastián, a slave from Guayama's Hacienda Bardeguez, for the murder of Juan Domingo, a slave from Hacienda Palmira. The two men fought on Sunday, 5 November, and Juan Domingo emerged so seriously injured that he died two days later. Their dispute had originated in a disagreement the previous night, when they were gambling with other slaves from different plantations at the *cuarteles* of Hacienda Bardeguez during a *baile de bomba*. In attendance were slaves from various Guayama plantations, although it is not known exactly how many. Witness testimonies before the court indicated that *bailes de bomba* were customarily held on Saturday evenings and that the gamblers included slaves from Haciendas Pica, Barrancas, Aurora, and Palmira.[9]

Given the fact that the island's slave code expressly restricted the slaves' recreational activities, it is not surprising that the Guayama district judge would question the administrator of Hacienda Bardeguez about such a permissive happening. Don Gerardo Garriga denied that slaves had been permitted to engage in "illicit games" (gambling) and stated that his policy was to deny entry to his plantation to slaves from other estates unless they were authorized to come by their masters, as the government regulations ordered. Garriga admitted, however, that he permitted the slaves of his plantation "to dance the *bomba* on certain Saturdays, and this recreation moves the slaves themselves to invite their friends from other haciendas, but as can be expected this is not authorized by [me] or by my subordinates. Yet when it does happen, we order all strangers to leave between eight and nine in the evening, leaving the rest to enjoy themselves until the time when the *mayordomo* orders them to return to their quarters."[10]

After abolition, *bailes de bomba* continued to be held on some of the plantations where many *libertos* remained resident. But with the migration of scores of freedmen and -women to the township, they naturally tried to perform their dances there as well. This new development, however, did not please the local white elite. On a Sunday in January 1882, for example, a group of people (presumably including a number of *libertos*) began a *baile de bomba* on Marina Street, a long north-south thoroughfare in Guayama with many *libertos* living at its south end. Mayor Calimano Martínez, a former planter, sent the chief of the municipal police to order the musicians, dancers, and bystanders to suspend the celebration. However, the municipal council found the mayor's actions insufficient. At a council meeting held a few days later, one of its members, Spanish attorney Don Miguel Zavaleta y Llompart, delivered a long and furious speech against the toleration of *bailes de bomba* inside the township. Zavaleta argued, among other things, that "the *baile de bomba* that was held the last Sunday on Marina Street demonstrated the undesirability of permitting such [events], and even less so in the center of the township, not only because of the boisterous [*escandaloso*] nature of the instruments used in these diversions but also because they are to some extent even immoral."

Zavaleta ended his attack by asking the council to adopt an ordinance that would expressly prohibit *bailes de bomba* in the township, allowing them only "at a long distance" away. The ordinance also ordered the local authorities to forbid people "from the second class" from attending the *bailes de bomba* ("*y que en ellos no se permita concurran las personas de la segunda clase*"), undoubtedly a reference to artisans.[11] The municipal council approved the ordinance, and the open celebration of *bailes de bomba* in the township of Guayama was forbidden thereafter. Thirty-three years later, on 4 February 1915, Guayama's city council ratified this prohibition but restricted it to the inner core of the urban perimeter, allowing for the first time "*bailes de bomba o tambor*" in the slums that had mushroomed around the township since the abolition of slavery.

A 1911 municipal ordinance also ratified the 1882 prohibition but allowed the celebration of other musical expressions regarded in Puerto Rico as of more "Hispanic" origin, such as *parrandas* and *serenatas*. As the nineteenth century progressed, Spanish and creole elites seem to have become increasingly uncomfortable with the character of Puerto Rican popular festivals. In 1878, for example, the Spanish governor issued a circular expressing his concern regarding the long duration of patron saint festivals (*fiestas patronales*), which, although slated to last for only "one, two, or three days are extended to fifteen, twenty, and sometimes up to a month." The governor saw no justification for this custom and sought local officials' advice as he prepared to issue a decree restricting these celebrations. The governor stated that he was appalled by their alleged negative effect, since the festivals "lead to upsetting the moral life of peoples, to fomenting vagrancy habits, so unfortunately prevalent in the island, [and] produce injury to moral and material interests in general."[12]

It is important not to overlook the other aspect of Zavaleta's 1882 ordinance, the prohibition on members "of the second class" attending the dances of those regarded as members of Guayama's lowest class and race stratum. The ordinance was consistent with the white propertied classes' views of the country's race and class structure and reflected the elite's fears that the mingling of *libertos* and artisans could produce an alliance that would challenge the existing class- and race-based structure.

Indeed, studying Guayama's history during the nineteenth and early twentieth centuries brings to the fore the powerful image of a society with a keen sense of class and racial order and place. In 1884, for example, when Don Hipólito Montes, a Haitian-born mulatto businessman, posted broadsides all over town announcing festivities to mark the opening of his new "Cafe-Restaurant y Hotel Español," he made an effort to allocate the proper time, space, and type of event for Guayama and Arroyo's three major social groups: the white elite, the artisans, and the *libertos*. The first evening would be capped by the inauguration of the establishment's carousel and a gala ("*baile de confianza*") for ladies and gentlemen and "enlightened" youth. The third day of festivities would be highlighted by a formal dance for the artisans held not in Montes's hotel but in another café. The celebrations would conclude with a formal dance ("*baile de etiqueta*") for the *libertos* to be held at the house of a mulatto mason, Hipólito Sargentón.[13] Of note here are not only the separate dates and places for the different groups' celebrations but also the order in which the different festivities were to be held.

Guayameses did not completely lose this sensitivity to proper order and space with the advent of U.S. colonialism and the passing of time. The 1931 festivities in honor of Guayama's patron saint, San Antonio, were marked by similar notions of class/race/ethnic status and space. On a Thursday, the fifth day of the "*grandes fiestas patronales*," the organizers planned a grand gala ("*suntuoso baile de sociedad*") at the Club Puertorriqueño, an elite private establishment. The highlight of the weeklong fiestas would occur on the seventh evening, when three different dances would be held: a "*gran baile de sociedad*" at the Casino Español at 9:30 P.M.; a "*baile de obreros*" (basically for the artisans who dominated the organized labor movement) at 10:00 at an unknown location; and an Afro–Puerto Rican dance ("*gran baile de bomba*") at 9:00 at an establishment run by Tito Curet, a descendant of the slaves of Hacienda Santa Elena.[14]

Conflict Within: Interpersonal Violence

The niceties of status and place reflected in these cultural events represented only one aspect of the expression and maintenance of Guayama's social order. To keep the mass of disenfranchised rural and urban folk at bay implied a need to maintain their correct civil behavior. At the time of abolition, the Spanish government as well as the planters were particularly concerned about the possibility that emancipation could bring about an increase in criminal activity among the ex-slaves. In June 1873, for example, Puerto Rico's Real Audiencia (the island's supreme court of justice) asked district judges to report on the number and types of criminal charges brought against ex-slaves. The court was expressing its fear that emancipation could propel the *libertos* into committing numerous acts of so-called antisocial behavior, but only a few months had passed since emancipation, and it was too soon for any major changes to have become evident in the criminal courts. Most *libertos* had been focused on celebrating the announcement of abolition, on beginning to experience their newly acquired freedom, and on responding to government and planter efforts to compel them to enter into new forced-labor contracts in the midst of the sugar harvest.

Some judges' comments in response to the *audiencia*'s request are, nevertheless, very telling about elite attitudes not only toward the *libertos* but also toward rural laborers in general. From Guayama, Judge Don Mariano Canencia y Castellanos responded that only four criminal cases had been filed against *libertos* in his district, so he had seen no direct negative effect of emancipation on behavior. In his response, however, he commented more on the failure of the regulations governing the process of *contratación* than on the criminality of the freedmen and -women.

The response of the judge from the eastern judicial district of Humacao was even more revealing, expressing the views of the generally conservative planter elite. The number of crimes committed by *libertos* in his district had been very few to that point, he said, but he expected an eventual increase because the ex-slaves' "instincts and inclinations have in general tended toward abhorring any type of work and because to sustain themselves in their ingrained habit of vagrancy and other vices inherent to it, they will necessarily have to conspire to attack property, taking what is not theirs, falling into all kinds of excesses from which the present system of forced [labor] contracting, even if modified, will not suffice to restrain them unless it is combined with another regulation that organizes productive labor . . . , and [unless] a vagrancy law is enforced."

Conversely, the response from the district judge from Ponce emphasized his belief that ex-slaves' crimes were and would remain only common crimes, like those committed by the rest of the island's population. He expected a rise in the number of cases of theft but only because that was "not a crime but a custom . . . that the *libertos*, especially those dedicated to agricultural work, have of pilfering . . . produce, which sometimes they eat and at other times they sell." This "custom," he added, had been part of their behavior during slavery, and abolition would not influence it except by increasing the number of prosecutions. Slave owners had either tolerated pilfering or punished it privately, but now punishment would come under the aegis of the criminal justice system.[15]

Were crimes against property the major "deviant" expression of the *libertos* or of other rural and urban folk in the 1870s? Clear answers are difficult to come by because of the absence of readily available criminal statistics or studies of criminality for the nineteenth century. Some information can be gathered, however, from the collection of criminal records of the Juzgado de Primera Instancia of the district of Guayama from 1870 to 1879. The 179 surviving *expedientes* include 35 cases of theft—5 for 1870–72, 7 for 1873–76, and 23 for 1877–79. In addition, the group includes 13 cases of burglary—6 for 1870–72, 2 for 1873–76, and 5 for 1877–79. Only a small fraction of those 48 cases involved ex-slave defendants: 3 cases of theft in 1873–76 (two involving the same individual), and 5 such cases in 1877–79. Physical assault and injury in a fight (*"lesiones"* and *"riñas"*) represented at this level of the criminal justice system a similar proportion of the cases from Guayama. Forty-eight such cases occurred during the 1870s: 15 in 1870–72, 9 in 1873–76, and 24 in 1877–79. In 3 1873–76 cases and 4 1877–79 cases, the defendants were *libertos*.

Yet these figures are limited by the fact that they represent *expedientes criminales*—that is, cases that merited formal investigations by the district judge—rather than criminal complaints or convictions. Moreover, because of the way the criminal justice system was structured at this time, the district court would investigate and prosecute only cases that appeared to be felonies. Both theft and burglary were felonies, but physical assault constituted a felony only if the victim took more than eight days to recover from his or her injuries. Therefore, other sources of information must be obtained on the "criminal behavior" of Guayama's rural folk during this period. A look at some of the surviving daily reports of Guayama's urban police, the Cuerpo de Orden Público, for 1877–78, for example, can assist in the determination of the kinds of social behavior that called the attention of township authorities. Of the ninety-nine persons arrested by the *guardias de orden público* during November–December 1877 and January–September 1878, thirty-six were cited for being without their identity papers, twenty-one for disturbing the peace (*"promoviendo escándalo"*), sixteen for being vagrants, three for fighting, and two for drunkenness. Eighteen others were arrested on the mayor's orders with no specific reason spelled out. Those arrested for lacking identity papers included people from places as far away as Vega Baja, a sugar *municipio* on the north-central coast.[16] In addition, the surviving daily reports of the Guayama municipal jail for February–May 1883 confirm that the most common offenses dealt with by the municipal judge were brawling or disturbing the peace, mistreatment or abuse (*"maltrato,"* often of a family member), and physical assault; only two individuals each were committed for trespassing, damaging property, and scuffling. Only five committed individuals could be identified as *libertos*.[17]

Conflict Without: Incidents of Protoproletarian Resistance

"Fire! Fire!" the plantation manager heard people shouting from the hacienda's central square. Dressing and running down the stairs as quickly as possible, Don Hutton Potts, the British manager of Arroyo's Hacienda Cuatro Calles, took charge of the *libertos'* firefighting efforts. A barn full of *bagazo* (haylike dried sugarcane refuse) was burning. The inferno raged all night, consuming the entire building. Potts realized that the barn that had burned was the only one on the plantation full of *bagazo* and that the fire had apparently started in a lower corner. His overseer, a Dane, Don Enrique Falsen, confirmed the suspicions: the fire had to be arson because the barn had been surrounded with fresh, moist bagasse to prevent the piles of dried bagasse in its interior from accidentally catching fire. Furthermore, the next morning, plantation officials noticed that the mesh fence that encircled the barn had been cut.[18]

If this fire was arson, who set it? Arroyo's mayor and the Guayama district judge began trying to answer that question on the night of the incident. The extant records of their investigation and the prosecution of the case are incomplete, without the section concerning the trial and adjudication, but the surviving documents, as well as the other criminal files dealing with hacienda fires in the district during the 1870s and 1880s, provide insight into some of the realities of plantation life and work in late-nineteenth-century Puerto Rico.

Not all threads in the social fabric of the sugar lowlands were characterized by state or planter measures of social control, conflicts among the plebes, or attempts to move away from the original plantation setting. As important as these threads were in creating this society's particular colors and patterns, another thread ran mostly beneath them, surfacing only occasionally. Those *libertos* and other *jornaleros* who remained or were pulled into the plantation orbit had to have ways of expressing their frustrations with plantation life and with planters' attempts to more completely control the labor force.

Yet Puerto Rico, still a Spanish colony, was not the best setting in which laborers could openly express their grievances against their employers and patrons. Spanish law made it illegal to organize labor unions as well as to walk off a job in combination with fellow workers as a means of expressing dislike of present conditions or of demanding improvements.[19] Consequently, laborers in Puerto Rico, as in many other similar societies, had to resort to other methods of expressing their grievances against laboring and living conditions or against particular planters and their proxies. More often than not, postemancipation plantation laborers resorted to tactics previously developed by slaves. The literature on slavery in the Americas has studied the various forms of resistance and protest used by plantation slaves, including shirking of assigned tasks and stealing ("taking") or sabotaging plantation property and/or produce. Indeed, the slaves developed a wide array of ways of demonstrating their feelings about the system as a whole and about specific acts or policies of particular planters, overseers, and drivers.[20]

Some scholars have outlined striking continuities in the forms in which slaves and ex-slaves and their descendants protested openly and directly against the propertied classes. Using slavery and postemancipation rebellions in Jamaica, Guyana, and Barbados, Michael Craton has pointed to the similarities between late-slavery and postemancipation revolts not only in formal terms but also in content, what he identifies as the struggle not merely to improve conditions of life but also to obtain, defend, or recover access to land for peasant class formation.[21] However, just as open revolts were not a yearly—let alone daily—occurrence during slavery, postemancipation plantation laborers had to resort to other forms of expressing immediate grievances or latent cravings for justice and/or revenge, particularly as long as organized and open forms of resistance were considered social or political crimes and the opportunity for open revolt had not yet emerged. Indeed, just as in the case of open revolt, it is necessary to ask how much continuity was maintained between everyday pre- and postemancipation forms of resistance and accommodation.

The answer involves a systematic study of forms of behavior for both the slavery and postslavery periods. Until 1870, Puerto Rico's southeastern *municipios* were part of a judicial district based in the town of Caguas, located in a central valley north of Guayama. This judicial district was abolished in 1870, and its records seem to have been lost. The criminal records of the new judicial district of Guayama, created in 1870, are extant, but they include proceedings from only the last three years of the slave period. Moreover, the investigation and prosecution of one of the

most potentially violent yet covert forms of protest on sugar plantations—the burning of estate fields, buildings, and produce—appears to
have been transferred from the civilian to the military judicial system as
part of the judicial reforms of the late 1880s.[22]

This particular type of crime, with its potential to represent a form of
protest, well illustrates many of the realities of life in the sugar coastlands
of postslavery southern Puerto Rico. Scholars have argued, for example,
that the intentional burning of plantation property trailed only theft as a
common slave offense in the U.S. South. Moreover, after emancipation
occurred in Trinidad, arson remained "one of the fears of the planter
class." Other writers, however, have questioned whether reading newspaper accounts or contemporary reports provides an accurate accounting
of the widespread nature of arson, since such documents reflect the bias
of the era's elite. Given the limited sophistication of forensic investigations into the causes of fires during most of the nineteenth century,
officials and victims often assumed intent and blamed the slaves. With
regard to the U.S. South, Eugene Genovese has argued that a "large
proportion of southern white opinion, especially in the cities, had so little
confidence in the loyalty, contentment, and docility of the slaves that it
regularly assumed the worst." But precisely because of arson's potential as
a covert "weapon of the weak," to use James Scott's phrase, it remained a
cause of planter and state concern after emancipation. Torching plantation property attacked directly the most tangible symbol of planter economic, social, and political domination.[23]

Law enforcement officials and planters had great difficulty determin-
ing whether fires had been accidental or provoked, and it is even more
difficult for historians to do so more than a hundred years later. Nevertheless, the value of studying these incidents goes beyond the issue of
whether they were ever proven to be arson. It is important to look beyond
the official criminal statistics, newspaper accounts, and contemporary
reports written by officials, planters, or "independent" observers and to
focus on the investigations and on prosecutions whenever they occurred.
Such an approach raises the question of what this behavior represented in
precapitalist societies such as postemancipation Puerto Rico.

I found complete records for twenty-seven southeastern coastal hacienda fires from the 1870s and 1880s. In addition, I located a reference to
an 1873 fire and the file of an 1884 fire that directly referred to two other
plantation fires that took place at another hacienda on the same evening.

Thus, a total of thirty hacienda fires are known to have occurred in the Guayama region between 1871 and 1887. Only two fires occurred before the end of slavery (one each in 1871 and 1872), eleven took place 1871 and 1878; and sixteen occurred between 1880 and 1887. For the period of the *contratación* (1873–76), files survive for only five hacienda fires, while thirteen files were located for 1880–84.

Nine affected haciendas were located in Guayama, nine were in Arroyo, four were in Patillas (all on the same estate), six were in Maunabo, and two were in Salinas. An 1880 fire in Arroyo affected four contiguous haciendas, and another plantation in Maunabo was set aflame in two different places on the same night. In total, these fires affected sixteen haciendas. Those that suffered the most were Palma in Arroyo (twice in 1880, once each in 1883 and 1884), Felícita in Patillas (1873, 1880, 1882, 1886), Deseada in Arroyo (1872, 1877, 1880), and Merced (1874, 1878) and Olimpo (1875, 1881) in Guayama.[24]

These surviving files represent fires reported to and investigated by the Juzgado de Primera Instancia of the judicial district of Guayama (mostly by the judge himself, but often by the municipal magistrates who during the 1870s served as the *alcaldes ordinarios* of the *municipios* where the incidents took place). Unreported fires or those that were not investigated because the initial report to the judge made it plain that they were accidents did not result in criminal proceedings. It follows, therefore, that the recorded fires were not prima facie accidents that arose from the normal day-to-day operations of a sugarcane plantation. As late as the 1970s, plantation managers often set cane fields on fire to destroy cane leaves and weeds and to facilitate the cutting, picking, and transportation of cane stalks.

Nineteenth-century plantations often conducted ongoing controlled burning of wood and cane refuse used to operate steam-powered grinding mills, to boil the cane juice and make molasses, and in some instances, especially toward the end of the century, to operate centrifugal machines to separate sugar crystals from molasses. Thus, an accident in any one of these operations could easily occur within or near the millhouse or the boiling house. Moreover, plantation dwellings of course included kitchens, where accidental fires could start. In either setting, when initial investigations determined that fires were accidental, no formal judicial file was generated.

Of the twenty-seven cases for which detailed information is available, eighteen were regarded by the plantation management and the court to be arson, although only four investigations resulted in the prosecution of specific individuals, three of whom were found not guilty and only one of whom was convicted. Eight other cases were thought to have been "casual" occurrences—the product of someone's carelessness in throwing a cigar—or the result of spontaneous combustion as a result of severe drought.[25]

The most common objects that burned in these plantation fires were the deposits of cane refuse, known as *ranchos de bagazo*. Fifteen fires completely or partially destroyed these *ranchos*, which were usually located next to the sugar mills. In one additional case, the fire was set on piles of *bagazo* sitting next to a barn. The frequency of *bagazo* fires should not be surprising given the highly combustible nature of the dried cane refuse.[26] The next-most-common subject of fires was the cane fields. Seven fires occurred in fields with standing cane, and three additional fires took place in harvested fields that had only cane ratoons or "cane pasture" standing. In another case, a plantation barn where clay bricks were made and stored was set on fire.

Most of these plantation fires took place during the sugar harvest months (January to June), and many occurred at nighttime: five fires occurred roughly between 7:00 and 9:00 P.M.; seven were set between 10:00 P.M. and midnight; seven took place between 1:00 and 5:00 A.M.; and eight fires took place between 6:00 A.M. and 1:00 P.M. It is important to note the time of the day of each fire to correlate it with the suspicion of arson. Did fires regarded as intentionally set occur more commonly during late night than during the daytime? Not necessarily. In fact, three fires believed to be arson occurred during daylight hours (from about 6:00 A.M. to 6:00 P.M.), four between 7:00 and 9:00 P.M., six between 10:00 P.M. and midnight, and five from 1:00 to 5:00 A.M.[27]

The most common explanation for fires where specific details of evidence suggesting foul play were lacking might be called the "cigar theory." Cane fields or deposits of cane refuse located near roads or accessible communal paths could be set on fire by the carelessness of a passing smoker who threw a still-ignited cigar into the field or *bagazo*.[28] In some instances, such a conclusion was reached by default when no direct evidence existed to rule out the possibility of an accident. Guayama's district attorney expressed well the frustration of the police and the court when he summed up his recommendation to discontinue action in one particular case: "Not having determined the cause of the fire and having exhausted all the prescribed methods to uncover it, it would be gratuitous to state that it was intentional or coincidental as well as to establish or not establish that there was a criminal element."

The feeling of frustration was particularly understandable in this case, in which the fire occurred between two and three in the morning, when the sugar mill was shut down and everyone was asleep, but frustration frequently recurred among the planters and authorities investigating and prosecuting hacienda fires.[29] Yet while the majority of the witnesses and/ or the judicial authorities deemed intentional only three of ten 1870s cases, all but three of seventeen fires during the following decade were considered the result of arson, including three cases in which charges were for the first time formally brought against hacienda laborers.

In another telling example, after an 1883 fire, the *mayordomos* of Hacienda Puerto of Guayama, Don Ignacio Peláez and Don Juan Cabrera, strongly suspected that five carts of cane refuse had been set on fire by one of the hacienda's resident peons, Gervasio Villodas, a *liberto*. But the court had to drop the case when Villodas came up with an alibi supported by his common-law wife and a neighbor. The basis of the overseers' suspicions was an earlier dispute when Villodas had asked Peláez for some money on credit and was turned down. Curiously, Villodas, a heavily indebted peon, had not been working on the hacienda most of the day yet suddenly appeared at the scene to help others extinguish the fire. An important factor in convincing the court not to bring formal charges against Villodas was the collection of testimonies of other hacienda laborers who disbelieved that Villodas's rage over the denial of credit could have made him take direct revenge against plantation property and who consistently put forth the theory that the *bagazo* had burned as a result of a cigar thrown by a passer-by.[30]

Even if this fire was labeled accidental, it did contain several key elements found in many other cases that were adjudged to be arson: the type and location of the burned objects, the location where the flames started, the behavior of laborers during the firefighting efforts, and the conflicting relationship between the laborers and the plantation owners, managers, and overseers. Even though only four cases resulted in arson prosecutions, in other instances plantation owners, managers, and *mayordomos* undoubtedly believed fires to be arson and suspected particular individuals. Indeed, the routine for plantation fire investigations involved asking the persons in charge of the plantation to assess whether they considered the fire to be intentional. If the plantation management believed that it could have been arson, the court would inquire about recent disputes with plantation laborers and about laborers' or neighbors' reactions to the firefighting effort.

Two consistent patterns emerge regarding judicial authorities' and plantation management's ability to ascertain the origins of hacienda fires, especially in cases where arson was clearly suspected. First, most plebeian witnesses tended to emphasize that they did their utmost to fight the flames and particularly to alert people about the fire and to help douse it. Such accounts appeared in the investigations of fires at Haciendas Carmen in Salinas (1871), Quebrada Salada in Arroyo (1878), Merced in Guayama (1878), and Palma in Arroyo (1880).[31]

The Palma fire of 1880 was perhaps the most revealing because the only suspect in this instance, *liberto* Antonio Viñas (originally from Guayama), was saved from prosecution by the single detail that he had rung the plantation bell to alert residents and neighbors in spite of the fact that he had an acute toothache (or so he claimed). Viñas had had a confrontation with the plantation's first overseer, Corsican Don Lázaro Parodi, just three hours before the fire was detected. At six in the morning, Parodi had ordered the seizure of a mare, property of Antonio, for grazing unauthorized in a cane field. According to Don Domingo Juliani, the deputy overseer, Viñas was furious about the action, especially since the mare had been sent to the Arroyo jail and Viñas would presumably have to pay a fine to retrieve the animal. Juliani also alleged that fifteen minutes before the fire started, Viñas had told the first overseer that if he did not return the animal, he "would pay for it."

José Rivera, another peon on the hacienda, added that he had heard Viñas say, "This man has crossed the line [el hombre había llegado a la raya]." Rivera then joined the overseers in declaring that he thought Viñas responsible for the fire. Yet Viñas had an alibi of sorts: he claimed that he had rung the plantation bell, signaling residents and neighbors to come help fight the fire. And this fact, grudgingly confirmed by Parodi, saved Viñas from certain prosecution and possible conviction.

This investigation is also quite representative of the second major pattern in the criminal records. Hacienda laborers rarely if ever confessed to having seen, heard, or known any information that might lead to the prosecution of another resident peon. José Rivera was the only hacienda laborer in the case of the 1880 fire at Palma to speak against a fellow *jornalero*; all the others steadfastly proclaimed Viñas's innocence. Paula Capó, Abraham Sansón, Enrique Fantauzzi, Pedro (Perico) Sánchez, and Jacinta Fantauzzi (Antonio's companion), among others, supported Viñas's claims to innocence. Although these laborers claimed not to have seen or heard anything, they nevertheless put forth the theory that the fire had to be an accident. Even when the judge carried out a "*careo*," or direct verbal confrontation between conflicting witnesses—in this case, the *mayordomos* and José Rivera—the rest of the hacienda's peons continued to support Viñas. As a result, the case was eventually closed for lack of evidence.[32]

Several reported hacienda fires also illustrate internal conflicts in the postemancipation plantation setting and the attitudes of both plantation management and laborers. Far from a bucolic image of laborers and planters getting along well in the context of paternalistic labor relations, relations between laborers and the plantation power structure were often antagonistic, especially on haciendas managed by administrators and overseers in the name of local merchant houses or absentee planters, an arrangement increasingly common in the late nineteenth century.

Plantations such as Reunión, Esperanza, Merced, Palmas, Cuatro Calles, and Felícita, for example, were acquired by merchant houses such as Amorós Hermanos, A. Hartman y Compañía, and Fantauzzi Hermanos in the 1880s and 1890s. In addition, several prominent planter families left the region and returned to Europe, particularly to Catalonia and France, to live off the profits generated by some of the most profitable sugar plantations. Such was the case, for example, for the Massó-Verdeguer and Virella families, owners of Haciendas Bardeguez and Cayures, respectively, as well as the Clausell family, former plantation owners in Guayama who retained Hacienda Garonne in Maunabo. The traditional image of a resident planter who developed and maintained paternalistic relations with his personnel, formerly slaves and now free peons, thus slowly gave way to more detached vertical life and work relationships.

Hacienda Cuatro Calles came under the control of the St. Thomas merchant house Lamb y Compañía during the 1870s (probably after Lamb repossessed the hacienda from its former owners). By the turn of the 1880s, an Arroyo merchant house, Fantauzzi Hermanos, leased and managed Cuatro Calles. When the 1876 fire occurred, both the manager and the overseer of the plantation were non-Hispanic foreigners, with Potts serving as administrator and Falsen as the overseer. As discussed earlier, the two men believed from the outset that the fire had been arson. Several elements contributed to their perception: this particular ranch was the only one full of bagasse, making it an ideal target; it caught fire even though it had been surrounded by wet cane refuse to protect it; the fire had started in the interior of the ranch; and finally, the encircling metallic mesh fence had been cut at the rear of the building. Potts and Falsen also believed that the fire had been set by a *liberto*, Martin Lind, with whom they had had a confrontation ten to twelve days earlier, when he had cut and extracted sugarcane from the hacienda without management's permission. The confrontation had resulted in Lind's punishment by the mayor of Arroyo and his dismissal from the plantation weeks before the end of the forced *liberto* contracting period in 1876. Lind had been punished with several days labor on public works and was reputed to be working on a nearby plantation at the time of the fire. Furthermore, Potts declared and Falsen and other plantation witnesses concurred that on the night of the fire, while the shack was still burning, "one of the watchmen of the *batey* called [Potts's] attention, telling him that the black Martin Lind was among those fighting the fire and that [Lind] had told him that 'like the black man suffered his punishment, the white man would suffer his too' [que así como el negro sufría castigo, también el blanco los sufriría]."[33]

When Lind was interrogated, he vehemently denied having committed the crime, adding that he had helped to extinguish the flames by operating a water pump he had brought to Cuatro Calles under the instructions of Don Luis Ramiú, another example of one of the key strategies for demonstrating innocence. More importantly, however, Lind also denied that he had uttered the phrase attributed to him and that he had had any conversation with the watchman, Antonelo Sánchez.[34]

It is not known whether Martin was formally charged, prosecuted, or convicted in this case. However, surviving records show that other cases resulted in formal prosecutions, including an 1881 fire at Hacienda Orleanesa in Maunabo, an 1884 fire at Hacienda Palma in Arroyo, and an 1886 fire at Hacienda Felícita in Patillas. The discolored, molded pages of these judicial files yield rich details on the evolving world of sugar plantation life in the 1880s. These cases are marked by previous incidents between plantation management and sugar workers. Such incidents were not necessarily considered causes for the fires, but they set the tone of plantation management *jornalero* relations.

On the evening of 22 June 1881, the mayor of Maunabo heard the public shouting "the general voice of fire" at Hacienda Orleanesa, property of Don Otto Riefkohl. A barn full of bagazo had caught fire, and from the outset, Riefkohl believed that it was arson. First, he argued, because it was late June, the harvest had ended and therefore no plantation operations being requiring the burning of fuel were taking place. Second, that month had been rainy, thus reducing the odds of an accidental fire.[35]

The overseer of the plantation, Madrid native Don Constancio Recio, was more precise. To Riefkohl's argument, Recio added the point that the kitchens of the old slave quarters still used by the *libertos* were far removed from the burned building, and he listed a series of incidents that led authorities to identify suspects. Two days before the fire, Recio asserted, he had admonished Francisco Ortiz, who "had used as a road an alley of the hacienda where [public] transit is prohibited," and Ortiz did not seem pleased by Recio's admonition. Second, the day before the fire, Recio had surprised Germán Inglés, a West Indian immigrant laborer, "taking molasses from a barrel" in the sugar mill and had rebuked him. Finally, the night before the fire, Recio had found a tin pot with some molasses in the room that *liberto* Juan Riefkohl occupied in the old slave *cuarteles*, and "I had to slap him a few times for the lie of having told me that Germán Inglés had given it to him, which was false." Recio had apparently been aware for some time that laborers had been stealing from the hacienda and had put the deputy overseers on alert to identify the culprits.[36]

Recio had indeed admonished Germán Inglés, a native of St. Thomas, for stealing, but Inglés testified that "the despicable thought of vengeance" had never crossed his mind (*"ni se le pasó por la mente la rastrera idea de venganza"*). Juan Riefkohl, also known as Colorao (probably because he was a red-haired mulatto), quickly explained that had not participated in firefighting efforts because he was tired and his leg was hurting but that he had never thought of seeking vengeance against the plantation's management. He claimed that "he neither harbored the least vengeful feelings against Señor Recio that would lead him to commit the crime of burning the *rancho* nor believed that others could harbor such an idea, because vengeance, besides being despicable, would only bring losses to the owner of the estate, to whom he is grateful because he was raised on the plantation."[37]

Francisco Ortiz also accepted that he had been wrong to trespass on forbidden lands, adding that Recio had "told him that it was not a highway and had punished him for having injured the [watch]dog. He took from him his machete and gave him some slaps and kicks [quien le dijo que aquello no era camino, le reprendió por lo de herir el perro, le quitó el espadín, y dándole unos pescozones y patadas]." Ortiz, a mulatto in his early thirties, also tried to distance himself from the idea that he could have thought of avenging himself by burning the bagasse barn, since he "understood that he was somewhat guilty, in that incident, [and] was resigned to the slaps, without any idea of vengeance" remaining in his mind. Questioned a second time about whether he participated in the efforts to stop the fire, Ortiz "was erratic, saying only that he had thrown plantain leaves and buckets of water on the fire, but he could not pinpoint where the *alcalde* who gave him the plantain leaves or the buckets of water was, how many people were there, if the water pump was used, etc., and always alleged that he could not remember." Indeed, another witness, a fisherman, declared that he had asked Ortiz to go with him to help stop the fire but that Ortiz had declined. Nonetheless, Judge Miguel Bustelo found Ortiz not guilty despite concluding that arson had been committed.[38]

Finally, the only recorded hacienda fire in which a suspect was convicted occurred at the Fantauzzi Hermanos' Hacienda Palma in Arroyo on 17 April 1884. At 10:30 A.M., a barn and some cartfuls of bagasse had been consumed by flames. The overseer, Martinique native Don José Maconduit, immediately alleged that the fire was intentional because a considerable distance apparently lay between the bagasse and the sugar mill, thus reducing the odds that a flying spark from the mill had accidentally set off the fire. If so, how was the deed done, and could the often powerless local *comisario de barrio* or the mainly urban Cuerpo de Policía catch the culprit or culprits?

Augusto Santel, a *jornalero*, declared the next day that Sofía Lind, a *liberta*, had told him that Alberto Sánchez had started the fire. Her evidence was not that she had seen him but that shortly before the fire started, he had complained of indigestion and had gone behind the barn. Lind confirmed her story to the Guardia Civil, adding that Sánchez had also asked for a cigar butt and some papers and that when he returned shortly before the fire started, he was "quite unsettled and scared." Furthermore, Lind asserted that she had heard other people say that Sánchez had later bragged that "just as he had set fire to [this] *rancho*, he would do it to the hacienda's other [one]."[39]

This case is remarkable because it is one of very few in which the dreaded rural paramilitary police, the Guardia Civil, took an active role, and members of the Guardia Civil were responsible for obtaining the incriminating declarations that led to Sánchez's conviction. Furthermore, the Guardia Civil had obtained—by what means remains unknown—the crucial testimony from Lind, Sánchez's common-law wife. Lind had originally not provided incriminating testimony to the authorities, but she was questioned a second time and confronted with Santel's declaration, and, presumably under the threat of perjury charges or more severe physical coercion, she changed her story. Santel apparently was believed to have courted Lind, although the record lacks any overt evidence on this issue.

The intervention of the Guardia Civil in this case foreshadowed what apparently became common after the 1889–91 judicial reforms: the transfer of plantation arson cases from civilian to military courts. It remains unknown whether the introduction of the Guardia Civil and the military tribunals ended the rash of hacienda fires of the 1880s. In this instance, did the colonial state deliver to planters the support in controlling their labor force that they had sought during the 1870s and most of the 1880s? Only future research in Spanish military and civilian archives will help answer these crucial questions.[40]

Conclusion

In trying to guarantee a smooth transition from slavery and coerced labor to free wage labor, Puerto Rico's planters tried to develop policies to govern both the narrow question of labor relations and the wider issue of social order and control. On both counts, the *hacendados* promoted the kinds of social relations that seemed not to look forward toward free labor but to hark back to the days of slavery. These policies hardly represented a clear path toward the formation of a free labor market. Indeed, substantial segments of the rural laboring class, including the recently freed slaves, seemed to have striven toward a truly more "proletarian" status than their rural lords were willing to accept. The basis for this contradiction seems to have rested not only on the structural economic constraints that planters faced as they tried to industrialize sugarcane agriculture but also on their attempts to maintain broader social and political control over the island's landless peons and small peasants. The planters wished to become "*capitalistas azucareros*" (sugar capitalists) while remaining "*amos y señores*" (masters and lords of their class and race inferiors).

CONCLUSION

More than fifty years ago, concluding his land-mark study of slavery in Puerto Rico, Luis Díaz Soler wrote that "the roots of the social democracy that has developed in Puerto Rico are found in the historic evolution of black slavery" on the island, particularly in its limited character, in the remarkable prevalence of racial miscegenation fostered by Spanish liberal attitudes, and in the relatively smooth transition from slavery to freedom. Miscegenation, Díaz Soler wrote, served as "an unequivocal proof of the deep sense of tolerance, equality, and democracy gestating in Puerto Rico." Moreover, abolition and its implementation, he asserted, "offered an example of high culture in the magnificent spectacle of equal rights, an essential factor in the true freedom of man."[1]

Díaz Soler came to these conclusions not simply because his analysis was constrained by an overreliance on a historiography dependent on institutional and legal evidence, but also because his mind-set was immersed in the intellectual and political climate of his generation. The island's intelligentsia of the 1940s and 1950s not only considered the existence of a long historical tradition of racial democracy in Puerto Rico to be a natural, self-evident truth but also wholeheartedly believed in the political and economic "liberation" and progress brought by the populist modernization project of the period.[2] Such statements would certainly provoke intense debate in the island's contemporary intellectual environment: the historical research and cultural production that emerged during the last quarter of the twentieth century challenged dramatically the earlier intelligentsia's picture of the island's past by posing new questions and offering new interpretations of the evolution of Puerto Rican society. This book is an effort to reconnect with the earlier impulses of that revisionist historiography with respect to the topic of slavery and its aftermath. I have shown how an array of social actors sought to define important aspects of their lives in the midst of major constraints imposed by the nature of the island's colonial order, its specific links to a wider Atlantic economy, and the interplay between these and the particular political projects, small and large, that sought to define Puerto Rico as a highly hierarchical society of racial castes at the service of a tiny settler elite and its local creole allies.

The demise of slavery in Puerto Rico seemed to have been forced on the slaveholders by the structural characteristics of their sugar industry, the demographic conditions of slavery on the island, and the haphazard dynamics of Spanish colonial politics. The relatively small and financially weak Puerto Rican sugar industry did not allow planters to accumulate the capital resources needed to keep the illegal slave trade flowing after midcentury, in contrast to the experience of the better endowed and more resourceful Cuban planters.

Yet the end of the slave trade did not by definition mean the eventual disappearance of the island's slave population by attrition; rather, this phenomenon arose because of the slave population's apparent inability to reproduce itself after midcentury. The study of slave demographic patterns remains beyond the scope of this study but certainly represents an important ingredient in the mix of societal expectations about the continuing viability of slavery. Francisco Scarano has discovered that the fertility levels of Ponce's slave population in 1838 outstripped those of comparable populations in Jamaica at the end of the slave trade, even though the proportion of African slaves was higher in Ponce (53 percent to 45 percent) and male slaves predominated there by a ratio of 175 to 100 while a virtually balanced sex ratio existed in Jamaica.[3]

Assuming that Ponce was representative of Puerto Rico's principal slaveholding districts, the possibility that slaves had positive rates of population growth could have created the expectation among planters that the slave population would sustain itself even after the end of the slave trade. Nonetheless, even if future studies confirm this phenomenon at the midcentury mark, the fact is that disaster struck shortly thereafter in the form of the devastating 1855–56 cholera epidemic. This and other biological and social factors seem to have reversed the pattern previously thought possible, so that the island's slave population declined sharply until abolition in 1873.

The fact that the Puerto Rican slave population declined after midcentury has been interpreted as a sign that the planters began to manumit substantial numbers of slaves, especially during the 1860s, as the *hacendados* saw the end of slavery nearing and some slaves as expendable. Chapter 3 gives a sharply different picture, however. Guayama's planters held onto the bulk of their slaves until abolition, and most manumissions during the last years of slavery likely represented token expressions of benevolence. Furthermore, many slaves who had allegedly been manumitted had in fact self-purchased their freedom or had relied on free kin or other subaltern brethren to provide the substantial sums of money needed for liberty. Either way, these *coartado* former slaves had earned their freedom and had not received it as a gift of masters bent on disbanding slavery as emancipation loomed.

The free society that these preabolition *libertos* and the almost two thousand others emancipated in Guayama in 1873 joined was not an unknown, radically foreign world. First, at the time of emancipation, less than one-fifth of Guayama's slaves had been born in Africa, and even this small proportion had spent at least twenty years on the island. But more importantly, the lower echelons of the free society were more heavily Afro–Puerto Rican, at least in Guayama, than previous studies have suspected. Centuries of miscegenation among the settlers of southeastern Puerto Rico, coupled with the immigration of black and mulatto artisans from the Caribbean region and the trickle of manumitted slaves, had produced a peasant and plebeian society in Guayama that contrasted with traditional notions of nineteenth-century Puerto Rican society. Free people of color were the majority racial group in all but one of Guayama's barrios, and almost 40 percent of the landed peasantry were classified as nonwhite, including 50 percent in the highland barrios of Guamaní and Palmas. Moreover, in the township and coastal barrios where most of the *libertos* lived, the landless laborers, the social grouping that the vast majority of ex-slaves joined, were almost exclusively nonwhite.

However, the proportion of people in Guayama classified as "mulatto" or "black" diminished in the final decades of the nineteenth century. What does this illustrate about late-nineteenth-century Puerto Rican society? Excluding the possibility of a large-scale migration of Afro-Guayameses (which is difficult to document), differential white and nonwhite fertility and mortality rates could point the way toward a reassessment of living conditions and social attitudes for the island's two major racial groups.

That miscegenation fostered the passing of thousands of mixed-blood Guayameses as whites in the context of a highly racially structured society also should not be excluded as a possible explanation, as indicated by the fact that the 1871 census listed seven slaves as racially "white." It seems that even in heavily Afro–Puerto Rican Guayama, distance from black ascriptions was a tempting proposition given the legacy of slavery that seems to have remained alive well into the early twentieth century. This preliminary finding and this range of explanations suggest that it is necessary to continue questioning the received myths about a mythical "social democracy" and to pose hard questions about the character of Puerto Rican society before the 1898 U.S. invasion.

Emancipation did not come to Guayama at the invitation of its slaveholders, nor was it implemented gradually, as in Cuba. The halfhearted implementation of the 1871 Moret Law was quickly followed less than two years later by full abolition.

Guayama's planters could not have been in a worse predicament when called to face abolition. Southeastern Puerto Rico had begun to experience a severe drought in 1872, and Guayama's planters had been unable to put in place the irrigation systems proposed since the 1860s that could have cushioned the drought's impact. Moreover, the sugar industry was about to face the need to modernize its technology and reorganize the traditional hacienda system. These goals required substantial capital investments at precisely the same time that the island's sugar planters were constrained by an archaic credit system. Cash-starved planters were now forced to pay cash wages to their ex-slaves. Furthermore, to retain the *libertos'* labor, planters now had to compete with other planters, some of whom enjoyed healthier lines of credit or had plans to expand production with modern mills.[4]

To compound the *hacendados'* problems, a liberal colonial governor, Rafael Primo de Rivera, ostensibly a true believer in free labor markets, published a set of regulations for the three-year forced-contracting period that permitted *libertos* to terminate contracts unilaterally and enter into new ones and to work for employers other than their former masters, including nonplantation employers. Many *libertos* seem to have seized the opportunity to give a better character to their new freedom than many planters had envisioned. Seventeen percent of the *libertos* in the sample contracted themselves out more than once in 1873; more importantly, however, as many as half may have changed "masters," including three out of every four female ex-slaves, who became domestic workers, as discussed in chapter 5. By removing themselves from the rigors of field labor, Guayama's *libertas* compounded the planters' labor supply problems: women had constituted almost half of the slave field labor force.

Although new regulations issued in 1874 seem to have somewhat rescued the planters, Guayama's sugar output declined by almost half between 1872 and 1873 as a consequence of the combined disruptions of drought and abolition. More importantly, the experience showed that many *libertos* were more interested in a free labor market than in their former masters. The series of proposed labor codes of the mid- to late 1870s reveal a planter class still insecure about its ability to guarantee a steady, dependent labor supply through the mechanisms of a free labor market and more than subliminally interested in preserving its social (not just economic) command over the chattel slaves of yesterday.

The issue of occupational and geographical mobility became contentious in the transition to free labor. Local geographical conditions, the scarcity of land on a relatively densely populated island, and the weak legacy of protopeasant slave experiences curtailed ex-slaves' ability to become peasants. Indeed, local notarial records show only twenty-four cases of *liberto* land purchases between 1873 and 1898, half of them in the first three years following emancipation and none in the last ten years of Spanish rule in Puerto Rico. Because by the 1860s unopened Crown lands in the highlands were no longer being sold, the possibilities for peasantization were minimal, especially when the free peasantry was being weakened in the last decades of the century. Chapter 6 offered much evidence on these issues.

Therefore, as an expression of their freedom, Guayama's *libertos* put a premium on freedom of movement within and beyond *municipio* boundaries. Many moved to the urban township, others relocated to districts east and west of Guayama, and many of those who remained on Guayama's haciendas moved to estates other than those where they had been slaves. Planters sought to limit this freedom of movement through old and new legal restrictions, but the colonial regime again failed to deliver the types of policies that many planters wanted. Indeed, as Rebecca Scott has suggested, former slaveholders' attempts to maintain the isolation of plantation life and work by restricting *liberto* mobility and the corresponding *liberto* attempts to break that isolation became key "elements in the struggle over the meaning of freedom."[5]

The issue for the *libertos* was more than just a simple preference regarding residential patterns. Instead, they sought to distance themselves from the specific setting of the old plantation *cuarteles* of their original haciendas and to live with at least some measure of freedom. Explaining similar efforts by ex-slaves in São Paulo, Brazil, George Reid Andrews has argued that the "overriding concern was to place as much distance between themselves and their former status as slaves, and to ensure that their new conditions of employment bore as little resemblance as possible to servitude." Indeed, even when remaining as plantation workers, Andrews adds, Paulista *libertos* moved to different *fazendas* and generally insisted that working and living conditions be different: no whips, no locks on the doors of the old barracks, and preferably the allocation of individual huts far from the main plantation house.[6]

On another level, Guayama's *libertos* appear to have attempted in practice to claim equal membership in Puerto Rico's civil society. After all, the end of the three-year period of forced labor would bring "civil" rights for the *libertos*, and article 7 of the 1873 Abolition Law had promised the extension of "political" rights to the ex-slaves by 1878. Yet, when 1876 arrived, the island's colonial governor did not emphasize the need to help the *libertos* become aware of and use their civil rights or order the island's mayors to guarantee ex-slaves' rights. Rather, he instructed the mayors to remind the *libertos* of their sacred obligation to work and to obey the law.[7] Indeed, Guayama's local elite also seemed oblivious to the express mandate of the Abolition Law when they restricted the *libertos'* right to hold festivals in the urban barrios to which they had moved. In addition, in court proceedings, the elites attempted to discredit the value of *liberto* testimony, arguing for the preeminence of considerations of authority and order over the administration of justice.

Puerto Rican courts do not seem to have been the preferred forum in which plantation laborers vented their complaints against real or perceived injustices on the part of overseers or planters. To be sure, laborers used judicial proceedings to their advantage in some instances. When confronted with conflicts with plantation management, however, some sugar workers appear to have resorted to other forms of resistance, including setting plantation property on fire, as discussed in chapter 7. A rash of hacienda fires in the late 1870s and 1880s suggests that labor relations in the Guayama plantation belt were soured by the implementation of new policies to reduce labor costs and secure a labor force by mechanisms of indebtedness and the payment of wages in nonstandard currency as well as by the emergence of more business oriented, less paternalistic labor relations as merchants began to displace traditional *hacendados* as plantation owners.

These diverse *liberto* responses to emancipation imply that even in conditions of continued subordination in terms of class and race, the ex-slaves sought to define their freedom in their own terms. Though perhaps unsuccessful on many counts, they did not respond merely passively to the changes brought by abolition and the planters' efforts to maintain economic and social oppression. Indeed, as Scott has pointedly argued, emancipation "was neither a transcendent liberation nor a complete swindle, but rather an occasion for reshaping—within limits—social, economic, and political relationships." As historians continue to explore the aftermath of emancipation, it is necessary to understand that subordination was not simply accepted without attempts to adapt and reshape the ordained strictures of the state and the planter class. Puerto Rico's freedmen and -women were not merely passive elements in the island's society, easily restricted and controlled by Madrid's laws, San Juan's decrees, and the actions of local overlords, but genuine actors in the drama of the formation of the island's modern society.[8]

Subaltern strategies and tactics of survival and adaptive resistance—in particular, those tied to the defense of what one could label "social maronage" and rearticulated notions of freedom—serve as reminders of Gramsci's call for a "war of maneuver" as the antithesis of a "war of position." Puerto Rican subalterns, like many of their counterparts elsewhere, chose to engage hierarchies of power, old and newly emerging, primarily through hit-and-run and hide-and-seek tactics. That they chose this means of contestation rather than engaging in frontal, open attacks on the sociopolitical order of Spanish colonialism has often been interpreted as a failure, an insufficiency, on the part of Puerto Ricans—or, to be more nuanced, Puerto Ricans in the making—during the long Spanish reign over the island. Putting aside comparisons with continental Spanish American revolutions, the quintessential comparison for Puerto Rico is Cuba and its insurrectionary activity from 1868 to 1898.[9]

However, at the risk of being overly polemical, an alternative reading would suggest that the contrast between an allegedly pliant, subdued Puerto Rico and a belligerent, revolutionary Cuba would posit that Puerto Rican subalterns did not perceive Spanish colonial power as strongly, fully constituted, and effective in blocking spaces for interstitial survival and adaptive resistance.[10] Such an alternative reading would represent far from a denial of all the ways in which Spanish colonialism was abusive, tyrannical, authoritarian, racist, and patriarchal. This alternative reading proposes that a radical subaltern Cuban response to Spanish colonialism emerged in a context in which Spanish colonialism had achieved an accomplished and self-reproducing level of articulation, creating a slave plantation system far more intensive and efficient than in Puerto Rico. Furthermore, I believe that this alternative approach to a comparative analysis of Cuba and Puerto Rico could open new avenues for interpreting the history of both islands in relation to the unfolding of Spanish colonial projects and domestic national projects over the course of the nineteenth century.

In the end, this examination of Guayama's past provides three new perceptions. First, historians of nineteenth-century Puerto Rico need more explicitly to tackle the contradictory role played by the Spanish colonial state in the island's transition to capitalism. Some historians have emphasized the Spanish government's provision of a series of regulations intended to guarantee the planters a smooth transition away from slavery, from the forced-labor codes of midcentury to the forced contracting of *libertos* in the 1870s. Later historiography has tended to suggest that local colonial authorities, particularly the judiciary, were quite responsive to planters' plight as they tried to survive the financial difficulties after emancipation and the declining fortunes of Puerto Rico's sugar industry in the last three decades of the century.[11] Yet the impression that emerges from this study of Guayama is that while local colonial officials tried to appease planter concerns in the area of labor relations, Madrid failed to deliver policies that could have ensured Puerto Rican planters a more tightly controlled transition from slavery to free labor as well as the successful modernization of the island's sugar industry.

Second, the importance of race in shaping Puerto Rican society and culture needs to be explored in more detail and confronted in all its implications, notwithstanding efforts in this direction in the recent revisionist historiography and the cultural writings of authors such as José Luis González.[12] It is indeed revealing, for example, that the discourse of Guayama's civil society apparently remained ingrained in the values inherited from its painful experience with slavery even after the end of the Spanish regime.

Finally, historians need to continue to pursue aggressively a line of inquiry that does not see 1898 and the change of colonial regimes as a radical rupture with the island's legacies of Spanish colonialism. Andrés Ramos Mattei's efforts to study the patterns of continuity between the last decades of the nineteenth century and the early 1900s in the transformation of the island's sugar economy, Fernando Picó's incisive study of peasant banditry during the 1898–1900 American military occupation, and Eileen Suárez Findlay's study of the interplay between race and gender politics in Ponce before and after the Spanish-American War point to the need to follow through with a study of Guayama's society in the early decades of the twentieth century that is informed by a better understanding of that society before the arrival of U.S. troops.[13]

To emphasize this point, I will end this study with a revealing story of how Guayama's plebeians reacted to the crisis of the Spanish-American War in late July and August 1898. U.S. troops took over Guayama on 5 August, and seven days later the new military authorities confirmed that Don Celestino Domínguez would remain as the *municipio*'s mayor. During the last two decades of the Spanish regime, Domínguez had been a staunch proponent of self-government for Puerto Rico and an opponent of the pro–Spanish conservative majority among the local elite. Yet when the turmoil of war prompted popular anti-Spanish responses among some Guayameses, Domínguez came to the rescue of his former opponents. As the records of the municipal council relate the story, Domínguez "did not consent that peninsular Spaniards should be attacked and assaulted or perhaps looted and robbed . . . on the day that the American troops arrived in this town. On that day, these unbridled plebeians [*ese populacho desbordado*] were denouncing [the Spaniards] to the American troops, taking about forty of them to the jail. But Señor Alcalde Domínguez, always noble and genteel before all this injustice, intervened with the American military authorities . . . to attest to the neutrality of those Spaniards attacked and jailed at the instigation of the mob [*populacho*]."[14]

At least for a moment, Guayama's plebeians seem to have tried to seize an opportunity to vent their grievances against the most obvious and immediate representatives of the falling Spanish regime under which many people or their ancestors had been made slaves, forced laborers, and impoverished peasants. In just a few years, the masses would turn their attention to what they viewed as new and old preservers of the old legacies. These targets included not only Domínguez but also the American and Puerto Rican sugar *centrales* that compelled the plebeian descendants of *libertos* to become rural proletarians in the vast cane fields of Guayama's revitalized plantation belt.

NOTES

Abbreviations

AGPR   Archivo General de Puerto Rico, San Juan
AM   Actas Municipales
BHPR   *Boletín Histórico de Puerto Rico*
DM   Documentos Municipales
FGE   Fondo de los Gobernadores Españoles
FJG   Fondo Judicial de Guayama
FMG   Fondo Municipal de Guayama
FPN   Fondo de Protocolos Notariales
PP   Great Britain, Parliament, House of Commons, *Irish University Press Series of British Parliamentary Papers, Slave Trade*

Introduction

1 In the past decade, many issues addressed in this book have been framed within broader concerns with the African diaspora in the Americas as a whole. Hine and McLeod, *Crossing Boundaries*, offers a collection of essays from this perspective.

2 Restall and Landers, "African Experience"; Schwartz, "Black Latin America"; Knight, "Blacks."

3 See Appelbaum, Macpherson, and Rosemblatt, *Race and Nation*.

4 Significant discussions of Puerto Rican historiography, including the works of scholars cited throughout this book, appear in F. Picó, "Historiography." For slavery and emancipation specifically, see Scarano, "Slavery and Emancipation." An earlier though still useful discussion appears in Bergad, "Recent Research." For developments during the 1980s and early 1990s, see also Matos Rodríguez, "New Currents."

5 Zenón, *Narciso*; Sánchez, *Guaracha*; Díaz Quiñones, *Conversación*; Díaz Quiñones, *Almuerzo*; Díaz Quiñones, "Estudio"; Vega and Lugo-Filippi, *Vírgenes y mártires*; Vega, *Encancaranublado*; Vega, *Falsas crónicas*. See also Rodríguez Juliá, *Entierro*.

6 See esp. the title essay, "El país de cuatro pisos," as well as "Plebeyismo y arte en el Puerto Rico de hoy," both in González, *País*.

7 Ibid., 11.

8 Ibid., 20. Two important studies on the subject of Afro–Puerto Rican history for

this early period appear in Sued Badillo and López Cantos, *Puerto Rico*. Sued Badillo's essay deals with the sixteenth century, while López Cantos concentrates on the seventeenth and eighteenth centuries. Two important contemporary anthropological studies addressing Afro–Puerto Rican identity are Torres, "Blackness," and Godreau-Santiago, "Missing the Mix." See also Den Tandt, "All That Is Black"; Torres, "Gran Familia."

9 For various critiques of "El país de cuatro pisos," see, e.g., Flores, "Puerto Rico"; Maldonado Denis, "En torno *El país*"; Méndez, "Arquitectura intelectual"; Quintero Rivera, *Historia*.

10 González, *El país*, 18–38.

11 Curet, "From Slave to *Liberto*"; Ramos Mattei, "Liberto"; Martínez-Vergne, *Capitalism*; Martínez-Vergne, "New Patterns."

12 Curet, "From Slave to *Liberto*," 278; Ramos Mattei, "Liberto," 123. Curet's documentary challenge when studying the municipality of Ponce, however, does not necessarily apply elsewhere on the island. For example, Nistal-Moret ("Pueblo," 324–25) reported in the late 1970s that the term *liberto* continues to appear in the local population censuses of the northern coastal municipality of Manatí at least until the late 1880s. The methodological problems confronting almost any study of ex-slaves after emancipation are not unique to the Puerto Rican case but have until recently also hampered the developing of such studies in Brazil, for example, as Stuart Schwartz observed while reviewing a set of studies on Brazilian slavery published up to the mid-1980s ("Recent Trends"). It is quite illustrative to compare this review with a more recent one, also by Schwartz, of works on colonial Brazilian history published during the decade that followed his 1988 review ("Somebodies and Nobodies").

13 Exceptions to this phenomenon in plantation studies up to the mid-1980s included Taussig, *Devil*, and, partially, Rodney, *History*. A more recent and quite successful effort is Peloso, *Peasants*.

14 The classic study in English of the process of Spanish abolition is Corwin, *Spain*, although Rebecca Scott's *Slave Emancipation* has now justifiably achieved the status of the new classic. Schmidt-Nowara's research, conversely, represents the most comprehensive and theoretically innovative body of work to date on the political culture, ideological discourses, and political events that led jointly to the rise of Spanish abolitionism and the termination of Spanish colonial slavery. See, e.g., Schmidt-Nowara, "National Economy"; Schmidt-Nowara, *Empire and Antislavery*.

   For Puerto Rico, the standard interpretation until the late 1970s was Díaz Soler, *Historia*. Within the revisionist historiography on Puerto Rican slavery that emerged in the late 1970s and early 1980s, the principal works dealing more exhaustively with the abolition process were written by José Curet; see, e.g., Curet, "From Slave to *Liberto*"; Curet, "De la esclavitud"; Curet, "About Slavery."

15 See, e.g., Adamson, *Sugar*; Mandle, *Plantation Economy*; Eisenberg, *Sugar Industry*.

16 Best, "Outlines"; Moreno Fraginals, *Ingenio*; Bengoa, "Plantaciones."

17 Craton and Walvin, *Jamaican Plantation*; Craton, *Searching*; *United Fruit Company*; Baralt, *Buena Vista*; Higman, *Montpelier*.

18 See, e.g., Hoernel, "Comparison"; Karch, "Transformation"; Albert and Greaves, *Crisis and Change*.

19 Gonzales, *Plantation Agriculture*; Huggins, *From Slavery to Vagrancy*; Trotman, *Crime*.

20 The literature on everyday forms of resistance and crime as a form of class conflict grew steadily during the 1980s and 1990s. Some excellent comparative perspectives as well as provocative theoretical and methodological ideas can be drawn from recent works discussing "everyday forms of resistance" in settings such as Southeast Asia and Africa. Recent work in the Caribbean and the American mainland is available in Hine and MacLeod, *Crossing Boundaries*, pt. 3, 179–315, and is analyzed in Torres and Whitten, "General Introduction."

21 Social Science Research Council, *Items* 37:1 (1983): 29.

22 See, e.g., Skidmore, "Workers and Soldiers"; Sofer, "Recent Trends;" Evans, "Results and Prospects"; Winn, "Urban Working-Class." Much new work comparing the Caribbean and Central America is available in Chomsky and Lauria, *At the Margins*.

23 Evans, "Results and Prospects," 37.

24 For example, a mid-1980s annotated bibliography on Jamaican history listed only two articles on predepression labor history by Eaton, "Trade Union Development." In the case of labor history in the Dominican Republic, Calderón Martínez's survey, "Movimiento," lists just three articles and one book/pamphlet-length work, Peña Valdez's *Breve historia*. Meanwhile, Cuban labor historiography for the period before the Great Depression has only recently begun to be better served thanks to the works of John Dumoulin; see Dumoulin, "Primer desarrollo"; Dumoulin, "Movimiento"; Dumoulin *Azúcar*; Casanovas, *Bread or Bullets!* The richer and earlier Puerto Rican labor historiography will be discussed in more detail later in this chapter

25 For a survey of Caribbean labor historiography, see Haraksingh, "Labour Movements."

26 Social Science Research Council, *Items* 38:2–3 (1984). The slow incorporation of new social history's concepts and methods to the study of Third World labor history did not occur exclusively in Latin American studies.

27 Albert argued, "Important as it is, an account of the causes and results of strikes and unrest gives little more than a one-dimensional view of the process of class formation. Much more needs to be known about the participants, the relationship between different groups of workers, about the cultural and social milieu on the estates and in the nearby towns, about how and why working and living conditions varied between estates and valleys and over time." Yet his study deals very little with the formation of Peru's sugar proletarians' culture and consciousness: "the intricate problem of consciousness," he adds, "demands a far more detailed treatment" (Albert, "Creation," 111–12).

28 On the incorporation of anthropological perspectives into historical studies, see, e.g., Thomas, "History and Anthropology"; E. P. Thompson, "Anthropology"; Mintz, "History and Anthropology"; San Miguel, "Falero," offers a recent and suggestive reformulation in the Puerto Rican context.

29 The literature on gender and class is too vast to summarize here, but recent surveys of the Latin American and Caribbean historiography on gender offer useful assessments. See esp. Stubbs, "Gender"; Caulfield, "History."

30 Ramos Mattei, *Hacienda*; Quintero Rivera, "Background."

31 General historical works on Guayama include Sued Badillo, *Guayama*; Camuñas Madera, "Orígen"; Porrata-Doria, *Guayama*. The only specialized historical research monograph on Guayama is Oquendo, "Inmigración."

32 While slaves never reached more than 15 percent of the nineteenth-century Puerto Rican population, slaves represented from a fifth to almost half of Guayama's population from 1821 to 1867, reaching a peak of 41.2 percent in 1842 (Puerto Rico, *Censo general*; Scarano, *Sugar and Slavery*, 30–31; Sued Badillo, *Guayama*, 92–100).

33 Excellent general discussions of various key issues in the postemancipation social history of former slaves include Mintz, "Slavery"; Klein and Engerman, "Transition"; R. Scott, "Exploring."

34 On the transition from slavery to free labor in the Caribbean, see, e.g., Bolland, "Systems"; Craton, *Searching*; Green, *British Slave Emancipation*; D. Hall, *Free Jamaica*; D. Hall, "Flight"; Marshall, "Notes"; Moreno Fraginals, Moya Pons, and Engerman, *Between Slavery and Free Labor*; R. Scott, *Slave Emancipation*. See also Reddock's stimulating comments on women and the transition to free labor in "Women."

35 The relative importance of town vis-à-vis the countryside in sugar plantation areas varied greatly. In "Cañamelar," 391–94, Mintz correctly pointed out to the relative unimportance of the *pueblo* in Santa Isabel, as does, for example, Klaren, *Formación*, chap. 4, esp. 138, for the case of Peru's northern coastal plantations. However, Dumoulin and the authors of *United Fruit Company* call attention to the importance of the town/city in the case of Cruces and Cienfuegos and Banes, Cuba, respectively; see, e.g., Dumoulin, *Azúcar*, 57–58, 61; *United Fruit Company*, 243–44.

36 General works on Puerto Rican labor history include Quintero Rivera, "Clase obrera," pts. 1–5; García and Quintero Rivera, *Desafío y solidaridad*; Silén, *Apuntes*; Galvin, *Organized Labor Movement*.

37 A rare contemporary work dealing with a strike in Guayama is Echevarría Morales, *Proceso*, which discusses the 1923 regional sugar workers' strike. An important work by the Taller de Formación Política, *¡Huelga en la caña! 1933–34* presents some evidence on the militancy of Guayama's sugar workers in the 1934 islandwide wildcat strike.

38 Dening, "Comaroffs."

39 For a recent review of issues and the literature about this period in Puerto Rican history, see Ayala and Bergad, "Rural Puerto Rico."

Chapter One

1   Vázquez, "Descripción topográfica," 250.

2   Porrata-Doria, *Guayama*, 10.

3   Baralt, *Esclavos rebeldes*, 47–56; Ramos Mattei, *Hacienda*, 23–24; Ramos Mattei, "Liberto," esp. 108, 110–11; Ramos Mattei, "Las haciendas del litoral sur, 1880–1910," in *Sociedad*, 53–84; Scarano, *Sugar and Slavery*, 14–34, 131–32, 151.

4   Sued Badillo, *Guayama*. See also Oquendo, "Inmigración," a well-researched study of the impact of foreign immigration in the early nineteenth century.

5   Porrata-Doria, *Guayama*, 103–8. While reviewing briefly the history of agriculture, trade, and industry in Guayama, Porrata-Doria usually discusses developments from the sixteenth to the eighteenth centuries and then conveniently leapfrogs into the late nineteenth century. When talking about sugar, for example, he jumps from some remarks about its emergence in the late eighteenth century to its state of decline in the 1950s–60s. While describing Guayama's trade, he reviews the development of Puerto Rico's export trade in the late eighteenth century, only to continue with an enumeration of the leading Guayama merchant houses of the end of the nineteenth century. Only when addressing the history of local rum production does he mention sugar mills in the middle of the nineteenth century, and he states merely that "it was not until the mid–nineteenth century that the first rudimentary sugar mills began to appear."

6   Vázquez, "Descripción topográfica," 250.

7   Porrata-Doria, *Guayama*, 48–49. Porrata-Doria dedicates one page to the 1821 conspiracy in which Guayama's slaves helped to spark a general rebellion against the white population and Spanish rule in Puerto Rico. He says merely that slaves were manipulated by proindependence conspirators who raised the banner of abolition. The best discussion of this conspiracy, which also included the slaves of the eastern municipality of Naguabo, appears in Baralt, *Esclavos rebeldes*, 47–56. For a literary view of slave conspiracies and rebellions in Puerto Rico, see Baralt et al., *El machete de Ogún*.

8   Porrata-Doria, *Guayama*, 91. Porrata-Doria also avoids the issue of slavery when he tries to explain Guayama's nickname, Ciudad Bruja (City of Shamans): "The African, when imported, brought with him his idiosyncrasy and his primitive art of healing the body and the soul of his fellow human beings." He adds that this phenomenon was evident from the early days of Spanish rule. Guayameses were involved in witchcraft to such an extent and, supposedly, with such success that their *brujos* eventually became famous throughout the island. However, Porrata-Doria adds, not until the 1920s did the nickname Ciudad Bruja begin to gain popularity, and it did so because Guayama's baseball teams always used the name Brujos de Guayama (*Guayama*, 95–99).

9   Adolfo Porrata-Doria is almost certainly a descendant of Don Santiago Porrata-Doria, mayor of Guayama in 1840 and owner of Hacienda Amparo in barrio Machete from the 1830s to the 1850s (Porrata-Doria, *Guayama*, 309; Oquendo, "Inmigración," 138, 260, 263–63).

10 Porrata-Doria's gesture of silence is reminiscent of the success with which this sort of writing has won many battles over the representation of Puerto Rican history that were filled with what Arcadio Díaz Quiñones, Memoria, has called a "broken memory." A testimony to the strong hegemonic power that such representations of nineteenth-century Puerto Rico have held over island intellectuals comes from the fact that many island professional historians and social scientists writing shortly after the publication of Porrata-Doria's book were still not far removed from the opinions of this local amateur historian. Until the research findings of Andrés Ramos Mattei, José Curet, Francisco Scarano, and Guillermo Baralt began to circulate in the late 1970s and early 1980s, even some charter members of the island's *nueva historia*—for example, Gervasio L. García and Angel G. Quintero Rivera—and younger scholars such as Kelvin Santiago continued for a while to hold onto the traditional view that slavery was marginal, patriarchal, and/or part of a notion of "natural economy" that echoed Porrata-Doria's image of a "pastoral life." See, e.g., García, *Primeros fermentos*; Quintero Rivera, *Conflictos*; Quintero Rivera, "Background"; Santiago, "Puerto Rico." For two recent analyses of the discursive strategies of late-nineteenth-century Puerto Rican liberal elites, the forebears Porrata-Doria, see, e.g. Cubano Iguina, "Political Culture"; Findlay, *Imposing Decency*, esp. 53–109.

11 For an excellent deployment of the concepts of second empire and second slavery to analyze nineteenth-century Spanish Caribbean history, see Schmidt-Nowara, *Empire and Antislavery*, esp. 3–6. On second slavery in general, see Tomich, " 'Second Slavery.' " Schmidt-Nowara bases his use of the concept of "second empire" in large part on Fradera, "Importáncia"; Fradera, "Why Were Spain's Special Overseas Laws Never Enacted?"; Fradera, "Quiebra."

12 Theoretically, on this issue of racial projects and racial formations I will draw on Omi and Winant, *Racial Formation*. More recently, innovative historical and theoretical work on race, region, and space in Latin America is available in Appelbaum, Macpherson, and Rosemblatt, "Racial Nations," 10–12.

13 The notion of a "frontier" in this context is rather distinct from the emerging historiography on frontiers in mainland regions of Latin America. See Guy and Sheridan, "On Frontiers."

14 Rodney, *History*, chap. 1.

15 R. Picó, *Geographic Regions*, 90–91. See also R. Picó, Buitrago de Santiago, and Berríos, *Nueva geografía*.

16 R. Picó, *Geographic Regions*, 93–94; Roberts, *Soil Survey*, 47–59.

17 Roberts, *Soil Survey*, 53.

18 Beishlag, "Trends"; Scarano, *Sugar and Slavery*, 38–39, 46–48; Bagué, *Del ingenio patriarcal*, 49; R. Picó, *Geographic Regions*, 94–96.

19 O'Reilly, "Memoria," 118; Miyares González, *Noticias*; Abbad y Lassiera, *Historia*, 111–13.

20 Vázquez, "Descripción topográfica," 244–46; Sued Badillo, *Guayama*, 13–14.

21 In 1869, Spanish colonial authorities transferred the rural barrio of Carite (11.5

square miles) from Guayama to Cayey, a curious yet potentially significant administrative measure.

22 Vázquez, "Descripción topográfica," 242–43.

23 Porrata-Doria, *Guayama*, 27–28; Sued Badillo, *Guayama*, 26–43.

24 Scarano, *Sugar and Slavery*, 3. For Cuba, see Knight, *Slave Society*; Moreno Fraginals, *Ingenio*; Bergad, *Cuban Rural Society*.

25 For a view of Puerto Rican history before the last third of the eighteenth century, see Gil-Bermejo, *Panorama*; López Cantos, *Historia*; López Cantos, *Miguel Enríquez*; F. Picó, *Historia general*; Scarano, *Puerto Rico*; Sued Badillo and López Cantos, *Puerto Rico*; Vila Vilar, *Historia*.

26 A 1775 report by the San Juan *cabildo* to the Crown summarized the division of Puerto Rico's exploited land into *hatos* and *estancias*. According to the report, 233 *hatos* and 5,581 *estancias* existed, but while just over half of the *hatos* were larger than two hundred *cuerdas* in size (one *cuerda* equals 0.97 acre), 5,309 of the *estancias* covered less than two hundred *cuerdas*. These figures illustrate two basic features of land tenure and use in eighteenth-century Puerto Rico: first, the concentration of land in cattle ranching *hatos* rather than agricultural *estancias*; and second, the preponderance of smaller properties, especially in the agriculturally oriented *estancias* (see "Informe del Cabildo"). An excellent overview of population and agrarian affairs up to the mid–eighteenth century appears in Scarano, *Puerto Rico*, 251–64, 286–93, 302–4.

27 Caro Costas, *Cabildo*, 2:87–88 nn. 19–20, give examples of these allocations by municipality for 1764 and 1770: in those two years, Guayama was allocated 100 and 700 out of a total of 2,400 and 10,000, respectively.

28 For sixteenth- and seventeenth-century Puerto Rico, see Porrata-Doria, *Guayama*, 27–28; Sued Badillo, *Guayama*, 26–43. For excellent identifications of the issues involved in Puerto Rican demographic history, along with several suggestive hypotheses, see F. Picó, *Historia general*, 98–114, 137–50; Scarano, *Puerto Rico*, 251–53, 268–69, 282–86; see also Díaz Soler, *Puerto Rico*, 133–352.

29 F. Picó, *Historia general*, 99; O'Reilly, "Memoria," 116–17.

30 Abbad y Lassiera, *Historia*, 153; Ormaechea, "Memoria," 228. On the study of the population growth in the late eighteenth and early nineteenth centuries, see also González Mendoza, "Parish"; Scarano, *Puerto Rico*, 328–51.

31 The best treatment of these issues appears in Scarano, "Congregate and Control," which relates two highly illustrative examples of these conflicts. In 1751 the San Juan *cabildo* sought the break up of two *hatos* in the north-central coastal district of Manatí out of fear of social unrest by *desacomodados* who demanded land. In 1758, Governor Antonio Guazo Calderón blocked the implementation of the measure granting property rights to *usufructurarios* (common-law land users) until a commission he had formed distributed marginal, uncultivated lands among landless peasants. Guazo Calderón, says Scarano, "justified the action to his superiors in Madrid by playing on the theme of the *hateros'* greed, 'for each one [of them] possessed by selfishness would like to own the entire island'" (34).

32 As will be discussed subsequently in this chapter, however, this conflict over agrarian policies had potentially larger ramifications that became more transparent during the period of political turmoil that engulfed Spain and its American empire in the aftermath of the Napoleonic occupation of Spain after 1808 and that extended until the dynastic succession civil war of the 1830s. For more on these land conflicts, see Gil-Bermejo, *Panorama*, 232–300; Caro Costas, *Cabildo*, 2:35–41, 64–83; F. Picó, *Historia general*, 106–10; F. Picó, *Amargo café*, 43–49.

33 Gil-Bermejo, *Panorama*, 256–60.

34 This should not be read as suggesting that generalized *hato* destruction ensued quickly. Most coastal regions may have still been involved in this process during the early phases of expansion of the sugar plantations in the early nineteenth century, and the redistribution of Crown lands in highland districts continued into midcentury. See, e.g., F. Picó, *Libertad*, 154–61. The most succinct and useful discussion of the vagaries of land reform in the late eighteenth century appears in Scarano, *Puerto Rico*, 320–24.

35 Gil-Bermejo, *Panorama*, esp. 275–99; Caro Costas, *Cabildo*, 2:80–83.

36 Scarano, *Sugar and Slavery*, 6. For the development and boom of nineteenth-century coffee agriculture, see esp. Bergad, *Coffee*; Buitrago Ortiz, *Origenes*; Buitrago Ortiz, *Haciendas*; F. Picó, *Libertad*; F. Picó, *Amargo café*; F. Picó, "Dehumanización"; F. Picó, *Al filo del poder*, esp. 27–45, 61–90, 147–60.

37 These issues enjoy a vast historiography. See, among many others, Lynch, "Institutional Framework"; Nadal and Tortella, *Agricultura*, esp. Izard, "Comercio libre."

38 On eighteenth-century contraband trade on the southern coast of Puerto Rico, see, e.g., Feliciano Ramos, "Comercio."

39 O'Reilly, "Memoria," 116–17; Abbad y Lassiera, *Historia*; Córdova, *Memorias*; on O'Reilly's writings and actions and the imperial military and economic concerns at the moment, see, e.g., Scarano, *Puerto Rico*, 304–24.

40 Izard, "Comercio libre," 295–99; Morales Carrión, *Puerto Rico*, 83–90; Ortiz, *Eighteenth-Century Reforms*, 75–76; Scarano, *Puerto Rico*, 298–324; Torres Ramírez, *Isla*, 71–93.

41 Moreno Fraginals, *Ingenio*, 1:52–62, 265–69; Morales Carrión, *Albores*; Scarano, *Puerto Rico*, 314–16. The 1789 slave-trading decree appears in *BHPR*, 9:122.

42 For Guayama, see O'Reilly, "Memoria," 118; Abbad y Lassiera, *Historia*, 153. For Río Piedras, see F. Picó, *Al filo del poder*, 108–9.

43 F. Picó, *Historia general*, 142–43; Szaszdi, "Credit," 148, 172; Szaszdi "Apuntes." See also Cifre de Loubriel, *Inmigración*.

44 On French and French-creole migration to western Puerto Rico, see esp. Morales, "Hispaniola Diaspora"; on Guayama, see Oquendo, "Inmigración."

45 Fernando Picó, first in his research on Utuado and later in his incisive general history of Puerto Rico and his research on San Juan's periphery, has helped to shift the traditional "birth" of Puerto Rican nationhood to the last three decades of the eighteenth century. See, e.g., F. Picó, *Historia general*, esp. chaps. 8–12; F. Picó, *Al filo del poder*, 9–26, 105–14, 133–46. Rodríguez Juliá has developed a similar view, this time in the realm of literature, in his novels *La renuncia del héroe Baltasar* and

La noche oscura del niño Avilés as well as in his extended essay on Puerto Rico's first major painter, free mulatto José Campeche, *Campeche o los diablejos de la melancolía.*

46 For the international economic context of the time as it relates to the sugar industry, and with an eye on explaining Cuban developments, see Moreno Fraginals, *Ingenio,* 1:39–47; Bergad, *Cuban Rural Society*; on Puerto Rican developments and their comparison to the Cuban case, see Scarano, *Sugar and Slavery,* 20–22.

47 Scarano, "Congregate and Control," 30, 31.

48 This discussion relies heavily on a critical essay that remains relevant well over a decade after its publication, Scarano's excellent "Congregate and Control," esp. 35–36. The most recent historiography has not superseded Scarano's essay, especially when discussing the Puerto Rican case in the broader Caribbean context. See Knight, "Blacks."

49 These petitions were elaborated by the five *cabildos* that existed in 1809: San Juan and San Germán, plus the new councils of Aguada (on the northwest coast), Arecibo (north-central coast), and Coamo (south coast). They were written in conjunction with a new colonial governor's selection (from a list of candidates supplied by the *cabildos*) of Don Ramón Power y Giralt as the Puerto Rican delegate to the assembly of deputies that would meet in Cádiz in 1810. Four of the five petitions, or "instructions," given to Power have been recovered (only Arecibo's seems lost) and published, first by Rafael Ramírez de Arellano in 1936 (San Juan's, Aguada's, and Coamo's) and then again (with the addition of San Germán's) in 1969 by Aida Caro Costas. San Juan's draft, written by its mayor and discussed in detail later in the chapter, was also reprinted by Eugenio Fernández Méndez in 1969 in a collection of documents of Puerto Rican history widely used in island colleges during the 1970s and 1980s. See Ramírez de Arellano, "Instrucciones"; Caro Costas, *Ramón Power y Giralt*; Fernández Méndez, *Crónicas.*

50 See, e.g., San Miguel, *Mundo,* 87, 132; Scarano, *Puerto Rico,* 371–74; Schmidt-Nowara, *Empire and Antislavery,* 40–41.

51 Caro Costas, *Ramón Power y Giralt,* 123–24. For a brief discussion of the political discourse of San Germán's text, see Scarano, *Puerto Rico,* 374.

52 "Informe dado por el Alcalde Don Pedro Yrizarri al Ayuntamiento de la Capital [15 September], 1809," and "Ynstrucciones de la Villa de Coamo," in Ramírez de Arellano, "Instrucciones," 9–31, 47–59; the petitions that the San Juan council finally approved appear on 33–46. On the similar nature of portions of Irizarri's and Coamo's texts, see, e.g., the identical, formulaic openings that precede their discussion of specific problems and solutions (10, 48), as well as when both reports introduce their views on the problem of labor organization (14, 50) and the issue of public education (22–23, 52). However, between their discussions of foreign immigration (from different perspectives) and their similar views on education, the Coamo text skips copying or even paraphrasing a substantial portion of Irizarri's report (14–22).

53 The list of historical, social science, and literary works that express this dichotomous paradigm of colonial elite conflicts in nineteenth-century Puerto Rico is too

vast to present here. Suffice it to say that it was the favorite paradigm of several generations of intellectuals. See, e.g., the works of Salvador Brau (commonly regarded as the first Puerto Rican professional historian), such as *Disquisiciones* and *Historia*; Cruz Monclova's massive *Historia*; Díaz Soler, *Historia*; Díaz Soler, *Puerto Rico*; Maldonado-Denis, *Puerto Rico*; Fernández Méndez, *Historia cultural*; Bothwell and Cruz Monclova, *Documentos*; Morales Carrión, *Ojeada*; Quintero Rivera, *Conflictos*; Bergad, *Coffee*.

One of the earliest and most consistent critics of this dichotomous approach in Puerto Rican historiography has been Gervasio García; see, e.g., García, *Historia crítica*; García, "Nuevos enfoques"; García, "Política." For other criticisms and responses to what is an ongoing debate in Puerto Rican historiography, see, e.g., Negrón Portillo and Mayo Santana, "Trabajo"; Quintero Rivera, *Patricios y plebeyos*, 292–93, 313–22; Castro, "De Salvador Brau"; Alvarez Curbelo, *País*.

Two important works produced by a new generation of Spanish scholars of the Spanish Caribbean have raised similar critiques of the creole-peninsular dichotomy; see Bahamonde and Cayuela, *Hacer las Américas*; Cayuela Fernández, *Bahía de Ultramar*. Schmidt-Nowara's *Empire and Antislavery*, an excellent study of the mid-nineteenth-century interplay between Spanish Caribbean creoles and peninsulars and metropolitan-resident Cuban and Puerto Ricans, especially in the antislavery campaigns of the 1860s and 1870s, is one of the best illustrations of the imbrication of creole and peninsular interests, both liberal and conservative. For a broader comparative perspective on the problems that such dichotomies create in the study of colonial societies in Africa, see Cooper, "Conflict and Connection," esp. 1518, 1527, 1544–45.

54 Ramírez de Arellano, "Instrucciones," 12–13, 20.
55 Ibid., 17.
56 Ibid., 50–57.
57 Omi and Winant, *Racial Formation*, 55, 60, 56, 60–61, 68.
58 Chinea, "Race and Labor," 107–8.
59 Schmidt-Nowara, *Empire and Antislavery*, esp. 1–13, 37–50, 139–60.

Chapter Two

1 Connerton, *How Societies Remember*. In this sense, beyond my more specific concerns with debates about slavery and emancipation in the Americas, this chapter echoes a recent trend in Latin American historiography regarding the politics of memory and the memory of politics. For excellent contributions in the cases of Brazil, El Salvador, and Chile, see Weinstein, "Decline"; Mahoney, "Past"; Gould, "Revolutionary Nationalism"; Mallon, "Bearing Witness."

2 Because an excellent historical study of these issues to 1850 already exists—Scarano's landmark *Sugar and Slavery*—I will concentrate on calling the attention to some specific aspects that provide a backdrop for the study of Guayama's economy and society after midcentury.

3 Ramírez de Arellano, "Instrucciones," 50.

4 On the outlook of the sugar industry and its challenges at midcentury, see, e.g., Ramos Mattei, *Hacienda*; Ramos Mattei, "Technical Innovations"; Ramos Mattei, *Sociedad*; Curet, "From Slave to *Liberto*"; Curet, "About Slavery."

5 On the notion of the plantation as a particular type of social institution see, e.g., E. T. Thompson, *Plantation Societies*; Wolf and Mintz, "Haciendas and Plantations"; Wolf and Mintz, "Aspectos específicos"; Curtin, *Rise*.

6 The term "systematized" is taken from Morales Carrión, *Puerto Rico*, 141. The best assessment of the Real Cédula de Gracias remains Scarano, *Sugar and Slavery*, 18–25. See also F. Picó, *Historia general*, 132–34; Scarano, *Puerto Rico*, 383–86; Bergad, *Coffee*, 4 n. 5.

7 Mascareñas, "Abolición," 270.

8 Tomich, "World Slavery," 302. See also Mintz, *Sweetness*.

9 Dietz, *Economic History*, 31.

10 Scarano, *Sugar and Slavery*, 62, 3–34; Bergad, *Coffee*, 3–67. For a look at this process in Cuba, see Guerra y Sánchez, *Sugar and Society*; Knight, *Slave Society*, 3–26; Le Riverend, *Historia*, 132–73; Moreno Fraginals, *Ingenio*.

11 Scarano, *Sugar and Slavery*, 32–34, 162. See also Nistal-Moret, "Pueblo," 119–21, 147–48; F. Picó, *Libertad*, 69–73; San Miguel, "Tierra," 15–16; Sued Badillo, *Guayama*, 59.

12 These classifications differed substantially from those in the United States. For example, the 1871 Census of Guayama discussed in chapter 3 shows seven "white" slaves—that is, seven individuals born to slave women whose phenotypical characteristics could have made them pass as whites had they been born to free mothers. The census also included individuals who were the offspring of two black parents but were classified as "mulattoes."

13 Knight, *Slave Society*, 22, 86.

14 For this interpretation, see, among many others, Díaz Soler, *Historia*. Even analyses with a sharply different theoretical framework than the legal-institutional view of these studies have assumed the same interpretation; see, e.g., History Task Force, *Labor Migration*, 71–74, 78–79.

15 Cruz Monclova, *Historia*, 2:2, 493.

16 Quoted in Curet, "From Slave to *Liberto*," 113.

17 Díaz Soler, *Historia*, 349.

18 See Carbonell Fernández, "Compra-venta," *Anales*; Curet, "From Slave to *Liberto*"; Curet, "De la esclavitud"; Curet, "About Slavery"; Nistal-Moret, "Pueblo"; Scarano, *Puerto Rico*; Scarano, *Sugar and Slavery*; Scarano, "Congregate and Control"; Scarano, "Slavery and Emancipation"; Vázquez Arce, "Compra-ventas." Beginning in the mid-1980s, however, the momentum of revisionist scholarly work on Puerto Rican slavery declined sharply, often taking on the topic of slavery only as context for the study of other issues. Of the many works from the mid-1980s, San Miguel, *Mundo*, is perhaps the only one to tackle directly the issue of slavery, the dynamics of slave demography, and the relationship between slave and free labor before emancipation. In the 1990s, Negrón Portillo and Mayo Santana published perhaps the only in-depth examinations of slavery, focusing primarily on San Juan and on a

new analysis of the 1872 Registro General de Esclavos that is distinct from the analysis carried out by a research team led by the late Nistal-Moret more than a decade earlier. See, e.g., Negrón Portillo and Mayo Santana, *Esclavitud*.

19 Scarano, *Sugar and Slavery*, xxiv, 14–16, 30–31, 63. Nistal-Moret, "Pueblo," for example, showed that the sugar *hacendado* class in Manatí (on the north-central coast) began to consolidate itself and grow further after 1850. Therefore, any increases in sugar production had to incorporate an internal slave trade (Nistal-Moret, "Pueblo," 215) and the use of larger numbers of free rural laborers (*jornaleros*).

20 Scarano, *Sugar and Slavery*, 16, 186; Bergad, *Coffee*, 54. Other significant though less developed sugar-producing centers were located around other coastal plains of the island, particularly in the southwest, on the eastern coast, and on the northern coastal periphery of San Juan. For 1828 data on these districts, see Scarano, *Sugar and Slavery*, 30, 185–86.

21 Scarano, *Sugar and Slavery*, 63.

22 Ibid., 70.

23 Ibid., 64–65.

24 Ibid., 71. Hoernel, "Comparison," 64, has also drawn attention to the fact that land on coastal plains and river valleys was both scarce and expensive in nineteenth-century Puerto Rico.

25 Scarano, *Sugar and Slavery*, 68–72.

26 Chinea, "Race and Labor," 78–79, 82, 136–37.

27 Dorsey, *Slave Traffic*, 29, 31.

28 AGPR, FPN, Guayama, Teodoro García, box 190, #108 (8 May 1871); #130 (28 May 1871); box 192, #65 (29 February 1872); Capó Alvarez, box 84, #173 (7 October 1881); box 111, #159 (6 July 1896); box 113, #294 (14 November 1896). The distinction made here between the fictitious and real owners of Hacienda Tuna refers to the fact that in the tax lists of this period, this hacienda appears as owned by some members of the Vázquez family, while deeds included in the notary records show that a series of real and simulated sales had occurred among family members to avoid the loss of the property to creditors.

29 Oquendo, "Inmigración."

30 Ibid.; AGPR, FPN, Guayama, Capó Alvarez, box 91, #53 (14 April 1885); box 95, #101 (14 July 1887); box 96, #118 (29 September 1888); box 99, #115 (30 June 1890); box 100, #93 (7 June 1891); box 120, #240 (9 October 1899).

31 AGPR, FPN, Guayama, Capó Alvarez, box 72, #181 (25 June 1877); box 86, #137 (18 August 1882); box 92, #125 (3 August 1885); box 100, #93 (7 June 1891); box 105, #75 (10 April 1894).

32 AGPR, FPN, Guayama, Teodoro García, box 190, #120 (20 May 1871); #333 (16 December 1871); box 192, #131 (4 May 1872); #153 (14 May 1871); Capó Alvarez, box 95, #107 (25 July 1887); box 113, #317 (21 December 1896); box 120, #240 (9 November 1899).

33 AGPR, FPN, Guayama, Capó Alvarez, box 72, #181 (25 June 1877); box 86, #137 (18

August 1882); box 92, #125 (3 August 1885); box 100, #93 (7 June 1891); box 105, #75 (10 April 1894).

34 AGPR, FPN, Guayama, Capó Alvarez, box 76, #120–21 (30 April 1878); box 96, #82 (17 July 1888); box 99, #137 (6 August 1890); box 100, #118 (3 July 1891).

35 AGPR, FPN, Guayama, Capó Alvarez, box 99, #166 (4 August 1890); box 102, #39 (7 April 1892); box 108, #103 (1 May 1895). Hacienda Esperanza seems to have been the original plantation founded early in the nineteenth century by Don Jacinto Texidor I, a Catalan who migrated to Guayama in the last decade of the eighteenth century, and given to Isabel and Juan as dowry.

36 Oquendo, "Inmigración," 102–3; Scarano, *Sugar and Slavery*, 7; Colón, *Datos*, 290–91.

37 AGPR, FGE, Censo y Riqueza, box 12, "Estado que manifiesta la riqueza y productos rurales del pueblo de Guayama formado para el presente año de 1818"; AGPR, FGE, Censo y Riqueza, box 12, "Partido de Guayama, noticia de los que poseen los vecinos de este partido y sus productos en el presente año. . . ."

38 AGPR, FGE, Censo y Riqueza, box 12, "Partido de Guayama, noticia de los que poseen los vecinos de este partido y sus productos en el presente año. . . ."

39 Future research on Guayama's slave plantation economy should explore not only similarities to Ponce but differences as well. This is especially true of the weight of the different production factors on Puerto Rican sugar haciendas. As discussed earlier, Scarano found that in the average Ponce hacienda in 1845, the value of land represented between 20 and 30 percent of the unit's total assets (Scarano, *Sugar and Slavery*, 64–65). I have been unable to uncover documentation for Guayama similar to that used by Scarano to prepare his profile.

40 Dorsey, *Slave Traffic*, 152, 171, 191, 195, 205.

41 Ibid., 152.

42 Colón, *Datos*, 290–91; *Balanzas mercantiles* (microfilm).

43 AGPR, FGE, DM, box 4 (1860–69), "Reparto de la riqueza agrícola del pueblo de Guayama para el año de 1864–1865."

44 See Bonnín, "Contratos," 126, graph 1.

45 Scarano, "Slavery and Free Labor," 558–59.

46 Curet, "From Slave to *Liberto*," 62–63.

47 Ibid., 64–65.

48 Oquendo, "Inmigración," 116; AGPR, FMG, DM, box 10 (1860–69).

49 Ramos Mattei, *Hacienda*, 19–20, 36.

50 Cubano Iguina has found a similar concentration of land in sugar production and consequent absence of small- and medium-sized haciendas in the *municipio* of Arecibo on the northern coast of the island for 1845, the same date as Scarano's data. See Cubano Iguina, "Trade and Politics," 38–40; Cubano Iguina, *Hilo*, 29–31.

51 For more information on Guadeloupean plantations in the final decades of slavery in the French Antilles, see Schnakenbourg, *Histoire*.

52 Scarano, *Sugar and Slavery*, 63.

53 Ponce had 34 oxen-driven and 4 water-driven sugar mills in 1866. Another impor-

tant south coast sugar district, Juana Díaz, a virtual satellite of Ponce's sugar industry, had 13 estates, 8 of them with steam-powered mills. As a whole, southern sugar districts from Guayanilla (west of Ponce) to Guayama had 132 haciendas, 50 with steam-powered mills, 60 with oxen *trapiches*, and 10 with water mills. See Bonnín, "Fortunas," 122; for Guayama, see AGPR, FMG, DM, box 10 (1860–69), "Planillas de riqueza sacarina de Guayama, 1866"; AGPR, FPN, Pedro Jiménez Sicardó, box 197, #249, fols. 91v–105v, 7 November 1870, "Venta de hacienda [Buena Esperanza a Don Wenceslao Lugo-Viñas]." Data for Buena Esperanza in the 1866 *planillas* are missing, but the deed of its sale to Lugo-Viñas in 1870 asserts that it had a steam-powered mill that was destroyed in a fire in December 1867.

54 AGPR, FPN, Teodoro García, 190, #6, fols. 7v–9, 11 January 1871; Capó Alvarez, 68, #234, fols. 948–90, 8 July 1876; Capó Alvarez, 69, #274, fols. 1179–1226, 4 August 1876; Pedro Jiménez Sicardó, 197, #249, fols. 91v–105v, 7 November 1870; AGPR, FJG, Expedientes Civiles, 1874, box 138, "Don Juan Vives de la Rosa: Sobre quita o espera de sus acreedores." Although the 1866 *planilla* of Hacienda Carlota has not been located, other sources indicate that it had 785 *cuerdas* when Don Wenceslao Lugo-Viñas obtained it in the 1850s, an amount that increased to one thousand *cuerdas* by the early 1880s.

55 AGPR, Fondo de Obras Públicas, Aguas, bundle 41, file 1452, "Sobre concesión á Don Juan Joubert y Don Florencio Capó para establecer un canal de riego en el río Guamaní-Guayama, 1859"; box 451, bundle 104, file 107, "Expediente sobre reparto de las aguas de la Quebrada 'Piedra Gorda'—Guayama, Año de 1850"; bundle 41, files 51, 1021, "Expediente sobre regularización de los riegos del río Guamaní—Guayama, 1890–1892."

56 AGPR, Fondo de Obras Públicas, Aguas, bundle 28, file 928, box 413, "Expediente sobre proyecto de riego general promovido por los hacendados de Guayama [1865–85]"; bundle 141, file 107, "Expediente promovido á instancias de varios hacendados de Guayama solicitando la concesión un canal para el riego de aquella lanura, 1866." See also AGPR, FPN, Guayama, Dionicio Díaz, 161, #335, 4 November 1864; 162, #260–62, 11 August 1865; 162, #94, 16 April 1866; 164, #81, 10 April 1867, #238, 22 August 1867.

57 Ramos Mattei, *Hacienda*, 34, graph 4; Ramos Mattei, "Technical Innovations," 160; Bonnín, "Contratos," 126.

58 Dávila Cox, *Este inmenso comercio*, 62–63.

59 On the impact of the development of the beet-sugar industry on Puerto Rico, see, e.g., Ramos Mattei, *Hacienda*, 29–35; Ramos Mattei, "Technical Innovations," 160–61; Ramos Mattei, *Sociedad*, 28–29; Bonnín, "Contratos," 127–30.

60 Dávila Cox, *Este inmenso comercio*, 62–66.

61 *Revista de Agricultura, Industria, y Comercio* 2 (1886): 11, 4 (1888): 3–4, 5 (1889).

62 Eltis, "Nineteenth-Century Transatlantic Slave Trade," 134, has estimated that 46,870 slaves arrived in Puerto Rico between 1811 and 1845.

63 Dorsey, *Slave Traffic*, 205.

64 Ibid., 150–52, 186–209; see 192 for Moret's petition.

65 Ramos Mattei, *Hacienda*, 12.

66 Scarano, *Sugar and Slavery*, xx–xxi; Curet, "From Slave to *Liberto*," 131–38, 159–63.

67 Curet, "From Slave to *Liberto*," 166–70, argues that the Reglamento de Jornaleros was a "fiasco" in terms of its purported aim of creating a large "free" labor pool, though the trends toward curtailing nonpropertied peasants' access to land (of which the *reglamento* was part) continued after the end of both the *reglamento* and slavery in 1873. The failure of the *libreta* system (as the *reglamento* was generally known, after the labor passbook it imposed) to create a large labor supply of peasant laborers, Curet concludes, "explains why *hacendados* hung onto their slaves up to the last day before abolition [was] decreed in 1873." Still, a degree of disagreement remains in Puerto Rican historiography over the *libreta* system's degree of success, and future scholars must be sensitive to distinctions between the older, more slave-dependent haciendas of the south coast and the newer haciendas established in more densely populated areas of the north coast, for example.

68 Future work on the historical demography of Guayama should explain these disparate growth rate figures for the free population (whether of those considered white or of color) and determine the influence of discrete demographical factors such as increases or reductions in birth and mortality rates and immigration as well as the role played by changing social and cultural factors that could have influenced the racial classification of individual Puerto Ricans during the middle of the nineteenth century.

69 The decline in Guayama's population between 1854 and 1858 also resulted from the formation by secession of a new municipality centered on the port of Arroyo in 1855. Arroyo had more than a dozen plantations and about one-third of the total slave population living in the old municipality of Guayama.

70 Porrata-Doria, *Guayama*, 58.

71 Archivo Histórico Nacional, Ultramar, Gobierno de Puerto Rico, bundle 5,082, file 1, microfilm copy at the Centro de Investigaciones Históricas, Universidad de Puerto Rico–Río Piedras. I thank Ramonita Vega for supplying me with a copy of this document.

72 Archivo Histórico Nacional, Ultramar, Gobierno de Puerto Rico, bundle 5,082, file 1; Scarano, "Slavery and Free Labor," 561. On the 1855–56 cholera epidemic, see Díaz Soler, *Historia*, 112–23; Curet, "From Slave to *Liberto*," 111–12.

73 Bergad, *Coffee*, presents evidence from 1864 on total slave and *jornalero* population on some selected municipalities that shows the weight of slave versus "free" (but coerced) labor on sugar, coffee, and mixed production districts. However, even these figures somewhat obscure the picture, for within municipal boundaries, the historical geography of slavery held, as rural barrios on coastal lowlands and river valleys with good sugarcane soil generally saw different land tenure and labor organization patterns than elsewhere within those *municipios*. See, e.g., Curet, "From Slave to *Liberto*," 50–51; Nistal-Moret, "Pueblo," 144–47, 212, 268 n. 31; Scarano, *Sugar and Slavery*, 116–19; Sued-Badillo, *Guayama*.

74 Ramos Mattei, *Hacienda*, 24, concludes that "the labor force maintained by the plantations in 1870 constitutes a good indication of how the *libreta* system did not represent an adequate long-term instrument for the solution of the estates' elastic

demand for workers. First, the planters did not do away with their slaves. . . . It is surprising, for example, that the inventory of the San Vicente plantation in Vega Baja [north coast] includes 201 slaves as property of the estate in 1864. Mercedita [a plantation in Ponce, conversely,] incorporated many leased slaves into its workforce until 1873." For more evidence on Hacienda Mercedita, see Ramos Mattei, *Hacienda*, 96–97.

75 Scarano, *Sugar and Slavery*, 32–33; see also xxii.

76 F. Picó, *Amargo café*, 22.

77 Bonnín, "Contratos"; Bonnín, "Fortunas"; Cubano Iguina, "Trade and Politics"; Cubano Iguina, *Hilo*; Martínez-Vergne, *Capitalism*; Ortiz Cuadra, "Crédito"; Ramos Mattei, *Hacienda*; San Miguel, *Mundo*; Vázquez Medina, *Hacienda*.

78 Oquendo, "Inmigración," 262.

Chapter Three

1 *Proceso abolicionista*, 2:446. In 1870, while the Spanish Cortes was debating various bills for the abolition of slavery in Cuba and Puerto Rico, conservative *diputado* Sebastián Plaja Vidol admonished that the emancipation of the slaves would bring ruin to the Spanish Antilles, murder to the slaveholders, "disgrace" to the freed slaves, and the breaking up of Spain's "national integrity," an expression used at the time to refer to the independence of the country's two remaining colonial possessions in the Americas. See Cruz Monclova, *Historia*, 2:108.

2 Patterson, *Slavery and Social Death*, 5.

3 Ibid., 7.

4 Ibid., 6. For a recent brief discussion of Patterson's concepts of social death and natal alienation in the context of a reexamination of postemancipation societies in the Atlantic world, see Cooper, Holt, and Scott, *Beyond Slavery*, 6–7.

5 On forms of slave control and slave resistance in the Caribbean context, see Beckles, "Social and Political Control"; Craton, "Forms."

6 Mintz first introduced the concept of a "protopeasantry" and its related notion, "reconstituted peasantry," in 1961 as a way of understanding the historical roots of the emergence of Afro-Caribbean peasantries after emancipation. Mintz argues that the formation of postemancipation Afro-Caribbean peasantries involved a process of "reconstitution," since slaves in many Caribbean societies had constituted some kind of a "protopeasantry" because of their dual role as laborers on plantations that produced staples for export and subsistence agricultural producers. See Mintz, "Question"; Mintz, *Caribbean Transformations*, 132–33; Mintz, "Slavery"; Mintz, "Caribbean Marketplaces"; Cardoso, *Agricultura*.

7 AGPR, FPN, Guayama, Pedro Jiménez Sicardó, box 201, 23 May 1873, no. 68, fols. 115v–16v.

8 The mechanism of *coartación* was available to slaves in both Spanish and Portuguese America and had evolved from legal codes, Crown rulings, and the experiences of colonial slavery from the sixteenth century onward. In Puerto Rico, the 1826 Reglamento de esclavos (title 9, art. 1) included provisions for *coartación* (see

Proceso abolicionista, 2:109). For more on manumissions and *coartaciones* in the Puerto Rican context, see, e.g., Díaz Soler, *Historia*, 226–27.

9 While I was able to study in detail the manumissions and *coartaciones* for 1870–72, information for 1860–69 was gathered by using only the index of notarized transactions in Guayama. At the time of my research, Héctor Martínez was preparing studying of Guayama's slave trade, manumissions, and *coartaciones* from 1808 to 1869. The index to notarized transactions gives the date, type of deed, and the names of the principal parties involved. Both manumissions and *coartaciones* appear under the rubric of *cartas de libertad*. It is therefore impossible to know from the index alone whether freedom was obtained by master manumission or self-purchase, the amount of money involved if the latter, and any other details that the parties might have provided in the documents themselves.

10 Campos, "Abolición."

11 This finding represents another piece of evidence that the so-called *libreta* labor system did not represent a viable alternative to substitute for dwindling numbers of slaves in the 1860s. See also Ramos Mattei, *Hacienda*, 24.

12 AGPR, FPN, Guayama, "Indice general de Salinas (1832–1873) y Guayama (1808–1913)."

13 Bowser, "Free Persons"; Johnson, "Manumission." Johnson, "Manumission," 262, summarizes the basic data from these studies on the distribution of manumissions by form, gender, age, and other variables.

14 Guayama had 1,722 slaves on 31 December 1871, while 256 men, women, and children classified as slaves had been emancipated by the provisions of the Moret Law—that is, they were either over sixty years old or born after 17 September 1868 (AGPR, FMG, DM, "Censo de almas de Guayama, 1871," special box).

15 AGPR, FPN, Guayama, Jiménez Sicardó, box 198, #77, 14 June 1871; Teodoro García, box 192, #37, 8 February 1872; Jiménez Sicardó, box 198, #59, 13 May 1871; #63, 17 May 1871; Teodoro García, box 192, #252, 2 August 1872.

16 AGPR, FPN, Jiménez Sicardó, box 198, #29, 2 March 1871; Teodoro García, box 192, #34, 7 February 1872.

17 Indeed, of the three children in this group, one, Félix (Pillot), age three, was freed gratis, and another, Loreta (Gaudinau), age ten, was *coartado* by a third party (AGPR, FPN, Guayama, Jiménez Sicardó, box 198, #59, 13 May 1871; Teodoro García, box 192, #72, 5 March 1872).

18 Johnson, "Manumission."

19 Schwartz, "Manumission," 616; Johnson, "Manumission," 263, 273, 276.

20 "Reglamento sobre la educación, trato y ocupaciones que deben dar a sus esclavos los dueños y mayordomos en esta Isla, 12 [de] agosto [de] 1826," in *Proceso abolicionista*, 2:103–12.

21 Baralt, *Esclavos rebeldes*, 68.

22 Ibid., 68–71.

23 The preamble appears in *BHPR*, 10:262–63.

24 *Proceso abolicionista*, 2:104.

25 Ibid., 105.

26 Ibid., 104.

27 Ibid., 107.

28 Ibid., 106.

29 Ibid., 106–7.

30 On the different roots and other types of food plants in Puerto Rico, see, e.g., Barrett, "Origins."

31 Victor Schoelcher, *Colonies étrangères et Haiti: Resultants de l'emancipation anglaise*, as quoted in Mathews, "Question," 303.

32 Brau, "Las clases jornaleras de Puerto Rico," in *Disquisiciones*, 30.

33 Díaz Soler's *Historia*, for example, contains two chapters that purportedly depict the slaves' daily life, but this description has the severe handicap of being almost wholly based on government regulations, not on actual plantation experiences. Curet, "From Slave to *Liberto*," 175–212 attempted to describe slave life and resistance on Ponce sugar haciendas, but his effort seems to have merely scratched the surface, as he studied only a very limited number of slave judicial complaints and secondary sources.

34 Martínez Diez, "Relación." The original appears as part of "Sumaria averiguacion instruida por orden de su excelencia por queja producida por cuatro siervos propiedad de D. José Martínez Diez hacendado en Guaynabo" (1843), in AGPR, FGE, entry 23, box 66.

35 Martínez Diez, "Relación," 81–82.

36 San Miguel, "Tierra," 16.

37 Scarano, *Sugar and Slavery*, 53, 49; Caraballo Román, "Origen," 37–38. Plantain groves were planted not only to feed slaves with their fruit but also because the leaves were used to cover the bottom of sugar hogsheads to filters sugar crystals out of molasses (Ramos Mattei, *Hacienda*, 49).

38 Flinter, *View*; Flinter, *Account*; Scarano, *Sugar and Slavery*, 26.

39 Flinter, *Examen* (1976), 16–17.

40 Scarano, *Sugar and Slavery*, 26–27.

41 Flinter, *Account*, 244–45.

42 Ibid., 246; also appears in Flinter, *Examen* (1976), 25.

43 Flinter, *Account*, 246–48.

44 Ibid., 249.

45 Walker, "Charles Walker's Letters," 43. In 1860, for example, the sugar *hacendados* of Dorado (on the northern coast) asked the government for permission to work their slaves on holidays during harvest time (roughly January to June). The planters said they would pay the slaves one to four reals (twelve to fifty cents) daily and that if they were not working, the slaves would waste their time being idle, perhaps even committing crimes. The government agreed to the request with exceptions for Thursday and Friday of Holy Week, Corpus Christi, and Holy Conception (Nistal-Moret, *Esclavos prófugos*, 197–201).

46 Walker, "Charles Walker's Letters," 46.

47 Nistal-Moret, *Esclavos prófugos*, 234.

48 Ibid., 236.

49   Ibid., 60.

50   Ibid., 61.

51   *Proceso abolicionista*, 1:186–87.

52   Ibid., 49.

53   Ibid., 50.

54   Díaz Soler, *Historia*, 227.

55   Vázquez Arce, "Compra-ventas," 64, 67–68. See also Carbonell Fernández, "Compra-venta," *Anales*, 21–22.

56   Vázquez Arce, "Compra-ventas," *Anales*, 57–58; Carbonell Fernández, "Compra-venta," *Anales*, 18. A number of slaves seem to have accumulated some capital and given it to their owners and thus to have been classified as *coartadas*, but it appears that after setting the process in motion, slaves had difficulty completing it, a phenomenon that might reflect planter efforts to block slaves' access to means of accumulating capital. See Carbonell Fernández, "Compra-venta," *Anales*, 111–12.

57   Carbonell Fernández, "Compra-venta," *Anales*, 114–15.

58   Vázquez Arce, "Compra-ventas," 58. In a study of the 1872 slave registry, Nistal-Moret, "Problems," 153, reported twice as many female as male slaves classified as *coartadas* (having paid a fraction of their value). See also Wessman, "Demographic Evolution," 245–47.

59   Scarano, *Sugar and Slavery*, 26–29.

60   Ibid., 184.

61   Ibid., 193.

62   Ibid., 177.

63   Ibid., 116.

64   In his brief review of the Puerto Rican case in "Slavery," 237, Mintz fails to address directly the question of the relationship between slavery and peasantry both before and after emancipation. Of the preabolition period, he concludes, "the data is simply not available, to my knowledge"; of the postabolition period, he asserts, "we are bothered again by the lack of enough data."

65   Commenting on the contradictions between legal prescriptions and historical practices in nineteenth-century Puerto Rico, Nistal-Moret says, "Those who have studied critically in primary sources the problem of slavery in Puerto Rico will have noted the frequent disregard of legal dispositions that protected the slaves. . . . After years of studying Spanish colonial slavery in Puerto Rico, one finds an unavoidable reality. From all the consulted documentation emerges a new image of slavery as an autonomous structure, segregated from the legal dispositions that were to limit it and controlled by other extralegal factors" ("Pueblo," 86, 89).

66   In contrast to the rosy picture of the slaves' daily life in Puerto Rico, Schoelcher depicted in 1842 a situation that made any slave opportunity for autonomously productive activities out of the question: "One is tempted to praise the charity of our planters when one sees how the unhappy creatures bowed under the great evil of slavery are treated in Puerto Rico. Completely given over to the discretion of the master, their work is only limited by his pleasure. At harvest time one sees the blacks going to the mill by three o'clock in the morning and continuing until eight

or nine in the evening, having as their only compensation the pleasure of eating cane. They never even get twenty-four hours of respite during the year. On Sundays and feast days they still have to go to work for two hours in the morning and often for two hours in the evening" (quoted in Scarano, *Sugar and Slavery*, 29). Schoelcher visited Puerto Rico during the harvest of 1841, precisely when the rigors of plantation life were most acute.

67 See, e.g., Curet, "From Slave to *Liberto*," 74–85; Szaszdi, "Credit"; Santiago de Curet, *Crédito*; Cubano Iguina, "Comercio"; Cubano Iguina, "Economía"; Pérez Vega, "Sociedades"; Bonnín, "Fortunas."

68 Quoted in Curet, "From Slave to *Liberto*," 91–94. The article, signed only "M.C.," was published in *El Ponceño* on 2 November 1853.

Chapter Four

1 The best treatments of the abolition of slavery in the Spanish Caribbean are the still useful Corwin, *Spain*; R. Scott's landmark study, *Slave Emancipation*; and more recently Schmidt-Nowara's excellent reinterpretation of the Spanish abolitionist movement, *Empire and Antislavery*. For specifically Puerto Rican aspects of the process, in addition to Schmidt-Nowara, *Empire and Antislavery*, see Díaz Soler, *Historia*, 265–375; Morales Carrión, "Ojeada"; Morales Carrión, "Abolición"; and more recently, Alvarez Curbelo's innovative analysis of the discourses of modernity contained in some of the writings of Puerto Rican abolitionists, "La ciudadanía abolicionista: La modernidad política," chap. 3 of *País*.

2 On the Sexenio, see, e.g., Lida and Zavala, *Revolución*; Tuñon de Lara, *Estudios*, chap. 3, "El problema del poder en el Sexenio"; Artola, *Burguesía revolucionaria*, 363–97; Espadas Burgos, *Alfonso II*; Tortella Casares, *Revolución*, 173–263; Carr, *Spain*, 305–46; Piqueras Arenas and Domingo, *Agiotistas*; Piqueras Arenas, *Revolución*. On the demise of the revolution, see also Varela Ortega, *Amigos*, 22–85.

3 Here I am adapting a notion and borrowing a term aptly coined by Rebecca Scott, who sees 1880 as such a pivot point for Cuba in terms of making the turn toward full emancipation rather than simply the liberation of children or elderly slaves. Of course, as Scott and many others have shown, the initial pivot point for both islands was the fall of 1868. The crucial difference was that abolition came to Puerto Rico within the context of the radicalization of Spain's revolutionary process in 1873, whereas slavery ended in Cuba in the aftermath of the conservative restoration of the Bourbon monarchy between 1874 and 1876 and the 1878 truce ending the Ten Years' War. See R. Scott, *Slave Emancipation*, 194.

4 Quoted by Maluquer, "Problema," 56–57.

5 Quoted in Corwin, *Spain*, 162–63.

6 See ibid., 176–83. See also Maluquer, "Problema," 57; R. Scott, *Slave Emancipation*, 37–38; Cubano Iguina, *Hilo*, 62–64. The best study of the formation of the Spanish abolitionist movement is now Schmidt-Nowara, *Empire and Antislavery*.

7 This perspective is shown, for example, in the organization of the documentation published in *Proceso abolicionista*, vol. 2, *Procesos y efectos de la abolición, 1866–*

1896, which starts with a section of documents on the Junta Informativa. See *Proceso abolicionista,* 2:1–42. On the link between the Junta Informativa and the rise of abolitionism, see Corwin, *Spain,* 186–214; Maluquer, "Problema," 57–58; R. Scott, *Slave Emancipation,* 39–41; Navarro Azcue, *Abolición,* 17–22; Cubano Iguina, *Hilo,* 39, 43–44; Schmidt-Nowara, *Empire and Antislavery,* 49, 106–8; Alvarez Curbelo, *País,* 95–139.

8 Ruiz Belvis, Acosta, and Quiñones, *Proyecto.* See also *Junta Informativa de Ultramar;* Ponce de León, *Información sobre reformas.*

9 Such is the interpretation, for example, of Cruz Monclova in his *Historia,* 1:378–79. On why abolitionism seems so entrenched among many western Puerto Rican elites, particularly those from Mayagüez, see Cubano Iguina, *Hilo,* 41–42, who points out correctly that the region's highlands became the island's center of coffee production during the second half of the nineteenth century and that its numerous free peasants had been incorporated into the sugar sector as free wage labor force since midcentury. Neither of these conditions applied to Guayama, with important consequences that will be examined in chapter 6. For an alternative or perhaps complementary interpretation that sees a link with the growth of an underground proindependence movement as well as with Spain's ruinous effort to reconquer the neighboring Dominican Republic during the 1860s, see Alvarez Curbelo, *País,* 115 n. 42.

10 On the Puerto Rican delegation to the Junta Informativa, see Cruz Monclova, *Historia,* 2:374–81, 388–428.

11 For detailed discussions of the Junta Informativa, see, e.g., Cruz Monclova, *Historia,* 2:486–90, 506–57; Díaz Soler, *Historia,* 272–85; Corwin, *Spain,* 184–214; Curet, "From Slave to *Liberto,*" 244–50. For recent alternative views, see Schmidt-Nowara, *Empire and Antislavery,* 106–25; Alvarez Curbelo, *País,* 114–39.

12 On Zeno's actions during the Junta Informativa, see Cubano Iguina, *Hilo,* 43–44; Navarro Azcue, *Abolición,* 18; Alvarez Curbelo, *País,* 128–30. Cubano Iguina also questions whether the proposals by the liberal delegates accurately represented the views of Puerto Rico's slaveholders.

13 On the period from the Junta Informativa to the Moret Law, see, e.g., Corwin, *Spain,* chaps. 13, 14; Cruz Monclova, *Historia,* 2:3–131; Díaz Soler, *Historia,* chap. 12; R. Scott, *Slave Emancipation,* chap. 3; Schmidt-Nowara, *Empire and Antislavery,* 126–37; Alvarez Curbelo, *País,* 139–52.

14 On Betances and Lares, see, e.g., Cruz Monclova, *Historia,* 2:429–37, 440–63; Maldonado Denis, *Puerto Rico,* 27–49; Bergad, "Towards Puerto Rico's Grito de Lares"; Bergad, "Hacia el Grito de Lares"; Jiménez de Wagenheim, *Grito de Lares;* Ramos Mattei, *Betances;* Cubano Iguina, *Hilo,* 44–45; Scarano, *Puerto Rico,* 430–33, 436–43. Remarkably, the story of Betances's and Ruiz Belvis's radical abolitionism and proindependence, nationalist project plays no role in Schmidt-Nowara's and Alvarez Curbelo's otherwise excellent analyses of Puerto Rican abolitionism in *Empire and Antislavery* and *País,* respectively.

15 On the role of the Ten Years' War in abolition, see R. Scott, *Slave Emancipation,* 45–83. See also Guerra y Sánchez, *Guerra;* Cepero Bonilla, *Azúcar;* Maluquer, "Prob-

lema"; Schmidt-Nowara, *Empire and Antislavery*, 129–35, 143–60, although special-
ists should also consult his doctoral dissertation, where his analysis extends to 1886
(Schmidt-Nowara, "Problem," 311–12, 317–21, 328, 332, 369–72, 414–15).

16 Artola, *Burguesía revolucionaria*, 366–70.

17 See Maluquer, "Problema," 59–62; Navarro Azcue, *Abolición*, 23–33; Schmidt-
Nowara, *Empire and Antislavery*, 141–54.

18 See the text of the Moret Law in *Proceso abolicionista*, 2:131–34.

19 Ibid., 131–32. Articles 6–11 cover the *patronato*.

20 "La Epoca," in ibid., 2:45.

21 "Ley [de] 4 [de] julio [de] 1870," art. 21, in ibid., 2:134.

22 R. Scott, *Slave Emancipation*, 65.

23 *Proceso abolicionista*, 2:48.

24 R. Scott, *Slave Emancipation*, 67–68.

25 Consul H. Augustus Cowper to Foreign Minister Granville, 10 November 1870, in
PP, 1871, 62:70–71. See also Ramos Mattei, "Technical Innovations," 167.

26 *PP*, 1871, 62:67.

27 Ibid., 69.

28 Ramos Mattei, "Technical Innovations," 167.

29 Cruz Monclova, *Historia*, 2:109–10; Díaz Soler, *Historia*, 309–10.

30 "Reglas a que deben ajustarse las autoridades y particulares para llevar a efecto la
ley de abolición parcial de la esclavitud," in *Proceso abolicionista*, 2:133–34.

31 *PP*, 1873, 65:1058.

32 "Documento no. 1," in Nistal-Moret, "Ocho documentos"; R. Scott, *Slave Emancipation*, 69; for her analysis of similar cases in Cuba, see 75–76, 78–82.

33 Díaz Soler, *Historia*, 310.

34 R. Scott, *Slave Emancipation*, 79–80, 86–87.

35 "Mentiras lícitas," *El Abolicionista* (Madrid), 1 December 1872, in *Proceso abolicionista*, 2:72–73.

36 Acosta used the metaphor to refer to the work of Puerto Rican abolitionist com-
missioners during the hearings of the 1866–67 Junta Informativa; quoted in Díaz
Soler, *Historia*, 285.

37 For a sample of these abolitionist pressures, see *Proceso abolicionista*, 1:395–473.

38 See the British consul in Puerto Rico's reports on island discussions of proslavery
counterprojects in late 1870 in *PP*, 1871, 62:68–71. On 23 November 1870, for example, Cowper reported, "The Commission of Planters of which I have spoken . . . is
still sitting here, the question which they were summoned [by the governor] to
discuss, the general emancipation of the effective slaves, has, I am informed, never
been mooted, and nothing but that of the 'Libreta,' or some other more stringent
substitute of slavery, has been under consideration" (*PP*, 1871, 62:71).

39 Cruz Monclova, *Historia*, 2:235–36; *Proceso abolicionista*, 2:135–38.

40 Cruz Monclova, *Historia*, 2:227–28.

41 *PP*, 1874, 62:1–2.

42 Cruz Monclova, *Historia*, 2:269; *PP*, 1874, 62:13.

43 See the text of the Abolition Law in *Proceso abolicionista*, 2:144, and in *PP*, 1874, 62:19.

44 Schmidt-Nowara, *Empire and Antislavery*, 152–53.

Chapter Five

1 Díaz Soler, *Historia*, 346–47. For additional testimonies of the immediate reaction to abolition, see Cruz Monclova, *Historia*, 2:272–77.

2 "Ley de abolición," *Proceso abolicionista*, 2:144. Both Curet, "From Slave to *Liberto*," 262, and Nistal-Moret, "Contratación," 52, have also commented on the brevity of the Abolition Law.

3 Cruz Monclova, *Historia*, 2:278–80; *PP*, 1875, 71:3. See also Schmidt-Nowara, "Problem," 380–83.

4 *Proceso abolicionista*, 2:418.

5 See the *reglamento* in *Proceso abolicionista*, 2:149–54.

6 For the functions of the *síndicos*, see, e.g., titles 14–16 of the 1826 slave code, the 1833 decision of the Real Audiencia de Puerto Rico (the island's supreme court) re-affirming the *síndicos'* role as "public defenders" of slaves in slave-initiated civil claims, and Governor Julián Pavía's 1868 defense of the institution of the *síndico* against some proposed reforms that would have allowed slaves to retain private attorneys as legal counsels in civil suits. All of these documents appear in *Proceso abolicionista*, 2:110–13, 126–30.

7 AGPR, FGE, Esclavos y Negros, "Contratos de libertos de Guayama," box 74; AGPR, FMG, DM, "Reparto de la riqueza agrícola de Guayama, 1872–73," box 18 (1870–79).

8 Bonnín, "Fortunas," 78–89. In Manatí as well, the *síndico* and deputy *síndico* at the time of the 1873 contracting of *libertos* were engaged simultaneously in contracting *libertos* for themselves. See Nistal-Moret, "Contratación," 53.

9 Díaz Soler, *Historia*, 194–95.

10 *Proceso abolicionista*, 2:147.

11 *Liberto* contracts have survived in Puerto Rican archives in only a few munici-palities, including Carolina, Manatí, Fajardo, Ponce, Hormigueros, and Guayama. The extant records often represent only a fraction of the total number of contracts formalized, making it very difficult to identify clear patterns within regions or across the island. Samples of *liberto* contracts can be found in the Archivo General de Puerto Rico. For example, Ponce's contracts are found in the FGE, Ponce, box 535; Fajardo's contracts can be found in the Fondo Municipal de Fajardo, book 607, 1868, Esclavos; and incomplete collections of the contracts of a few other munici-palities are located in AGPR, FGE, Esclavos y Negros.

12 "Papers Relating to the Emancipation of the Negroes of Puerto Rico," *PP*, 3:22.

13 Navarro Azcue, *Abolición*, 155, 158. Unfortunately, Navarro Azcue is not alone in holding these rather simplistic and often erroneous views (for example, no such banking institutions existed in Puerto Rico in 1873). A few other Spanish scholars

have held onto a historiographical perspective whose main feature is the replication of an outdated approach bent on both glorifying the ideas and actions of Spanish and Puerto Rican liberals and abolitionists and reproducing the notion that emancipation in Puerto Rico was a smooth transition resulting from the enforcement of strict state regulations, the unimportance of slave labor, the zeal of creole and *hacendado* abolitionism, and the "mature behavior" of Puerto Ricans, especially the slaves. Other studies that have approached the topic include Cabrero, "Abolición"; Cabrero, "Integración"; Mascareñas, "Abolición"; Pérez-Prendes y Muñoz de Araco, "'El Abolicionista'"; Hernández Ruigómez, "Abolición."

14 Curet, "From Slave to *Liberto*," 263; Ramos Mattei, "Liberto," 106; Ramos Mattei, "Technical Innovations," 169–70.

15 Curet, "From Slave to *Liberto*," 263–64; Ramos Mattei, "Liberto," 106; Nistal-Moret, "Problems," 144–46. Nistal-Moret samples 12,512 slaves out of the total slave population of 31,000 in 1872 and finds that 17.5 percent were under ten and over fifty-five years old and 11.9 percent were aged between ten and fourteen. Since slaves aged eleven to fourteen and fifty-five to fifty-eight in 1872 would have been eligible for forced contracting in 1873, it is reasonable to estimate that the under-twelve and over-sixty groups represented no more than 20 percent of the total *liberto* population in 1873.

16 Ramos Mattei, "Liberto," 121–22.

17 Curet, "From Slave to *Liberto*," 279; F. Picó, "Introducción," 4.

18 Ramos Mattei, "Liberto," 123.

19 Scarano, "Slavery and Free Labor," 561.

20 Nistal-Moret, *Esclavos prófugos*, 24–25.

21 The last contract in this group is numbered 1,668 and is dated 20 October 1873. Given the fact that by that time of the year, an average of only one contract per calendar day was registered, it is reasonable to assume approximately 1,670 contracts were registered between 26 April and 20 October.

22 As mentioned earlier, Curet cited a report by the colonial governor to his superiors in the Ministry of Overseas Territories in Madrid that indicated that some 27,000 *libertos* had been contracted by September 1873, while Ramos Mattei used a report by the governor published in the Puerto Rican press that 21,584 libertos had been contracted by December 1873. The great disparity between these figures raises the specter of statistics "cooked" for the benefit of different audiences. Examples of the weekly summary reports sent to the Negociado de Libertos are found in AGPR, FGE, Esclavos y Negros, box 73, 76.

23 The conversion was done on the basis of twenty-four working days per month, from Monday through Saturday. However, since domestic laborers could also have been compelled to work on Sundays, their daily wage rates could have been even lower.

24 However, these contracts did not specify whether agricultural work was to take place either in the field or in the mill.

25 See Ramos Mattei, *Sociedad*, 36–39. Ramos Mattei was unable to gather more complete information on Boyrie, who gained planter status by marrying Luisa

Pillot, owner of Hacienda Luisa in Maunabo. As chapter 2 discussed, the Boyrie and Pillot families were among the pioneering French immigrant families that developed sugar plantations in Guayama in the 1810s–40s. Luis Boyrie was the son of Juan Bautista Boyrie, owner of Hacienda Algarrobos, while Luisa Pillot was one of the heirs of Arístides Pillot, owner of Hacienda Barrancas. Other individuals who contracted many of the 527 *libertos* involved in this batch of contracts included Don Jesús María Texidor y Vázquez, owner of Hacienda Gregoria and co-owner of Haciendas Puerto and Josefa (25 *libertos*); and Don Luis Cabassa, co-owner and manager of Hacienda (Gregoria) Pica, of the *sucesión* (estate) of Don Matías Pica, Cabassa's late father-in-law (20 *libertos*).

26 Cruz Monclova, *Historia*, 2:287, 510, 512. Although Lugo-Viñas was elected to the Cortes as deputy for the district of Utuado, a highland municipality halfway across the island from Guayama, I have found no evidence that he ever had property or lived there. For one of the better treatments of the manipulation of elections in late-nineteenth-century Spain, see Varela Ortega, *Amigos*.

27 Ramos Mattei, *Sociedad*, 71. Ramos Mattei cited this complaint to AGPR, FGE, Esclavos y Negros, box 69, but I have been unable to locate it.

28 Ibid.

29 AGPR, FGE, Esclavos y negros, "Contratos de libertos de Guayama, 1873," box 74, contract 1,017; AGPR, FMG, DM, "Censo de almas de Guayama, 1871," special box.

30 AGPR, FGE, Esclavos y Negros, "Contratos de libertos de Guayama, 1873," box 74, contracts 79, 80, 81, 1,043, 1,044, 1045.

31 AGPR, FGE, Esclavos y Negros, "Contratos de libertos de Guayama, 1873," box 75, contracts 82, 83, 84, 105, 106, 107, 108.

32 AGPR, FGE, Esclavos y Negros, "Contratos de libertos de Guayama, 1873," box 74; AGPR, FMC, DM, "Censo de almas de Guayama, 1871," special box.

33 AGPR, FGE, Esclavos y Negros, "Contratos de libertos de Guayama, 1873," box 74, contracts 1,054, 1,653, 1,047; AGPR, FMG, DM, "Censo de almas de Guayama, 1871," special box.

34 F. Picó, *Libertad*; San Miguel, *Mundo*, 156–63. My use of the term "resistant adaptation" is based on Stern, "New Approaches," esp. 11. It is important, however, not to gloss over the numerous instances in which subordinated peoples in Guayama and other locations are enmeshed in relations of class, racial, or gender hierarchies often characterized by domination and the exercise of power, albeit in different ways than between elites and subalterns, as Rosalind O'Hanlon has correctly pointed out in her poignant critique of the Indian subaltern studies group. As O'Hanlon, "Recovering," warns, it is essential to avoid restoring an impression of "unity and consensus, of the absence of relationships of power," among various categories of subaltern people and to look at the operations of power among subordinated folks. See also similar warnings, emphasizing particularly the issue of gender domination among subordinated groups, in Spivak, "Subaltern Studies"; Mallon, "Promise and Dilemma."

35 Curet, "From Slave to *Liberto*," 264–65.

36 Nistal-Moret, "Pueblo," 325–26; Nistal-Moret, introduction to *Esclavos prófugos*,

24–25; see also the discussion of labor mobility in the 1870s–90s in chapters 6–7 of this volume.

37   *Proceso abolicionista,* 2:418–19.

38   *PP,* 1874, 62:22.

39   "Papers Relating to the Emancipation of the Negroes," 24; Cruz Monclova, *Historia,* 2:380–81. Moreover, in early 1874 the elimination of the municipal bureaus of *libertos* was proposed to the governor as a response to the futility of enforcing the requirement that all *libertos* to work regularly as well as to the alleged "general state of vagrancy" in which many *libertos* lived (*Proceso abolicionista,* 2:435).

40   For Sanz's first term as governor, see Cruz Monclova, *Historia,* 2:3–47; Gómez Acevedo, *Sanz.*

41   *Proceso abolicionista,* 2:399–417.

42   Quoted in Curet, "From Slave to *Liberto,*" 265–66.

43   All of us owe gratitude to Rebecca Scott for her unflinching emphasis that slavery was much more than a labor system and that emancipation was a contest over values. See R. Scott, *Slave Emancipation,* 282; R. Scott, "Defining," 70. My approach to Sanz's and later to Segundo de la Portilla's discourses on the *libertos* is obviously influenced by Guha, "Prose," as well as Spivak, "Rani." My comment about the constitution of *libertos* exclusively within the folds of elite discourse occurs in response to what appears as a sort of elitism returning through the kitchen door in Prakash, "Subaltern Studies," esp. 1480–81. For two different critical stands on this and other issues regarding the approaches advocated by Prakash and by some within the Indian subaltern studies group, see, e.g., O'Hanlon, "Recovering," esp. 217; Mallon, "Promise and Dilemma"; Cooper, "Conflict and Connection."

44   *Proceso abolicionista,* 2:162–64.

45   Several contemporary accounts testify to high day-laborer wage rates during the 1870s. See, e.g., the remarks of Governors Primo de Rivera and de la Portilla in Cruz Monclova, *Historia,* 2:361, 496; see also *PP,* 1875, 76:804. Ramos Mattei, "Liberto," 107, mentions the case of a *hacendado* who, "anticipating the events, proposed on 25 March 1873 that current daily wage rates be reduced [from 50 to 62 cents] to 28 to 30 cents, so that the laborers could not satisfy their consumption needs but by working more [days a week]." On the rise in wages in a highland coffee municipality during the 1870s, see Bergad, "Coffee," 94–95.

46   "Trabajadores," *Boletín Mercantil,* 4 July 1873, reprinted in *Proceso abolicionista,* 2:302–4.

47   On the contracted immigration of West Indian laborers, see *PP,* 1875, 76:804; 1876, 75:908; 1877, 83:1530. See also Ramos Mattei, "Importación."

48   See, e.g., the complaints brought by the Spanish Abolitionist Society to the Spanish overseas minister in *Proceso abolicionista,* 2:331–35. For British diplomatic correspondence, see "Papers Relating to the Emancipation of the Negroes"; "Papers Respecting the Abolition of Slavery and the Condition of the Libertos of Porto Rico," *PP,* vol. 71.

49   "Los libertos," *Boletín Mercantil,* 15 April 1874, reprinted in *Proceso abolicionista,* 2:336–40.

50 According to Ramos Mattei, "Liberto," 112, no "public manifestations" occurred against Sanz's new code.

51 Nistal-Moret, *Esclavos prófugos*, 190–96.

52 Rebecca Scott, "Defining," esp. 75, 90, has also suggested that one of the key issues of contention in the aftermath of emancipation in Louisiana and Cuba was not only the length of labor contracts but also whether they were for gang labor or task labor.

53 De la Portilla's decree on vagrancy appears in *Proceso abolicionista*, 2:448–50. On the Spanish government's rejection of the decree during Sanz's second term, see Gómez Acevedo, *Organización*, 281–95.

54 The Sociedad de Agricultura de Ponce submitted this proposal for reimposing forced-labor laws to the Spanish government in August 1877. The file of the case is found in *Proceso abolicionista*, 2:356–78; a detailed discussion of the proposal and the process that ended with its rejection by the Spanish government appears in Gómez Acevedo, *Organización*, 297–304, 381–87. For more on planter efforts to obtain postemancipation regulations for labor relations, see chapters 6–7 in this volume.

55 *Proceso abolicionista*, 2:446.

56 Ibid.

57 Guha, *Elementary Aspects*, 18–76; O'Hanlon, "Recovering," 204–5.

Chapter Six

1 Many of the issues can be traced in Klein and Engerman, "Transition"; Bolland, "Systems."

2 AGPR, FPN, Guayama, Teodoro García, box 192, #252, 3 August 1872; García, box 192, #275, 3 September 1872, fols. 397v–98v; García, box 195, #196, 10 August 1874, fols. 404–7v; AGPR, FMG, DM, "Censo de almas de Guayama, 1871," special box; FPN, Guayama, José M. Capó Alvarez, box 94, #65, 13 May 1887, fols. 311–16. I did not examine the notarial records pertaining to the municipalities neighboring Guayama, where Valentín Gual and other *libertos* could have purchased land. However, the fact that José Mariano Capó y Alvarez, Guayama's most important notary, covered the registration of deeds in Arroyo and Patillas a few times after abolition permitted the discovery of Valentín's land purchases. Other such cases include those of Juan Nepomuceno Texidor, who bought ten *cuerdas* in Barrio Real of Patillas in 1876, and of Enriqueta Texidor (or Sabater), who in February 1876 obtained 2.75 *cuerdas* in the piedmont barrio of Yaurel in Arroyo. Enriqueta sold her land to José Morales of Arroyo on 19 November 1877 (FPN, Guayama [Patillas], Capó Alvarez, box 67, #102, 24 March 1876, fols. 437–41; FPN, Guayama [Arroyo], Capó Alvarez, box 74, #356, 19 November 1877, fols. 1793–98).

3 AGPR, FPN, Guayama, Teodoro García, box 190, #224, 225, 23–24 August 1871, fols. 329–31; box 194, #255, 8 November 1873, fols. 353v–54v; Capó Alvarez, box 67, #64, 21 February 1876, fols. 249–51; Capó Alvarez, box 67, #96, 16 March 1876, fols. 379–80. Although there seems to be a disparity between the date of the final payment of

the inheritance (31 August 1871) and of the purchase of these two properties (23–24 August 1871) this might by explained by the possibility that the payment of the last installment occurred a few days before it was registered with the notary. Although the amount of land sold in 1873 appears originally to have been sixty-five cuerdas, in actuality it measured forty cuerdas, as Adelaida clarified in the 1876 deed. In all of these transactions, Adelaida was represented by her surviving son, Pedro. Cristian sold this land five years later to a wealthy farmer, Don Francisco Navarro Colón.

4 AGPR, FPN, Guayama, Teodoro García, box 195, #97, 1874, fols. 134–35v; Capó Alvarez, box 69, #316, 31 October 1876, fols. 1560–62; Capó Alvarez, box 70, #361, 17 November 1876, fols. 1624–28; Capó Alvarez, box 72, #135, 28 May 1877, fols. 671–79; Capó Alvarez, box 169, 12 July 1894, fols. 1027–30.

5 AGPR, FPN, Guayama, Dionicio Díaz, 26 November 1860, fols. 336; Capó Alvarez, box 79, #143, 6 August 1879, fols. 838–42; Capó Alvarez, box 95, #112, 27 July 1887, fols. 578–80.

6 F. Picó, "Dehumanización," 196–206; see also F. Picó, *Libertad*.

7 The value of these various coins does not add up to 147 pesos because the contract stipulated that Ceferino and Ruperta would pay Emilio 20 pesos after the surveyor had officially measured the exact dimensions of the parcel and possibly because of errors in the *escritura*.

8 AGPR, FPN, Guayama, Teodoro García, box 194, #153, 7 August 1873, fols. 210v–11; García, box 194, #162, 11 August 1873, fols. 223–24; Capó Alvarez, box 66, #369, 4 November 1875, fols. 1589–91. In 1891, Don Enrique Amy also bought the two *cuerdas* that the *liberto* brothers José Ramón and Pablo Texidor had purchased in barrio Guamaní five months after abolition.

9 AGPR, FPN, Guayama, Capó Alvarez, box 65, #353, 26 October 1875, fols. 1514–16; Capó Alvarez, box 79, #176, 25 September 1879, fols. 1023–29; Capó Alvarez, box 93, #16, 10 February 1886, fols. 102–5; Capó Alvarez, box 107, #32, 13 February 1895, fols. 122–23; AGPR, FMG, DM, "Padrón de la riqueza agrícola de Guayama, 1885–1886," box 18 (1880–89), "Padrón de la riqueza agrícola de Guayama, 1898–1899," box 5 (1890–99). Angelina Viñas apparently did marry Juan de la Cruz Texidor, thus explaining her absence from the latter's transactions or from any other deed in which she sold or transferred her share of the property to Juan.

10 AGPR, FMG, DM, "Padrón de la riqueza agrícola de Guayama, 1885–1886," box 18 (1880–89), "Padrón de la riqueza agrícola de Guayama, 1898–1899," box 5 (1890–99).

11 AGPR, FPN, Guayama, Teodoro García, box 195, #98, 20 April 1874, fols. 135–36; Capó Alvarez, box 79, #134, 25 July 1879, fols. 790–95v.

12 AGPR, FPN, Guayama, Capó Alvarez, box 77, #242, 22 November 1878, fols. 1269–73; Capó Alvarez, box 89, #15, 4 February 1884, fols. 67–70; Capó Alvarez, box 96, #60, 25 June 1888, fols. 313–16.

13 AGPR, FPN, Guayama, Teodoro García, box 194, #74, 12 May 1873, fols. 103–103v; Capó Alvarez, box 82, #167, 14 September 1880, fols. 894–98.

14 AGPR, FPN, Guayama, Teodoro García, box 190, #299, 16 November 1871, fols. 433–34; box 190, #322, 11 December 1871, fols. 461v–62; box 192, #62, 28 February 1872, fols. 87v–88v; box 192, #262, 17 August 1872, fols. 383–84; box 192, #281, 7 September 1872, fols. 404v–5; box 192, #344, 13 November 1872, fols. 487v–88v; box 192, #367, 13 December 1872, fols. 519v–20.

15 Machete's ratio surpasses that of other sugar plantation areas on the southern coast. In Arroyo, for example, the most skewed index was found in barrios Guásimas (4.7) and Cuatro Calles (2.9), both sugar districts, while in Ponce, sugar barrios Vayas (2.8), Sabanetas (2.4), and Bucaná (2.1) showed indexes far below that of Guayama's Machete. See Ubeda y Delgado, *Isla*, 217, 249, 272.

16 See Mintz, "Culture History"; Mintz, "Cañamelar."

17 AGPR, FPN, Capo Alvarez, vol. 100, #108, 18 June 1891, fols. 597–600; vol. 110, #11, 27 January 1896, fols. 49–464v.

18 Ramos Mattei, *Hacienda*, 47, 100–103; Ramos Mattei, "Liberto," 108–9. See also Brau, *Disquisiciones*, 70–71; Mintz, *Caribbean Transformations*, 109–13.

19 Ramos Mattei, *Hacienda*, 25; Ramos Mattei "Liberto," 95.

20 R. Scott, *Slave Emancipation*, 99.

21 Gómez Acevedo, *Organización*; F. Picó, *Libertad*, chap. 5; Scarano, *Sugar and Slavery*, xx–xxi, 34; Curet, "From Slave to *Liberto*," 131–38, 159–63.

22 F. Picó, *Amargo café*.

23 F. Picó, *Libertad*, 117–24; Gómez Acevedo, *Organización*, 130–215; BHPR, 11:177, "Circular de 13 de julio de 1873, suprimiendo por completo el uso de las libretas de jornaleros." The opinions of Guayama's municipal council and planters during the 1866 inquiry appear in Gómez Acevedo, *Organización*, 139, 141, 146, 163–64; the proposed local Reglamento de Jornaleras appears in AGPR, FMG, DM, box 4 (1860–69).

24 Gómez Acevedo, *Organización*, 39–40, 120, 272–73, 275–76.

25 Ibid., 39–40; F. Picó, *Libertad*, 124.

26 AGPR, FMG, AM, box 7, 15 October 1879, fols. 208–9v. The preoccupations of Capó and the rest of the Guayama municipal council seem to have been at least somewhat well founded, as illustrated by the case of Portalatín Colón, Baldomero Ramos, and Manuel Martínez Vázquez, three *jornaleros* from the neighboring municipio of Salinas whom the mayor of Salinas requested be arrested and returned so that they could be compelled to pay their overdue *prestaciones personales*. The mayor of Salinas had received information that Colón and Ramos were working in the *estancia* (formerly the sugar hacienda) of Don Isidoro Crouzet in barrio Jobos while Martínez Vázquez was working for the commercial house of Amorós in the township of Guayama (AGPR, FMG, DM, 24 July 1880, box 4 [1880–89]). I was unable to locate evidence indicating whether these *jornaleros* were found and sent to Salinas.

27 Ramos Mattei, "Technical Innovations," 163.

28 *Proceso abolicionista*, 2:340–56, doc. 254.

29 Madrid also responded by instructing the governor to limit his actions to the

enforcement of the vagrancy code "of your predecessor," a somewhat confusing order since the Ministry of Overseas Territories apparently rejected Sanz's vagrancy code in 1874.

30 *Proceso abolicionista*, 2:356–80, docs. 255–61; Gómez Acevedo, *Organización*, 297–304, 381–87.

31 See AGPR, FMG, DM, box 16 (1870–79), "Informe del Círculo Agrícola de Guayama, [15 October 1877]."

32 Ibid., fols. 2–3, 7, 12–14.

33 For 1874, see AGPR, FMG, DM, transcripts of correspondence, book 24, 7 January 1874, Cayetano Granel from Guayama found undocumented in Fajardo; book 24, 5 February 1874, Ramón Suárez from Guayama undocumented in Cayey; book 12, 14 March 1874, Francisco Santiago from Guayama in Bayamón; book 24, 8 May 1874, Dionicio de la Cruz from Hato Grande in Guayama; box 13 (1870–79), 11 May 1874, Santiago Villodas [*liberto*] from Guayama in Arroyo; box 13 (1870–79), 20 May 1874, Luis Mariano Gaudinau (*liberto*), from Guayama in Coamo; book 12, 23 May 1874, Luis Ferrer from Guayama in Arroyo; book 23, 12 June 1874, José Vázquez from Caguas in Guayama; book 23, 13 June 1874, Juan de Dios (no surname), unknown origin, in Guayama; book 23, 19 June 1874, Clemente Cortés, unknown origin, in Guayama; box 13 (1870–79), 19 August 1874, Juan José Martinez from Guayama in Arroyo; box 13 (1870–79), 7 October 1874, Antonio José Rodríguez from Aibonito in Guayama; box 2 (1870–79), 21 December 1874, Alfonso Serrano from Guayama in Ponce; box 2 (1870–79), 25 December 1874, Román a.k.a. Primo de Rivera (*liberto*) from Guayama in Coamo. Francisco Santiago was in Bayamón with documents authorizing him to reside there but was arrested on the order of the Bayamón mayor for suspicion of vagrancy and theft of a horse. He was immediately sent back to Guayama. For 1875, see AGPR, FMG, DM, box 2 (1870–79): 4 January 1875, Eduardo Domínguez (*liberto*) from Guayama in Yabucoa; 20 July 1875, Domingo Villodas (*liberto*) from Guayama in Maunabo; 12 August 1875, Antonio Margarito from Guayama in Ponce; 19 August 1875, Antonio Rodríguez from Guayama in Salinas; 31 August 1875, Juan de Dios Sánchez from Guayama in Arroyo; 1 September 1875, José Sánchez from Guayama in Yabucoa; 28 September 1875, unknown from Guayama in Patillas; 30 September 1875, Juan de los Angeles (no surname given) from Guayama in Maunabo; 5 October 1875, Miguel Alvarez from Patillas in Guayama; 7 October 1875, Laureano Viñas (*liberto*) from Guayama in Maunabo; 19 October 1875, Roman García from Guayama in Arroyo; 13 December 1875, Celestino Villega from Guayama in Arroyo; 24 December 1875, José Antonio (*liberto*) (no surname given) from Guayama in Salinas.

34 See, e.g., the cases of Bernabé Soria and Leonarda Quiles. Bernabé was a carpenter from Guayama with permission to reside and work in the southwestern municipio of Yauco, but the mayor of Guayama asked for Soria's immediate return to Guayama, where he had "abandoned his wife and children in the greatest misery and with no person who could help them. Such behavior," the mayor of Guayama added, "induces me to plead with you that you order his immediate return to the Alcaldía, either to take his family back with him or to support it" (AGPR, FMG,

DM, transcript book 12). Juan Anastacio Alicea, the "legitimate husband" of Leonarda Quiles, asked the mayor of Ponce, where he was residing, to ask the mayor of Guayama to order his wife to "follow him" to his new place of residence. Leonarda was living at a farm in barrio Pozo Hondo of Guayama, and as the mayor of Ponce put it, she "resisted following her husband, who is claiming her." She should be immediately ordered to present herself and their two children at the Ponce *alcaldía* (AGPR, FMG, DM, box 2 [1870–79]). On 2 October 1874, Isidro López, a peon at Guayama's Hacienda Carlota, was "*requerido*" (asked for) by the authorities of his home municipio of Arroyo to "solve a complaint" there, but no additional details were given (AGPR, FMG, DM, transcript book 23).

35 AGPR, FMG, DM, 14 March 1874, transcript book 12.

Chapter Seven

1 In 1878, for example, José Gallardo, a peasant from the highland barrio of Palmas, quarreled with his *comisario de barrio*, who wanted to force Gallardo to pay his share of the *prestación personal* (road tax). Gallardo disputed the order with receipts for previous payments. Gallardo told the man in charge of the road-maintenance gangs in Palmas that he was "fed up" with the *prestaciones*, and in the heat of the discussion hit him and went to the township to state his claims in the *alcaldía*. He was arrested en route, and witnesses said that as he was being carried to jail he shouted that he just wanted to see the mayor to show his receipts (AGPR, FJG, Expedientes Criminales, "Contra José Gallardo, por atentado contra un comisario de barrio, 1878," box 262, fols. 6v, 9v, 11v–14v, 41v–43v; "Contra José Gallardo, por lesiones a Don Francisco Vázquez, 1878," box 268; "Contra José Gallardo, por resistencia y lesiones a un guardia de orden público, 1878," box 267, fols. 15–23v, 45–46, 48v). Gallardo was sentenced to two years in prison, one for resisting the orders of the *comisario* and another for resisting arrest. The physical assault charge was reduced to a misdemeanor. See also AGPR, FJG, Expedientes Criminales, "Contra Raimundo Hernández, por desobediencia y falta de respeto a un comisario de barrio, 1873," box 244; "Contra Carlos Sánchez Marqués, por lesiones a Don Francisco Lopez [jefe de orden público], 1880," box 291; "Contra Julio Vázquez, por atentado a un agente de la autoridad, 1881," box 304; "Contra Rodulfo Vázquez, y Monserrate Vázquez, por desobediencia y resistencia a un agente de la autoridad, 1883," box 319; "Contra Felix Cora, por desacato a un comisario de barrio, 1885," box 350.

2 Gómez Acevedo, *Sanz*, 115–16.

3 "Sobre la creación y aumento de la Guardia Civil en el reyno español y Puerto Rico," AGPR, FGE, Agencias: Guardia Civil, 1880–83, box 325. On the creation of the Guardia Civil in Spain, see López Garrifo's excellent analysis in *Guardia Civil*. Also important is Ballbé's *Orden público*, a juridical study on the issue of public order and the restriction of civil rights, especially freedom of meeting, in Spain in the nineteenth and twentieth centuries.

4 Hacienda Felicidad was constituted with about half of the original Hacienda Santa

Elena after Doña Catalina Curet y Lozada and her sister, Doña Josefina (Joaquín Villodas's wife), decided in 1883 to divide their inheritance. For more details, see Figueroa, "From Slaves to Proletarians," chap. 5.

5 AGPR, FJG, Expedientes Criminales, "*vs.* Don José González, por lesiones, 1884," box 335, fols. 1–2v, 5–6, 8v–14, 18, 25–29v, 32v–36, 52–54, 56–61v. On 13 June 1885, the Real Audiencia de Puerto Rico upheld González's conviction but upgraded his sentence to four months plus the indemnification. González was committed on 6 October 1885 and was released on 7 February 1886. Ledeé "*generosamente*" (graciously) renounced the indemnification on 11 October 1886. This was not the only criminal case against González, however. In 1879 he was sentenced to six months in prison for firing a weapon at Don Adolfo Porrata-Doria, a member of a lesser planter family (AGPR, FJG, Expedientes Criminales, "*vs.* Don José González, por disparo de arma, 1879," box 279). González was convicted by the local district judge, but his sentence was revoked by the Real Audiencia, the island's supreme court.

Three years after the incident with Angel Maria Ledeé, Don José González was again involved in an incident directly related to the discipline of the labor force of a plantation under his supervision. This time, however, the confrontation took place on Hacienda Carlota and González was on the receiving end. At 7:00 P.M. on 13 March 1887, Bernardo Santiago Burgos and other peons of Hacienda Carlota were engaged in a lively conversation in the hacienda compound, but the conversation apparently became too loud for González's liking and he promptly expelled all those involved from the hacienda. Burgos exchanged words with González, and threw a rock at him, hitting him in the forehead. Burgos immediately fled the plantation and Guayama. Burgos evaded punishment until a year later, when he was arrested in his hometown of Patillas and sentenced to two months in jail for hitting González (AGPR, FJG, Expedientes Criminales, "*vs.* Bernardo [Santiago] Burgos, por lesiones a Don José González, 1887," box 372, fols. 5–6, 20–24, 26–29, 40v–41, 49–49v, 103–6, 116–18v).

6 Vega Druet, "Historical and Ethnological Survey"; Padín, "Redefinition." I am grateful to José Padín, to whom I owe this reference.

7 For example, in the summer of 1826, a group of slaves of some of Ponce's plantations conspired to start a rebellion that would commence during a *baile de bomba* on one of the haciendas. See Baralt, *Esclavos rebeldes*, 65–67.

8 "Reglamento sobre la educación, trato y ocupaciones que deben dar a sus esclavos los dueños y mayordomos en esta Isla, 12 [de] agosto [de] 1826," *Proceso abolicionista*, 2:103–12, doc. 179, esp. chap. 7, arts. 1–3, 107.

9 The events at Hacienda Bardeguez echo the lyrics of one of Puerto Rico's most popular *bomba* songs, which says, in part, "A la Bardeguez, a la Bardeguez, mi mama not quiere que yo vaya a la Bardeguez [To the Bardeguez, to the Bardeguez, my mom doesn't want me to go to the Bardeguez]." On the Puerto Rican *bomba*, its African origins, and its diverse regional genres, see, e.g., Vega Druet, "Historical and Ethnological Survey."

10 AGPR, FJG, Expedientes Criminales, "*vs.* Sebastián, esclavo de la Hacienda Barde-

guez, por muerte de Juan Domingo, esclavo de la Hacienda Palmira, 1871," box 218, fols. 33–38v, 69v–72. Sebastián was found not guilty of murder because the autopsy could not certify conclusively whether Juan Domingo died as a result of a blow to his stomach by Sebastián or as a result of peritonitis that had been developing from sometime before their fight (fols. 80–80v, 122–32v).

11 AGPR, FMG, AM, vol. 22, box 8, fol. 9, 19 January 1882.

12 AGPR, FMG, AM, Actas del Concejo Municipal, box 34, fol. 58, 4 February 1915; AGPR, FMG, DM, Oficios de 1878, box 14 (1870–79), "Gobierno general de la isla de Puerto Rico, secretaría, negociado 30, [circular] no. 1776, 22 October 1878." See Actas de Concejo Municipal, box 33, fols. 275–76v, 12 October 1911. For a discussion of planter and state efforts elsewhere to restrict Afro-Caribbean revelry during the same period, see, e.g., Campbell, "Carnival."

13 AGPR, FJG, Expedientes Criminales, box 347, "vs. Don Hipólito Montes, por incendio de una casa en esta villa, 1885," pt. 2, fols. 231–33. The events organized to coincide with the inauguration of the Café-Restaurant y Hotel Español were originally set to take place 20–24 August 1884. However, for reasons that remain unclear, on 20 August the alcaldía of Guayama used its wide powers of local regulation to order the suspension of the festivities based on a vague concern for the "health" of the population. Many districts in the island, the alcaldía expressed in its order, were suffering "unhealthy circumstances," and since many visitors were expected to flock to Guayama to participate in the events, they could bring disease. Montes rescheduled the festivities to begin on 23 August, but they apparently never took place (perhaps because of the same order). Original copies of the broadsides and related information are part of the evidence in a criminal case against Montes for arson in the fire that destroyed the establishment on 7 March 1885.

14 AGPR, FMG, DM, printed matter box 2, Programa de las grandes fiestas patronales de Guayama en honor a San Antonio de Padua, que se celebrarán durante los días 7, 8, 9, 10, 11, 12, 13, y 14 de junio de 1931. The head of the organizing committee for the 1934 fiestas was a prominent member of a family of nineteenth-century planters and merchants, and two committee members (including the secretary) were descendants of libertos from Guayama and Arroyo. The program for the 1934 fiestas also included a great ball at the Club Puertorriqueño, a baile de artesanos at the alcaldía, and two "popular" dances at the town's main square, all on separate evenings. Somewhat similar provisions were made in the 1936 program. For more on the role of artisan leisure activities in the formation of Puerto Rico's urban working class in the late nineteenth century, see, e.g., García, Primeros fermentos; García and Quintero Rivera, Desafío y solidaridad, chap. 1; Quintero Rivera, "Socialista y tabaquero." It is not known whether this Tito Curet is a relation of the island's foremost salsa music composer, the recently deceased Tite Curet Alonso, but he was indeed the descendant of Guayama slaves, as he expressed to the author in an August 1998 conversation.

15 Proceso abolicionista, 2:393–98, doc. 266.

16 AGPR, FMG, DM, Partes de Novedades de Orden Público, box 14 (1870–79), transcript book 23.

17 AGPR, FMG, DM, box 4 (1880–89), "Año de 1883: Antecedentes referentes a los individuos que han cumplido condenas impuestas por el juzgado municipal de esta villa." There are 175 reports covering orders and notifications to commit specific people to the municipal jail, the dates of their entry into the jail to serve time, and the dates of their release. Most of the people were committed to serve less than a week for *escándalo*, *maltrato*, and *riña*. The term for *lesiones* varied according to the working days that the victim lost in recovery, since the aggressor was expected to pay an indemnity to the victim, which rarely occurred except through serving time in the municipal jail. Individuals served terms of eight, eleven, fifteen, and thirty days for *lesiones*. The five persons that I have been able to identify as *libertos* were Felícita Gaudinau, Pilar Sabater, Ramón Texidor, Julio Villodas, and Antonio Texidor. Felícita was originally a slave of Hacienda Melanía but appeared in 1883 as a resident of Don Jesús M. Texidor's Hacienda Gregoria. She was committed for sixteen days for physically assaulting another *liberta*, Simona Gual. Pilar Sabater was committed initially on 3 March 1883 for two days for *escándalo* and disobeying the authorities (probably resisting her arrest), and for three days for the same charges on 14 March (again, probably for resisting her arrest): she was finally arrested for the first offense on 11 March. Ramón Texidor served eleven days for assaulting Gumersindo Texidor, while Antonio Texidor served five days for disturbing the peace, damaging private property, and disobeying the authorities. Another individual, Luis Anés, was involved in and served time for the same incident as Antonio but does not appear in the 1871 census as a slave, although his elite surname coupled with his plebeian status suggests that he might have been a manumitted slave or a descendant of slaves.

18 AGPR, FJG, Expedientes Criminal, 1876, box 251, "Sobre incendio en la Hacienda Cuatro Calles de Arroyo, 1876," fols. 1v–5.

19 *Código penal*, 138. See also García, *Primeros fermentos*; García and Quintero Rivera, *Desafío y solidaridad*, chap. 1.

20 See Genovese, *Roll, Jordan, Roll*, 285–324, on time, work, and "laziness"; 599–612, on stealing; 613–15, on arson; 598, on an interpretation of these forms of protest as prepolitical; Stein, *Vassouras*, 86 n. 23, 140–47, 171–73. See also, among others, R. Bauer and Bauer, "Day to Day Resistance"; Fredrickson and Lasch, "Resistance"; Craton, *Searching*; Queiros de Mattoso, *To Be a Slave*; Machado, *Crime*.

21 Craton, "Continuity and Change."

22 Trías Monge, *Sistema*, 38–40. Not a single investigation and/or prosecution related to fires on Guayama sugar plantations was located among the hundreds of criminal proceedings over the last eleven years of Spanish rule in Puerto Rico. More than a decade earlier, a series of fires on sugar plantations throughout the island provoked Governor Sanz to seek to shift the investigation and prosecution of these cases from the regular civilian justice system to special military courts set up to handle political crimes against Spanish colonialism. The Ministry of Overseas Territories in Madrid rejected such a permanent transfer on the grounds that political turmoil had not reached a critical stage but stated that the governor had the power to intervene in the investigation and prosecution of hacienda fires "every time that

their frequent repetition induces sound suspicions that they were committed with the sinister aim of subverting order and peace in the townships or in the countryside and that ordinary judicial courts would not suffice to correct them" (Gómez Acevedo, *Sanz*, 241–43). Indeed, during the 1880s, the Guardia Civil increased its presence in the investigation of hacienda fires and was responsible for "solving" the only case found in which someone was convicted of arson in a hacienda fire.

23 Genovese, *Roll, Jordan, Roll*, 613; Stampp, *Peculiar Institution*, 127–28; Trotman, *Crime*, 64–65, 126–27. For more on arson on sugarcane plantations, see, e.g., Gonzales, *Plantation Agriculture*, 107; Takaki, *Pau Hana*, 128–29. For two analyses of arson in rural but nonplantation settings, see E. P. Thompson, "Crime," esp. 277–78; Peacock, "Village Radicalism," 30–31.

24 To provide at least a sense of the relative magnitude of these thirty fires over an eighteen-year period, Takaki, *Pau Hana*, 128, for example, obtained information on nine fires in Hawaii from 1865 to 1915, and Gonzales, *Plantation Agriculture*, 107, mentions that Hacienda Cayalti in northern Peru suffered two fires between 1878 and 1888 that resulted in the punishment of laborers.

25 The eighteen cases in which the fires were thought to be arson are 1871, Hacienda Carmen in Salinas; 1872, Hacienda Deseada in Arroyo; 1873, Hacienda Barrancas in Guayama; 1874, Hacienda Merced in Guayama; 1875, Hacienda Olimpo in Guayama; 1876, Hacienda Cuatro Calles in Arroyo; 1880, Hacienda Palma in Arroyo, Hacienda Felícita in Patillas; 1881, Hacienda Orleanesa in Maunabo, Hacienda Olimpo; 1882, Hacienda Felícita, the hacienda of Mattey and Sécola in Salinas; 1883, Hacienda Palma; 1884, Hacienda Palma, Haciendas Luisa and Bordelaise in Maunabo, both on the same evening; 1886, Hacienda Felícita, Hacienda Aguirre in Salinas; 1887, Hacienda Josefa in Guayama. The eight cases considered "casual" or unintentional, though not always conclusively, were 1877, Hacienda Deseada in Arroyo; 1878, Haciendas Quebrada Salada (Cora) in Arroyo, Merced in Guayama; 1880, Hacienda Palma in Arroyo, Hacienda Bordelaise in Maunabo; 1882, Hacienda Carlota in Guayama; 1883, Hacienda Puerto in Guayama, Hacienda Bordelaise. This group includes a fire in which a disagreement surfaced over the interpretation of the fire's origins: the plantation *mayordomo* declared it arson, while the court labeled it casual. In another case, the court could not reach either conclusion ("Sobre incendio en la Hacienda Garona, [Maunabo], 1877," box 257).

26 Trotman, *Crime*, 64, found a similar pattern in Trinidad after emancipation.

27 Eighteen out of twenty-eight cases for which the precise date of occurrence is known took place during the harvest months. In addition, another fire took place in December, when the sugarcane stalks were mature and the final preparations for the harvest were taking place. However, the timing of fires thought to be the result of drought conditions and spontaneous combustion also needs to be considered. Only two such cases were found, with both occurring in late morning in a year regarded as particularly dry: a fire in the abandoned cane fields of a defunct Guayama plantation and a large fire that charred 364 acres of cane fields of Haciendas Palma, Deseada, Emilia, and Cuatro Calles in Arroyo. The fire started once again on the arson-prone Hacienda Palma owned by the Corsican Fantauzzi

brothers (AGPR, FJG, Expedientes Criminales, "Sobre incendio en pastos de los Sres. Clausell Hermanos, Guayama, 1880," box 289; "Sobre incendio en los pastos de las haciendas Palma, Emilia, Cuatro Calles, y Deseada, Arroyo, 1880," box 290). Fires supposedly resulting from the carelessness of smokers were evenly distributed during the day: two occurred during the daytime, with one each during the early evening, late evening, and early morning.

28   In Trinidad, the planters' and the authorities' realization that the bagasse ranches had turned into an attractive object for arsonists led to the banning of smoking on plantation grounds. "By so doing," Trotman argues, "estate owners reduced the risk of fire on the estates and ruled out a legal defence for those apprehended on charges of arson" (*Crime*, 64–65).

29   AGPR, FJG, Expedientes Criminales, "Sobre incendio en la Hacienda Garona, de Fantauzzi Hnos., Maunabo, 1877," box 257. The six cases where the "cigar theory" was used to explain the origin of the fire were at Hacienda Merced in Guayama in 1874 and 1878; at Hacienda Cora (Quebrada Salada) in Arroyo in 1878 (AGPR, FJG, Expedientes Civiles, box 145); at Hacienda Carlota in Guayama in 1882 (Expedientes Criminales, box 312); at Hacienda Puerto in Guayama in 1883 (box 321); and at Hacienda Bordelaise in Maunabo in 1883 (box 317).

30   AGPR, FJG, Expedientes Criminales, "Sobre incendio en la Hacienda Puerto, Guayama, 1883," box 321, fols. 5v–6v, 22–26.

31   AGPR, FJG, Expedientes Criminal, 1871, box 234, #3, "Sobre incendio en una pieza de cañas de la Hacienda Carmen [de Salinas]"; 1878, box 267, #124, "Sobre incendio en la Hacienda Merced del barrio Jobos [de Guayama]"; 1880, box 289, #59, "Sobre incendio en la Hacienda Palma [de Arroyo]."

32   "Sobre incendio en la Hacienda Palma, 1880," fols. 4–5v, 6–7v, 11v, 23–25v. These patterns of confessed ignorance, which sometimes seem to have taken the form of a "law of silence," were not restricted to arson investigations but also appeared in cases of physical aggression and even murder. See, e.g., AGPR, FJG, Expedientes Criminal, 1880, box 285, "*vs.* Petrona Sabater y Rufino Virella, por lesiones [mutuas] en riña," Guayama, Hacienda Cayures; 1883, box 319, "*vs.* Juan Jaime alias 'Santiago Inglés,' por lesiones"; 1886, box 357, "*vs.* Isaías Soto y Genraro Ortiz alias 'Guayama,' por homicidio de Celestino Sánchez," Hacienda Patillas. In this case, Soto y Genraro Ortiz tried but failed to silence witnesses.

33   AGPR, FJG, Expedientes Criminal, 1876, box 251, "Sobre incendio en la Hacienda Cuatro Calles de Arroyo, 1876," fol. 2v. Falsen quoted Lind's alleged phrase somewhat differently: "that like the black is punished, so to the white man would suffer [*que así como se castiga al negro, así también el blanco sufriría*]." Potts version is, however, identical to that of the watchman, Antonelo Sánchez, a black, to whom Lind had allegedly spoken (fols. 4v, 9).

34   Ibid., fols. 12–14v, 25v–26.

35   AGPR, FJG, Expedientes Criminal, box 301, #95, "*vs.* Francisco Ortiz, alias 'Viejo,' por incendio en la Hacienda Orleanesa de D. Otto Risffkohl [*sic*], Maunabo, 1881," fols. 1–4.

36   Ibid., fols. 4v–6v, 10–10v. The "*tercer mayordomo*," Don Simón Maezo, another

Castilian, confirmed that Recio suspected that laborers routinely stole molasses from the sugar mill.

37 Ibid., fols. 18–19v, 24–24v.

38 Ibid., fols. 22v–23, 35v–39, 75–75v, 98–101.

39 AGPR, FJG, Expedientes Criminal, box 322, #93, "*vs.* Alberto Sánchez, por incendio en la Hacienda Palma, Arroyo, 1884," esp. fols. 4–6v, 29–30v, 44v–46v.

40 The FGE at the AGPR has a section containing documents from the Guardia Civil's central San Juan headquarters, but these items represent only a fraction of the documentation that such an important agency should have generated. I suspect that scholars need to search Spanish military and civilian archives for more records pertaining to Guardia Civil activities in the Spanish Antilles.

Conclusion

1 Díaz Soler, *Historia*, 373–75.

2 See also, e.g., Fernández Méndez, *Historia cultural*, 207–321, esp. 240, 265.

3 Scarano, *Sugar and Slavery*, 142.

4 Ramos Mattei, *Sociedad*; Martínez-Vergne, *Capitalism*.

5 R. Scott, "Exploring," 19.

6 Andrews, "Black and White Workers," 108–9. Martínez-Vergne, "New Patterns," 66–69, found similar residential patterns in Vega Baja.

7 *Proceso abolicionista*, 2:144, doc. 203, "Ley de Abolición [del 22 de marzo de 1873]," 446–47; doc. 279, "Circular [del Excelentísimo Señor Gobernador General Don Segundo de la Portilla]," 17 April 1876.

8 R. Scott, "Exploring," 2, 19.

9 On race and Cuba's anticolonial and postcolonial struggles, see Ferrer, *Insurgent Cuba*; Guerra, "From Revolution to Involution."

10 On radical subaltern projects and postslave societies in the French and British Caribbean, see Sheller, *Democracy*.

11 See, e.g., Scarano, "Slavery and Free Labor"; Cubano Iguina, "Trade and Politics." For a quite nuanced view of the colonial state's role in the coffee highlands, see F. Picó, *Libertad*.

12 One of the initial, principal criticisms of González's "El país de los cuatro pisos" focused on his stress of race's role in shaping Puerto Rican history since the sixteenth century. Yet one important strain in the island's cultural production over the past few decades has been a growing interest in issues dealing with race. This is evident in the literary works cited in the introduction to this book as well as in controversies ranging from the naming of cultural centers to the commemoration of the five-hundredth anniversary of Columbus's voyage to the Americas.

13 Ramos Mattei, *Sociedad*; F. Picó, *1898*; Findlay, *Imposing Decency*. Some of the points made here also apply to Guerra, *Popular Expression*.

14 AGPR, FMG, AM, 16 September 1898, box 13, v. 32, fols. 148–148v. For a detailed study of similar events, many leading to the emergence of peasant and plebeian banditry in 1898–99, see F. Picó, *1898*.

BIBLIOGRAPHY

Note on Primary Sources

Almost all unpublished and printed primary sources consulted for this study are located in archives and libraries in Puerto Rico. The Centro de Investigaciones Históricas of the Universidad de Puerto Rico in Río Piedras contains an excellent and rapidly improving collection of microfilms. I relied on the centro primarily for the *Balanzas mercantiles del comercio exterior de la Isla de Puerto Rico* (also known as *Estadística del comercio exterior . . .*). The Biblioteca y Hemeroteca Puertorriqueña of the Biblioteca General José M. Lázaro at the Universidad de Puerto Rico in Río Piedras is the main depository of nineteenth-century Puerto Rican books and serials, both in print and on microfilm.

The Archivo General de Puerto Rico (AGPR) in San Juan contains the major unpublished primary sources used in this study. The AGPR is the treasure chest, albeit underfunded, of Puerto Rican historians. The major record groups I consulted there included the municipal records of Guayama (Fondo Municipal de Guayama [FMG]), the Guayama judicial district criminal and civil records (Fondo Judicial de Guayama [FJG], Expedientes Criminales, and Expedientes Civiles), the notarial records of Guayama (Fondo de Protocolos Notariales [FPN]), and the records of the Spanish Governors of Puerto Rico (Fondo de los Gobernadores Españoles [FGE]). These record groups vary in terms not only of the source generating the documentation but also of the degree of organization of the documents: the notarial records are well organized, but the municipal and judicial records almost completely lack any sort of order. Indeed, I found using these two record groups quite frustrating and spent six months as an *ad honorem* assistant archivist at the AGPR to gain access to the rich judicial *expedientes*. I again express my gratitude in this regard to the chief archivist at the time, the late Eduardo León, and his staff for enabling me to consult some of the records that had been closed before my stay in Puerto Rico. What follows is a description of the major record groups (*fondos*) and the kinds of information that they yield.

Fondo Municipal, Serie Guayama, Subseries:
Actas Municipales and Documentos Municipales

The municipal records of Guayama have no official classifications by source or type, but I have divided them for reasons of clarity between two provisional subgroups (or *subseries* in Spanish). First, the Actas Municipales (AM) include all the surviving proceedings of the Guayama municipal council, whether or not these proceedings are included in the existing provisional classification by the same name (not all are) and regardless of the actual name of the municipal council at any given moment (*corregimiento, ayunta miento, junta municipal, consejo municipal,* or *asamblea municipal*). Second, the Documentos Municipales (DM) include the rest of the surviving documentation kept by the *alcaldía* (town hall) of Guayama and rescued by AGPR personnel in the early 1970s, regardless of the source that produced it, the type of documentation, or its physical configuration (manuscripts, bound volumes, printed materials).

During the Spanish regime, the municipal council was known at different times either as *ayuntamiento* or as *junta municipal*. At different times, its members were named by the governor or elected by the small number of males holding the franchise. The volumes of *actas* under the Spanish regime were numbered, a good practice that was discontinued with the coming of U.S. rule. The *actas* contain useful information on the municipality's economic situation, taxing and budget debates and actions, growth of working-class neighborhoods on the periphery of the original urban center (*pueblo*), organization and functioning of local police, and enactment of ordinances to regulate all sorts of social behavior (from business hours of stores, cafés, and bars to political activities, prostitution, and public dancing).

As mentioned previously, the Documentos Municipales have not been organized beyond being grouped in boxes by decade, and even that classification turned out to be full of errors, which I corrected when I found them. The boxes had no further labeling other than by decade. No one knew how many boxes there were, and previous researchers had just marked the boxes with symbols or diminutive numbers, with no obvious order. I tried to correct this situation, at least provisionally, by numbering the boxes within a decade (since additional boxes emerged to include incorrectly classified documents).

Following is a list of the type of documents included in these files. In addition to the ones described here, the DM includes an extensive collection of demographic documents from the local office of the civil registry (individual declarations of births, marriages, deaths, and burials) that should be a gold mine for detailed prosopographical studies of Guayama's population.

Oficios: This general heading includes the correspondence received by the mayor's office. Surprisingly few letters written by the mayor have survived from the period 1870–99. Most of the extant correspondence of this era from the mayor's office consists of materials sent to him by central government authorities in San Juan, by other mayors (mostly from the same region), and by local officials (like *comisarios de barrios*, municipal or district judges, municipal police, or the Guardia Civil [discussed subsequently]). A great deal of the letters written by other mayors deals with individuals from Guayama found in other municipalities without identification and internal passport papers, which were required as a measure of social control. Correspondence from the central government deals with various aspects of the administration of the municipalities and the island (taxes, accounting records, and so forth), as well as other subjects such as foreign immigration and specific decrees by the governor (for example, controlling the establishment of small stores in the countryside for the peasantry, regulating the celebration of patron saint festivities, and so on).

Informes de los Comisarios de Barrios: These *comisarios* (sometimes also called *inspectores*) were deputies of the municipality's mayor. There were as many *comisarios* as the municipal budget could allow, either one for each barrio or one for a group of neighboring barrios. Guayama had nine rural barrios during the period of this study as well as three to four urban barrios. These reports, of which just a few survive, consist mostly of references on the conduct and recent employment data of individuals charged with crimes.

Partes del Cuerpo de Orden Público: These are the daily forms sent to the mayor by the municipal police chief (normally a sergeant). They give dates, name of individuals arrested, and reasons for the arrests. Most of the arrests were made for *escándalos*—personal fights, drunkenness, vagrancy, petty theft—and for being undocumented. Not many of these reports survive, and they lack the kind of continuity that would be desirable: They have survived only in bundles for several groups of months and years rather than for the thirty-year period as a whole. Yet they constitute an excellent resource for gathering information about particular individuals and provide a glimpse of the kinds of behavior that the authorities commonly defined as unlawful or undesirable.

Libro diario de servicios de policía: This is one volume reporting the arrests and interventions of municipal police forces in the Guayama department between May 1883 and June 1885. It gives the date of each intervention, the municipality, the name of the policeman involved, the name and "class" (*paisano, mujer, Don,* law enforcement official) of the individual(s) intervened with, and the reason/charges for the intervention.

Actas de la Junta Departamental de Agricultura, Industria y Comercio: This was a government-organized regional board that was supposed to deal with the development of the economy, although little could be done in that direction under Spanish rule. These juntas were at times even suspected of engaging in political activities and were repeatedly dissolved and reconstituted. From the junta for the department of Guayama, I located a few very important *actas* dealing, not surprisingly, with the region's late-nineteenth-century sugar crisis and with attempts to overcome it, including the establishment of modern central processing mills, irrigation facilities, and more beneficial tariff agreements with the United States.

Censo de habitantes de Guayama, 1871: This census is complete and in excellent condition. It lists everyone in Guayama on 31 December 1871 by residential district and household, giving full name (both last names if the person was not born illegitimate); "social condition" (color, gender, and social status [free or slave]); native country; age; marital status; occupation; and level of literacy.

Economic documentation: The municipal budget and tax commission documents are divided into three groups of files. The first group is composed of "Expedientes sobre la formación del presupuesto municipal" and "Expedientes sobre la formación del reparto municipal." These are stitched but usually unbound thick volumes that include the records used to prepare the annual municipal budget and tax (*reparto*) lists. The budget volumes usually contain copies of the annual general tax lists, and the *reparto* formation volumes usually include preliminary tax lists, appeal letters from individuals who claim less income than in the previous year, and the commission's correspondence. The second group includes "Padrones de riqueza   " and "Repartos de la riqueza . . ." The *padrones* are lists detailing the data on production, income, or property value for the four types of *riquezas*—agriculture, livestock, and urban property. The *repartos* are lists that summarize the data in the *padrones* and detail the amount of money in proportional taxes to be paid. The third group contains "Expedientes para la formación de la matrícula de industria y comercio" and "Matrículas de industria y comercio," which are grouped together since the *expedientes* usually include the final *matrícula* or tax list. These *matrículas* are the equivalent of the *repartos* for "industrial" (mostly artisan manufacture and services) and commercial (wholesale and retail) businesses. The commercial section is of great importance not only for studying general business activity or the merchant classes (as has been done in some recent studies) but also for studying the petty commercial concerns in urban and rural areas where peasants, laborers, and slaves/*libertos* bought produce and commodities and gathered to interact socially as they sold tobacco, rum, and other spirits.

Fondo de Gobernadores Españoles (formerly Records of the Spanish Governors of Puerto Rico at the U.S. National Archives)

Serie Asuntos políticos y civiles, Subserie: Esclavos (negros y libertos): This record group contains, among other rich and diverse materials on Afro–Puerto Ricans, copies of the *liberto* labor contracts of 1873 used in chapter 5.

Serie Municipios, Subserie: Guayama: This subseries includes documents from the gubernatorial offices dealing with municipal affairs. Only five boxes contain documents on Guayama (boxes 454, 455, 456, 457, 458).

Serie Agencias Gubernamentales, Subserie: Guardia Civil: The Guardia Civil was a paramilitary law-enforcement institution created in Puerto Rico in 1869–70. It still exists in Spain. It was commanded by the governor's office in San Juan, and its members were distributed geographically throughout the island. Its served primarily as a rural and sometimes political police force. The collection contains only two boxes of surviving Guardia Civil documents for the period 1870–98, although some historians believe that Spanish officials perhaps took home with them some of the Guardia Civil documentation when they left the island in 1898. Some amount of local documentation produced by the Guardia Civil is found scattered in the surviving Fondos Municipales.

Serie Agencias Gubernamentales, Subserie: Seguridad Pública: These are the files of the central office of the Cuerpo de Orden Público y Policía Municipal (COP). This institution was created in 1879 and served mainly as an urban police force. There are four boxes of these files in the FGE. Local documentation of the COP is found in the Fondos Municipales.

Fondo Judicial, Serie Tribunal General de Justicia, Guayama, Subserie:
Expedientes Criminales

This group of records can be divided into three distinctive sets. Just three boxes contain cases dating from 1812–68 because at that time, Guayama was part of another judicial district, and its cases for this early period should be part of the files of that district, which is one of two that have yet to turn over their files to the AGPR. In 1870, Guayama became the head of a new judicial district. The great problem with this record group is that these files are not fully classified by year and by municipality where the criminal act took place, as has been done with every other judicial district whose files are at the AGPR.

These records are an excellent source for social history. Many of them contain rich qualitative and quantifiable information that helps to reconstruct the social and cultural patterns that emerged during the processes of transition to free labor, development of capitalist plantation agriculture, and formation of the rural proletariat class and class consciousness. Court depositions and testimonies often contain spirited and unstructured social commentary. Used with care and systematically and supplemented by other primary and secondary sources, these records offer a marvelous opportunity to explore the cultural values and symbols that inform the development of the various class, gender, and racial conflicts and solidarities that form part of the transition to capitalism. Although the majority of these *expedientes* have survived in poor physical condition, most include an index of contents that directs the researcher to the original complaint, the declarations by witnesses, and the sentence reached by the judge. The judicial system during this period did not have jury trials, and the judicial process combined the functions of both investigation and adjudication that today are performed by the police, district attorney, judiciary, and juries.

Fondo de Protocolos Notariales

These volumes are classified by judicial district, *municipio*, and notary public. Guayama has one of the most complete collections, and the volumes for the late nineteenth century are generally in excellent condition. Moreover, there is a useful chronological listing of ExCrim transactions by notary from early 1808 to 1913. Also, from the mid-1870s to shortly after the turn of the century, only one *notario público* existed. These factors tremendously facilitate work with these materials, which are among the richest types of historical documentation in Latin America.

Published Primary Sources

Abbad y Lassiera, Fray Iñigo. *Historia geográfica, civil, y natural de la Isla de San Juan Bautista de Puerto Rico*. Madrid: Imprenta de Valladares, 1788. Reprint, annotated and with an introduction by Isabel Gutiérrez del Arroyo. 3d ed. Río Piedras, P.R.: Editorial Universitaria, 1970.

Balanzas mercantiles del comercio exterior de Puerto Rico. Microfilm. Universidad de Puerto Rico, Recinto de Río Piedras, Centro de Investigaciones Históricas.

Boletín Histórico de Puerto Rico. San Juan: Cantero Fernández, 1914–27.

Código penal para las provincias de Cuba y Puerto-Rico y Ley provisional de enjuiciamiento criminal, mandados observar por real decreto de 23 de mayo de 1879. Madrid: Imprenta Nacional, 1879.

Córdova, Pedro Tomás de. *Memorias geográficas, históricas, económicas, y estadísticas de la Isla de Puerto Rico* [1831–33]. San Juan: Instituto de Cultura Puertorriqueña, 1968.

"Expediente sobre la abolición de la esclavitud (Juncos, Puerto Rico, 1873)." *Historia y Sociedad* 1 (1988): 182–88.

Fernández Méndez, Eugenio, ed. *Crónicas de Puerto Rico, desde la conquista hasta nuestros días, 1493–1955*. Río Piedras, P.R.: Editorial U.P.R., 1969.

Fernández Umpierre, Manuel. *Manual práctico de la agricultura de la caña de azúcar.* [San Juan]: Imprenta Boletín Mercantil, 1884.

Flinter, George. *An Account of the Present State of the Island of Puerto Rico*. London: Longman, Reese, Orme, Brown, Green, and Longman, 1834.

———. *A View of the Present Condition of the Slave Population of Puerto Rico.* Philadelphia: Waldie, 1832. Published in Spanish as *Examen del estado actual de los esclavos de la Isla de Puerto Rico bajo el dominio español*. New York: Imprenta Española del Redactor, 1832. Reprinted as *Examen del estado actual de los esclavos de Puerto Rico*. San Juan: Instituto de Cultura Puertorriqueña, 1976.

Great Britain. Parliament. House of Commons. *Irish University Press Series of British Parliamentary Papers. Slave Trade.* 8 vols. Shannon: Irish University Press, 1968–74.

"Informe del Cabildo de San Juan al Rey, 1775." *Boletín Histórico de Puerto Rico* 2:262–70.

Junta informativa de Ultramar: Extracto de las contestaciones que las comisiones elegidas por las Islas de Cuba y Puerto Rico han dado al interrogatorio que se ha puesto a su discusión, etc. Madrid: n.p., 1869.

Martínez Diez, José. "Relación del trato que doy a mi peonage en mi Hacienda Pueblo Viejo." *Anales de Investigación Histórica* 3:1 (1976): 80–83.

Miyares González, Fernando de. *Noticias particulares de la Isla de Puerto Rico y Plaza de San Juan Bautista de Puerto Rico* [1775]. 2d ed. San Juan: Universidad de Puerto Rico, 1957.

Nistal-Moret, Benjamín, ed. *Esclavos prófugos y cimarrones: Puerto Rico, 1770–1870*. Río Piedras: Editorial de la Universidad de Puerto Rico, 1984.

———. "Ocho documentos legales para el estudio de la esclavitud en Puerto Rico, 1797–1873." *Caribbean Studies* 20:2 (1980) 81–109.

O'Reilly, Alejandro. "Memoria de D. Alejandro O'Reilly a su magestad sobre la Isla de Puerto Rico en 1765." *Boletín Histórico de Puerto Rico* 8:116–17.

Ormaechea, Darío de. "Memoria acerca de la agricultura, el comercio y las rentas internas de la Isla de Puerto Rico" [1847]. *Boletín Histórico de Puerto Rico*, vol. 2.

Ponce de León, Néstor, ed. *Información sobre reformas en Cuba y Puerto Rico*. 2 vols. New York: Imprenta de Hallet and Breen, 1867.

El proceso abolicionista en Puerto Rico: Documentos para su estudio. 2 vols. San Juan: Centro de Investigaciones Históricas, Universidad de Puerto Rico, and Instituto de Cultura Puertorriqueña, 1974, 1978.

Puerto Rico. *Censo general de habitantes de 1867*. Computer data set. Río Piedras: Centro Académico de Computos de Ciencias Sociales, Universidad de Puerto Rico, 1983.

Ramírez de Arellano, Rafael W., ed. "Instrucciones al diputado Don Ramón Power y Giralt." *Boletín de la Universidad de Puerto Rico* 7:2 (1936).

"Relación del trato que doy a mi peonage en mi Hacienda Pueblo Viejo." *Anales de Investigación Histórica* 3:1 (1976): 80–83.

Revista de Agricultura, Industria, y Comercio. San Juan: Imprenta del Boletín Mercantil, 1886–91.

Ruiz Belvis, Segundo, José Julián Acosta, and Francisco Mariano Quiñones. *Proyecto para la abolición de la esclavitud en Puerto Rico, 1867*. San Juan: Instituto de Cultura Puertorriqueña, 1969.

Turnbull, David. *Travels in the West: Cuba; with Notices of Porto Rico, and the Slave Trade* [1840]. New York: AMS Press, 1973.

Ubeda y Delgado, Manuel. *Isla de Puerto Rico: Estudio histórico, geográfico, y estadístico de la misma*. San Juan: Imprenta del Boletín, 1878.

U.S. Department of War. Bureau of the Census of Puerto Rico. *Informe sobre el Censo de Puerto Rico*. Washington, D.C.: U.S. Government Printing Office, 1900.

Vázquez, José Antonio. "Descripción topográfica del pueblo de Guayama [1848]." *Boletín Histórico de Puerto Rico* 12:242–54.

Walker, Charles. "Charles Walker's Letters from Puerto Rico, 1835–1837." Annotated and with an introduction by Kenneth Scott. *Caribbean Studies* 5:1 (1965): 37–50.

Secondary Sources

Adamson, Alan H. *Sugar without Slaves: The Political Economy of British Guiana*. New Haven: Yale University Press, 1972.

Adas, Michael. "From Avoidance to Confrontation: Peasant Protest in Pre-Colonial Southeast Asia." *Comparative Studies in Society and History* 23:2 (1981): 217–45.

Aimes, Hubert H. "*Coartación*: A Spanish Institution for the Advancement of Slaves into Freedom." *Yale Review* 17 (1909): 412–31.

Albert, Bill. "The Creation of a Proletariat on Peru's Coastal Sugar Plantations." In *Crisis and Change in the International Sugar Economy, 1860–1914*, edited by Bill Albert and Adrian Greaves, 111–12. Norwich, Eng.: ISC Press, 1984.

Albert, Bill, and Adrian Greaves, eds. *Crisis and Change in the International Sugar Economy, 1860–1914*. Norwich, England: ISC Press, 1984.

Alvarez Curbelo, Silvia. *Un país del porvenir: El afán de modernidad en Puerto Rico (siglo XIX)*. San Juan: Callejón, 2001.

Andrews, George Reid. "Black and White Workers: São Paulo, Brazil, 1888–1928." In *The Abolition of Slavery and the Aftermath of Emancipation in Brazil*, 85–118. Durham, N.C.: Duke University Press, 1988.

Appelbaum, Nancy P., Anne S. Macpherson, and Karin A. Rosemblatt. "Racial Nations." In *Race and Nation in Modern Latin America*, edited by Nancy P. Appelbaum, Anne S. Macpherson, and Karin A. Rosemblatt, 1–31. Chapel Hill: University of North Carolina Press, 2003.

———, eds. *Race and Nation in Modern Latin America*. Chapel Hill: University of North Carolina Press, 2003.

Artola, Miguel. *La burguesía revolucionaria (1808–1874)*. Madrid: Alianza, 1974.

Ayala, César J., and Laird W. Bergad. "Rural Puerto Rico in the Early Twentieth Century Reconsidered: Land and Society, 1899–1915." *Latin American Research Review* 37:2 (2002): 65–97.

Bagué, Jaime. *Del ingenio patriarcal a la central azucarera*. Mayagüez, P.R.: Taller Gráfico de la Oficina de Información y Publicaciones del Colegio de Agricultura y Artes Mecánicas, 1968.

Bahamonde, Angel, and José Cayuela. *Hacer las Américas: Las élites coloniales españolas en el siglo XIX*. Madrid: Alianza, 1992.

Ballbé, Manuel. *Orden público y militarismo en la España constitucional, 1812–1983*. Madrid: Alianza, 1985.

Baralt, Guillermo A. *Buena Vista: Life and Work on a Puerto Rican Hacienda, 1833–1904*. Translated by Andrew Hurley. Chapel Hill: University of North Carolina Press, 1999.

———. *Esclavos rebeldes: Conspiraciones y sublevaciones de esclavos en Puerto Rico (1795–1873)*. Río Piedras, P.R.: Huracán, 1982.

Baralt, Guillermo A., Carlos Collazo, Lydia Milagros González, and Ana Lydia Vega. *El machete de Ogún: Las luchas de los esclavos en Puerto Rico (siglo 19)*. Río Piedras, P.R.: Centro de Estudios de la Realidad Puertorriqueña, 1990.

Barrett, O. W. "The Origins of Food Plants in Puerto Rico." *Scientific Monthly* 37:3 (1933): 241–56.

Bauer, Arnold J. "Rural Workers in Spanish America: Problems of Peonage and Oppression." *Hispanic American Historical Review* 59:1 (1979): 34–63.

Bauer, Raymond A., and Alice H. Bauer. "Day to Day Resistance to Slavery." *Journal of Negro History* 27:4 (1942): 388–419.

Beckles, Hilary McD. "Social and Political Control in the Slave Society." In *General History of the Caribbean*, vol. 3, *The Slave Societies of the Caribbean*, edited by B. W. Higman, 194–221. London: UNESCO Publishing and Macmillan Education, 1997.

Beishlag, George. "Trends in Land Use in Southeastern Puerto Rico." In *Symposium on the Geography of Puerto Rico*, edited by Clarence F. Jones and Rafael Picó. Río Piedras: University of Puerto Rico Press, 1955.

Bengoa, José. "Plantaciones y agroexportación: Un modelo teórico." In *Desarrollo agrario y la América Latina*, edited by J. E. G. de Araujo and Antonio García, 162–81. Mexico: Fondo de Cultura Económica, 1981.

Bergad, Laird W. "Coffee and Rural Proletarianization in Puerto Rico, 1840–1898." *Journal of Latin American Studies* 15:1 (1983): 83–100.

———. *Coffee and the Growth of Agrarian Capitalism in Nineteenth-Century Puerto Rico*. Princeton: Princeton University Press, 1983.

———. *Cuban Rural Society in the Nineteenth Century: The Social and Economic History of Monoculture in Matanzas*. Princeton: Princeton University Press, 1990.

———. "Hacia el Grito de Lares: Café, estratificación social, y conflictos de clase, 1828–1868." In *Inmigración y clases sociales en el Puerto Rico del siglo XIX*, edited and translated by Francisco A. Scarano, 143–85. Río Piedras, P.R.: Huracán, 1981.

——. "Recent Research on Slavery in Puerto Rico." *Plantation Society in the Americas* 2:1 (1983): 99–109.

——. "Towards Puerto Rico's Grito de Lares: Coffee, Social Stratification, and Class Conflicts, 1828–1868." *Hispanic American Historical Review* 60:4 (1980): 617–42.

Best, Lloyd. "Outlines of a Model of Pure Plantation Economy." *Social and Economic Studies* 22 (1968): 283–326.

Blackburn, Robin. *The Overthrow of Colonial Slavery, 1776–1848*. London: Verso, 1988.

Blanco, Tomás. *El prejuicio racial en Puerto Rico*. Río Piedras, P.R.: Huracán, 1985.

Bolland, O. Nigel. "Reply to William Green's 'The Perils of Comparative History.' " *Comparative Studies in Society and History* 26:1 (1984): 120–25.

——. "Systems of Domination after Slavery: The Control of Land and Labor in the British West Indies after 1838." *Comparative Studies in Society and History* 23:4 (1981): 591–619.

Bonnín, María Isabel. "Los contratos de refacción y el decaimiento de la hacienda tradicional en Ponce: 1865–1880." *Op. Cit.: Boletín del Centro de Investigaciones Históricas de la Universidad de Puerto Rico* 3 (1987–88): 123–50.

——. "Las fortunas vulnerables: Comerciantes y agricultores en los contratos de refacción de Ponce, 1865–1875." Master's thesis, Universidad de Puerto Rico, 1984.

Bothwell, Reece, and Lidio Cruz Monclova, eds. *Los documentos . . . ¿Qué dicen?: 1869–1899*. 2d ed. Río Piedras: Editorial Universitaria, Universidad de Puerto Rico, 1974.

Bourgois, Philippe I. *Ethnicity at Work: Divided Labor on a Central American Plantation*. Baltimore: Johns Hopkins University Press, 1989.

Bowser, Frederick P. "The Free Persons of Color in Lima and Mexico City: Manumission and Opportunity, 1580–1650." In *Race and Slavery in the Western Hemisphere: Quantitative Studies*, edited by Stanley L. Engerman and Eugene D. Genovese. Princeton: Princeton University Press, 1974.

Brana-Shute, Rosemary. "Approaching Freedom: The Manumission of Slaves in Suriname, 1760–1828." *Slavery and Abolition* 10:3 (1989): 40–63.

Brau, Salvador. *La colonización de Puerto Rico*. 2d ed. Annotated by Isabel Gutierrez del Arroyo. San Juan: Instituto de Cultura Puertorriqueña, 1966.

——. *Disquisiciones sociológicas y otros ensayos*. Río Piedras, P.R.: Edil, 1971.

——. *Historia de Puerto Rico*. 1904; San Juan: Coquí, 1966.

Buitrago Ortiz, Carlos. *Haciendas cafetaleras y clases terratenientes en el Puerto Rico decimonónico*. Río Piedras, P.R.: Huracán, 1982.

——. *Los orígenes de la sociedad pre-capitalista en Puerto Rico*. Río Piedras, P.R.: Huracán, 1976.

Bush, Barbara. *Slave Women in Caribbean Society, 1650–1838*. Bloomington: Indiana University Press, 1990.

Cabrero, Leoncio. "La abolición de la esclavitud en Puerto Rico." In *Estudios sobre la abolición de la esclavitud*, edited by Francisco de Solano, 181–215. Madrid: Consejo Superior de Investigaciones Científicas, Centro de Estudios Históricos, Departamento de Historia de América, 1986.

——. "La integración de los libertos puertorriqueños a la comunidad ciudadana." In *Esclavitud y derechos humanos: La lucha por la libertad del negro en el siglo XIX,* edited by Francisco de Solano and Agustín Guimerá, 293–314. Madrid: Consejo Superior de Investigaciones Científicas, Centro de Estudios Históricos, Departamento de Historia de América, 1990.

Calderón Martínez, Rafael. "El movimiento obrero dominicano, 1870–1978." In *Historia del movimiento obrero en América Latina*, edited by Pablo González Casanova, 1:253–357. Mexico: Siglo XXI, 1984.

Campbell, Susan. "Carnival, Calypso, and Class Struggle in Nineteenth-Century Trinidad." *History Workshop Journal* 26 (1988): 1–27.

Campos, Ricardo. "La abolición de la esclavitud en Puerto Rico: Una interpretación." *Avance*, 26 March 1973, 61–63.

Camuñas Madera, Ricardo. "Orígen y desarrollo de Guayama." *Horizontes* 24:48 (1981): 91–102.

Caraballo Román, Eurípides. "Origen y desarrollo de la Central San Francisco." Master's thesis, Universidad de Puerto Rico, 1983.

Carbonell Fernández, Rubén. "La compra-venta de esclavos en San Juan, 1817–1873." *Anales de Investigación Histórica* 3:1 (1976): 1–41.

——. "La compra-venta de esclavos en San Juan, 1818–1873." Master's thesis, Universidad de Puerto Rico, 1976.

Cardoso, Ciro F. S. *Agricultura, Escravidão, e Capitalismo*. Petrópolis, Brazil: Vozes, 1979.

Caro Costas, Aida. *El cabildo o régimen municipal puertorriqueño en el siglo XVIII*. 2 vols. San Juan: Municipio de San Juan and Instituto de Cultura Puertorriqueña, 1965–74.

——, ed. *Ramón Power y Giralt, diputado puertorriqueño a las Cortes Generales y Extraordinarias de España, 1810–1812: Compilación de documentos*. San Juan: n.p., 1969.

Carr, Raymond. *Spain, 1808–1975*. 2d ed. Oxford: Clarendon, 1982.

Casanovas, Joan. *Bread or Bullets! Urban Labor and Spanish Colonialism in Cuba, 1850–1898*. Pittsburgh: University of Pittsburgh Press, 1998.

Castro, María de los Angeles. "De Salvador Brau hasta la 'novísima' historia: Un replanteamiento y una crítica." *Op. Cit.: Boletín del Centro de Investigaciones Históricas de la Universidad de Puerto Rico* 4 (1988–89): 9–55.

Caulfield, Sueann. "The History of Gender in the Historiography of Latin America." *Hispanic American Historical Review* 81:3–4 (2001): 449–90.

Cayuela Fernández, José G. *Bahía de Ultramar: España y Cuba en el siglo XX: El control de las relaciones colonials*. Madrid: Siglo XXI, 1993.

Cepero Bonilla, Raúl. *Azúcar y abolición* [1948]. Barcelona: Editorial Crítica, 1976.

Chalhoub, Sidney. "Slaves, Freedmen, and the Politics of Freedom in Brazil: The Experience of Blacks in the City of Rio." *Slavery and Abolition* 10:3 (1989): 64–84.

Chinea, Jorge L. "Race and Labor in the Hispanic Caribbean: The West Indian Immigrant Worker Experience in Nineteenth-Century Puerto Rico, 1800–1850." Unpublished manuscript, 2003.

Chomsky, Avi, and Aldo Lauria, eds. *At the Margins of the Nation-State: Identity and*

Struggle in the Making of the Laboring Peoples of Central America and the Hispanic Caribbean, 1860–1960. Durham, N.C.: Duke University Press, 1998.

Cifre de Loubriel, Estela. *La inmigración a Puerto Rico durante el siglo XIX.* San Juan: Instituto de Cultura Puertorriqueña, 1964.

Colón, Edmundo. *Datos sobre la agricultura en Puerto Rico antes de 1898.* San Juan: Cantero Fernández, 1930.

Connerton, Paul. *How Societies Remember.* Cambridge: Cambridge University Press, 1989.

Cooper, Frederick. "Conflict and Connection: Rethinking Colonial African History." *American Historical Review* 99:5 (1994): 1516–45.

——. *From Slaves to Squatters: Plantation Labor and Agriculture in Zanzibar and Coastal Kenya, 1890–1925.* New Haven: Yale University Press, 1980.

Cooper, Frederick, Thomas C. Holt, and Rebecca J. Scott. *Beyond Slavery: Explorations of Race, Labor, and Citizenship in Post-Emancipation Societies.* Chapel Hill: University of North Carolina Press, 2000.

Córdova Iturregui, Félix. "Las huelgas azucareras de 1905." Paper presented at the Encuentro de Historiadores, Universidad de Puerto Rico, Recinto de Río Piedras, Departamento de Historia, 15–17 February 1990.

Corwin, Arthur F. *Spain and the Abolition of Slavery in Cuba, 1817–1886.* Austin: University of Texas Press, 1967.

Craton, Michael. "Continuity and Change: The Incidence of Unrest among Ex-Slaves in the British Caribbean, 1838–1876." *Slavery and Abolition* 9:2 (1988): 144–70.

——. "Forms of Resistance to Slavery." In *General History of the Caribbean*, vol. 3, *The Slave Societies of the Caribbean*, edited by B. W. Higman, 222–70. London: UNESCO Publishing and Macmillan Education, 1997.

——. *Searching for the Invisible Man: Slaves and Plantation Life in Jamaica.* Cambridge: Harvard University Press, 1978.

——. *Testing the Chains: Slave Rebellion in the British Caribbean.* Ithaca: Cornell University Press, 1982.

——. "The Transition from Slavery to Free Wage Labor in the Caribbean, 1780–1890: A Survey with Particular Reference to Recent Scholarship." Paper presented at the Conference of the Latin American Studies Association, 3–5 April 1991, Washington, D.C.

——, ed. *Roots and Branches: Current Directions in Slave Studies.* Toronto: Pergamon, 1979.

Craton, Michael, and James Walvin. *A Jamaican Plantation: The History of Worthy Park, 1670–1970.* Toronto: University of Toronto Press, 1970.

Cruz Monclova, Lidio. *Historia de Puerto Rico (siglo XIX).* 6 vols. Madrid: Editorial Universidad de Puerto Rico, 1952–64.

Cubano, Astrid. "Comercio y hegemonía social: Los comerciantes de Arecibo, 1857–1887." Master's thesis, Universidad de Puerto Rico, 1979.

——. "Economía y sociedad en Arecibo en el siglo XIX: Los grandes productores y la inmigración de comerciantes." In *Inmigración y clases sociales en el Puerto Rico de siglo XIX*, edited by Francisco A. Scarano, 67–124. Río Piedras, P.R.: Huracán, 1981.

——, "El estudio de las elites económicas y la política en Puerto Rico en el siglo XIX." *Op. Cit.: Boletín del Centro de Investigaciones Históricas de la Universidad de Puerto Rico* 4 (1988–89): 124–33.

——. *El hilo en el laberinto: Claves de la lucha política en Puerto Rico, siglo XIX*. Río Piedras, P.R.: Huracán, 1990.

——. "Paz pública y propiedad territorial: La discusión sobre la política agraria en Puerto Rico, 1880–1889." *Op. Cit.: Boletín del Centro de Investigaciones Históricas de la Universidad de Puerto Rico* 5 (1990): 11–36.

——. "Political Culture and Male Mass-Party Formation in Late-Nineteenth-Century Puerto Rico." *Hispanic American Historical Review* 78:4 (1998): 631–62.

——. "Sugar Trade and Economic Elites in Puerto Rico: Response to the Sugar Crisis in the Arecibo Region, 1878–1898." *Historia y Sociedad* 2 (1989): 70–89.

——. "Trade and Politics in Nineteenth-Century Puerto Rico." Ph.D. diss., Princeton University, 1988.

Cumper, G. E. "Labour Demand and Supply in the Jamaican Sugar Industry, 1830–1950." *Social and Economic Studies* 2:4 (1954): 37–86.

Curet, José. "About Slavery and the Order of Things: Puerto Rico, 1845–1873." In *Between Slavery and Free Labor: The Spanish-Speaking Caribbean in the Nineteenth Century*, edited by Manuel Moreno Fraginals, Frank Moya Pons, and Stanley L. Engerman, 117–40. Baltimore: Johns Hopkins University Press, 1985.

——. *Los amos hablan: Conversaciones entre un esclavo y su amo publicadas en "El Ponceño" 1853–1854*. Río Piedras, P.R.: Cultural, 1986.

——. "De la esclavitud a la abolición: Transiciones económicas en las haciendas azucareras de Ponce, 1845–1873." In *Azúcar y esclavitud*, edited by Andrés Ramos Mattei, 59–86. Río Piedras: Universidad de Puerto Rico, Recinto de Río Piedras, Biblioteca General José M. Lázaro, Departamento de Selección y Canje, 1982.

——. "From Slave to *Liberto*: A Study on Slavery and Its Abolition in Puerto Rico, 1840–1880." Ph.D. diss., Columbia University, 1980.

Curtin, Philip D. *The Rise and Fall of the Plantation Complex: Essays in Atlantic History*. New York: Cambridge University Press, 1990.

Dávila Cox, Emma. *Este inmenso comercio: Las relaciones mercantiles entre Puerto Rico y Gran Bretaña, 1844–1898*. San Juan: Editorial de la Universidad de Puerto Rico and Instituto de Cultura Puertorriqueña, 1996.

Deer, Noel. *The History of Sugar*. 2 vols. London: Chapman and Hall, 1949–50.

Dening, Greg. "The Comaroffs Out of Africa: A Reflection Out of Oceania." *American Historical Review* 108:2 (2003): 471–78.

Den Tandt, Catherine. "All That Is Black Melts into Air: Negritud and the Nation in Puerto Rico." In *Caribbean Romances: The Politics of Regional Representation*, edited by Belinda Edmondson. Charlottesville: University Press of Virginia, 1999.

Díaz Quiñones, Arcadio. *El almuerzo en la hierba (Lloréns Torres, Palés Matos, René Marqués)*. Río Piedras, P.R.: Huracán, 1982.

——. *Conversación con José Luis González*. Río Piedras, P.R.: Huracán, 1976.

———. "Estudio introductorio." In Tomás Blanco, *El prejuicio racial en Puerto Rico*, edited by Arcardio Díaz Quiñones, 13–91. Río Piedras, P.R.: Huracán, 1985.

———. *La memoria rota*. Río Piedras, P.R.: Huracán, 1993.

Díaz Soler, Luis. *Historia de la esclavitud negra en Puerto Rico*. 1953; Río Piedras: Editorial Universitaria, Universidad de Puerto Rico, 1981.

———. *Puerto Rico, desde sus orígenes hasta el cese de la dominación española*. Río Piedras: Editorial de la Universidad de Puerto Rico, 1994.

Dorsey, Joseph C. *Slave Traffic in the Age of Abolition: Puerto Rico, West Africa, and the Non-Hispanic Caribbean, 1815–1859*. Gainesville: University Press of Florida, 2003.

Dumoulin, John. *Azúcar y lucha de clases, 1917*. Havana: Editorial de Ciencias Sociales, 1980.

———. "El movimiento obrero en Cruces, 1902–1925: Corrientes ideológicas y formas de organización en la industria azucarera." *Islas* 62 (1979): 83–121.

———. "El primer desarrollo del movimiento obrero y la formación del proletariado azucarero: Cruces, 1886–1902." *Islas* 48 (1974): 3–66.

Eaton, George. "Trade Union Development in Jamaica." *Caribbean Quarterly* 8:1 (1962): 43–53; 8:2 (1962): 69–75.

Echevarría Morales, Moisés. *El proceso de Catalino Figueroa; o, La víctima de un error judicial*. Ponce: El Día, 1932.

Eisenberg, Peter L. *The Sugar Industry of Pernambuco: Modernization without Change, 1840–1910*. Berkeley: University of California Press, 1974.

Eltis, David. "The Nineteenth-Century Transatlantic Slave Trade: An Annual Time Series of Imports into the Americas Broken Down by Region." *Hispanic American Historical Review* 67:1 (1987): 109–38.

Espadas Burgos, Manuel. *Alfonso II y los orígenes de la Restauración*. Madrid: Consejo Superior de Investigaciones Científicas, 1990.

Evans, Judith. "Results and Prospects: Some Observations on Latin American Labor Studies." *International Labor and Working-Class History* 16 (1979): 29–39.

Feliciano Ramos, Héctor R. "El comercio de contrabando en la costa sur de Puerto Rico (1750–1778)." *Revista/Review Interamericana* 14 (1984): 80–99.

Fernández Méndez, Eugenio. *Historia cultural de Puerto Rico*. 3d ed. San Juan: El Cemí, 1971.

Ferrer, Ada. *Insurgent Cuba: Race, Nation, and Revolution, 1868–1898*. Chapel Hill: University of North Carolina Press, 1999.

Figueroa, Luis A. "Facing Freedom: The Transition from Slavery to Free Labor in Guayama, Puerto Rico, 1860–1898." Ph.D. diss., University of Wisconsin–Madison, 1991.

———. "From Slave to Peasant: Comparative Perspectives on Ex-Slave Class Formation in Puerto Rico." Master's Thesis, University of Wisconsin–Madison, 1985.

Findlay, Eileen J. Suárez. *Imposing Decency: The Politics of Sexuality and Race in Puerto Rico, 1870–1920*. Durham, N.C.: Duke University Press, 1999.

Flores, Juan. "The Puerto Rico José Luis González Built: Comments on Cultural History." *Latin American Perspectives* 11:3 (1984): 173–84.

Fradera, Josep M. "La importáncia de tenir colonies." In *Catalunya i ultramar: Poder i negoci a les colònies espanyoles (1750–1914)*, edited by Josep Maria Fradera, 22–52. Barcelona: Ambit Serveis, 1995.

——, "Quiebra imperial y reorganización política en la Antillas españolas, 1810–1868." *Op. Cit.: Boletín del Centro de Investigaciones Históricas de la Universidad de Puerto Rico* 9 (1997): 289–317.

——. "Why Were Spain's Special Overseas Laws Never Enacted?" In *Spain, Europe, and the Atlantic World: Essays in Honour of John H. Elliott*, edited by Richard L. Kagan and Geoffrey Parker, 335–49. New York: Cambridge University Press, 1995.

Fredrickson, George, and Christopher Lasch. "Resistance to Slavery." *Civil War History* 13 (1967): 315–39.

Frucht, Richard. "A Caribbean Social Type: Neither 'Peasant' nor 'Proletarian.'" *Social and Economic Studies* 16 (1967): 295–300.

Galloway, J. H. *The Sugar Cane Industry: An Historical Geography from Its Origins to 1914*. Cambridge: Cambridge University Press, 1989.

Galvin, Miles. "The Early Development of the Organized Labor Movement in Puerto Rico." *Latin American Perspectives* 3:3 (1976): 17–35.

——. *The Organized Labor Movement in Puerto Rico*. Cranbury, N.J.: Associated University Presses, 1979.

García, Gervasio L. *Historia crítica, historia sin coartadas: Algunos problemas de la historia de Puerto Rico*. Río Piedras, P.R.: Huracán, 1985.

——. "La historia de los trabajadores en la sociedad pre-industrial: El caso de Puerto Rico (1870–1900)." *Op. Cit.: Boletín del Centro de Investigaciones Históricas de la Universidad de Puerto Rico* 1 (1985–86): 17–26.

——. "Nuevos enfoques, viejos problemas." *Op. Cit.: Boletín del Centro de Investigaciones Históricas de la Universidad de Puerto Rico.*

——. "La política de la historia en Puerto Rico." *Op. Cit.: Boletín del Centro de Investigaciones Históricas de la Universidad de Puerto Rico* 2 (1986–87): 39–50.

——. "Las primeras actividades de los honrados hijos del trabajo: 1873–1898." *Op. Cit.: Boletín del Centro de Investigaciones Históricas de la Universidad de Puerto Rico* 5 (1990): 179–247.

——. *Primeros fermentos de organización obrera en Puerto Rico, 1873–1898*. Río Piedras, P.R.: Centro de Estudios de la Realidad Puertorriqueña, 1974.

García, Gervasio L., and Angel G. Quintero Rivera. *Desafío y solidaridad: Breve historia del movimiento obrero en Puerto Rico*. Río Piedras, P.R.: Huracán, 1982.

García Ochoa, María Asunción. *La política española en Puerto Rico durante el siglo XIX*. Río Piedras: Editorial de la Universidad de Puerto Rico, 1982.

Gaspar, David Barry. "Slavery, Amelioration, and Sunday Markets in Antigua, 1823–1831." *Slavery and Abolition* 9:1 (1988): 1–28.

Genovese, Eugene. *Roll, Jordan, Roll: The World the Slaves Made*. New York: Random House, 1974.

Gil-Bermejo, Juana. *Panorama histórico de la agricultura en Puerto Rico*. Seville: Escuela de Estudios Hispanoamericanos, 1970.

Godreau-Santiago, Isar Pilar. "Missing the Mix: San Antón and the Racial Dynamics of 'Nationalism' in Puerto Rico." Ph.D. diss., University of California–Santa Cruz, 1999.

Gómez Acevedo, Labor. *Organización y reglamentación del trabajo en el Puerto Rico del siglo XIX (propietarios y jornaleros)*. San Juan: Instituto de Cultura Puertorriqueña, 1970.

———. *Sanz: Promotor de la concienca separatista de Puerto Rico*. San Juan: Ediciones de la Universidad de Puerto Rico, 1956.

Gonzales, Michael. *Plantation Agriculture and Social Control in Northern Peru, 1875–1933*. Austin: University of Texas Press, 1985.

González, José Luis. *El país de los cuatro pisos y otros ensayos*. Río Piedras, P.R.: Huracán, 1980.

González Mendoza, Juan. "Demografía y sociedad en San Germán: Siglo XVIII." *Anales de Investigación Histórica* 9:1–2 (1982): 1–64.

———. "The Parish of San Germán de Auxerre in Puerto Rico, 1765–1850: Patterns of Settlement and Development." Ph.D. diss., State University of New York at Stony Brook, 1989.

Gould, Jeffrey L. "Revolutionary Nationalism and Local Memory in El Salvador." In *Reclaiming the Political in Latin American History*, edited by Gilbert M. Joseph, 138–71. Durham, N.C.: Duke University Press, 2001.

———. *To Lead as Equals: Rural Protest and Political Consciousness in Chinandega, Nicaragua, 1912–1979*. Chapel Hill: University of North Carolina Press, 1990.

Graden, Dale. "The Abolition of Slavery in Bahia, 1790–1900." Ph.D. diss., University of Connecticut, 1991.

Green, William A. *British Slave Emancipation: The Sugar Colonies and the Great Experiment, 1830–1865*. Oxford: Clarendon, 1976.

———. "The Perils of Comparative History." *Comparative Studies in Society and History* 26:1 (1984): 112–19.

Greenfield, Sidney M. "The Organization of Large Scale Agricultural Labor in Barbados and Minas Gerais, Brazil: A Comparison of Two Responses to Emancipation." *Anthropological Quarterly* 40:4 (1967): 201–16.

Guerra, Lillian. "From Revolution to Involution in the Early Cuban Republic: Conflicts over Race, Class, and Nation, 1902–1906." In *Race and Nation in Modern Latin America*, edited by Nancy P. Appelbaum, Anne S. Macpherson, and Karin A. Rosemblatt, 132–69. Chapel Hill: University of North Carolina Press, 2003.

———. *Popular Expression and National Identity in Puerto Rico: The Struggle for Self, Community, and Nation*. Gainesville: University Press of Florida, 1998.

Guerra y Sánchez, Ramiro. *La guerra de los diez años, 1868–1878*. 2d ed. 1950; Havana: Pueblo y Educación, 1986.

———. *Sugar and Society in the Caribbean*. New Haven: Yale University Press, 1964.

Guha, Ranajit. *Elementary Aspects of Peasant Insurgency in Colonial India*. Delhi: Oxford University Press, 1983.

———. "The Prose of Counter-Insurgency." In *Subaltern Studies*, edited by Ranajit Guha, 2:1–42. Delhi: Oxford University Press, 1983.

Guha, Ranajit, and Gayatri Chakravorty Spivak, eds. *Selected Subaltern Studies*. New York: Oxford University Press, 1988.

Gutman, Herbert. *The Black Family in Slavery and Freedom, 1750–1925*. New York: Pantheon, 1976.

Guy, Donna J., and Thomas E. Sheridan. "On Frontiers. The Northern and Southern Edges of the Spanish Empire in the Americas." In *Contested Ground: Comparative Frontiers on the Northern and Southern Edges of the Spanish Empire*, edited by Donna J. Guy and Thomas E. Sheridan, 3–15. Tucson: University of Arizona Press, 1998.

Hall, Douglas G. "The Apprenticeship Period in Jamaica, 1834–1838." *Caribbean Quarterly* 3:3 (1953): 142–66.

——. "The Flight from the Estates Reconsidered: The British West Indies, 1838–1842." *Journal of Caribbean History* 10–11 (1978): 7–24.

——. *Free Jamaica, 1838–1865: An Economic History*. New Haven: Yale University Press, 1959.

Hall, Gwendolyn Midlo. *Social Control in Slave Plantation Societies: A Comparison of St. Domingue and Cuba*. Baltimore: Johns Hopkins University Press, 1971.

Hall, Irwin. "International Conference of History of the Labor Movement." *International Labor and Working-Class History* 26 (1984): 102–3.

Handler, Jerome S., and Frederick W. Lange. *Plantation Slavery in Barbados: An Archaeological and Historical Investigation*. Cambridge: Harvard University Press, 1978.

Haraksingh, Kusha. "Labour Movements in the Caribbean." In *General History of the Caribbean*, vol. 6, *Methodology and Historiography of the Caribbean*, edited by B. W. Higman, 283–307. London: UNESCO Publishing and Macmillan Education, 1999.

Hernández Ruigómez, Almudena. "La abolición de la esclavitud en Puerto Rico: Introducción al estudio de las mentalidades anti-esclavistas." *Quinto Centenario* 14 (1988): 27–41.

Higman, B. W. *Montpelier, Jamaica: A Plantation Community in Slavery and Freedom, 1739–1912*. Mona, Jamaica: Press University of the West Indies, 1998.

Hine, Darlene Clark, and Jacqueline McLeod, eds. *Crossing Boundaries: Comparative History of Black People in Diaspora*. Bloomington: Indiana University Press, 1999.

History Task Force, Centro de Estudios Puertorriqueños, City University of New York. *Labor Migration under Capitalism: The Puerto Rican Experience*. New York: Monthly Review Press, 1979.

Hoernel, Robert B. "A Comparison of Sugar and Social Change in Puerto Rico and Oriente, Cuba, 1898–1959." Ph.D. diss., Johns Hopkins University, 1977.

Huggins, Martha Knisely. *From Slavery to Vagrancy in Brazil: Crime and Social Control in the Third World*. New Brunswick, N.J.: Rutgers University Press, 1985.

Izard, Miguel. "Comercio libre, guerras coloniales, y mercado Americano." In *Agricultura, comercio colonial, y crecimiento económico en la España contemporánea*, edited by Jordi Nadal and Gabriel Tortella. Barcelona: Ariel, 1974.

James, Daniel. *Resistance and Integration: Peronism and the Argentine Working Class, 1946–1976*. New York: Cambridge University Press, 1988.

Jiménez de Wagenheim, Olga. *El Grito de Lares: Sus causas y sus hombres*. Río Piedras, P.R.: Huracán, 1985.

Johnson, Lyman. "Manumission in Colonial Buenos Aires, 1776–1810." *Hispanic American Historical Review* 59:2 (1979): 258–79.

Jones, Jacqueline. *Labor of Love, Labor of Sorrow: Black Women, Work, and the Family from Slavery to the Present*. New York: Basic Books, 1985.

Joseph, Gilbert M., ed. *Reclaiming the Political in Latin American History: Essays from the North*. Durham, N.C.: Duke University Press, 2001.

Joseph, Gilbert M., and Allen Wells. "The Possibilities for and Limitations of Resistance on Yucatán's Henequén Estates, 1880–1915." Paper presented at the Eighth Latin American Labor History Conference, Princeton University, April 1991.

Karch, Cecilia Ann. "The Transformation and Consolidation of the Corporate Plantation Economy in Barbados, 1860–1977." Ph.D. diss., Rutgers University, 1979.

Klaren, Peter. *La formación de las haciendas azucareras y los orígenes del APRA*. Lima: Instituto de Estudios Peruanos, 1976.

Klein, Herbert S. *African Slavery in Latin America and the Caribbean*. New York: Oxford University Press, 1986.

———. *The Middle Passage: Comparative Studies in the Atlantic Slave Trade*. Princeton: Princeton University Press, 1978.

———. *Slavery in the Americas: A Comparative Study of Cuba and Virginia*. Chicago: University of Chicago Press, 1967.

Klein, Herbert S., and Stanley L. Engerman. "The Transition from Slave to Free Labor: Notes on a Comparative Economic Model." In *Between Slavery and Free Labor: The Spanish-Speaking Caribbean in the Nineteenth Century*, edited by Manuel Moreno Fraginals, Frank Moya Pons, and Stanley L. Engerman, 255–69. Baltimore: Johns Hopkins University Press, 1985.

Knight, Franklin W. "Blacks and the Forging of National Identity in the Caribbean, 1840–1900." In *Blacks, Coloureds, and National Identity in Nineteenth-Century Latin America*, edited by Nancy Priscilla Naro, 81–94. London: University of London, Institute of Latin American Studies, 2003.

———. *Slave Society in Cuba during the Nineteenth Century*. Madison: University of Wisconsin Press, 1970.

Knisely Huggins, Martha. *From Slavery to Vagrancy in Brazil: Crime and Social Control in the Third World*. New Brunswick, N.J.: Rutgers University Press, 1985.

Le Riverend, Julio. *Historia económica de Cuba*. Havana: Ensayo Book Institute, 1967.

Levy, Claude. "Barbados: The Last Years of Slavery, 1823–1833." *Journal of Negro History* 44:4 (1959): 308–45.

———. *Emancipation, Sugar, and Federalism: Barbados and the West Indies, 1833–1876*. Gainesville: University Presses of Florida, 1980.

Lida, Clara E., and Iris M. Zavala, eds. *La revolución de 1868: Historia, pensamiento, literatura*. New York: Las Américas, 1970.

López Cantos, Angel. *Historia de Puerto Rico, 1650–1700*. Seville: Escuela de Estudios Hispanoamericanos, 1975.

———. *Miguel Enríquez: Corsario boricua del siglo XVIII*. San Juan: Puerto, 1994.

López Garrifo, Diego. *La Guardia Civil y los orígenes del estado centralista en España*. Barcelona: Crítica, 1982.

Luque de Sánchez, María Dolores. "Aportaciones y apropiaciones extranjeras: Los inmigrantes en la historiografía puertorriqueña." *Op. Cit.: Boletín del Centro de Investigaciones Históricas de la Universidad de Puerto Rico* 4 (1988–89): 59–79.

Lynch, John. "The Institutional Framework of Colonial Spanish America." *Journal of Latin American Studies* 24:Quincentenary Supplement (1992): 69–81.

Machado, María Helena Pereira Toledo. *Crime e escravidão: Trabalho, luta, e resistencia nas lavouras paulistas, 1830–1888*. São Paulo: Editora Brasiliense, 1987.

Mahoney, Mary Ann. "A Past to Do Justice to the Present: Collective Memory, Historical Representation, and Rule in Bahia's Cacao Area." In *Reclaiming the Political in Latin American History*, edited by Gilbert M. Joseph, 102–37. Durham, N.C.: Duke University Press, 2001.

Maldonado Denis, Manuel. "En torno *El país de los cuatro pisos*." *Casa de las Americas* 135 (1982): 151–59.

——. *Puerto Rico: Una interpretación histórico-social*. Mexico City: Siglo XXI, 1969.

Mallon, Florencia E. "Bearing Witness in Hard Times: Ethnography and *Testimonio* in a Postrevolutionary Age." In *Reclaiming the Political in Latin American History*, edited by Gilbert M. Joseph, 311–54. Durham, N.C.: Duke University Press, 2001.

——. "Labor Migration, Class Formation, and Class Consciousness among Peruvian Miners: The Central Highlands, 1900–1930." In *Proletarians and Protest*, edited by Michael Hanagan and Charles Stephenson, 198–230. Westport, Conn.: Greenwood 1986.

——. "The Promise and Dilemma of Subaltern Studies." *American Historical Review* 99:5 (1994): 1491–1515.

Maluquer, Jordi. "El problema de la esclavitud y la revolución de 1868." *Hispania: Revista Española de Historia* 31:117 (1971): 55–75.

Mandle, Jay R. *The Plantation Economy: Population and Economic Change in Guyana, 1838–1960*. Philadelphia: Temple University Press, 1973.

Marshall, Woodville K. "Commentary One [on Sidney Mintz's 'Slavery and the Rise of Peasantries']." In *Roots and Branches: Current Directions in Slave Societies*, edited by Michael Craton, 243–48. Toronto: Pergamon, 1979.

——. "The Establishment of a Peasantry in Barbados, 1840–1920." In *Social Groups and Institutions in the History of the Caribbean: Papers Presented at the Sixth Annual Conference of Caribbean Historians, Puerto Rico, April 4–9, 1974*, 85–104. Mayagüez, P.R.: Association of Caribbean Historians, 1975.

——. "Notes on Peasant Development in the West Indies since 1838." *Social and Economic Studies* 17:3 (1968): 252–63.

Martínez-Vergne, Teresita. *Capitalism in Colonial Puerto Rico: Central San Vicente in the Late Nineteenth Century*. Gainesville: University Press of Florida, 1992.

——. "New Patterns for Puerto Rican Sugar Workers: Abolition and Centralization at San Vicente, 1873–1892." *Hispanic American Historical Review* 68:1 (1988): 45–74.

——. "La transición en Caribe: Reflexiones en torno a *Between Slavery and Free Labor*." *Historia y Sociedad* 2 (1989): 148–64.

Mascareñas, M. Tona. "La abolición en Puerto Rico: Un proceso irremediable." In *Esclavitud y derechos humanos: La lucha por la libertad del negro en el siglo XIX*, edited by Francisco de Solano and Gabriel Guimará, 269–78. Madrid: Consejo Superior de Investigaciones Científicas, Centro de Estudios Históricos, Departamento de Historia de América, 1990.

Mathews, Thomas G. "The Question of Color in Puerto Rico." In *Slavery and Race Relations in Latin America*, edited by Robert Brent Toplin, 299–323. Westport, Conn.: Greenwood, 1974.

Matos Rodríguez, Félix V. "New Currents in Puerto Rican History: Legacy, Continuity, and Challenges of the 'Nueva Historia.'" *Latin American Research Review* 32:3 (1997): 193–208.

McAvoy-Weissman, Muriel. "Brotherly Letters: The Correspondence of Henry Cabot Lodge and J. D. H. Luce, 1898–1913." *Historia y Sociedad* 1 (1988): 99–122.

Méndez, José Luis. "La arquitectura intelectual de *El país de los cuatro pisos*." *Claridad*, 16–22 April 1982; 23–29 April 1982.

Mintz, Sidney. "Cañamelar: The Sub-Culture of a Rural Sugar Plantation Proletariat." In Julian H. Steward et al., *The People of Puerto Rico: A Study in Social Anthropology*. Urbana: University of Illinois Press, 1956.

———. "Caribbean Marketplaces and Caribbean History." *Radical History Review* 27 (1983): 110–20.

———. *Caribbean Transformations*. 1974; Baltimore: Johns Hopkins University Press, 1984.

———. "The Culture History of a Puerto Rican Sugar-Cane Plantation, 1876–1946." *Hispanic American Historical Review* 33:2 (1953): 224–51.

———. Foreword to *Sugar and Society in the Caribbean*, by Ramiro Guerra. New Haven: Yale University Press, 1964.

———. "History and Anthropology: A Brief Reprise." In *Race and Slavery in the Western Hemisphere: Quantitative Studies*, edited by Stanley Engerman and Eugene Genovese, 477–94. Princeton: Princeton University Press, 1975.

———. "Labor and Sugar in Puerto Rico and Jamaica, 1800–1850." *Comparative Studies in Society and History* 1:3 (1959): 273–83.

———. "The Question of Caribbean Peasantries: A Comment." *Caribbean Studies* 1:3 (1961): 31–34.

———. "The Role of Forced Labor in Nineteenth-Century Puerto Rico." *Caribbean Historical Review* 1:2 (1951): 134–51.

———. "Slavery and the Rise of Peasantries." In *Roots and Branches: Current Directions in Slave Studies*, edited by Michael Craton, 213–53. Toronto: Pergamon, 1979.

———. *Sweetness and Power: The Place of Sugar in Modern History*. New York: Viking, 1985.

———. "Was the Plantation Slave a Proletarian?" *Review—Fernand Braudel Center for the Study of Economies, Historical Systems, and Civilizations* 2:1 (1978): 81–98.

Mintz, Sidney, and Richard Price. *An Anthropological Approach to the Afro-American Past: A Caribbean Perspective*. Philadelphia: Institute for the Study of Human Issues, 1976.

Morales, José. "The Hispaniola Diaspora, 1791–1850: Puerto Rico, Cuba, Louisiana, and Other Host Societies." Ph.D. diss., University of Connecticut, 1986.

Morales Carrión, Arturo. "La abolición de la trata y las corrientes abolicionistas en Puerto Rico." In *Esclavitud y derechos humanos: La lucha por la libertad del negro en el siglo XIX*, edited by Francisco de Solano and Agustín Guimerá, 44/ 68. Madrid: Consejo Superior de Investigaciones Científicas, Centro de Estudios Históricos, Departamento de Historia de América, 1990.

———. *Albores históricos del capitalismo en Puerto Rico*. Río Piedras: Editorial Universitaria, Universidad de Puerto Rico, 1972.

———. *Auge y decadencia de la trata negrera en Puerto Rico (1820–1860)*. San Juan: Centro de Estudios Avanzados de Puerto Rico y el Caribe and Instituto de Cultura Puertorriqueña, 1978.

———. "Ojeada a las corrientes abolicionistas en Puerto Rico." *Anuario de Estudios Americanos* 43 (1986): 295–309.

———. *Ojeada al proceso histórico y otros ensayos*. San Juan: Cordillera, 1974.

———. *Puerto Rico and the Non-Hispanic Caribbean: A Study in the Decline of Spanish Exclusivism*. Río Piedras: University of Puerto Rico Press, 1952.

Moreno Fraginals, Manuel. *La historia como arma y otros estudios sobre esclavos, ingenios y plantaciones*. Barcelona: Crítica, 1983.

———. *El Ingenio: Complejo económico social cubano del azúcar*. 3 vols. Havana: Editorial de Ciencias Sociales, 1978.

Moreno Fraginals, Manuel, Frank Moya Pons, and Stanley L. Engerman, eds. *Between Slavery and Free Labor: The Spanish-Speaking Caribbean in the Nineteenth-Century*. Baltimore: Johns Hopkins University Press, 1985.

Morrissey, Marietta. *Slave Women in the New World: Gender Stratification in the Caribbean*. Lawrence: University Press of Kansas, 1989.

Nadal, Jordi, and Gabriel Tortella, eds. *Agricultura, comercio colonial, y crecimiento económico en la España contemporánea*. Barcelona: Ariel, 1974.

Náter Vázquez, Laura. "El '98 en la historiografía puertorriqueña: Del político entusiasta al héroe popular." *Op. Cit.: Boletín del Centro de Investigaciones Históricas de la Universidad de Puerto Rico* 4 (1988–89): 102–22.

Navarro Azcue, Concepción. *La abolición de la esclavitud negra en la legislación española, 1870–1886*. Madrid: Instituto de Cooperación Iberoamericana, Ediciones Cultura Hispánica, 1987.

Negrón Portillo, Mariano. "Comentarios sobre el libro *1898: La guerra después de la guerra*, de Fernando Picó." *Revista de Ciencias Sociales* 27:3–4 (1988): 173–78.

Negrón Portillo, Mariano, and Raúl Mayo Santana. *La esclavitud urbana en San Juan*. Río Piedras, P.R.: Huracán, 1992.

———. "Trabajo, producción, y conflictos en el siglo XIX: Una revisión crítica de las nuevas investigaciones históricas en Puerto Rico." *Revista de Ciencias Sociales* 24:3–4 (1985): 472–97.

Nistal-Moret, Benjamín. "La contratación de los libertos de Manatí, 1873–1876." *Revista del Instituto de Cultura Puertorriqueña* 61 (1973): 51–59.

———. "Problems in the Social Structure of Slavery in Puerto Rico during the Process of Abolition, 1872." In *Between Slavery and Free Labor: The Spanish-Speaking Caribbean in the Nineteenth Century*, edited by Manuel Moreno Fraginals, Frank

Moya Pons, and Stanley L. Engerman, 141–57. Baltimore: Johns Hopkins University
Press, 1985.

——. "El Pueblo de Nuestra Señora de la Candelaria y el Apóstol San Matías de Manatí,
1800–1880: Its Ruling Classes and the Institution of Black Slavery." Ph.D. diss., State
University of New York at Stony Brook, 1977.

O'Hanlon, Rosalind. "Recovering the Subject: *Subaltern Studies* and Histories of
Resistance in Colonial South Asia." *Modern Asian Studies* 22:1 (1988): 189–224.

Omi, Michael, and Howard Winant. *Racial Formation in the United States: From the
1960s to the 1990s.* New York: Routledge, 1994.

Oquendo, Elí. "Inmigración y cambio social en Guayama, 1815–1840." Master's thesis,
Universidad de Puerto Rico, 1986.

Ortiz, Altagracia. *Eighteenth-Century Reforms in the Caribbean: Miguel de Muesas,
Governor of Puerto Rico, 1769–1776.* Rutherford, N.J.: Fairleigh Dickinson University
Press, 1983.

Ortiz Cuadra, Cruz M. "Crédito y azúcar: Los hacendados de Humacao ante la crisis
del dulce, 1865–1900." Master's thesis, Universidad de Puerto Rico, 1985.

Padín, José A. "The Redefinition of National Identity: The Afro-Caribbean Sources
of Puerto Rican Culture and Music." Master's thesis, University of Wisconsin–
Madison, 1989.

Patterson, Orlando. *Slavery and Social Death: A Comparative Study.* Cambridge:
Harvard University Press, 1982.

Peacock, A. J. "Village Radicalism in East Anglia, 1800–1850." In *Rural Discontent in
Nineteenth-Century Britain*, edited by J. P. D. Dunbabin. London: Faber, 1974.

Peloso, Vincent C. *Peasants on Plantations: Subaltern Strategies of Labor and Resistance.*
Durham, N.C.: Duke University Press, 1999.

Peña Valdez, Julio Augusto de. *Breve historia del movimiento sindical dominicano.* Santo
Domingo: Dominicanas Populares, 1977.

Pérez-Prendes y Muñoz de Araco, J. M. "La Revista 'El Abolicionista' (1865–1876) en la
génesis de la abolición de la esclavitud en las Antillas españolas." *Anuario de
Estudios Americanos* 43 (1986): 215–40.

Pérez Vega, Ivette. "Las sociedades mercantiles en Ponce, 1817–1825." *Anales de
Investigación Histórica* 6:2 (1979).

Picó, Fernando. *Amargo café: Los pequeños y medianos caficultores de Utuado en la
segunda mitad del siglo XIX.* Río Piedras, P.R.: Huracán, 1981.

——. "Dehumanización del trabajo y cosificación de la naturaleza: Los comienzos del
auge del café en el Utuado del siglo XIX." In *Inmigración y clases sociales en el Puerto
Rico del siglo XIX*, edited by Francisco A. Scarano, 187–206. Río Piedras, P.R.:
Huracán, 1981.

——. *1898: La guerra después de la guerra.* Río Piedras, P.R.: Huracán, 1987.

——. "Esclavos, cimarrones, libertos, y negros libres en Río Piedras, 1774–1873."
Anuario de Estudios Americanos 43 (1986): 25–33.

——. *Al filo del poder: Subalternos y dominantes en Puerto Rico, 1739–1910.* Río Piedras,
P.R.: Editorial de las Universidad de Puerto Rico, 1993.

——. "Fuentes para la historia de las comunidades rurales en Puerto Rico durante los siglos 19 y 20." *Op. Cit.: Boletín del Centro de Investigaciones Históricas de la Universidad de Puerto Rico* 1 (1985–86): 1–14.

———. *Historia general de Puerto Rico*. Río Piedras, P.R.: Huracán, 1986.

———. "Historiography of Puerto Rico." In *General History of the Caribbean*, vol. 6, *Methodology and Historiography of the Caribbean*, edited by B. W. Higman, 417–50. London: UNESCO Publishing and Macmillan Education, 1999.

———. "Introducción." In *Azúcar y esclavitud*, edited by Andrés A. Ramos-Mattei, 1–4. San Juan: Universidad de Puerto Rico, Recinto de Río Piedras, Biblioteca General José M. Lázaro, Departamento de Selección y Canje, 1982.

———. *Libertad y servidumbre en el Puerto Rico del siglo XIX (los jornaleros utuadeños en vísperas del auge del café)*. Río Piedras, P.R.: Huracán, 1979.

Picó, Rafael. *The Geographic Regions of Puerto Rico*. Río Piedras: University of Puerto Rico Press, 1950.

Picó, Rafael, Zayda Buitrago de Santiago, and Héctor H. Berríos. *Nueva geografía de Puerto Rico: Física, económica, y social*. Río Piedras: Editorial Universitaria, Universidad de Puerto Rico, 1969.

Piqueras Arenas, José A. *La revolución democrática, 1868–1874: Cuestión social, colonialismo, y grupos de presión*. Madrid: Ministerio de Trabajo y Seguridad Social, 1992.

Piqueras Arenas, José A., and Enric Sebastiá Domingo. *Agiotistas, negreros, y partisanos: Dialéctica social en vísperas de la Revolución Gloriosa*. Valencia: Ediciones Alfons el Magnánim, Institució Valenciana d'Estudis i Investigació, 1991.

Porrata Doria, Adolfo. *Guayama: Sus hombres y sus instituciones*. Barcelona: Porrata Doria, 1972.

Prakash, Gyan. "Subaltern Studies as Postcolonial Criticism." *American Historical Review* 99:5 (1994): 1475–90.

Queiros de Mattoso, Katia. *To Be a Slave in Brazil*. New Brunswick, N.J.: Rutgers University Press, 1986.

Quintero Rivera, Angel G. "Background to the Emergence of Imperialist Capitalism in Puerto Rico." *Caribbean Studies* 13:3 (1973): 31–63.

———. "La clase obrera y la política en Puerto Rico." *Revista de Ciencias Sociales* 18:1 (1974): 147–98; 18:3–4 (1974): 61–107; 19:1 (1975): 49–99; 19:3 (1975): 263–98; 20:1 (1976): 3–47.

———. "Clases sociales e identidad nacional: Notas sobre el desarrollo nacional puertorriqueño." In *Puerto Rico: Identidad nacional y clases sociales*, edited by Angel G. Quintero Rivera, José Luis González, Ricardo Campos, and Juan Flores, 13–44. Río Piedras, P.R.: Huracán, 1979.

———. *Conflictos de clase y política en Puerto Rico*. San Juan: Centro de Estudios de la Realidad Puertorriqueña; Río Piedras, P.R.: Huracán, 1976.

———. *Historia de unas clases sin historia: Notas para el analisis cultural*. Río Piedras, P.R., 1983.

———. *Patricios y plebeyos: Burgueses, hacendados, artesanos, y obreros: Las relaciones de clase en el Puerto Rico de cambio de siglo*. Río Piedras, P.R.: Huracán, 1988.

——. "Socialista y tabaquero: La proletarización de los artesanos." *Revista sin Nombre* 8:4 (1977): 100–137.

——, ed. *Lucha obrera en Puerto Rico: Antología de grandes documentos en la historia obrera puertorriqueña*. San Juan: Centro de Estudios de la Realidad Puertorriqueña, 1971.

Ramos Mattei, Andrés. *Betances en el ciclo revolucionario antillano, 1867–1875*. Río Piedras, P.R.: Instituto de Cultura Puertorriqueña, 1987.

——. "Las centrales olvidadas: Formación de capital y los cambios técnicos en la industria azucarera puertorriqueña, 1873–1880." *Historia y Sociedad* 1 (1988): 81–98.

——. *La hacienda azucarera: Su crecimiento y crisis en Puerto Rico (siglo XIX)*. San Juan: Centro de Estudios de la Realidad Puertorriqueña, 1981.

——. "La importación de trabajadores contratados para la industria azucarera puertorriqueña, 1860–1880." In *Inmigración y clases sociales en el Puerto Rico del siglo XIX*, edited by Francisco Scarano, 125–41. Río Piedras, P.R.: Huracán, 1981.

——. "El liberto en el régimen de trabajo azucarero de Puerto Rico, 1870–1880." In *Azúcar y esclavitud*, edited by Andrés Ramos Mattei, 91–124. San Juan: Universidad de Puerto Rico, Recinto de Río Piedras, Biblioteca General José M. Lázaro, Departamento de Selección y Canje, 1982.

——. *Los libros de cuentas de la Central Mercedita, 1861–1900*. San Juan: Centro de Estudos de la Realidad Puertorriqueña, 1975.

——. *La sociedad del azúcar en Puerto Rico, 1870–1910*. Río Piedras: Universidad de Puerto Rico, Recinto de Río Piedras, 1988.

——. "Technical Innovations and Social Change in the Sugar Industry of Puerto Rico, 1870–1880." In *Between Slavery and Free Labor: The Spanish-Speaking Caribbean in the Nineteenth Century*, edited by Manuel Moreno Fraginals, Frank Moya Pons, and Stanley L. Engerman, 158–78. Baltimore: Johns Hopkins University Press, 1985.

——, ed. *Azúcar y esclavitud*. San Juan: Universidad de Puerto Rico, Recinto de Río Piedras, Biblioteca General José M. Lázaro, Departamento de Selección y Canje, 1982.

Reddock, Rhoda E. "Women and Slavery in the Caribbean: A Feminist Perspective." *Latin American Perspectives* 12:1 (1985): 63–80.

Restall, Mathew, and Jane Landers. "The African Experience in Early Spanish America." *The Americas* 57:2 (2000): 167–70.

Richardson, David, ed. *Abolition and Its Aftermath: The Historical Context, 1790–1916*. London: Cass, 1985.

Rivière, W. Emanuel. "Labour Shortage in the British West Indies after Emancipation." *Journal of Caribbean History* 4 (1972): 1–30.

Roberts, Ray Carlton. *Soil Survey, Puerto Rico*. Washington, D.C.: U.S. Government Printing Office, 1942.

Rodney, Walter. *A History of the Guyanese Working People, 1881–1905*. Baltimore: Johns Hopkins University Press, 1981.

Rodríguez Juliá, Edgardo. *Campeche o los diablejos de la melancolía*. San Juan: Instituto de Cultura Puertorriqueña, 1986.

——. *El entierro de Cortijo*. Río Piedras, P.R.: Huracán, 1982.

——. *La noche oscura del niño Avilés*. Río Piedras, P.R.: Huracán, 1984.

——. *La renuncia del héroe Baltasar*. Río Piedras, P.R.: Cultural, 1986.

Rubin, Vera, and Arthur Tuden, eds. *Comparative Perspectives on Slavery in New World Plantation Societies*. New York: New York Academy of Sciences, 1977.

Sánchez, Luis Rafael. *La guaracha del Macho Camacho*. Buenos Aires: Ediciones de la Flor, 1976.

San Miguel, Pedro L. "Falsos (además de confusos) comienzos de una digresión sobre historia y antropología." *Op. Cit.: Revista del Centro de Investigaciones Históricas* 11 (1999): 33–61.

——. *El mundo que creó el azúcar: Vega Baja*. Río Piedras, P.R.: Huracán, 1988.

——. "Tierra, trabajadores, y propietarios: Las haciendas en Vega Baja, 1828–1865." *Anales de Investigación Histórica* 6:2 (1979): 1–51.

Santiago, K. Antonio. "El Puerto Rico del siglo XIX: Apuntes para su análisis." *Homines* 5 (1981): 7–23

Santiago de Curet, Ana Mercedes. *Crédito, moneda, y bancos en Puerto Rico durante el siglo XIX*. San Juan: Centro de Estudios Avanzados de Puerto Rico y el Caribe, 1991.

Scarano, Francisco A. "Congregate and Control: The Peasantry and Labor Coercion in Puerto Rico, 1750–1820." *New West-Indian Guide* 63:1–2 (1989): 23–40.

——. "Población esclava y fuerza de trabajo: Problemas del análisis demográfico de la esclavitud en Puerto Rico." *Anuario de Estudios Americanos* 43 (1986): 3–24.

——. *Puerto Rico: Cinco siglos de historia*. Santafé de Bogotá: McGraw-Hill, 1993.

——. "Slavery and Emancipation in Caribbean History." In *General History of the Caribbean*, vol. 6, *Methodology and Historiography of the Caribbean*, edited by B. W. Higman, 232–82. London: UNESCO Publishing and Macmillan Education, 1999.

——. "Slavery and Free Labor in the Puerto Rican Sugar Economy, 1815–1873." In *Comparative Perspectives on Slavery in New World Plantation Societies*, edited by Vera Rubin and Arthur Tuden, 553–63. New York: New York Academy of Sciences, 1977.

——. *Sugar and Slavery in Puerto Rico: The Plantation Economy of Ponce, 1800–1850*. Madison: University of Wisconsin Press, 1984.

——, ed. *Inmigración y clases sociales en el Puerto Rico del siglo XIX*. Río Piedras, P.R.: Huracán, 1981.

Schmidt-Nowara, Christopher. *Empire and Antislavery: Spain, Cuba, and Puerto Rico, 1833–1874*. Pittsburgh: University of Pittsburgh Press, 1999.

——. "National Economy and Atlantic Slavery: Protectionism and Resistance to Abolitionism in Spain and the Antilles, 1854–1874." *Hispanic American Historical Review* 78:4 (1998): 603–29.

——. "The Problem of Slavery in the Age of Capital: Abolitionism, Liberalism, and Counter-Hegemony in Spain, Cuba, and Puerto Rico, 1833–1886." Ph.D. diss., University of Michigan, 1995.

Schnakenbourg, Christian. *Histoire de l'industrie sucrière en Guadeloupe aux XIXe–XXe siècles*. Vol. 1, *La crise du système esclavagiste, 1835–1847*. Paris: L'Harmattan, 1980.

Schwartz, Stuart B. "Black Latin America: Legacies of Slavery, Race, and African Culture." *Hispanic American Historical Review* 82:3 (2002): 429–33.

———. "The Manumission of Slaves in Colonial Brazil: Bahia, 1684–1745." *Hispanic American Historical Review* 54:4 (1974): 603–35.

———. "Recent Trends in the Study of Slavery in Brazil." *Luso-Brazilian Review* 25:1 (1988): 1–25.

———. "Somebodies and Nobodies in the Body Politic: Mentalities and Social Structures in Colonial Brazil." *Latin American Research Review* 31 (1996): 113–34.

Scott, James C. *Domination and the Arts of Resistance: Hidden Transcripts.* New Haven: Yale University Press, 1990.

———. "Protest and Profanation: Agrarian Revolt and the Little Tradition." *Theory and Society* 4:1 (1977): 1–38; 4:2 (1977): 211–46.

———. "Resistance without Protest and without Organization: Peasant Opposition to the Islamic *Zakat* and the Christian Tithe." *Comparative Studies in Society and History* 29:3 (1987): 417–52.

———. *Weapons of the Weak: Everyday Forms of Peasant Resistance.* New Haven: Yale University Press, 1985.

Scott, Rebecca J. "Comparing Emancipations: A Review Essay." *Journal of Social History* 20:3 (1987): 565–83.

———. "Defining the Boundaries of Freedom in the World of Cane: Cuba, Brazil, and Louisiana after Emancipation." *American Historical Review* 99:1 (1994): 70–102.

———. "Explaining Abolition: Contradiction, Adaptation, and Challenge in Cuban Slave Society, 1860–1886." *Comparative Studies in Society and History* 26:1 (1984): 83–111.

———. "Exploring the Meaning of Freedom: Post-Emancipation Society in Comparative Perspective." *Hispanic American Historical Review* 68:3 (1988): 407–28.

———. *Slave Emancipation in Cuba: The Transition to Free Labor, 1868–1895.* Princeton: Princeton University Press, 1985.

Scott, Rebecca J., Seymour Drescher, Hebe Maria Mattos de Castro, George Reid Andrews, and Robert Levine. *The Abolition of Slavery and the Aftermath of Emancipation in Brazil.* Durham, N.C.: Duke University Press, 1988.

Sheller, Mimi. *Democracy after Slavery: Black Publics and Peasant Radicalism in Haiti and Jamaica.* Gainesville: University Press of Florida, 2000.

Silén, Juan Angel. *Apuntes para la historia del movimiento obrero puertorriqueño.* Río Piedras, P.R.: Cultural, 1978.

Skidmore, Thomas E. "Workers and Soldiers: Urban Labor Movements and Elite Responses in Twentieth-Century Latin America." In *Elites, Masses, and Modernization in Latin America*, edited by Virginia Bernhard, 79–126. Austin: University of Texas Press, 1979.

Social Science Research Council. *Items* 37:1 (1983): 29.

———. *Items* 38:2–3 (1984).

Sofer, Eugene F. "Recent Trends in Latin American Labor Historiography." *Latin American Research Review* 15:1 (1980): 167–76.

Spivak, Gayatri Chakravorty. "The Rani of Sirmur: An Essay in Reading the Archives." *History and Theory* 24:3 (1985): 247–72.

———. "Subaltern Studies: Deconstructing Historiography." In *Selected Subaltern*

Studies, edited by Ranajit Guha and Gayatri Chakravorty Spivak, 3–32. New York: Oxford University Press, 1988.

Stampp, Kenneth M. *The Peculiar Institution: Slavery in the Ante Bellum South.* New York: Knopf, 1956.

Stein, Stanley J. *Vassouras: A Brazilian Coffee County, 1850–1900.* Cambridge: Harvard University Press, 1957. Reprint, Princeton: Princeton University Press, 1985.

Stern, Steve J. "New Approaches to the Study of Peasant Rebellion and Consciousness: Implications of the Andean Experience." In *Resistance, Rebellion, and Consciousness in the Andean World: Eighteenth to Twentieth Centuries*, edited by Steve J. Stern, 3–25. Madison: University of Wisconsin Press, 1988.

Steward, Julian H., et al. *The People of Puerto Rico.* Urbana: University of Illinois Press, 1956.

Stubbs, Jean. "Gender in Caribbean History." In *General History of the Caribbean*, vol. 6, *Methodology and Historiography of the Caribbean*, edited by B. W. Higman, 95–135. London: UNESCO Publishing and Macmillan Education, 1999.

Sued Badillo, Jalil. *Guayama: Notas para su historia.* San Juan: Comité Historia de los Pueblos, 1983.

Sued Badillo, Jalil, and Angel López Cantos, *Puerto Rico negro.* Río Piedras, P.R.: Cultural, 1985.

Szaszdi, Adam. "Apuntes sobre la esclavitud en San Juan de Puerto Rico, 1800–1811." *Anuario de Estudios Americanos* 24 (1967): 1433–77.

———. "Credit without Banking in Early Nineteenth-Century Puerto Rico." *The Americas* 19:2 (1962): 149–71.

———. "Los registros del siglo XVIII en la parroquia de San Germán." *Historia*, n.s., 1:1 (1962): 56–66.

Takaki, Ronald. *Pau Hana: Plantation Life and Labor in Hawaii, 1835–1920.* Honolulu: University of Hawaii Press, 1983.

Taller de Formación Política. *¡Huelga en la caña! 1933–1934.* Río Piedras, P.R.: Huracán, 1982.

Taussig, Michael. *The Devil and Commodity Fetishism in South America.* Chapel Hill: University of North Carolina Press, 1980.

Taylor, Bruce M. "Emancipation in Barbados, 1830–1850: A Study in Planter Accommodation." Ph.D. diss., Fordham University, 1973.

Thomas, Keith "History and Anthropology." *Past and Present* 24 (1963): 3–24.

Thompson, E. P. "Anthropology and the Discipline of Historical Context." *Midland History* 1:3 (1972).

———. "The Crime of Anonymity." In *Albion's Fatal Tree: Crime and Society in Eighteenth-Century England*, edited by Douglas Hay et al. London: Allen Lane, 1975.

———. *Customs in Common.* New York: New Press, 1991.

———. "Eighteenth-Century Society: Class Struggle without Class?" *Social History* 3:2 (1978): 133–65.

———. *The Making of the English Working Class.* 1963; New York: Vintage, 1966.

———. "The Moral Economy of the English Crowd." *Past and Present* 50 (1971): 76–136.

———. "Patrician Society, Plebeian Culture." *Journal of Social History* 7:4 (1974): 382–405.

——. "Time, Work-Discipline, and Industrial Capitalism." *Past and Present* 38 (1967): 56–97.

——. *Whigs and Hunter: The Origin of the Black Act*. New York: Pantheon, 1975.

Thompson, Edgar T. *Plantation Societies, Race Relations, and the South: The Regimentation of Populations: Selected Papers of Edgar T. Thompson*. Durham, N.C.: Duke University Press, 1975.

Tomich, Dale. "The 'Second Slavery': Bonded Labor and the Transformation of the Nineteenth-Century World Economy." In *Rethinking the Nineteenth Century: Contradictions and Movements*, edited by Francisco O. Ramírez, 103–17. New York: Greenwood, 1988.

——. *Slavery and the Circuit of Sugar: Martinique and the World Economy, 1830–1848*. Baltimore: Johns Hopkins University Press, 1990.

——. "World Slavery and Caribbean Capitalism: The Cuban Sugar Industry, 1760–1868." *Theory and Society* 20:3 (1991): 297–319.

Torres, Arlene. "Blackness, Ethnicity, and Cultural Transformations in Southern Puerto Rico." Ph.D. diss., University of Illinois at Urbana-Champaign, 1995.

——. "La Gran Familia Puertorriqueña 'Ej Prieta de Belda' (The Great Puerto Rican Family Is Really Black)." In *Blackness in Latin America and the Caribbean: Social Dynamics and Cultural Transformations*, edited by Arlene Torres and Norman E. Whitten Jr., 2:285–306. Bloomington: Indiana University Press, 1998.

Torres, Arlene, and Norman E. Whitten Jr. "General Introduction: To Forge the Future in the Fires of the Past: An Interpretive Essay on Racism, Domination, Resistance, and Liberation." In *Blackness in Latin America and the Caribbean: Social Dynamics and Cultural Transformations*, edited by Arlene Torres and Norman E. Whitten Jr., 2:3–33. Bloomington: Indiana University Press, 1998.

Torres Ramírez, Bibiano. *La isla de Puerto Rico*. San Juan: Instituto de Cultura Puertorriqueña, 1968.

Tortella Casares, Gabriel, ed. *Revolución, burguesía, oligarquía, y constitucionalismo (1834–1923)*. Barcelona: Labor, 1981.

Trías Monge, José. *El sistema judicial de Puerto Rico*. Río Piedras: Editorial Universitaria, Universidad de Puerto Rico, 1978.

Trotman, David Vincent, *Crime in Trinidad: Conflict and Control in a Plantation Society, 1838–1900*. Knoxville: University of Tennessee Press, 1986.

Tuñon de Lara, Manuel. *Estudios sobre el siglo XIX español*. Madrid: Siglo XXI de España, 1972. *United Fruit Company: Un caso del dominio imperialista en Cuba*. Havana: Editorial de Ciencias Sociales, 1976.

Varela Ortega, José. *Los amigos políticos: Partidos, elecciones, y caciquismo en la restauración (1875–1900)*. Madrid: Alianza, 1977.

Vázquez Arce, María Consuelo. "Las compra-ventas de esclavos y cartas de libertad en Naguabo durante el siglo XIX." *Anales de Investigación Histórica* 3:1 (1976): 42–79.

Vázquez Medina, Angel, *La hacienda Monserrate de Manatí: Desde su fundación hasta que se convirtió en central en el 1894*. San Juan: Centro de Estudios Avanzados de Puerto Rico y el Caribe, 1986.

Vega, Ana Lydia. *Encancaranublado y otros cuentos de naufragio*. Río Piedras, P.R.: Antillana, 1982.

———. *Falsas crónicas del sur*, Río Piedras: Editorial de la Universidad de Puerto Rico, 1991.

Vega, Ana Lydia, and Carmen Lugo-Filippi. *Vírgenes y mártires*. Río Piedras, P.R.: Cultural, 1981.

Vega Druet, Héctor. "Historical and Ethnological Survey on the Probable African Origins of the Puerto Rican *Bomba*, Including a Description of the Santiago Apóstol Festivities in Loíza, Puerto Rico." Ph.D. diss., Wesleyan University, 1979.

Vila Vilar, Enriqueta. *Historia de Puerto Rico, 1600–1650*. Seville: Escuela de Estudios Hispano-Americanos, 1974.

Villegas, Gregorio. "Fluctuaciones de la poblaciónde Guaynabo en el periodo 1780–1830." *Anales de Investigación Histórica* 8:1–2 (1981): 80–125.

Viotti da Costa, Emília. *Da senzala à colônia*. São Paulo: Difusão Européia do Livro, 1966.

Weinstein, Barbara. "The Decline of the Progressive Planter and the Rise of Subaltern Agency: Shifting Narratives of Slave Emancipation in Brazil." In *Reclaiming the Political in Latin American History*, edited by Gilbert M. Joseph, 81–101. Durham, N.C.: Duke University Press, 2001.

Wessman, James W. "Demographic Evolution and Agrarian Structure of a Sugar Cane Region in Puerto Rico." Ph.D. diss., University of Connecticut, 1976.

Wimberly, Fayette Darcell. "The African '*Liberto*' and the Bahian Lower Class: Social Integration in Nineteenth-Century Bahia, Brazil, 1870–1900." Ph.D. diss., University of California–Berkeley, 1988.

Winn, Peter. "The Urban Working-Class and Social Protest in Latin America." *International Labor and Working-Class History* 14–15 (1979): 61–64.

———. *Weavers of Revolution: The Yarur Workers and Chile's Road to Socialism*. New York: Oxford University Press, 1986.

Wolf, Eric R., and Sidney W. Mintz. "Aspectos específicos del sistema de plantaciones en el Nuevo Mundo." In *Sistemas de plantaciones en el Nuevo Mundo*, edited by Vera Rubin, 150–61. Washington, D.C.: Unión Panamericana, 1960.

———. "Haciendas and Plantations in Middle America and the Antilles." *Social and Economic Studies* 6 (1957): 386–412.

Wolfe, Joel "The Rise of Brazil's Industrial Working Class: Community, Work, and Politics in São Paulo, 1900–1955." Ph.D. diss., University of Wisconsin–Madison, 1990.

Zenón, Isabelo. *Narciso descubre su trasero*. 2 vols. Humacao, P.R.: Euridi, 1974.

INDEX

Fertility of slaves, 202–3

Festivities and cultural events, 180–84, 206, 243 (nn. 13–14)

Fiestas patronales (patron saint festivals), 183, 184

Fígaro, Manuel, 116–17

Figueroa Flores, Manuel, 154

Findlay, Eileen Suárez, 209

Finquitas (diminutive farms), 157, 159

Fires at sugar plantations, 187, 189–98, 207, 244–45 (n. 22), 245–47 (nn. 24–29)

Flinter, George, 95–96, 101–3

Food: for slaves, 92, 93, 95, 96, 104; for *libertos*, 133, 135, 140, 141, 142, 146

Forced-labor contracts. *See* Contracts with *libertos/as*

Foreign immigrants. *See* Immigrants

France and French immigrants, 31, 32, 34, 47, 56–57, 194, 235 (n. 25)

Freedmen and freedwomen. See *Libertos/as*

Free people of color: population of (1776–1899), 48, 50, 58, 73–74, 203, 225 (n. 68); as employers of *libertos*, 132, 134

French immigrants. *See* France and French immigrants

Gallardo, José, 241 (n. 1)

Gambling, 181

García, Gervasio L., 216 (n. 10)

García, Isidro, 140

García, Don José, 57, 87

García, Juan, 141

García, Micaela, 157

García, Monserrate, 162

García, Pedro, 140

García, Valentín, 157

García, Victoriana, 163

García de Sergés, Doña Belén, 155

García Orozco, Don Joaquín, 87

Garriga, Don Gerardo, 181–82

Gaudinau, Dionicio, 141

Gaudinau, Felícita, 244 (n. 17)

Gaudinau, Don Félix, 67

Gaudinau family, 87

Gender: and emancipation of slaves, 88–89, 90, 100, 229 (n. 58); and *liberto* contracts, 128, 130–33, 135; and domestic labor contracts, 131, 132, 133, 135, 138, 141, 205; and occupational mobility, 131–33; and wages for *libertos/as*, 138, 141; and house purchases, 162; and urban migration, 162, 163; and slave field labor force, 205

Genovese, Eugene, 189

González, Don José, 178–80, 242 (n. 5)

González, José Luis, 4–6, 12, 209, 247 (n. 12)

Gramsci, Antonio, 207

Grande marronage, 82

Great Britain: and Cuba, 29, 30, 47; and slave trade, 30, 31, 62, 72; and irrigation system in Puerto Rico, 70; and sugar exports, 71; and abolition of slavery, 117, 118

Guadeloupe, 64, 65, 66

Gual, Ignacio, 153, 162

Gual, Miguel (Chivo), 82–84, 120

Gual, Tomas, 157

Gual, Valentín, 153–54, 178, 237 (n. 2)

Gual y Frías, Don José, 59, 67, 82–85, 87, 89, 153

Guamaní, 154, 157, 159, 238 (n. 8)

Guardia Civil, 149, 177–78, 197–98, 245 (n. 22), 247 (n. 40)

Guayama: immigrants to, 1–2, 57, 59; languages spoken in, 2; reasons for study of, 10–13; town versus country dynamic in, 11; sugar workers' strikes in, 11, 214 (n. 37); Afro-Caribbean heritage of, 11–12, 63; nickname for, 11–12, 215 (n. 8); Caribbeanness in, 12, 19–20; Vázquez on, 15–18, 23, 78; Porrata-Doria on, 15–18, 45, 77–78, 215 (nn. 5, 7–8); physical environment of, 18–23, 67, 70; establishment and early history of, 23–24; slave population statistics on, 31–32, 53, 54, 58, 60, 62, 73, 74, 78,

Peru, 88, 245 (n. 24)

Petite marronage, 82

Pezuela, Juan de la, 116, 142, 166

Physical environment of Guayama, 18–23, 67, 70

Pica, Don Matías, 235 (n. 25)

Picó, Fernando, 26, 127, 142, 156, 166, 209, 218 (n. 45)

Picó, Rafael, 21

Pillot, Don Arístides, 87, 155

Pillot, Carlota, 159

Pillot, Felicidad, 159

Pillot, Félix, 159

Pillot, José, 140

Pillot, Juana, 159

Pillot, Luisa, 234–35 (n. 25)

Pillot, Martina, 162

Pillot, Don Mauricio, 87, 89, 159

Pillot, Petrona, 163

Pillot, Zenón, 155

Plaja Vidol, Sebastián, 226 (n. 1)

Plantain, 95, 228 (n. 37)

Plantation system. *See* Sugar plantations

Planters (*hacendados*): ethnic origins of, 57, 59; and consolidation of sugar plantations, 67; and importation of slaves after legal end of slave trade, 72; and *coartación*, 82–90, 100–101, 120, 229 (n. 56); manumission of slaves by, 84–90, 203; compensation to, for abolition of slavery, 119, 122; and *liberto* contracts, 127–28, 132–33, 135–39, 146, 147; and immigration of agricultural workers, 146–47; and *jornaleros*, 171–72; and social control of laborers, 178–83, 199; in Manatí, 222 (n. 19). *See also* Sugar plantations; *and specific planters*

Police, 149, 172–73, 177–78, 186, 197–98, 241 (n. 1), 245 (n. 22)

Political rights for *libertos*, 119, 122, 149, 206

Ponce: slavery in, 52, 61–62, 64, 72, 75, 76, 202; sugar plantations in, 52–55, 60–62, 64–67, 95, 223 (n. 39), 223–24 (n. 53),

226 (n. 74); *jornaleros* in, 76; slave life and resistance in, 98, 228 (n. 33); slave transit beyond hacienda perimeters in, 98–99; delegate to Junta Informativa from, 109; and Moret Law, 116; and Abolition Law (1873), 121; *liberto* contracting in, 124, 233 (n. 11); *libertos* on sugar plantations in, 164; and labor code (1876–77), 170; *indocumentados* in, 172; crime by *libertos* in, 185; sugar mills in, 223 (n. 53); households per dwellings in, 239 (n. 15)

Population: of Puerto Rico, 26, 31–32, 48, 49, 50, 58, 214 (n. 32); of slaves in Puerto Rico, 31–32, 48, 50, 54, 76, 96, 214 (n. 32); of slaves in Guayama, 31–32, 53, 54, 58, 60, 62, 73, 74, 78, 86, 214 (n. 32), 227 (n. 14); of Guayama, 31–32, 53, 58, 59–60, 73–74, 214 (n. 32), 225 (nn. 68–69); of free people of color, 48, 50, 58, 73–74, 225 (n. 68); of whites, 48, 50, 58, 74; of *jornaleros*, 76; population density in Puerto Rico, 152

Porrata-Doria, Don Adolfo, 15–18, 45, 74, 77–78, 215 (n. 5), 215–16 (nn. 7–10), 242 (n. 5)

Porrata-Doria, Don Santiago, 215 (n. 9)

Potts, Don Hutton, 187, 195

Power y Giralt, Don Ramón, 34, 219 (n. 49)

Prakash, Gyan, 236 (n. 43)

Prestaciones personales (road tax), 167–68, 173, 177, 239 (n. 26), 241 (n. 1)

Prices: for slaves, 62, 72; for sugar, 65, 70, 71, 77; for *coartación*, 83, 89–90, 153; for land, 153–57, 161; for houses, 159, 162

Primo de Rivera y Sobremonte, Rafael, 122–29, 142, 143, 145, 148, 167, 168, 204–5

Prim y Prats, Juan, 98–99, 112, 113

Proletarianization, 152, 155–56, 164–65, 176–84, 198–99

Protector de libertos, 123

Protopeasantry: slaves' protopeasant activities, 90–104, 205; and Sunday and holiday activities for slaves, 92, 93, 95, 97, 228 (n. 45), 230 (n. 66); marketing of crafts and food by slaves, 93, 94, 97, 98, 99–100; and slave transit beyond hacienda perimeters, 93, 97–100; subsistence agriculture by slaves, 94–97, 101–2; and *coartación*, 100–101, 104, 229 (n. 56); Mintz on, 226 (n. 6), 229 (n. 64)

Protoproletarian resistance, 187–98

Proyecto de Reglamento sobre las Relaciones entre el Capital y el Trabajo Destinados a la Industria Agrícola, 169–72

Pueblo of Guayama. *See* Guayama township

Puerto Rico: immigrants to, 1–2, 32, 47, 55–57, 59; social formation in, 2–6; patterns of history and identity in, 2–7; historiography of, 2–9, 15–18, 35, 45, 51–52, 216 (n. 10), 221–22 (n. 18); *jíbaro* identity in, 3, 12, 42, 51; U.S. military occupation of and colonial policies in, 10, 14, 209–10; land tenure in, 19, 24–28, 217 (nn. 26, 31), 218 (n. 34); in eighteenth century, 24–34; population of, 26, 31–32, 48, 49, 50, 58, 214 (n. 32); and trade, 28–32, 56, 110; Abbad y Lassiera's report on, 29, 30, 31; O'Reilly's report on, 29–30, 31, 33–34; Córdova's report on, 30; slave population of, 31–32, 48, 50, 54, 76, 96, 202–3, 214 (n. 32); labor organization in, 33–41; cholera epidemic in, 66, 74, 203; slave code in, 91–94, 97, 99, 124, 181–82; usury in, 103; currency problems in, 103, 156, 164; political reforms in, and Junta Informativa, 110–11; population density in, 152; land purchases in, 152–62, 164–65, 205. *See also* Abolition of slavery; Emancipation of slaves; Guayama; Slavery; Sugar plantations

Quiles, Leonarda, 241 (n. 34)

Quiñones, Francisco M., 108–11

Quintero Rivera, Angel G., 218 (n. 10)

Racial classifications, 221 (n. 12)

Racial formation, 40

Racial projects, 40–41

Ramírez de Arellano, Rafael, 219 (n. 49)

Ramiú, Don Luis, 195

Ramos, Baldomero, 239 (n. 26)

Ramos Mattei, Andrés: significance of research by, 7, 216 (n. 10); on labor force, 72–73, 164, 168, 169, 225–26 (n. 74); on sugar industry, 73, 209; on *liberto* contracts, 126–27, 138, 234 (n. 22); on *libreta* system, 168, 225–26 (n. 74); on Boyrie, 234 (n. 25); on daylaborer wages, 236 (n. 45)

Ranches (*hatos*), 17, 25–28, 39, 217 (nn. 26, 31), 218 (n. 34)

Real Cédula de Gracias, 32, 47, 55–56, 57

Recio, Don Constancio, 196, 247 (n. 36)

Reconstituted peasantry, 226 (n. 6)

Registros de jornaleros, 170

Reglamento de Jornaleros (Day Laborer Code), 73, 116, 148, 166–67, 225 (n. 67)

Reglamento para . . . la Contratación del Servicio de los Libertos, 123–24

Residential patterns of *libertos*, 161–65, 205–6

Resistance: crime as, 8, 213 (n. 20); by slaves, 81–82, 91, 188, 215 (n. 7), 242 (n. 7); and *coartación*, 82–90, 100–101, 104, 120, 229 (n. 56); slave code for repression of, 91; to *liberto* contracts, 142, 147–48; arson as, 187, 189–98, 207, 244–45 (n. 22), 245–46 (nn. 24–29); protoproletarian resistance, 187–98; by *libertos* generally, 206–8

Riefkohl, Don Otto, 196–97

Río Piedras, 54

Rivera, José, 193–94

Rivera, José Victor, 156

Rivera y Texidor, Doña Isabel, 59, 223 (n. 35)

Road tax, 167–68, 173, 177, 239 (n. 26), 241 (n. 1)

Rodney, Walter, 20

Rodríguez, Doña Gregoria, 88–89

Rodriguez, Don Luis, 154

Rodríguez, Manuel, 156

Rodríguez Juliá, Edgardo, 218–19 (n. 45)

Roubert, Nicomedes, 153

Rubio, Don Bautista, 154

Rubio, Don Roque, 137, 138

Ruiz Belvis, Segundo, 108–12

Rum production, 61, 215 (n. 5)

Runaway *libertos*, 127, 143

Runaway slaves, 41–42, 91, 97–98

Sabater, Don José, 87

Sabater, Pilar, 244 (n. 17)

Saint Domingue, 32, 49, 56. *See also* Haiti

Salinas, 70, 172, 190, 193, 239 (n. 26)

Sambolín, Don Vicente, 148

Sánchez, Alberto, 197–98

Sánchez, Antonelo, 195

Sánchez, Castora, 162, 163

San Germán: *cabildo* in, 25, 34, 219 (n. 49); slavery in, 54; delegate to Junta Informativa from, 109; and Moret Law, 116–17

San Juan: and land tenure, 25–28, 217 (nn. 26, 31); *cabildo*'s reports from, 34–38, 41, 42, 219 (n. 49); and peasants, 36; and slavery, 36–38, 54; and slave trade, 37–38; and racial project, 42

San Lorenzo, 172

San Miguel, Pedro L., 95, 142, 221 (n. 18)

Santa Isabel, 164

Santel, Augusto, 197

Santiago, Francisco, 173, 240 (n. 33)

Santiago, Kelvin, 216 (n. 10)

Sanz, José Laureano, 118, 143–48, 167–69, 240 (n. 29), 244–45 (n. 22)

Sargentón, Hipólito, 184

Saunión, Don Joaquín, 140, 178

Scarano, Francisco A.: on *cahiers des doléance*, 34; on land for sugar production, 49, 55, 60, 102, 223 (n. 39); on sugar plantations, 53, 61, 65, 95; on slave importation, 62; on peasants, 75, 77; on Flinter, 95–96, 101; on fertility of slaves, 202; significance of research by, 216 (n. 10), 219 (n. 48), 220 (n. 2); on *hatos*, 217 (n. 31)

Schmidt-Nowara, Christopher, 119, 212 (n. 14), 216 (n. 11), 220 (n. 53), 230 (n. 1)

Schoelcher, Victor, 94, 229–30 (n. 66)

Schwartz, Stuart, 89, 90, 212 (n. 12)

Scott, James, 189

Scott, Rebecca, 117, 164, 206, 207, 212 (n. 14), 230 (nn. 1, 3), 236 (n. 43), 237 (n. 52)

Sebastián (slave), 181, 243 (n. 10)

Self-purchase. See *Coartación*

Sergés, Don Luis, 155

Serrano, Francisco (Duke of Torre), 10, 112, 113

Síndico protector de libertos, 123–24, 148, 233 (nn. 6, 8)

Slave code, 91–94, 97, 99, 124, 181–82

Slave conspiracies and revolts, 188, 215 (n. 7), 242 (n. 7)

Slaveholders. *See* Planters

Slavery: in eighteenth century, 6, 30–32; emancipation of slaves, 6, 226 (n. 1); Porrato-Doria on, 18, 45, 78, 215 (n. 7); population statistics on, 31–32, 48, 50, 54, 58, 60, 62, 73, 74, 76, 78, 86, 96, 116, 202–3, 214 (n. 32), 217 (n. 14); Irizarri on, 36–38; San Juan *cabildo*'s report on, 36–38, 54; Coamo *cabildo*'s report on, 38–40, 41, 46; runaway slaves, 41–42, 91, 97–98; in Guayama, 44–45; and sugar plantations in 1810s–1840s, 46, 50–55, 61–63; in Cuba, 50, 72, 109, 148; in Ponce, 52, 61–62, 64, 72, 75, 76; regional diversity in, 52–55; capital investment in, 61; prices for slaves, 62, 72; in Louisiana, 64; in Guadeloupe,

64, 66; and sugar plantations in 1850s–1860s, 64, 68–69, 72–76, 225–26 (n. 74); in Mayagüez, 72, 75, 76; deaths of slaves from cholera epidemic, 74, 203; Patterson on social death and natal alienation of slaves, 80–81; social relationships of slaves, 81; resistance by slaves, 81–82, 91, 188, 215 (n. 7); autonomous economic activities of slaves, 90–103; protopeasant slave activities, 90–104, 205; and slave code in Puerto Rico, 91–94, 97, 99, 124, 181–82; food for slaves, 92, 93, 95, 96, 104; hours of work for slaves, 92, 93, 228 (n. 45), 229–30 (n. 66); Sunday and holiday activities for slaves, 92, 93–95, 97, 228 (n. 45), 230 (n. 66); in Jamaica, 92, 188, 202; work tools used by slaves, 93; marketing of crafts or food by slaves, 93, 94, 97, 98, 99–100; slave transit beyond hacienda perimeters, 93, 97–100; subsistence agriculture by slaves, 94–97, 101–2; Flinter on, 96; and *baile de bomba*, 181–82, 242 (n. 7); Díaz Soler on, 201; fertility of slaves, 202–3. *See also* Abolition of slavery; Emancipation of slaves; Slave trade

Slave trade: end of, in Spanish colonies, 18, 46, 66, 72, 77, 108, 202; and Great Britain, 30, 31, 62, 72; in eighteenth century, 30–32; Irizarri on, 36–38; Coamo *cabildo*'s report on, 38–40, 41, 46; illicit slave trade in 1830s–1840s, 51, 52, 62, 72; and Real Cédula de Gracias, 56; statistics on, 72; internal slave trade, 100. *See also* Slavery

Social control of laborers, 165–72, 176–84, 199

Socialist Party, 11

Sociedad Abolicionista Española (Spanish Abolitionist Society), 108

Sociedad Agrícola Hermanas Curet, 59, 136

Soria, Bernabé, 240 (n. 34)

Spain: and end of slave trade, 13, 46, 66, 72, 77, 108, 202; trade policy of, 28–32, 56, 110; immigrants from, to Puerto Rico, 57, 59; Sexenio or Revolución Gloriosa in, 105–6, 111, 112–13; and Junta Informativa, 108–12; and Moret Law, 113–17; and Abolition Law (1873), 117–20; and Topete bill, 118; blacks' involvement in abolitionist rallies in, 119–20; military coup (1874) in, 143; and reconquest of Dominican Republic, 231 (n. 9)

Spanish-American War, 14, 209–10

Spivak, Gayatri Chakravorty, 235 (n. 34)

Storer, C. F., 169

Strikes by sugar workers, 11, 214 (n. 37)

Sued Badillo, Jalil, 212 (n. 8)

Sugar industry: strikes by sugar workers, 11, 214 (n. 37); in eighteenth century, 24; statistics on, 24; growth of, in 1810s–1840s, 24, 45–63; in Saint Domingue, 32, 49; in Jamaica, 32, 53, 101, 111; and sugar mills, 45, 60, 66–69, 136, 223–24 (n. 53), 247 (n. 36); and slavery, 46, 50–55; structural constraints on, during 1850s–1860s, 46, 63–77; in Cuba, 49, 53, 71; and immigrants, 55–57, 59; and sugar exports, 60, 63, 67, 70; prices for sugar, 65, 70, 71, 77; decline of, in 1870s, 205; Porrata-Doria on, 215 (n. 5). *See also* Sugar plantations

Sugar mills, 59, 60, 66–69, 136, 223–24 (n. 53), 247 (n. 36)

Sugar plantations: in early nineteenth century, 27–28; growth of, in 1810s–1840s, 45–63; in Caribbean, 46; and slavery, 46, 50–55, 61–63, 68–69, 72–75, 225–26 (n. 74); structural constraints on, during 1850s–1860s, 46, 63–77; acreage of, 49, 60, 67, 68–69, 78, 224 (n. 54); peasants as day laborers on, 51, 73, 75, 104, 164, 166; in Mayagüez, 52–53, 54, 62, 65; in Ponce, 52–55, 60–62, 64–67, 95, 223 (n. 39), 223–24 (n. 53),